WATER SYSTEMS OPERATION AND MAINTENANCE

VIDEO TRAINING SERIES

Learning Booklet

Office of Water Programs
California State University, Sacramento
and
California State Department of Health Services

2004

NOTICE

This *LEARNING BOOKLET* provides additional helpful information for operators, managers, owners, and elected board members using the *WATER SYSTEMS OPERATION AND MAINTENANCE VIDEO TRAINING SERIES*. The titles of the seven videos are as follows:

1. Wellhead Protection,

2. Hypochlorination,

3. Water Storage Tanks,

4. Sampling and Testing,

5. Inspecting a Pump Station,

6. Distribution Systems, and

7. Approaches to Compliance With Standards.

ISBN 1-59371-007-0

OPERATOR TRAINING MATERIALS

OPERATOR TRAINING MANUALS AND VIDEOS IN THIS SERIES are available from the Office of Water Programs, California State University, Sacramento, 6000 J Street, Sacramento, CA 95819-6025, phone: (916) 278-6142, e-mail: wateroffice@csus.edu, FAX: (916) 278-5959, or website: www.owp.csus.edu.

1. *SMALL WATER SYSTEM OPERATION AND MAINTENANCE,**

2. *WATER DISTRIBUTION SYSTEM OPERATION AND MAINTENANCE,*

3. *WATER TREATMENT PLANT OPERATION,* 2 Volumes,

4. *UTILITY MANAGEMENT,*

5. *MANAGE FOR SUCCESS,*

6. *SMALL WASTEWATER SYSTEM OPERATION AND MAINTENANCE,* 2 Volumes,

7. *OPERATION OF WASTEWATER TREATMENT PLANTS,* 2 Volumes,

8. *OPERATION AND MAINTENANCE OF WASTEWATER COLLECTION SYSTEMS,* 2 Volumes, (Spanish edition available),

9. *COLLECTION SYSTEMS: METHODS FOR EVALUATING AND IMPROVING PERFORMANCE,*

10. *ADVANCED WASTE TREATMENT,*

11. *INDUSTRIAL WASTE TREATMENT,* 2 Volumes,

12. *TREATMENT OF METAL WASTESTREAMS,* and

13. *PRETREATMENT FACILITY INSPECTION.*

* Other training materials and training aids developed by the Office of Water Programs to assist operators in improving small water system operation and maintenance and overall performance of their systems include the *SMALL WATER SYSTEMS VIDEO INFORMATION SERIES.* This series of 15- to 59- minute videos was prepared for the operators, managers, owners, and elected officials of very small water systems. The videos provide information on the responsibilities of operators and managers. They also demonstrate the procedures to safely and effectively operate and maintain surface water treatment systems, groundwater treatment systems, and distribution and storage systems. Other topics covered include monitoring, managerial, financial, and emergency response procedures for small systems. These videos are used with a *LEARNING BOOKLET* that provides additional essential information and references. The videos complement and reinforce the information presented in *SMALL WATER SYSTEM OPERATON AND MAINTENANCE.*

The Office of Water Programs at California State University, Sacramento, has been designated by the U.S. Environmental Protection Agency as a *SMALL PUBLIC WATER SYSTEMS TECHNOLOGY ASSISTANCE CENTER.* This recognition will provide funding for the development of training videos for the operators and managers of small public water systems. Additional training materials will be produced to assist the operators and managers of small systems.

PREFACE TO THE LEARNING BOOKLET

The purposes of this Water Systems Operation and Maintenance Video Training Series are as follows:

1. To develop new qualified water treatment and distribution system operators,

2. To expand the abilities of existing operators, permitting better service to both their employers and the public,

3. To prepare operators for civil service and *CERTIFICATION EXAMINATIONS*,[1]

4. To help operators earn contact hours or continuing education units (CEUs) to renew their licenses, and

5. To inform systems managers and board members of their roles and responsibilities.

To provide you with the knowledge and skills needed to operate and maintain water treatment and distribution systems as efficiently and effectively as possible, experienced operators helped prepare the scripts for these videos and participated in the videoing of the field demonstration procedures.

Water systems vary from village to village and from region to region. The material contained in this video training series is presented to provide you with an understanding of the basic operation and maintenance aspects of your system and with information to help you analyze and solve operation and maintenance problems. This information will help you operate and maintain your system in a safe and efficient manner. Information also is provided on how to successfully manage and finance water systems, as well as be in compliance.

Water treatment and distribution system operation, maintenance, management, financing, and compliance are rapidly advancing fields. To keep pace with scientific and technological advances, the information in these videos must be periodically revised and updated. *THIS MEANS THAT YOU, THE OPERATOR, THE MANAGER, THE OWNER, OR THE GOVERNING BOARD MEMBER, MUST RECOGNIZE THE NEED TO BE AWARE OF NEW ADVANCES AND THE NEED FOR CONTINUOUS TRAINING BEYOND THIS PROGRAM.*

We are indebted to the many operators, managers, and other persons who contributed to this training video series. Every effort was made to acknowledge material from the many excellent references in the water treatment and distribution system field. Special thanks go to Dave Bender, who hosted the videos, and Mike Cherniak, who contributed his time and effort to the production of the videos and served as resident expert. Video guests included Peggy Zarriello, Environmental Health Specialist, Department of Environmental Health, Nevada County; Richard Beskeen, Supervising Plant Operator, Department of Utilities, City of Sacramento; Brad Stone, Water Treatment Plant Operator, Carmichael Water District; Steve Nugent, Manager, Carmichael Water District; Mel Davis, Operator, Bitney Springs Center, Grass Valley; Greg Stinson, Water Treatment Plant Operator, Carmichael Water District; Scott Bair, Superintendent, Carmichael Water District; Chris Nelson, Foreman, Carmichael Water District; Chris Mayer, Utilities Coordinator, San Juan Water District; Steve Mindt, Staff Environmentalist, California Department of Health Services; Alex Peterson, P.E., Principal, Kennedy/Jenks Consultants; Maria Tikkanen, Ph.D., Senior Scientist, Kennedy/Jenks Consultants; Fred J. Stafford, Water Production Supervisor, East Valley Water District; Teresa Tanaka, General Manager, Linden County Water District; Richard Haberman, Supervising Sanitary Engineer, California Department of Health Services; Bryan Zinn, Senior Project Engineer, Basin Water; and Gary Young, Water Quality Technician, East Valley Water District. Consultants included Dave Long, Chet Anderson, Steve Nugent, and Kurt Ohlinger, who also assisted with the review of the *LEARNING BOOKLET*. The videos were produced by Creative Services, California State University, Sacramento.

KENNETH D. KERRI

2004

---

[1] *Certification Examination. An examination administered by a state agency that small water supply system operators take to indicate a level of professional competence. In the United States, certification of small water system operators is mandatory.*

OBJECTIVES OF THIS VIDEO TRAINING SERIES

Proper installation, inspection, operation, maintenance, repair, and management of water treatment and distribution systems have a significant impact on the operation and maintenance costs and effectiveness of the systems. The objective of this video training series is to provide water treatment and distribution system operators and others with the knowledge and skills required to operate and maintain these systems effectively, thus eliminating or reducing the following problems:

1. Health hazards created by the delivery of unsafe water to the consumer's tap;

2. System failures that result from the lack of proper installation, inspection, preventive maintenance, surveillance, and repair programs designed to protect the public investment in these facilities;

3. Tastes and odors caused by water system problems;

4. Corrosion damages to pipes, equipment, tanks, and structures in the water system;

5. Complaints from the public or local officials due to the unreliability or failure of the water system to perform as designed; and

6. Fire damage caused by insufficient water and/or inadequate pressures at a time of need.

SCOPE OF THIS VIDEO TRAINING SERIES

Operators with the responsibility for wells, pumps, disinfection, and water treatment plant distribution systems will find this video training series very helpful. This video training series contains the following information:

1. What water treatment and distribution systems operators do,

2. Sources and uses of water,

3. How to operate and maintain wells and pumps,

4. Operation and maintenance of surface water and groundwater treatment plants,

5. Disinfection of new and repaired facilities as well as water delivered to consumers,

6. Operation and maintenance of water storage tanks and distribution systems,

7. Development and implementation of water system monitoring programs,

8. Techniques for recognizing hazards and developing safe procedures and safety programs, and

9. Procedures for effectively managing resources for a water treatment and distribution systems O & M program,

10. How to identify procedures to keep your system in compliance.

Material in this video training series furnishes you with information concerning situations encountered by most water treatment and distribution system operators in most areas. These materials provide you with an understanding of the basic operational and maintenance concepts for water systems and with an ability to analyze and solve problems when they occur. Operation and maintenance programs for water systems will vary with the age of the system, the extent and effectiveness of previous programs, and local conditions. You will have to adapt the information and procedures in this video training series to your particular situation.

Technology is advancing very rapidly in the fields of operation, maintenance, management, financial, and compliance aspects of small water systems. To keep pace with scientific advances, the material in this program must be periodically revised and updated. This means that you, the water system operator, must be aware of new advances and recognize the need for continuous personal training reaching beyond this program.

TRAINING OPPORTUNITIES EXIST IN YOUR DAILY WORK EXPERIENCE, FROM YOUR ASSOCIATES, AND FROM ATTENDING MEETINGS, WORKSHOPS, CONFERENCES, AND CLASSES.

USES OF THIS VIDEO TRAINING SERIES

This video training series was developed to serve the needs of operators in several different situations. The format used was developed to serve as a home-study or self-paced instruction course for operators in remote areas or persons unable to attend formal classes either due to shift work, personal reasons, or the unavailability of suitable classes. This home-study video training series uses the concepts of self-paced instruction where you are your own instructor and work at your own speed. In order to certify that a person has successfully completed this video training series, an objective test for each chapter is included with each enrollment in the course.

Also, this video training series can serve effectively as a supplement to a textbook in the classroom. Many colleges and universities have used the manuals *WATER TREATMENT PLANT OPERATION*, Volumes I and II, as textbooks in formal classes (often taught by operators). In areas where colleges are not available or are unable to offer classes in the operation of water systems, operators and utility agencies can join together to offer their own courses using the manuals and this video series.

Cities or utility agencies can use the videos and the manual in several types of on-the-job training programs. In one type of program, a manual and *LEARNING BOOKLET* are purchased for each operator. A senior operator or a group of operators are designated as instructors. These operators help answer questions when the persons in the training program have questions or need assistance. The instructors grade the objective tests at the end of each chapter, record scores, and notify California State University, Sacramento, of the scores when a person successfully completes this program. This approach eliminates any waiting while tests are being graded and returned by CSUS.

The video training series was prepared to help operators operate and maintain their water treatment and distribution systems. Please feel free to use the video training series in the manner that best fits your needs and the needs of your operators. We will be happy to work with you to assist you in developing your training program. Please feel free to contact:

Program Director
Office of Water Programs
California State University, Sacramento
6000 J Street
Sacramento, California 95819-6025

Phone: (916) 278-6142
Fax: (916) 278-5959
e-mail: wateroffice@csus.edu

INSTRUCTIONS TO PARTICIPANTS IN THE HOME-STUDY COURSE

Procedures for watching the videos, reading the *LEARNING BOOKLET*, and answering the objective test questions are contained in this section.

To progress steadily through this program, you should establish a regular study schedule. For example, many operators in the past have set aside two hours during two evenings a week for study.

The study material is contained in seven videos. Some videos are longer and more difficult than others. The time required to complete a video will depend on your background and experience. Some people might require 45 minutes to complete a video and some might require an hour to two hours, but that is perfectly all right. *THE IMPORTANT THING IS THAT YOU UNDERSTAND THE MATERIAL IN THE VIDEO.*

NOTICE: Please be sure you carefully study the videos and the material in the *LEARNING BOOKLET.* Some of the questions in the objective test are designed to ensure that people watch the entire video and read the entire video section in the *LEARNING BOOKLET* before taking the objective test.

You are your own teacher in this program. You could merely copy the answers from someone else, but you would not understand the material. Consequently, you would not be able to apply the material to the operation of your facilities nor recall it during an examination for certification or a civil service position.

YOU WILL GET OUT OF THIS PROGRAM WHAT YOU PUT INTO IT.

SUMMARY OF PROCEDURES

A. OPERATOR (YOU)

1. Watch each video one at a time. Read what you are expected to learn in each video (the video objectives).

2. Rewatch the video if you wish.

3. Read the material in the *LEARNING BOOKLET*.

4. Mark your answers to the objective test on the answer sheet provided by the Program Director or by your instructor.

5. Mail material to the Program Director. (Send *ONLY* your completed answer sheet.)

> Program Director
> Office of Water Programs
> California State University, Sacramento
> 6000 J Street
> Sacramento, California 95819-6025

B. PROGRAM DIRECTOR

1. Mails answer sheet for each video to operator.

2. Corrects tests, answers any questions, and returns results to operator, including explanations and solutions for missed questions.

C. ORDER OF WATCHING VIDEOS

To complete this program you will have to watch all of the videos. You may proceed in numerical order or in any order that meets your needs.

SAFETY IS A VERY IMPORTANT TOPIC. Everyone working in a water system must always be safety conscious. Every day operators encounter situations and equipment that can cause a serious disabling injury or illness if the operator is not aware of the potential danger and does not exercise adequate precautions. In each video, *SAFE PROCEDURES ARE ALWAYS STRESSED.*

WATER SYSTEMS OPERATION AND MAINTENANCE

VIDEO TRAINING SERIES

COURSE OUTLINE

NOTE: The five operator training manuals listed below and on the next two pages contain information helpful to operators of water systems. All of them are available from the Program Director, Office of Water Programs, California State University, Sacramento.

SMALL WATER SYSTEM OPERATION AND MAINTENANCE

(Wells, Small Treatment Plants, and Rates)

COURSE OUTLINE

WATER DISTRIBUTION SYSTEM OPERATION AND MAINTENANCE

COURSE OUTLINE

UTILITY MANAGEMENT
by Lorene Lindsay

COURSE OUTLINE

WATER TREATMENT PLANT OPERATION, VOLUME I

COURSE OUTLINE

WATER TREATMENT PLANT OPERATION, VOLUME II
COURSE OUTLINE

WATER SYSTEMS OPERATION AND MAINTENANCE VIDEO TRAINING SERIES

CHAPTER (VIDEO) 1

WELLHEAD PROTECTION

VIDEO 1 SUMMARY

Video 1, WELLHEAD PROTECTION, provides operators with the knowledge, skills, and abilities they need to inspect, protect, and maintain wellheads. Information is provided on how to inspect small system and large distribution system wellheads. Emphasis is placed on how to maintain a well and also how to troubleshoot wells and well pump problems. Procedures are provided regarding how to design and implement a wellhead protection program.

CONTENTS OF VIDEO 1

WELLHEAD PROTECTION VIDEO

INTRODUCTION

INSPECTING A WELLHEAD

     Small Systems

     Large Distribution Systems

QUALITY

     Collecting Samples

     Monitoring

DRAWDOWN TEST OR SOUNDING TEST

     Purpose

     Measuring Distance Down to Water Surface

DESIGN AND IMPLEMENTATION OF A WELLHEAD PROTECTION PROGRAM

     Involve Community

     Sources of Contamination

SUMMARY

CONTENTS OF CHAPTER 1
**WELLHEAD PROTECTION
LEARNING BOOKLET**

OBJECTIVES

Chapter (Video) 1.   WELLHEAD PROTECTION

Following completion of Video 1 and Chapter 1, you should be able to:

1. Identify sources of groundwater contamination and take corrective actions,

2. Protect a well from contamination,

3. Maintain a well,

4. Inspect a well and pumping station,

5. Troubleshoot a well and pumping system,

6. Collect samples from a well and pumping system, and

7. Design and implement a wellhead protection program.

LEARNING BOOKLET STUDY MATERIAL

This section of the *LEARNING BOOKLET* contains important information. Read this section after watching the video and before attempting to take the Objective Test for this chapter.

Material in this section will help you to better understand the material presented in the video. Also some critical information is easier to present in the *LEARNING BOOKLET*, such as illustrating forms and calculations.

Chapter (Video) 1. WELLHEAD PROTECTION

1.0 WELLHEAD PROTECTION

1.00 Purpose of Wellhead Protection

Statement of the Problem

Groundwater contamination can originate on the surface of the ground or in the ground above or below the water table. Table 1.1 shows the types of activities that can cause groundwater contamination at each level. The contaminant may be microorganisms or toxic substances.

Where a contaminant originates is a factor that can affect its actual impact on groundwater quality. For example, if a contaminant is spilled on the surface of the ground or injected into the ground above the water table, it may have to move through numerous layers of soil or other materials before it

TABLE 1.1 ACTIVITIES THAT CAN CAUSE GROUNDWATER CONTAMINATION [a]

Origin	Activity	
GROUND SURFACE	Infiltration of polluted surface water Land disposal of wastes Stockpiles Dumps Sewage sludge disposal	De-icing salt use and storage Animal feedlots Fertilizers and pesticides Accidental spills Airborne source particulates
ABOVE WATER TABLE	Septic tanks, cesspools, and privies Holding ponds and lagoons Sanitary landfills Underground storage tank leaks	Underground pipeline leaks Artificial recharge Sumps and dry wells Graveyards Waste disposal in excavations
BELOW WATER TABLE	Waste disposal in wells Drainage wells and canals Underground storage	Exploratory wells Abandoned wells Water-supply wells Groundwater withdrawal Mines

[a] *CITIZEN'S GUIDE TO GROUNDWATER PROTECTION*, Office of Groundwater Protection, U.S. Environmental Protection Agency, Washington, DC 20460. EPA 440/6-90-004, April 1990.

reaches the groundwater. As the contaminant moves through these layers of soil, a number of treatment processes are in operation in the soil (for example, filtration, ion exchange, adsorption, dilution, oxidation, biological decay) that can lessen the eventual impact of the contaminant once it finally reaches the groundwater. The effectiveness of these processes also is affected by both the distance between the groundwater and where the contaminant is introduced and the amount of time it takes the substance or microorganism to reach the groundwater. If the contaminant is introduced directly into the area below the water table, the primary process that can affect the impact of the contaminant is dilution by the surrounding groundwater.

Cleaning up a contaminated groundwater supply is a complicated, costly, and sometimes impossible process. In general, a community whose groundwater supply has been contaminated has five options:

1. Contain the contaminants to prevent their migration from their source,

2. Withdraw the pollutants from the aquifer,

3. Treat the groundwater where it is withdrawn or at its point of use,

4. Rehabilitate the aquifer by either immobilizing or detoxifying the contaminants while they are still in the aquifer, and

5. Abandon the use of the aquifer and find alternative sources of water.

Given the importance of groundwater as a source of drinking water for so many communities and individuals and the cost and difficulty of cleaning up groundwater, the best way to guarantee continued supplies of clean groundwater is to prevent contamination. The National Program for Wellhead Protection is designed to protect groundwater supplies of drinking water.

Community Involvement and Support

Effective wellhead protection programs require control of sources of contaminants; this requires land use planning and control of certain types of development activities on private and public lands. Control of land use is difficult to achieve and requires support of the public and also public officials. Success in this effort must start with a program to educate the public and public officials on the nature of the problem and ways the problem can be controlled. Once everyone understands the problem, support to control or prevent the problem should be easier to achieve.

"What are the threats to our groundwater drinking supply?" is a question of concern to all responsible citizens in a community. Community involvement can start with this question and an explanation of the existing situation. Citizens should be informed that the quality of the groundwater is at risk (1) if a land use presents the capacity to leach contaminants into a groundwater supply that is used for drinking water, and (2) if the contaminants are of sufficient quantity and type to endanger human health. Contamination of groundwater that is not used for drinking does not present an immediate threat because there would not be the potential for health consequences unless the water could be used for drinking in the future. Similarly, just because a land use *MAY* contaminate groundwater does not necessarily mean that there is a threat to public health; the contamination may be in quantities small enough that no adverse health consequences would result.

The importance of broad public support and the fullest possible participation cannot be overstressed. Time and effort spent at this stage educating the community about the goals and process of establishing a wellhead protection program will greatly improve the chance of successfully implementing the program.

Relative Levels of Risk

Not all threats to groundwater quality are of equal significance. Some land uses, while appearing on a list (Table 1.2) of businesses that present risks for groundwater contamination, present a low risk. This determination is based upon the types of contaminants, how they interact with the environment, how they degrade in soil and water, how fast they move, and how dangerous they are to human health. It is important in the analysis of threats to groundwater that the specific characteristics of the community are taken into consideration. Many types of activities identified in Table 1.2 may not occur in a specific community. Therefore, it is an important step to identify which land uses with potential risk to groundwater do occur in a given community and to determine the level of risk they present. Railroad tracks, yards, and maintenance stations are listed as a *SLIGHT* risk in Table 1.2. However, in some communities in certain locations a railroad yard could be considered a *SEVERE* risk. Also, any other types of activities that there is a reason to be concerned about but which have not appeared in the Table should be identified and included.

1.01 Well Casing Vent

A well casing vent is provided to prevent vacuum conditions inside a well by admitting air during the *DRAWDOWN*[1] period when the well pump is first started. If vacuum conditions are allowed to develop, contamination may be sucked into the well through some hidden defect in the well or *CONDUCTOR CASING*[2] or through the top of the well at the pump base.

The well casing vent also prevents pressure buildup inside the well casing by allowing excess air to escape during the well recovery (refilling) period after the well pump shuts off. If pressures are allowed to build up, they will loosen and blow out the sealing compound around the pump base.

TABLE 1.2   RELATIVE LEVELS OF RISK FROM LAND USES TO GROUNDWATER
Taking Into Consideration Volume, Likelihood of Release, Toxicity of Contaminants, and Mobility

(Compiled and Analyzed by Vermont Department of Health, 1988)

SEVERE
- Dry Cleaners
- Gas Stations
- Car Wash With Gas Station
- Service Station—full or minor repairs
- Painting and Rust Proofing
- Junk Yards
- Highway De-Icing—application and storage
- Right-of-Way Maintenance
- Dust Inhibitors
- Parking Lot Runoff
- Commercial Size Fuel Tanks
- Underground Storage Tanks
- Injection Wells: automobile service station disposal wells, industrial process water, and waste disposal wells
- Hazardous Waste Disposal
- Landfills
- Salt Stockpiles

SEVERE TO MODERATE
- Machine Shops: metal working, electroplating, machining
- Chemical and Allied Products
- Industrial Lagoons and Pits
- Septic Tanks, Cesspools, and Privies
- Septic Cleaners
- Septage
- Household Cleaning Supplies
- Commercial Size Septic Systems
- Chemical Stockpiles
- Clandestine Dumping

MODERATE
- Carpet and Upholstery Cleaners
- Printing and Publishing
- Photography and X-Ray Labs
- Funeral Homes
- Pest Control
- Oil Distributors
- Paving and Roofing
- Electrical Component Industry
- Fertilizers and Pesticides
- Paint Products
- Automotive Products
- Home Heating Oil Tanks, Greenhouses, and Nurseries
- Golf Courses
- Landscaping
- Above Ground Fuel Tanks
- Agricultural Drainage Wells
- Raw Wastewater Disposal Wells, Abandoned Drinking Wells

MODERATE TO SLIGHT
- Water Softeners
- Research Laboratories
- Above Ground Manure Tanks
- Storm Water and Industrial Drainage Wells
- Stump Dumps
- Construction

SLIGHT
- Beauty Salons
- Car Wash
- Taxidermists
- Dyeing/Finishing of Textiles
- Paper and Allied Products
- Tanneries
- Rubber and Miscellaneous Plastic Products
- Stone, Glass, Clay, and Concrete Products
- Soft Drink Bottlers
- Animal Feedlots, Stables, and Kennels
- Animal Burial
- Dairy Wastes
- Poultry and Egg Processing
- Railroad Tracks, Yards, and Maintenance Stations
- Electrical Power Generation Plants and Powerline Corridors
- Mining of Domestic Stones
- Meat Packing, Rendering, and Poultry Plants
- Open Burning and Detonation Sites
- Aquifer Recharge Wells
- Electric Power and Direct Heat Reinjection Wells
- Domestic Wastewater Treatment Plant and Effluent Disposal Wells
- Radioactive Waste

[1] *Drawdown.   (1) The drop in the water table or level of water in the ground when water is being pumped from a well. (2) The amount of water used from a tank or reservoir. (3) The drop in the water level of a tank or reservoir.*
[2] *Conductor Casing.   The outer casing of a well. The purpose of this casing is to prevent contaminants from surface waters or shallow groundwaters from entering a well.*

A properly sized and constructed vent should allow the unrestricted flow of air into and out of the well interior. A vent of at least three inches (75 mm) in diameter should be provided. Dual venting is desirable on wells over 14 inches (350 mm) in diameter.

All well vents should be constructed so that openings are in a vertical downward position. Openings should be a minimum of 36 inches (900 mm) in height above the finished surface of the well lot (yard) and should be covered with a fine mesh screen or similar device to keep insects from the well interior.

1.02   Well Pumps

Once a well is completed and water is available from an aquifer, some type of pump must be installed to lift the water from the well and deliver it to the point of use. The intent of this section is to discuss the general characteristics of well pumps operators are likely to encounter.

Well pumps are generally classified into two basic groups:

1. *POSITIVE DISPLACEMENT* pumps which deliver the same volume or flow of water against any *HEAD*[3] within their operating capacity. Typical types are piston (reciprocating) pumps and screw or squeeze displacement (diaphragm) pumps; and

2. *VARIABLE DISPLACEMENT* pumps which deliver water with the volume or flow varying inversely with the head (the *GREATER* the head, the *LESS* the volume or flow) against which they are operating. The major types are centrifugal, jet, and air-lift pumps.

Either of these types of pumps can be used for pumping water from a well. However, centrifugal pumps are by far the most commonly used pump in the waterworks field because of their capability to deliver water in large quantities, against high as well as low heads, and with high efficiencies.

A centrifugal pump raises the water by a centrifugal force which is created by a wheel, referred to as an *IMPELLER*, revolving inside a tight *CASING*. In operation, the water enters the pump at the center of the impeller, called the *EYE*. The impeller throws the water outward toward the inside wall of the casing by the centrifugal force resulting from the revolution of the impeller. The water passes through the channel or diffuser vanes between the rim of the impeller and the casing and emerges at the discharge under pressure.

Centrifugal pumps are used almost exclusively in the waterworks field. Advantages of centrifugal pumps include: (1) relatively small space needed for any given capacity, (2) rotary rather than reciprocating motion, (3) adaptability to high-speed driving mechanisms such as electric motors and gas engines, (4) low initial cost, (5) simple mechanism, (6) simple operation and repair, and (7) safety against damage from high pressure because of limited maximum pressure that can be developed. Centrifugal pumps are generally classed as *VOLUTE* or *TURBINE* pumps.

The volute type of centrifugal pump has no diffuser vanes (see Figure 1.1). The impeller is housed in a spiral-shaped case in which the velocity of the water is reduced upon leaving the impeller, with a resultant increase in pressure. Ordinarily, the volute-type pump is of single-stage design and used in the water utility field for large-capacity, low-head application, and for low- to mid-range booster pump operations.

The turbine type of centrifugal pump is the one most commonly used for well pump operations (see Figure 1.2). In the turbine-type pump, the impeller is surrounded by diffuser vanes which provide gradually enlarging passages in which the velocity of the water leaving the impeller is gradually reduced, thus transforming velocity head to pressure head.

Use of multi-stage pumps is standard practice in well pumping operations. The stages are bolted together to form a pump bowl assembly and it is not uncommon to assemble a pump bowl assembly with 10 or more stages. The function of each stage is to add pressure head capacity; the volume capacity and efficiency are almost identical for each stage.

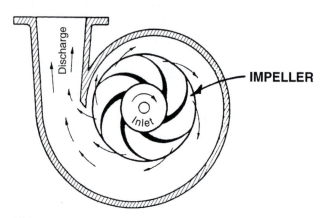

Volute-type centrifugal pump has no diffuser vanes or guides.

Fig. 1.1   Volute-type pump
(Source: *GROUNDWATER AND WELLS*,
permission of Johnson Division, UOP, St. Paul, Minn.)

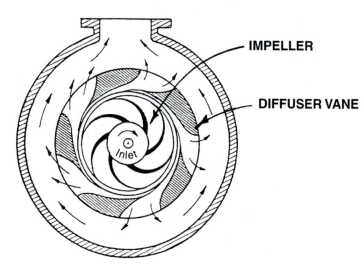

In turbine-type pump, water leaving the impeller moves out through the curved passages between diffuser vanes.

Fig. 1.2   Turbine-type pump
(Source: *GROUNDWATER AND WELLS*,
permission of Johnson Division, UOP, St. Paul, Minn.)

---

[3] *Head.   The vertical distance (in feet) equal to the pressure (in psi) at a specific point. The pressure head is equal to the pressure in psi times 2.31 ft/psi.*

1.03 Sand in the Well

Sources of Sand

Nearly all wells produce a certain amount of sand. Every reasonable effort should be made to prevent sand particles from entering the distribution system.

Wells drilled in *ALLUVIAL*[4] formations, where the water-bearing aquifers consist of numerous layers of sand and gravel deposits, are susceptible to sand production. In many localities, formations of sand and gravel are the only water-bearing formations of sufficient yield available to a community. Properly designed and constructed wells can be drilled in these types of formations that produce high yields while at the same time are virtually sand free. A carefully designed gravel envelope well, with selected louvers or well screen, supported by an engineering filter pack, should operate many years without producing any significant quantities of sand. However, the typical perforated casing or open-bottom well that has penetrated water-bearing sand formations is likely to produce sand. Some wells produce sand from the very beginning while others may be in use for some length of time before it is evident that the quantity of sand produced by the well is causing problems.

Problems Associated With Sand

The abrasive action of sand can damage well pumping facilities, customers' fixtures and appliances, water meters, and precision equipment. In addition, sand can accumulate in the mains in the distribution system, thereby reducing their carrying capacity and increasing *FRICTION LOSS*.[5] Sand can also be carried into the customers' premises with resultant complaints. Excessive sand production from a well could create cavities in the water-bearing formations and result in the eventual collapse of unstable overlying strata (layer of soil) and damage to the well. Tests have demonstrated that it is the sand particles larger than 200 mesh (74 microns) that cause the most trouble. Almost all sand contained in well water is this size or coarser.

Several methods are available to the well system operator to reduce sand production to an acceptable level. One method is to install a sand separator designed to remove the objectionable sand and other solids from the well water. Another method would be to pump the well at various rates of flow to determine if a lower rate of flow would reduce the amount of sand to an acceptable level. Many times a small change in water production will make a large change in sand production. In addition, if the system hydraulics permit, the well or wells producing objectionable amounts of sand could be operated on a continuous basis by either raising the cutoff pressure or, preferably, by controlling the operation of the well pump by means of a time clock. An alternative, and perhaps less desirable, approach would be to keep the sand-producing well in an emergency or standby mode. This can be done by setting the cut-in (start) and cutoff (stop) pressure 10 pounds (psi) below the other pumps in the system.

If sand production from a well cannot be controlled by the methods described, rehabilitation of the well or eventual abandonment may be necessary.

1.1 GROUNDWATER—CRITICAL LINK TO WELLS

1.10 Importance of Groundwater

The function of a well is to intercept groundwater moving through *AQUIFERS*[6] and bring water to the surface for use by people. Although we are concerned with wells and their construction and maintenance, we must also be concerned with the lifeline to these wells. The aquifers and the quality of water in the aquifers must be maintained if we are going to preserve this precious source of water. Pollution and misuse of the aquifers can seriously affect a good water source. Pollution can render a supply useless while excessive use of our wells can affect both volume and rate of output causing permanent damage to the water-bearing formations of the earth's surface.

Approximately 45 percent of the water used in the United States comes from underground sources. In many locations, water from wells or springs is the only water available to a community. Estimates indicate that there are between 10,000,000 and 20,000,000 water wells scattered throughout the United States. Most are situated in valleys or river-bottom land, although many are located in hilly and mountainous regions. They range from shallow hand-dug wells to carefully designed, large production wells.

---

[4] *Alluvial (uh-LOU-vee-ul). Relating to mud and/or sand deposited by flowing water. Alluvial deposits may occur after a heavy rainstorm.*

[5] *Friction Losses. The head, pressure or energy (they are the same) lost by water flowing in a pipe or channel as a result of turbulence caused by the velocity of the flowing water and the roughness of the pipe, channel walls, or restrictions caused by fittings. Water flowing in a pipe loses head, pressure or energy as a result of friction losses.*

[6] *Aquifer (ACK-wi-fer). A natural underground layer of porous, water-bearing materials (sand, gravel) usually capable of yielding a large amount or supply of water.*

The principal reasons for using groundwater are:

1. Groundwater is generally available in most localities although quantities may be very limited in certain areas;

2. Well and pumping facilities cost less than surface treatment facilities;

3. Groundwater is usually clear and, with few exceptions, can meet turbidity requirements;

4. Conditions for growth and survival of bacteria and viruses in groundwater are generally unfavorable when compared with surface waters;

5. The mineral content for a given well is usually uniform;

6. Well water usually has a more constant and lower temperature during the summer; and

7. *WELL SUPPLIES ARE PARTICULARLY SUITED TO THE NEEDS OF SMALLER COMMUNITIES IN MANY AREAS.*

1.11 Water (Hydrologic) Cycle[7] (Figure 1.3)

The earth's water cycle, or hydrologic cycle, is the continuous circulation of water (including moisture) on our planet. The cycle has neither a beginning nor an end, but the concept of the hydrologic cycle commonly begins with the waters of the ocean, since they cover about three-fourths of the earth's surface.

Water that infiltrates the soil is called subsurface water, but not all of it becomes groundwater. Basically, three things may happen to that water. First, it may be pulled back to the surface by capillary forces and be *EVAPORATED*[8] into the atmosphere, thus skipping much of the journey through the water cycle we have described. Second, it may be absorbed by plant roots growing in the soil and then re-enter the atmosphere by a process known as *TRANSPIRATION*.[9] Third, water that has infiltrated the soil deeply enough may be pulled on downward by gravity until it reaches the level of the *ZONE OF SATURATION*[10]—*THE GROUNDWATER RESERVOIR THAT SUPPLIES WATER TO WELLS.* Groundwater conditions directly affect the design, operation, and performance of a water well.

1.12 Aquifers

An aquifer, shown in Figure 1.4, is an underground layer of pervious material, such as sand, gravel, cracked rock, limestone, and/or other porous soil material capable of transporting and storing water. At the bottom of the aquifer will be an impervious layer of clay or rock which holds the aquifer in place.

If the water table is unconfined, the aquifer is known as a water table aquifer and a well in this aquifer is called a table well. If the aquifer is confined between two impervious layers, it is known as an artesian aquifer and from this type of aquifer we get what is referred to as an artesian well. Both types of aquifers and wells are shown in Figure 1.4. The artesian aquifer is under pressure and quite often this natural pressure reduces pumping requirements and thereby reduces pumping costs.

For a saturated material to qualify as an aquifer, it must have: (1) POROSITY,[11] area, and thickness sufficient to store an adequate water supply; (2) sufficient SPECIFIC YIELD[12] to allow the stored water to drain into a well; and (3) hydraulic TRANSMISSIVITY[13] to permit a well to drain water from the aquifer fast enough to meet flow requirements.

1.120 *Porosity and Specific Yield*

Porosity (usually expressed as a percentage) is a measure of the openings or voids (PORES[14]) in a particular soil. Porosity measurements represent (quantify) the amount of water that a particular soil type or rock can store.

$$\text{Porosity, \%} = \frac{(\text{Volume of Voids})(100\%)}{\text{Total Volume of Soil Sample}}$$

EXAMPLE:

$$V_v = \text{Volume of Voids} = 0.2 \text{ cu ft}$$

$$V_s = \text{Total Volume of Soil Sample} = 1.0 \text{ cu ft}$$

$$\text{Porosity, \%} = \frac{(V_v)}{(V_s)}(100\%)$$

$$= \frac{(0.2 \text{ cu ft})}{(1.0 \text{ cu ft})}(100\%)$$

$$= 20\%$$

Large porosities are usually associated with fine-grained, highly sorted materials while small porosities are representative of dense rock and soils.

---

[7] *Hydrologic (HI-dro-LOJ-ick) Cycle. The process of evaporation of water into the air and its return to earth by precipitation (rain or snow). This process also includes transpiration from plants, groundwater movement, and runoff into rivers, streams and the ocean. Also called the water cycle.*

[8] *Evaporation. The process by which water or other liquid becomes a gas (water vapor or ammonia vapor).*

[9] *Transpiration (TRAN-spur-RAY-shun). The process by which water vapor is released to the atmosphere by living plants. This process is similar to people sweating.*

[10] *Zone of Saturation. The soil or rock located below the top of the groundwater table. By definition, the zone of saturation is saturated with water.*

[11] *Porosity. (1) A measure of the spaces or voids in a material or aquifer. (2) The ratio of the volume of spaces in a rock or soil to the total volume. This ratio is usually expressed as a percentage.*

$$\text{Porosity, \%} = \frac{(\text{Volume of Spaces})(100\%)}{\text{Total Volume}}$$

[12] *Specific Yield. The quantity of water that a unit volume of saturated permeable rock or soil will yield when drained by gravity. Specific yield may be expressed as a ratio or as a percentage by volume.*

[13] *Transmissivity (TRANS-miss-SIV-it-tee). A measure of the ability to transmit (as in the ability of an aquifer to transmit water).*

[14] *Pore. A very small open space in a rock or granular material. Also called an interstice, void, or void space.*

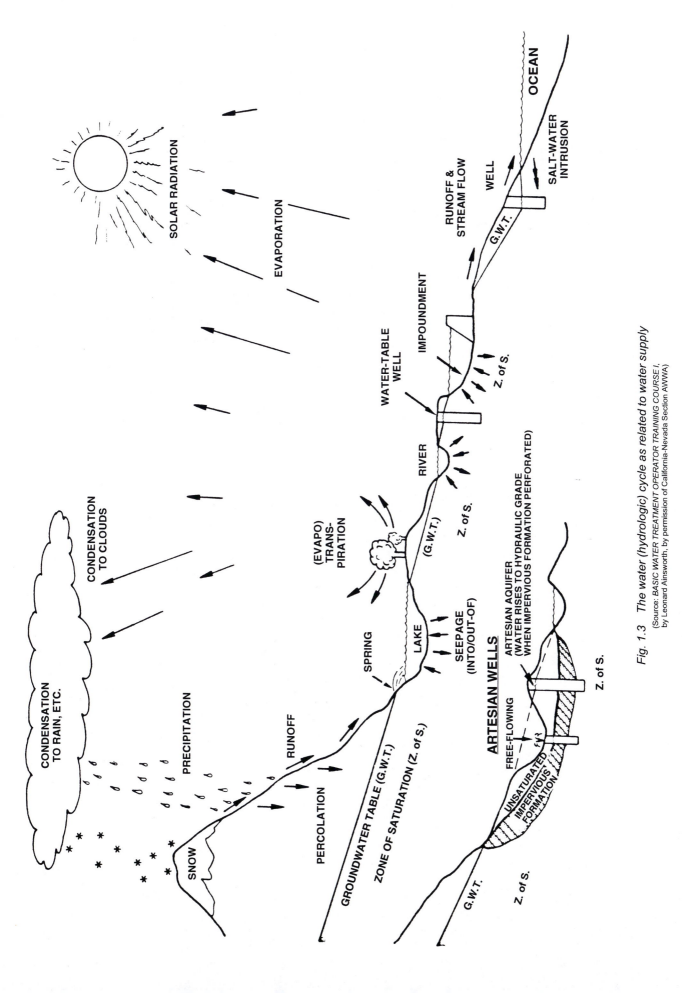

Fig. 1.3   The water (hydrologic) cycle as related to water supply
(Source: *BASIC WATER TREATMENT OPERATOR TRAINING COURSE I*,
by Leonard Ainsworth, by permission of California-Nevada Section AWWA)

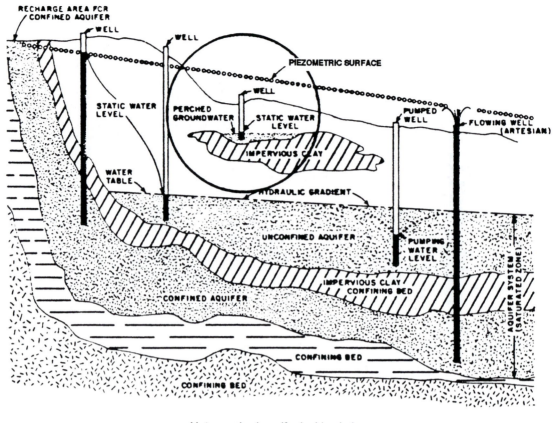

Note perched aquifer inside circle

Fig. 1.4   Water (hydrologic) cycle as related to groundwater
(Source: *WATER WELLS AND PUMPS: THEIR DESIGN, CONSTRUCTION, OPERATION AND MAINTENANCE,*
Division of Agricultural Sciences, University of California, Davis)

Only a portion of the stored water can be used to supply water to wells or aquifers. A certain amount of water will be retained and not affected by forces of gravity. The water volume that can move through the pores in the rock is affected by gravitational forces and is termed the specific yield (Y_{sp}). Table 1.3 shows the relationship in percentage between porosity and specific yield of various types of soil. Notice that although high porosity may be a good indicator of water storage capacity, it does not necessarily guarantee a high specific yield. Clay, for example, has a high porosity but a low specific yield.

1.121   Overdraft [15]

Aquifers have a certain *YIELD* [16] that can normally be replaced each year through recharge due mainly to precipitation. This yield, commonly called safe yield, is determined during well development through analysis by a qualified *HYDROGEOLOGIST.* [17]   Overdraft (overpumping) of the aquifer can cause permanent damage to the water storage and transmitting properties of the aquifers. If an excessive amount of water is removed (overdraft) from an aquifer, the soil may settle and cause compaction of the aquifers, which results in closing the pores through which water moves and in which the water is stored. This compaction and closing of pores also produces what we call subsidence (sub-SIDE-ence) of the land. Over the past three decades, ground subsidence has been measured from 0.91 foot (0.27 meter) in Savannah, Georgia, to over 27 feet (8 meters) in the San Joaquin Valley in California. Sink holes in Florida can also be attributed to overdraft of the groundwater supplies.

---

[15] *Overdraft.   The pumping of water from a groundwater basin or aquifer in excess of the supply flowing into the basin. This pumping results in a depletion or "mining" of the groundwater in the basin.*

[16] *Yield.   The quantity of water (expressed as a rate of flow—GPM, GPH, GPD, or total quantity per year) that can be collected for a given use from surface or groundwater sources. The yield may vary with the use proposed, with the plan of development, and also with economic considerations.*

[17] *Hydrogeologist (HI-dro-gee-ALL-uh-gist).   A person who studies and works with groundwater.*

TABLE 1.3   SELECTED VALUES OF POROSITY AND SPECIFIC YIELD[a]

Materials	Porosity[b]	Specific Yield[b]
Soil	55	40
Clay	50	2
Sand	25	22
Gravel	20	19
Limestone	20	18
Sandstone (semiconsolidated)	11	6
Granite	0.1	0.09
Basalt (young)	11	8

[a] *BASIC GROUNDWATER HYDROLOGY*, U.S. Geological Survey Water Supply Paper 2220. Prepared by Ralph C. Heath in cooperation with the North Carolina Department of Natural Resources and Community Development.
[b] Values in percent by volume.

1.122   Salt Water Intrusion

A special phenomenon occurs where salt water comes in contact with fresh water. A natural boundary (Figure 1.5) exists because of the differences in *SPECIFIC GRAVITIES*[18] of the two waters. The specific gravity of salt water is greater than the specific gravity of fresh water. This boundary prevents mixing of fresh and salty waters. As long as the natural movement of fresh water within the aquifer replaces water drawn by a well, the boundary between fresh and salty water will remain stable and little mixing will occur. When more fresh water is removed (by overpumping or overdraft) than can be replaced naturally, the salt water will intrude into the aquifer and may be drawn into the well.

Care must be exercised when installing or operating wells near any salt water source to prevent intrusion and pollution of those and neighboring wells. Any well operated in the fresh water area of Figure 1.5(a) will create a *CONE OF DEPRESSION*[19] from the salty groundwater upward toward the well as shown in Figure 1.5(b); a second cone of depression will form from the surface of the water table downward toward the aquifer. Excessive drawdown can bring the salt water into the aquifer and close enough to the well that salt water will be drawn into the cone of depression and into the well. As a general operating guideline, the ratio of "d" to "h" (shown in Figure 1.5(a)) should be at least 40 to 1; for example, if "h" equals 1 foot, "d" would equal 40 feet.

Salt water intrusion is a common problem along coastlines, but also occurs inland where groundwater supplies contain more than 1,000 mg/L of total dissolved solids. Figure 1.6 shows areas within the United States where salt water intrusion could be a problem. Local geologic conditions need to be known prior to placing wells in salt water areas.

1.13   Pollution

1.130   Pollution Control

Groundwater moves very slowly through the soil purifying itself of suspended particles as it travels. If water should be contaminated on its journey to a well and the distance from the source of contamination is far, there is a possibility that we will not see adverse effects at the well. The soil mantle acts as a natural filter for suspended material to bring us a good, clean product. Unfortunately, the soil mantle does not always filter out or remove dissolved pollutants and contaminants (such as organic chemicals) found in water. Chemicals used for farming, waste disposal pits, wastewater disposal, mining, leaks from gas storage tanks, oil spills, hazardous waste disposal, and urban drainage are a few of the factors contributing to groundwater pollution. Human wastes containing pathogenic organisms are also a source of pollution.

If sources of pollution are allowed to increase without limit and without regard to proximity to our wells, the earth's surface will become saturated with pollutants which no known treatment process can remove. Since water moves so slowly through the soil, we may end up with a water supply that cannot be used for years, even after the sources of pollution are eliminated.

Cleaning a polluted aquifer is difficult and expensive at best. Aquifers contaminated with oil spills and other chemical problems are almost impossible to clean up. The most reasonable course against groundwater pollution is prevention. Common sense and strict adherence to health agencies' requirements will go a long way in protecting this vital resource. The Environmental Protection Agency, and others, are making positive strides in keeping our groundwater supplies clean and safe, but a vigorous effort and awareness from all the public (and especially the public water supplier) are necessary.

The well operator has a responsibility to preserve the quality of wells through preventive maintenance of the aquifers. Be alert for any construction that might result in wastes entering the groundwater stream. Septic tanks, subsurface leaching systems, mining operations, agricultural practices, solid waste disposal sites, and wastewater collection facilities are all potential sources of groundwater pollution. Any such activity should be reported to the proper authorities so that adequate safeguards can be taken. Also you must make sure that none of your wells allow direct contamination of an aquifer due to inadequate grouting or seals. Although unsanitary conditions are not as common in the United States as in some countries, they still pose potential problems to our groundwater supplies.

Operators must always be alert for potential sources of groundwater pollution to the aquifers providing drinking water to their communities. Some of the possible sources include[20]:

1. Leaks from oil and gas pipelines,

2. Leaks from storage tanks,

---

[18] *Specific Gravity.   (1) Weight of a particle, substance, or chemical solution in relation to the weight of an equal volume of water. Water has a specific gravity of 1.000 at 4°C (39°F). Particulates in raw water may have a specific gravity of 1.005 to 2.5. (2) Weight of a particular gas in relation to the weight of an equal volume of air at the same temperature and pressure (air has a specific gravity of 1.0). Chlorine has a specific gravity of 2.5 as a gas.*

[19] *Cone of Depression.   The depression, roughly conical in shape, produced in the water table by the pumping of water from a well. Also called the cone of influence.*

[20] *Source: The Johnson Drillers Journal, Second Quarter, 1982.*

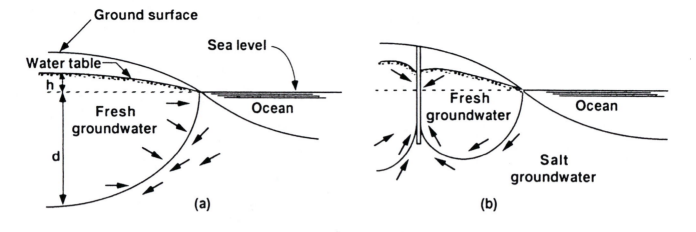

Fig. 1.5   (a) Salt water intrusion along coastal areas;
(b) Effect of excessive drawdown near a salt water source

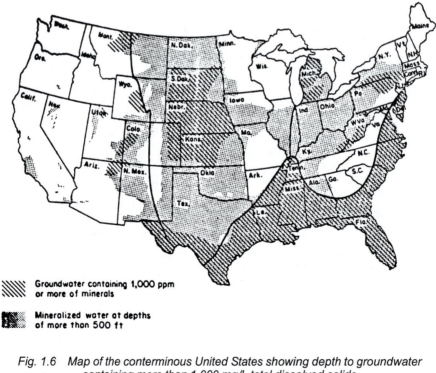

NNN Groundwater containing 1,000 ppm
      or more of minerals

██ Mineralized water at depths
      of more than 500 ft

*Fig. 1.6   Map of the conterminous United States showing depth to groundwater
containing more than 1,000 mg/L total dissolved solids*

(From paper by Bill Katz, *TREATING BRACKISH WATER FOR COMMUNITY SUPPLIES*,
published in Proceedings in "Role of Desalting Technology," a series of
Technology Transfer Workshops presented by
the US EPA Office of Water Research and Technology)

3. Fertilizers, pesticides, and irrigation water,

4. Improper management of animal wastes,

5. Liquid wastes and solid-waste tailing piles from surface and underground mining operations,

6. Drainage from abandoned mines,

7. Salt water encroachment from saline aquifers and the ocean,

8. Improper construction and use of injection wells for the disposal of industrial, nuclear, and hazardous wastes,

9. Accidental spills or liquid wastes, toxic fuels, gasoline and oil, and

10. Abandoned wells which were not properly destroyed.

1.131   Geologic and Hydrologic Data

If operators are going to protect aquifers, something must be known about them. Recordkeeping can be an invaluable tool for understanding the aquifer and its performance. Geologic data from the well driller's logs (records of depths of various layers of soil and type of soil in each layer), mining operations in the area, and data from the U.S. Geological Surveyor, U.S. Natural Resources Conservation Service, and from other sources will help operators to understand how water is getting into a well. Consultation with a geologist is recommended for a more complete understanding of the underground formation.

Records of pumping amounts and dates, depths of water at start and end of pumping, time of pumping, and water quality results remain the best sources of information about a well's performance. Using past performance data, an engineer, hydrologist, geologist, and well operator can predict the well's performance with a high degree of accuracy. Recordkeeping is very important and it is not possible for operators to accumulate too much information. So, if records are not now being kept, a program should be started immediately.

1.2   WELL MAINTENANCE AND REHABILITATION

1.20   Importance of Well Maintenance

If the well casing, well screen, filtering material, and other appurtenances of a well are properly designed and correctly installed by a qualified well driller, maintenance of a well will be minimized. However, wells, like all other waterworks facilities, need periodic routine maintenance in the interest of a continuous high level of performance and a maximum useful life. The usual attitude toward maintenance of wells is "out of sight—out of mind." Consequently, very little or no attention is

paid to wells until problems reach crisis levels, often resulting in the complete loss of the well. The importance of a routine maintenance program for the prevention, early detection, and correction of problems that reduce well performance and useful life cannot be overemphasized. A maintenance program can pay handsome dividends to a well owner and will certainly result in long-term benefits that exceed the cost of implementation and continuation of the program.

1.21   Factors Affecting the Maintenance of Well Performance

1.210   Adverse Conditions

The factors affecting the maintenance of well performance or yield are numerous. Care should be taken to distinguish between factors associated with the normal wearing of pump parts and those directly associated with changing conditions in and around the well. A perfectly functioning well, for example, can show a reduced yield because of a reduction in the capacity of the pump due to excessively worn parts. On the other hand, the excessive wearing of pump parts may be due to the pumping of sand that entered the well through a corroded well screen. Corrosion may reduce the pump capacity but, at the same time have little or no effect on a properly designed well. There will be some overlap in what is called well maintenance and what is called pump maintenance. Conditions (which we'll consider well maintenance problems) that should be guarded against are overpumping and lowering of the water table, clogging or collapse of a screen or perforated section, and corrosion or incrustation.

1.211   Overpumping

Overpumping was discussed in Section 1.121, "Overdraft," so we'll only summarize the problems here. Overpumping an aquifer can damage the aquifer by reducing the storage and production capacity of groundwater systems. The net result is consolidation of the water-bearing formations which provides less storage space, a lowering of the water table, and a reduced yield from the well. Other problems that may develop from overpumping or installing the pump suction too high include pumping air and also water cascading into the well. The well production rate is normally determined by the well driller and hydrogeologist at the time the well is drilled and developed.

Overpumping may cause sand pumping. This will subject the pump to excessive wear, which over time can reduce its operating efficiency. Under severe conditions, the pump may become sand locked, either during pumping or after shut-off. Should sand locking occur, the pump must be pulled, disassembled, cleaned, and repaired, if necessary, before being placed back into service.

1.212   Clogging or Collapse of Screen

A decrease in the capacity of a well most commonly results from clogging of the well screen openings and the water-bearing formation immediately around the well screen by incrusting deposits. These incrusting deposits may be of the hard, cement-like form typical of the carbonate and sulfate compounds of calcium and magnesium, the soft, sludge-like forms of the iron and manganese hydroxides, or the gelatinous slimes of iron bacteria. Iron may also be deposited in the form of ferric oxide with a reddish-brown, scale-like appearance. Less common is the deposit of soil materials such as silt and clay. More will be said about incrustation later.

Well screens are designed to fit individual well formations and are composed of numerous slits as shown on Figure 1.7.

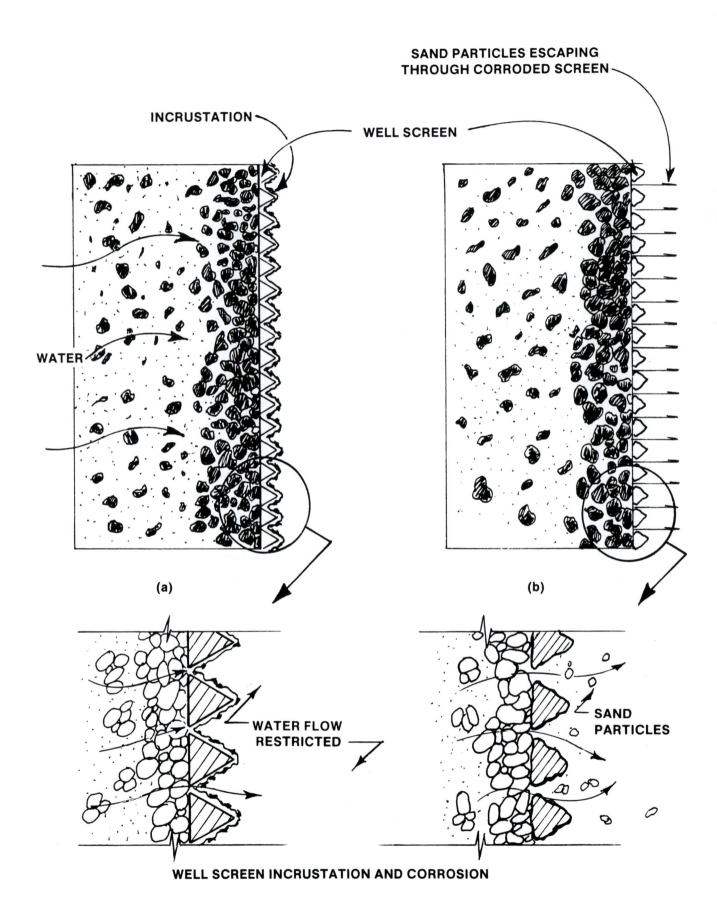

Fig. 1.7   Well screen incrustation and corrosion

As can be seen from this figure, if the slits in the casing become incrusted and blocked, the available area for water to move through is severely limited. If corrosion should occur, the slits may enlarge enough for grit and sand to be carried into the well along with water. This, in turn, will damage the pump and appurtenances. If the corrosion is severe enough, total collapse of the screen could occur.

1.213 Corrosion or Incrustation

Corrosion is a process which results in the gradual decomposition or destruction of metals. Corrosive waters are usually acidic and may contain relatively high concentrations of dissolved oxygen which is often necessary for and increases the rate of corrosion. High concentrations of carbon dioxide, total dissolved solids, and hydrogen sulfide (with its characteristic odor of rotten eggs) are other indications of a possibly corrosive water.

Besides water quality, other factors such as velocity of flow and dissimilarity of metals also contribute to the corrosion process. The greater the velocity of flow, the greater is the removal of the protective corrosion end products from the surface of the metal and hence the exposure of that surface to further corrosion. This is another important reason for keeping the velocity through screen openings within acceptable limits. The use of two or more different types of metals such as stainless steel and ordinary steel, or steel and brass or bronze should be avoided whenever possible. Corrosion is usually greatest at the points of contact of the different metals or where they come closest to contact.

Casing failure by corrosion ruins a well as fast as failure of the screen. Failure can cause the introduction of clay and polluted or otherwise unsatisfactory water into the well. Corrosive well waters have been known to destroy steel casings in less than six months, thus ruining many wells.

Incrustation, unlike corrosion, results not in the destruction of metal, but in the deposition of minerals on the metal and in the aquifer immediately around a well. Physical and chemical changes in the water in the well and the adjacent formation cause dissolved minerals to change to their insoluble states and settle out as deposits. These deposits block the screen openings and the pore spaces immediately around the screen with a resulting reduction in the yield of the well.

Incrusting waters are usually alkaline or the opposite of corrosive waters, which are acidic. Excessive carbonate hardness is a common source of incrustation in wells. Scale deposits of calcium carbonate (lime scale) occur in pipes carrying hard waters. Iron and manganese, to a lesser extent, are other common sources of incrustation in wells. Iron causes characteristic reddish-brown deposits while those of manganese are black.

Iron bacteria are often associated with groundwater that contains iron. These tiny living organisms aid in the deposition of iron but are not dangerous to health. However, iron bacteria produce accumulations of slimy, jelly-like material which block well screen openings and aquifer pore spaces.

1.22 Preventive Maintenance and Repairs

The best possible procedure for a good maintenance program is adequate recordkeeping. This aspect of the operator's responsibility cannot be overemphasized. Regular water level measurements in the well before and after pumping, flow rates, water quality samples, length of time pumping, and accurate data on pump repairs and causes are a few of the records that should be routine. The records should be kept neatly and in logical order. This collected data will be an in-

valuable tool in the hands of an engineer, hydrogeologist, chemist, or skilled operator. Operators should monitor this data to look for early warnings of potential problems such as overpumping. In areas where extensive oil and/or gas exploration is being conducted, operators should be alert for changes in water quality which could indicate pollution of an aquifer.

1.23 Casing and Screen Maintenance

The types of materials that go into the well are very important. Wells composed of materials with little or no resistance to corrosion can be destroyed beyond usefulness by a highly corrosive water within a few months of completion. This will be the case no matter how excellent the other aspects of design, construction, and maintenance. A poor selection of materials can also result in collapse of the well due to inadequate strength. All these factors have a considerable influence on the useful life of a well.

1.230 Surging

Surging, which is a form of plunging, is a procedure used for opening pores in the screen and for cleaning the gravel pack around the screen. A typical surge arrangement is shown in Figure 1.8.

Surging is commonly used for new well development to remove sand from the area around the well screen. However, it is also an effective procedure in combating incrustation when used with acid treatment. Care must be exercised when using surge plungers within the screen area itself and in wells in which aquifers contain large amounts of clay. In cleaning screens, the plunger can become sand-locked by the settling of sand above it. In cleaning the gravel pack around the screen, the action of the plunger can cause the clay to plaster over the screen surface. Plungers should be used only under the supervision of someone experienced in their use.

1.231 High-Velocity Jetting

High-velocity jetting is the spraying of water at a high velocity. This is an effective form of backwashing which, when used with acid treatment, is another procedure for removing incrustation from well screens and casings. Jetting can also be used for re-opening the pores of the aquifer and removing sand from the immediate vicinity of the well screen.

A simple form of jetting tool for use in wells is shown in Figure 1.9. An appropriately sized coupling with a steel plate welded over one end is screwed or welded to a pipe. The jetting tool's outside diameter will vary depending on the inside diameter of the well. The maximum and minimum difference in diameter between the jet tool and well screen are two inches

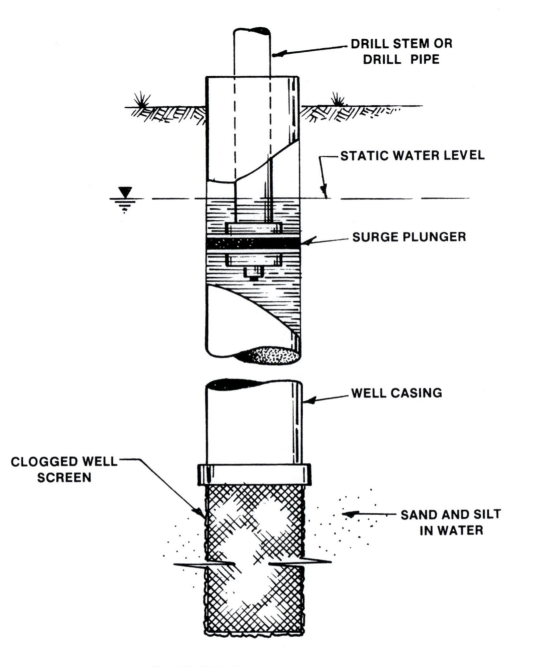

Fig. 1.8   Typical surge plunger arrangement

(50 mm) and one inch (25 mm) respectively. That is, if the well screen has a 10-inch (250-mm) inside diameter, then the jet tool should have an outside diameter between eight and nine inches (200 and 225 mm). Two to four $^{3}/_{16}$- or $^{1}/_{4}$-inch (5- or 6-mm) diameter holes, equally spaced around the circumference, are drilled through the full thicknesses of the coupling and the jetting pipe at a fixed distance along the coupling from the near surface of the steel plate. Better results can be obtained if properly shaped nozzles are used instead of the straight, drilled holes shown in Figure 1.9, but these are also acceptably effective.

The procedure is to lower the tool on the jetting pipe to a point near the bottom of the screen. The upper end of the pipe is connected through a swivel and hose to the discharge end of a high-pressure pump such as the mud pump used for hydraulic rotary drilling. The pump should be capable of operating at a pressure of at least 100 pounds per square inch (psi) (690 kPa or 7 kg/sq cm) and preferably at about 150 psi (1,040 kPa or 10.5 kg/sq cm) while delivering 10 to 12 gallons per minute (GPM) (0.6 to 0.8 L/sec) for each $^{3}/_{16}$-inch (5-mm) nozzle or 16 to 20 GPM (1.0 to 1.25 L/sec) for each $^{1}/_{4}$-inch (6-mm) nozzle on the tool. For example, a tool with two $^{3}/_{16}$-inch (5-mm) diameter nozzles would require a pumping rate of about 20 to 24 GPM (1.25 to 1.5 L/sec), while a tool with three $^{1}/_{4}$-inch (6-mm) diameter nozzles would require a pumping rate of 48 to 60 GPM (3.0 to 3.8 L/sec). While pumping water through the nozzles and screen into the formation, the jetting tool is slowly rotated, thus washing and developing the formation near the bottom of the well screen. The jetting tool is then

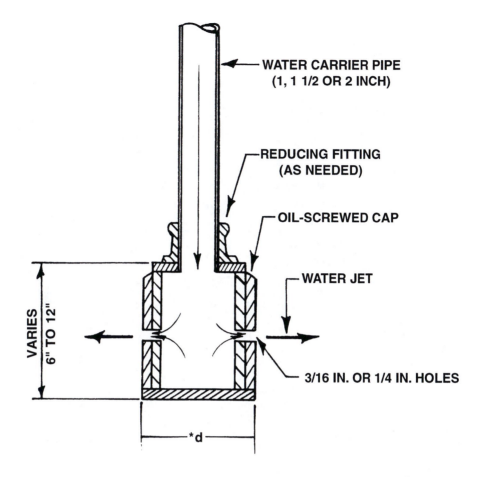

WATER CARRIER PIPE
(1, 1 1/2 OR 2 INCH)

REDUCING FITTING
(AS NEEDED)

OIL-SCREWED CAP

WATER JET

VARIES
6" TO 12"

3/16 IN. OR 1/4 IN. HOLES

*d

***d VARIES FROM 1 IN. TO 2 IN. LESS THAN
INSIDE DIAMETER OF WELL SCREEN**

Fig. 1.9   Simple jetting tool

raised at intervals of a few inches and the process repeated until the entire length of screen has been backwashed and fully developed. Where possible, it is very desirable to pump the well at the same time the jetting operation is in progress.

As shown in Figure 1.10, the area of concentration of the spray is very small. Because of this concentration, the jet spraying procedure becomes one of the most effective procedures for screen cleaning and well development.

1.232   Acid Treatment

Acid treatment may be the only effective procedure available to loosen incrustation so that it may be removed from the well casing and well. Acids normally used are hydrochloric or sulfamic. Both of these acids readily dissolve calcium and magnesium carbonate, though hydrochloric acid does so at a faster rate. Strong hydrochloric acid solutions also dissolve iron and manganese hydroxides. The simultaneous use of an inhibitor serves to slow up the tendency of the acid to attack steel casing. The use of chemicals in a well requires the proper selection of well materials at the time of construction to avoid damage to the materials by the chemicals.

Hydrochloric acid should be used at full strength. Each treatment usually requires 1 1/2 to 2 times the volume of water in the screen or pipe to be cleaned. This provides enough acid to fill the area to be cleaned and additional acid to maintain adequate strength as the chemical reacts with the incrusting materials. Figure 1.11 illustrates a method of placing acid in a well. Acid can be introduced into the well by means of a wide-mouthed funnel and 3/4- or 1-inch (18- or 25-mm) plastic pipe. Acid is heavier than water which it tends to displace but with which it also mixes readily to become diluted.

The acid solution in the well should be agitated by means of a surge plunger or other suitable means for 1 to 2 hours. Following this, the well should be bailed until the water is relatively clear. The driller usually can detect an improvement in the yield of the well while running the bailer. The well may, however, be pumped to determine the extent of improvement. If the results are less than expected, the treatment may be repeated using a longer period of agitation before bailing. Additional treatment may even be undertaken.

The procedure is sometimes varied to alternate acid treatment and chlorine treatment. The chlorine helps to remove

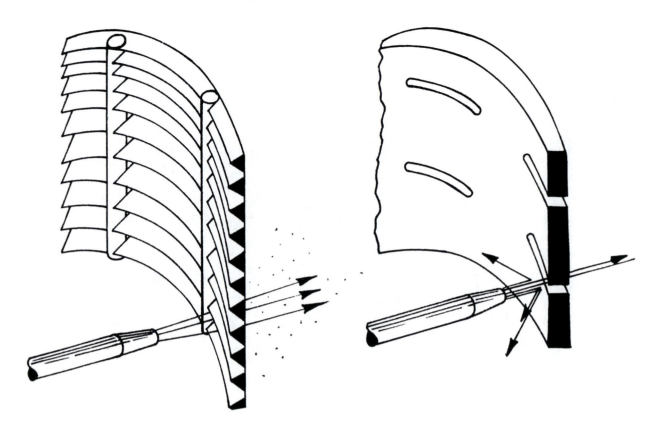

Fig. 1.10   Use of jet spray on well screen

the slime deposited by iron bacteria. Sulfamic acid offers a number of advantages over hydrochloric acid as a means of treating incrustation in wells. Sulfamic acid can be added to a well in either its original granular form or as an acid solution mixed on site. Granular sulfamic acid is nonirritating to dry skin and its solution gives off no fumes except when reacting with incrusting materials. Spillage, therefore, presents no hazards and handling is easier, cheaper, and safer. Sulfamic acid also has a markedly less corrosive effect on well casing and pumping equipment. Sulfamic acid dissolves calcium and magnesium carbonate compounds to produce very soluble products. The reaction is, however, slower than that using hydrochloric acid and a somewhat longer contact period in the well is required. Again, agitation must be provided by some sort of plunger. The quantity of acid added in this case should be based on the total volume of water standing in the well—*NOT* on the volume of just the part of the well to be cleaned (as is the case if the acid is applied in solution form). A little extra granular sulfamic acid may be added to keep the solution up to maximum strength while it is being used up through reaction with the incrusting material. The addition of a low-foaming, non-ionic wetting agent improves the cleansing action to some extent.

A number of precautions must be exercised in using any strong acid solution. Goggles and waterproof gloves should be worn by all persons handling the acid. When preparing an acid solution, *ALWAYS POUR THE ACID SLOWLY INTO THE WATER.* In view of the variety of gases, some of them very toxic, produced by the reaction of acid with incrusting materials, adequate ventilation must be provided in pump houses or other confined spaces around treated wells. Do not allow personnel to stand in a pit or depression around the well during treatment because some of the toxic gases (such as hydrogen sulfide) are heavier than air and will tend to settle in the lowest areas. After a well has been treated, it should be pumped to waste to ensure the complete removal of all acid (measure pH) before it is returned to normal service.

1.233   Chlorine Treatment

Chlorine treatment of wells is more effective than acid treatment in loosening bacterial growths and slime deposits which often accompany the deposition of iron oxide. Because of the very high concentrations required, 100 to 200 mg/L of *AVAILABLE CHLORINE*,[21] the process is often referred to as shock treatment with chlorine. Calcium or sodium hypochlorite may be used as the source of chlorine.

> NOTE: Either calcium or sodium hypochlorite can be used. They are *NEVER* used together. Extreme heat or an explosion could occur.

---

[21] *Available Chlorine.   A measure of the amount of chlorine available in chlorinated lime, hypochlorite compounds, and other materials that are used as a source of chlorine when compared with that of elemental (liquid or gaseous) chlorine.*

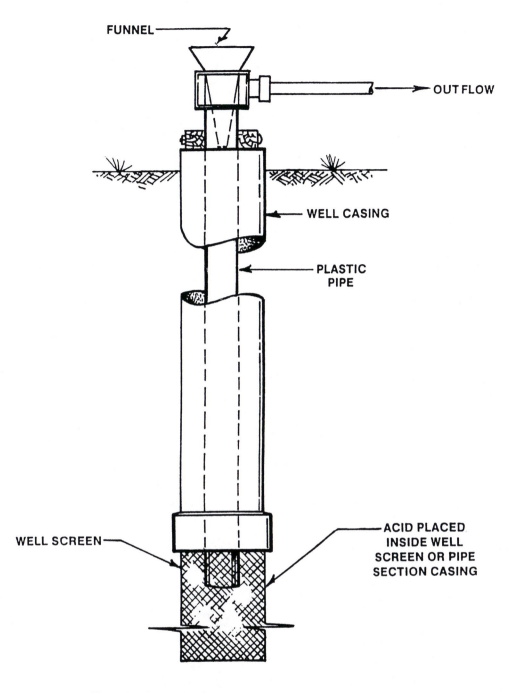

FUNNEL

OUT FLOW

WELL CASING

PLASTIC PIPE

WELL SCREEN

ACID PLACED INSIDE WELL SCREEN OR PIPE SECTION CASING

Fig. 1.11   Procedure for introducing acid into well for purpose of cleaning incrustations from screen and casing

The chlorine solution in the well must be agitated. This may be done by using the high-velocity jetting technique or by surging with a surge plunger or other suitable technique. The recirculation provided with the use of the jetting technique greatly improves the effectiveness of the treatment.

The treatment should be repeated 3 or 4 times in order to reach every part of the formation that may be affected. This treatment may also be alternated with acid treatment, but use the acid first.

1.234   Polyphosphates

Polyphosphates, or glassy phosphates as they are commonly called, effectively disperse silts, clays, and the oxides and hydroxides of iron and manganese. The dispersed materials can be easily removed by pumping. In addition, the polyphosphates are safe to handle and are often used in the chemical treatment of wells.

1.235   Explosive Charges

Small explosive charges have been used to clean plugged well screens. Experts in this field should be consulted before attempting this procedure.

1.236   Summary

Although many forms of well cleaning and maintenance have been discussed here, you are cautioned to exercise care in the application of any of these. Always observe manufacturers' recommendations. Obtain expert advice if you are not sure which chemical to use, how to apply the chemical or how to remove it from the well.

1.24   Water Quality Monitoring

Well performance can be affected by the quality of the groundwater. Similarly, water quality, both physical and chemical, is a good indicator of existing or potential problem areas and should be monitored regularly for clues to problems. For example, excessive sand production indicates problems with the well completion procedure and will produce excessive pump wear. The chemical quality of water indicates the type of dissolved minerals in the groundwater and will help in the design of a maintenance program if mineral deposition is suspected to be a cause of decreased well performance.

1.25   Downhole Video Inspection

Downhole video inspection can aid in well maintenance. Cameras take both still photographs and motion pictures of the well with the pumping equipment removed. The tape recorded "video log" of the well can then be reviewed as an aid in designing a maintenance or rehabilitation program. Specific problem areas, such as mineral deposition or other incrustation, corrosion of screen perforations or casing, and mechanical collapse or other failure, can be identified, permitting more precise procedures to correct problems.

1.26   Troubleshooting

1.260   Decline in Yield

The yield of any water supply well depends on three factors: the aquifer, the well, and the pump. A decline in yield is due to a change in at least one of these factors, and correction of the problem depends on identification of the factor that is involved. This identification in many cases can be made only if data are available on the depth to the water level in the well and the pumping rate. Inability to identify reasons for a decline in yield frequently results in discontinuing the use of the groundwater and developing more expensive supplies from either groundwater or surface water sources. Table 1.4 is a summary analysis of the causes of declines in well yields and potential corrective actions.

The specific capacity test is a measure of the adequacy of an aquifer or well. Specific capacity of a well is determined measuring the yield of a well in gallons per minute per unit of drawdown during a specific time period, usually 24 hours. For example, if a well yield was 150 GPM and the drawdown was 15 feet, the specific capacity would be 150 GPM/15 ft or 10 GPM/ft of drawdown. Specific capacity generally varies with the duration of pumping; as pumping time increases, specific capacity decreases. Also, specific capacity decreases and discharge increases in the same well.

1.261   Changes in Water Quality

Deterioration in water quality may result from changes in the quality of water in the aquifer or changes in the well. These changes may affect the biological quality, the chemical quality, or the physical quality of the water. Deterioration in biological and chemical quality generally results from conditions in the aquifer whereas changes in physical quality result from changes in the well. Both the biological and chemical quality of water from new public water supply wells must be analyzed before the wells are placed in use to determine if the water meets drinking water standards and, if it does not, what treatment is required. Table 1.5 is a summary analysis of the causes of changes in water quality and possible corrective actions.

1.27   Summary

Maintenance operations should not be put off until problems become serious. When this happens, rehabilitation of a well becomes more difficult and sometimes impossible or impractical. Incrustation not treated early enough can so thoroughly clog the well screen and the formation around it that it becomes extremely difficult (and even impossible) to diffuse or circulate a chemical solution to all affected points in the formation. At this point, any attempts at rehabilitation would most likely prove unsuccessful.

No methods have yet been developed for the complete prevention of incrustation in wells. Various steps can be taken to delay the process and reduce the magnitude of its effects. Among these are the proper design of well screens and the reduction of pumping rates, both aimed at reducing entrance velocities into screens and drawdown in wells. For example, it may be worthwhile to share the pumping load among a larger number of wells in order to reduce the rate of incrustation. However, the ultimate or final solution will be in a regular cleaning program. Incrusting wells are usually treated with chemicals which either dissolve the incrusting deposits or loosen them from the surfaces of the well screen and formation materials so that the deposits may be easily removed by bailing. Corkscrew-shaped brushes have been rotated in wells to remove incrustations.

Recordkeeping is a must. Only with data on the well's performance can problems be identified or predictions be accurately estimated. Start a recordkeeping program when a well is constructed. If such steps were not taken at the time of construction, they should be started as soon as possible.

1.3   WELL PUMPS AND SERVICE GUIDELINES

1.30   Purpose of Well Pumps

1.300   Well Pumps

Once a well is completed and water is available from an aquifer, some type of pump must be installed to lift the water from the well and deliver it to the point of use. The intent of this section is to discuss the general characteristics of well pumps operators are likely to encounter.

Well pumps are generally classified into two basic groups:

1. *POSITIVE DISPLACEMENT* pumps which deliver the same volume or flow of water against any *HEAD*[22] within their operating capacity. Typical types are piston (reciprocating) pumps, and screw or squeeze displacement (diaphragm) pumps; and

2. *VARIABLE DISPLACEMENT* pumps which deliver water with the volume or flow varying inversely with the head (the

---

[22] *Head.   The vertical distance (in feet) equal to the pressure (in psi) at a specific point. The pressure head is equal to the pressure in psi times 2.31 ft/psi.*

TABLE 1.4   ANALYSIS OF DECLINES IN WELL YIELDS [a]

Symptom	Cause	Corrective Action
Decline in available drawdown, no change in specific capacity.	The aquifer, due to a decline in groundwater level resulting from depletion of storage caused by decline in recharge or excessive withdrawals.	Increase spacing of new supply wells. Institute measures of artificial recharge.
No change in available drawdown, decline in specific capacity.	The well, due to increase in well head loss resulting from blockage of screen by rock particles or by deposition of carbonate or iron compounds; or reduction in length of the open hole by movement of sediment into the well.	Redevelop the well through the use of a surge block or other means. Use acid to dissolve incrustations.
No change in available drawdown, no change in specific capacity.	The pump, due to wear of impellers and other moving parts or loss of power from the motor.	Recondition or replace motor, or pull pump and replace worn or damaged parts.

[a] *BASIC GROUNDWATER HYDROLOGY.* United States Geological Survey (USGS) Water Supply Paper 2220.

TABLE 1.5   ANALYSIS OF CHANGES IN WATER QUALITY [a]

Change in Quality	Cause of the Change	Corrective Action
Biological	Movement of polluted water from the surface or near-surface layers through the *ANNULAR SPACE.*[b]	Seal annular space with cement grout or other impermeable material and mound dirt around the well to deflect surface runoff.
Chemical	Movement of polluted water into the well from the land surface or from shallow aquifers.	Seal the annular space. If sealing does not eliminate pollution, extend the casing to a deeper level (by telescoping and grouting a smaller diameter casing inside the original casing).
	Upward movement of water from zones of salty water.	Reduce the pumping rate and (or) seal the lower part of the well.
Physical	Migration of rock particles into the well through the screen or from water-bearing fractures penetrated by open-hole wells.	Remove pump and redevelop the well.
	Collapse of the well screen or rupture of the well casing.	Remove screen, if possible, and install new screen. Install smaller diameter casing inside the original casing.

[a] *BASIC GROUNDWATER HYDROLOGY.* United States Geological Survey (USGS) Water Supply Paper 2220.
[b] Annular (AN-you-ler) Space.   A ring-shaped space located between two circular objects, such as two pipes.

GREATER the head, the *LESS* the volume or flow) against which they are operating. The major types are centrifugal, jet, and air-lift pumps.

Either of these types of pumps can be used for pumping water from a well. However, centrifugal pumps are by far the most commonly used pump in the waterworks field because of their capability to deliver water in large quantities, against high as well as low heads, and with high efficiencies.

1.301 Shallow Well Pumps

A pump installed above a well is often called a *SHALLOW WELL PUMP*; this pump takes water from the well by *SUCTION LIFT.*[23] Such a pump can be used for either a deep well or a shallow well providing the pumping level is within the suction lift capability of the pump (maximum of 20-feet (6-m) lift).

1.302 Deep Well Pumps

A pump installed in the well with the *PUMP BOWL*[24] inlet submerged below the pumping level in the well is generally referred to as a *DEEP WELL PUMP*. This type of pump may be used for any well, regardless of depth, where the pumping level is below the limit of suction lift.

---

[23] *Suction Lift.   The NEGATIVE pressure [in feet (meters) of water or inches (centimeters) of mercury vacuum] on the suction side of a pump. The pressure can be measured from the centerline of the pump DOWN TO (lift) the elevation of the hydraulic grade line on the suction side of the pump.*
[24] *Pump Bowl.   The submerged pumping unit in a well, including the shaft, impellers and housing.*

1.31   Types of Well Pumps

1.310   Centrifugal Pumps

A centrifugal pump raises the water by a centrifugal force which is created by a wheel, referred to as an *IMPELLER*, revolving inside a tight *CASING*. In operation, the water enters the pump at the center of the impeller, called the *EYE*. The impeller throws the water outward toward the inside wall of the casing by the centrifugal force resulting from the revolution of the impeller. The water passes through the channel or diffuser vanes between the rim of the impeller and the casing, and emerges at the discharge under pressure. Centrifugal pumps are used almost exclusively in the waterworks field. Advantages of centrifugal pumps include: (1) relatively small space needed for any given capacity, (2) rotary rather than reciprocating motion, (3) adaptability to high-speed driving mechanisms such as electric motors and gas engines, (4) low initial cost, (5) simple mechanism, (6) simple operation and repair, and (7) safety against damage from high pressure because of limited maximum pressure that can be developed. Centrifugal pumps are generally classed as *VOLUTE* or *TURBINE* pumps.

1.311   Volute-Type Pumps

This type of centrifugal pump has no diffusion vanes (see Figure 1.12). The impeller is housed in a spiral-shaped case in which the velocity of the water is reduced upon leaving the impeller, with a resultant increase in pressure. Ordinarily, the volute-type pump is of single-stage design and used in the water utility field for large-capacity, low-head application, and for low- to mid-range booster pump operations.

1.312   Turbine-Type Pumps

This type of centrifugal pump is the one most commonly used for well pump operations (see Figure 1.13). In the turbine-type pump, the impeller is surrounded by diffuser vanes which provide gradually enlarging passages in which the velocity of the water leaving the impeller is gradually reduced, thus transforming velocity head to pressure head.

Use of multi-stage pumps is standard practice in well pumping operations. The stages are bolted together to form a pump bowl assembly and it is not uncommon to assemble a pump bowl assembly with 10 or more stages. The function of each stage is to add pressure head capacity; the volume capacity and efficiency are almost identical for each stage. As an example, in the case of a 10-stage pump rated at 500 gallons per minute (32 liters/sec) at 250 feet (75 m) of required head, utilizing 40 *BRAKE HORSEPOWER*[25] (30 kW), the first stage would pump 500 gallons per minute (32 liters/sec) at 25 feet (7.5 m) of head, the next stage would not increase the GPM but would add 25 feet (7.5 m) more of head; each of the remaining eight stages would also add 25 feet (7.5 m) of head making the total 250 feet (75 m) of head. The capacity would remain at 500 GPM (32 *L*/sec). However, the brake horsepower for each stage is also additive (as is head). Therefore, if each stage requires 4 BHP (3 kilowatts), then the total for the 10 stages would amount to 40 BHP (30 kilowatts).

Well pumps for water utility operation are generally of the turbine design and often are referred to as variable-displacement deep well centrifugal pumps or more simply, *DEEP WELL TURBINE* pumps.

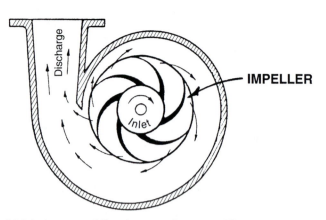

Volute-type centrifugal pump has no diffuser vanes or guides.

Fig. 1.12   Volute-type pump
(Source: *GROUNDWATER AND WELLS*,
permission of Johnson Division, UOP, St. Paul, Minn.)

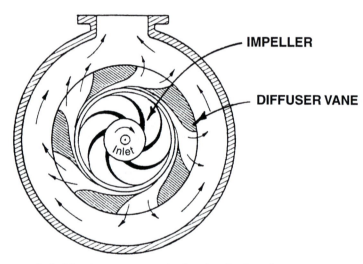

In turbine-type pump, water leaving the impeller moves out through the curved passages between diffuser vanes.

Fig. 1.13   Turbine-type pump
(Source: *GROUNDWATER AND WELLS*,
permission of Johnson Division, UOP, St. Paul, Minn.)

1.313   Deep Well Turbine Pumps

There are two classifications of deep well turbine pumps, depending upon the location of the prime mover (electric motor or engine).

1. *STANDARD DEEP WELL TURBINE* pumps are driven through a rotating shaft (lineshaft) connected to an electric motor or engine mounted on top of the well (see Figure 1.14). This type of pump requires lubrication of the lineshaft connecting the motor and the pump. Manufacturers have

---

[25] *Brake Horsepower.   (1) The horsepower required at the top or end of a pump shaft (input to a pump). (2) The energy provided by a motor or other power source.*

incorporated both *OIL LUBRICATION* and *WATER LUBRICATION* into this design.

a. In *WATER LUBRICATED* models, the lineshaft is supported in the center of the pump column pipe by means of stainless-steel lineshaft sleeves equipped with neoprene bearings which are lubricated by the water as it flows upward in the column pipe (see Figure 1.15).

This type of pump is most commonly used for large capacity wells and is designed specifically for each well and for its intended function.

Pumping capacities generally range from 200 to 2,000 gallons per minute (12.6 to 126 liters per second).

b. *OIL LUBRICATED* models have a watertight oil tube surrounding the lineshaft and oil is fed from the surface (see Figure 1.16).

Although both oil and water lubricated pumps are used in water utility operation, oil lubricated pumps are most often used.

2. *SUBMERSIBLE DEEP WELL TURBINE* pumps use a pumping bowl assembly similar to the standard deep well turbine except that the motor is mounted directly beneath the bowl assembly. This eliminates the need for the lineshaft and oil tube (see Figure 1.17). Unit efficiency approaches that of a lineshaft turbine pump.

Submersible pumps are available in a wide range of capacities from 5 to 2,000 gallons per minute (0.3 to 126 liters/sec), and are used by individual well owners as well as by small and large water system operators.

Submersible pumps are ideally suited to small water system operation where source capacities range from 25 to 1,000 gallons per minute (1.5 to 63 liters/sec). Maintenance is minimal, the noise level is very low, and they are suited to installations that have limited building areas.

1.314 Other Pumps

There are numerous types of pumps that may be used in the water utility field such as those discussed in the following paragraphs.

1. *JET PUMPS*

These were used for years on individual wells prior to the development of submersible pumps. They are low in efficiency and are generally restricted to lifts of 100 feet (30 m) or less (see Figure 1.18).

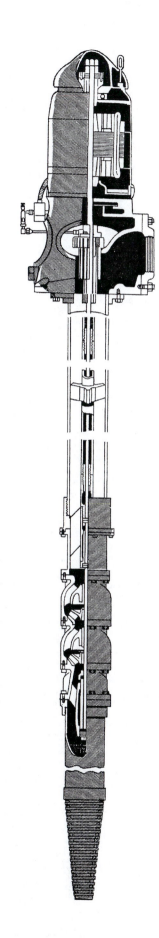

Fig. 1.14   Standard deep well turbine pump
(Permission of Jacuzzi Brothers, Inc.)

Water Lubricated

Oil Lubricated

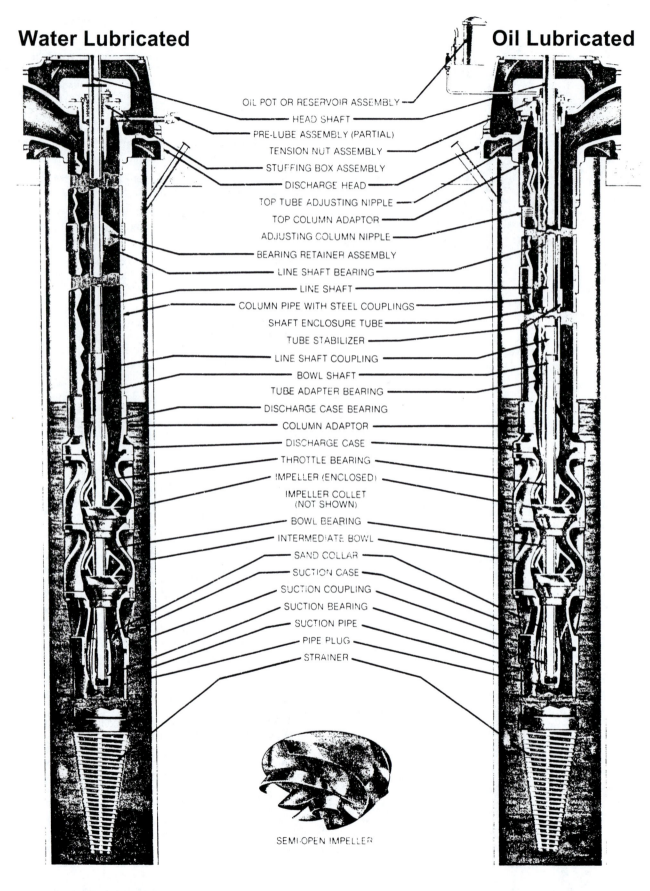

OIL POT OR RESERVOIR ASSEMBLY
HEAD SHAFT
PRE-LUBE ASSEMBLY (PARTIAL)
TENSION NUT ASSEMBLY
STUFFING BOX ASSEMBLY
DISCHARGE HEAD
TOP TUBE ADJUSTING NIPPLE
TOP COLUMN ADAPTOR
ADJUSTING COLUMN NIPPLE
BEARING RETAINER ASSEMBLY
LINE SHAFT BEARING
LINE SHAFT
COLUMN PIPE WITH STEEL COUPLINGS
SHAFT ENCLOSURE TUBE
TUBE STABILIZER
LINE SHAFT COUPLING
BOWL SHAFT
TUBE ADAPTER BEARING
DISCHARGE CASE BEARING
COLUMN ADAPTOR
DISCHARGE CASE
THROTTLE BEARING
IMPELLER (ENCLOSED)
IMPELLER COLLET
(NOT SHOWN)
BOWL BEARING
INTERMEDIATE BOWL
SAND COLLAR
SUCTION CASE
SUCTION COUPLING
SUCTION BEARING
SUCTION PIPE
PIPE PLUG
STRAINER

SEMI-OPEN IMPELLER

Fig. 1.15   Water lubricated pump

Fig. 1.16   Oil lubricated pump

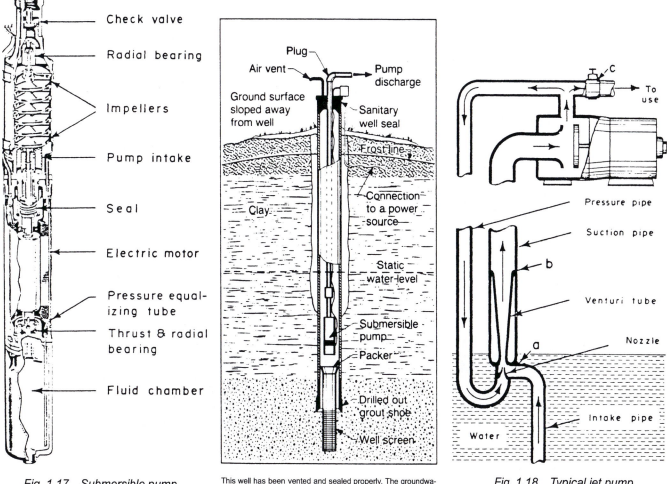

Fig. 1.17   Submersible pump

(Source: *GROUNDWATER AND WELLS*,
Johnson Division, UOP, Inc., St. Paul, Minn.)

This well has been vented and sealed properly. The groundwater surface around the top of the casing has been graded to slope away in all directions. *(After U.S. Environmental Protection Agency, 1973)*

Fig. 1.18   Typical jet pump

(Source: *GROUNDWATER AND WELLS*,
Johnson Division, UOP, Inc., St. Paul, Minn.)

2. PISTON PUMPS

All piston pumps function by means of a piston movement which displaces water in a cylinder. The flow is controlled by valves. They are restricted to low capacity-high pressure applications and are being phased out in favor of turbine-type pumps (see Figure 1.19).

3. ROTARY PUMPS

The rotary pump uses cogs or gears, rigid vanes and flexible vanes. When rotated, a gear-type pump squeezes the water from between the close-fitting gear teeth, moving the water from the inlet side to the outlet side of the pump. A typical rigid-vane rotary pump has a series of dividers or vanes fitted into a slotted rotor. When rotated, these vanes move radially to conform to the contour of the pump housing. The pump housing is eccentric with relation to the rotor, so that the water is pushed from the pump in a continuous flow ahead of the vanes. In flexible-vane rotary pumps, the vanes are elastic blades (usually rubber) which bend to provide the change in displacement volume which forces the water along its path. Rotary pumps are usually used for booster purposes and are generally used in conjunction with another pump (see Figure 1.20).

The above-mentioned pumps have a very limited application and are discussed in this section for the purpose of familiarizing operators with pumps that could be found in water utility operations.

1.32   Column Pipe

Operators should be aware of the functions of the pump column pipe in a deep well turbine pumping installation. The column pipe is an integral part of the pump assembly and serves three basic purposes: (1) the column pipe connects to the bottom of the surface discharge head, extends down into the well and connects to the top of the well pump (bowl unit) thereby supporting the pump in the well, (2) the column pipe delivers water under pressure from the well pump to the surface, and (3) keeps the lineshaft and shaft enclosing (oil) tube assembly in straight alignment. Column pipe assemblies for both water and oil lubricated pumps are shown in Figures 1.21 and 1.22.

1.33   Right-Angle Gear Drives (Figures 1.23 and 1.24)

Right-angle gear drives for water utility operations have two distinct applications and provide an economical, efficient, and positive power transmission from a horizontal prime mover (electric motor or engine) to a vertical shaft.

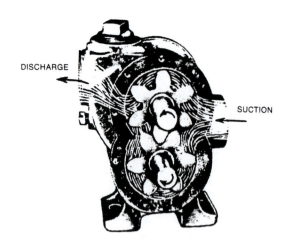

Rotary gear pump

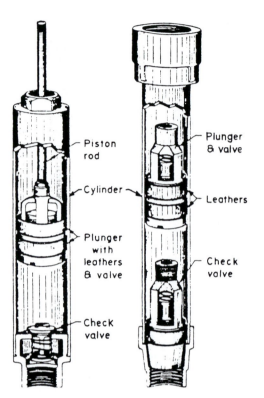

NOTE: Leathers are O-rings or gaskets used to provide a seal between the piston and the side wall.

(Source: GROUNDWATER AND WELLS, permission of
Johnson Division, UOP, St. Paul, Minn.)

(Source: GROUNDWATER AND WELLS, permission of
Johnson Division, UOP, St. Paul, Minn.)

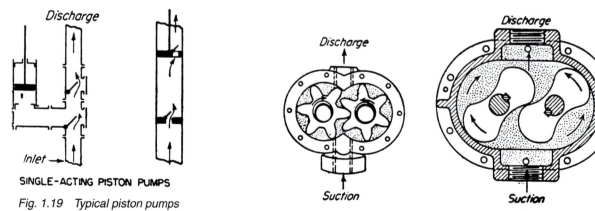

SINGLE-ACTING PISTON PUMPS

Fig. 1.19   Typical piston pumps

(Reprinted from WATER SUPPLY ENGINEERING by Babbit, Dolan, and Cleasby,
Sixth Edition, by permission. Copyright 1962, McGraw-Hill Book Company)

Fig. 1.20   Rotary pumps

(Reprinted from WATER SUPPLY ENGINEERING by Babbit, Dolan, and Cleasby,
Sixth Edition, by permission. Copyright 1962, McGraw-Hill Book Company)

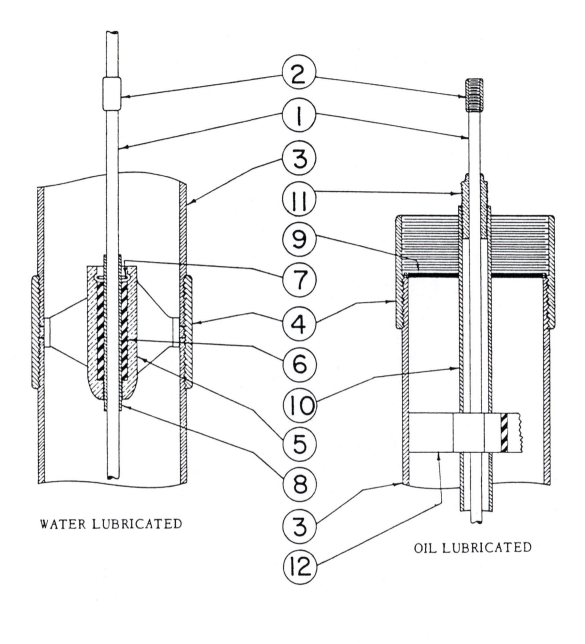

WATER LUBRICATED

OIL LUBRICATED

1 LINESHAFT	7 SNAP RING
2 SHAFT COUPLING	8 SHAFT SLEEVE
3 COLUMN PIPE	9 COLUMN PIPE SPACER RING (OPTIONAL)
4 COLUMN PIPE COUPLING	10 OIL TUBE
5 BEARING CAGE	11 LINESHAFT BEARING
6 RUBBER SHAFT BEARING	12 TUBE STABILIZER

Fig. 1.21   Column pipe assembly for
water lubricated pumps

Fig. 1.22   Column pipe assembly for
oil lubricated pumps

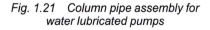

(Permission of Peabody Floway, Inc., Fresno, CA)

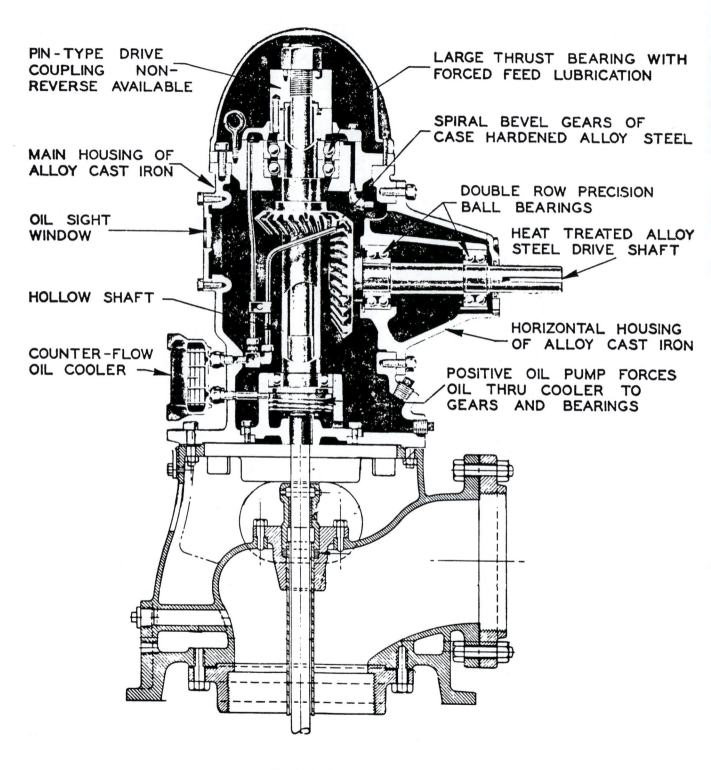

PIN - TYPE DRIVE COUPLING NON-REVERSE AVAILABLE

LARGE THRUST BEARING WITH FORCED FEED LUBRICATION

SPIRAL BEVEL GEARS OF CASE HARDENED ALLOY STEEL

MAIN HOUSING OF ALLOY CAST IRON

DOUBLE ROW PRECISION BALL BEARINGS

HEAT TREATED ALLOY STEEL DRIVE SHAFT

OIL SIGHT WINDOW

HOLLOW SHAFT

HORIZONTAL HOUSING OF ALLOY CAST IRON

COUNTER-FLOW OIL COOLER

POSITIVE OIL PUMP FORCES OIL THRU COOLER TO GEARS AND BEARINGS

Fig. 1.23   *Right-angle gear drive*

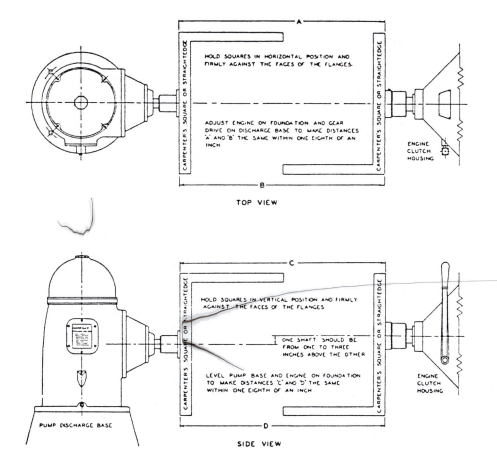

Fig. 1.24   Alignment of right-angle gear drive
(Source: Amarillo Right Angle Pump Drive, Amarillo, Texas)

In one application, the right-angle gear drive replaces the electric motor on top of the well and is used on either a full-time or part-time basis.

In a second application, the right-angle gear drive is used with the electric motor. The gear drive is mounted on top of the well discharge head and the electric motor is connected to the right-angle gear drive. An extra long headshaft (an extension of the lineshaft) connects both prime movers to the bowl unit in the well. In most applications, the electric motor is the lead prime mover and the right-angle gear drive unit is used for standby or emergency purposes only. The unit is usually set up for automatic operation.

In either application, the prime mover could be in the form of a gasoline, natural gas, diesel, or propane-powered engine connected to the gear head by means of a flexible drive shaft.

1.34 Selecting a Pump

Before a pump can be intelligently selected for any installation, accurate information about required capacity, location and operating conditions, and total head is needed. With this data available, a selection of the type, class, and size of pump can be made.

After the best type of pump has been determined on the basis of available data, an individual pump must be selected which will best fit each situation. This selection is particularly important if a well is the source of water supply and must take into account differences in pumping head caused by seasonal variations of static water level, temporary lowering of the pumping water level as a result of long periods of continuous pumping, and interference from other wells in the area.

1.35 Service Guidelines

DEEP WELL TURBINE, OIL LUBRICATED pumps are usually equipped with an automatic electric oiler system that is activated by means of an electric solenoid valve when the well pump starts. An adjusting needle and sight glass are part of this assembly. The needle valve is adjusted to feed approximately five drops per minute plus one drop of oil per minute for each 20 feet (6 m) of column during the first week of operation. The drip rate may thereafter be reduced to one drop per minute for each 40 feet (12 m) of column. Under no circumstances should the drip rate be less than five drops per minute, regardless of the length of column.

A good grade of turbine oil (mineral base) SAE 10 is used as the lubricant. Automotive or diesel engine lubricating oils cannot be used as a lineshaft lubricant. The oils listed in Table 1.6 are recommended for lubricating the lineshaft bearings. This list does not include all acceptable oils.

DEEP WELL TURBINE, WATER LUBRICATED pumps are self-lubricating and normally require little or no lineshaft maintenance. In a few cases where the static water level is over 100 feet (30 m) and the pump is operated on an intermittent

TABLE 1.6   OILS RECOMMENDED FOR LUBRICATING THE LINESHAFT BEARINGS [a]

OIL	SOURCE
Turbine Oil, Light	Atlantic Refining
Teresso, #43	ESSO Standard
Gulfcrest, #44	Gulf
Turbo, #27	Shell
DTE, #797	Socony Mobil
Chevron OC Turbine, #9	Standard Oil of California
Nonpareil, Medium L5803	Standard Oil of Indiana
Sunvise, #916	Sun Oil
Regal, R & O	The Texas Company
Pacemaker, #1	Cities Service

[a] JOHNSTON VERTICAL TURBINE PUMPS, INSTALLATION, OPERATION AND MAINTENANCE MANUAL, Glendora, CA.

basis, a special small-diameter, pressurized water line may be used to keep the bearings above the water level lubricated.

1.36   Motors

Vertical, hollow-shaft motors for deep well turbine pumps (motor on top of well) require some degree of routine maintenance. The motor bearings at the top and bottom of the motor are enclosed within a weatherproof oil bath container. The oil in this container should be changed annually. Most motors are equipped with a lubrication instruction plate attached to the motor that specifies the proper type and viscosity of oil required for various operating temperatures.

On small motors, the bearings are generally grease lubricated and require weekly attention during the heavy pumping season. Do not use excess grease because the bearings will overheat. The motor manufacturer's instruction manual should specify the type of grease recommended for various applications.

1.4   TROUBLESHOOTING

1.40   Need for Troubleshooting

Approximately 75 percent of well pump and control problems are associated with electricity. The well pump operator should have a good working knowledge of electric circuits and circuit testing instruments before attempting to service or troubleshoot the electric circuits and components commonly used in well pump operations. The operator should not undertake any electrically related troubleshooting or repair job until instructions have been received on how to do it properly and until the operator has been authorized to perform that job.

Small water utilities that do not have a knowledgeable operator or electrician on their staff should arrange with a local electrical firm or pump service company to perform this service.

1.41   Troubleshooting Guide

The "Troubleshooting Guide" on the following pages is designed to assist the operator or service personnel in diagnosing and correcting the most common problems associated with well pumping facilities.

TO USE THE GUIDE:

1. Find the appropriate condition in the SYMPTOM column or section.

2. Find the cause in the PROBABLE CAUSE column.

3. Perform the CORRECTIVE ACTION listed in the third column. The remedy is listed briefly and the procedures may not be detailed enough to cover every possibility.

The operator should not proceed if there is any doubt as to what is meant or what course of action should be taken to correct a given problem.

1.5   ADDITIONAL READING

To obtain information regarding the topics in this chapter, review the appropriate chapters and sections in the following operator training manual:

SMALL WATER SYSTEM OPERATION AND MAINTENANCE. Obtain from the Office of Water Programs, California State University, Sacramento, 6000 J Street, Sacramento, CA 95819-6025, phone (916) 278-6142 or visit the website at www.owp.csus.edu. Price, $45.00.

1.6   ACKNOWLEDGMENT

TROUBLESHOOTING GUIDE

Symptom	Probable Cause	Corrective Action
1.410 *Pump Will Not Start*	Circuit breaker or overload relay tripped, motor cold.	Reset breaker or reset manual overload relay.
	Fuses burned out.	Check for cause and correct, replace fuses.
	No power to switch box.	Confirm with multimeter by checking incoming power source, notify power company.
	Motor is hot and overload relay has tripped.	Allow motor to cool. Check supply voltage. If low, notify power company. If normal, reset overload relay, start motor, check amperage; if above normal, call electrician.
	Loose or broken wire, or short.	Tighten wiring terminal, replace any broken wires, check for shorts and correct.
	Low line voltage.	Check incoming power, use multimeter; if low, notify power company.
	Defective motor.	*MEG*[26] out motor; if bad, replace.
	Defective pressure switch.	With contact points closed, check for voltage through switch; if no voltage, replace switch; if low voltage, clean contact points; if full voltage, proceed to next item.
	Line to pressure switch is plugged or valve in line has accidentally been shut off.	Open valve if closed. Clean or replace line.
	Pump control valve malfunctioning.	Check limit switch for proper travel and contact. Adjust or replace as required.
	Defective time delay relay or pump start timer.	Check for voltage through relay or timer — replace as necessary — check for loose linkage.
	Float switch or transducer malfunctioning.	If pump is activated by float switch or pressure transducer on storage tank, check for incoming signal; if no signal, check out switch or transducer with multimeter. If OK, look for broken cable between storage tank and pump station.
1.411 *Pump Will Not Shut Off*	Defective pressure switch.	Points in switch stuck or mechanical linkage broken, replace switch.
	Line to pressure switch is plugged or valve in line has been accidentally shut off.	Open valve if closed. Clean or replace plugged line.
	Cutoff pressure setting too high.	Adjust setting.
	Pump control valve malfunctioning.	Check limit switch for proper travel and contact. Adjust or replace as required.
	Float switch or transducer malfunctioning.	Defective incoming signal, check and replace components as required. Check cable.
	Defective timer in pump stop mode.	Check for voltage through pump stop timer, replace if defective.
1.412 *Pump Starts Too Frequently*	Pressure switch cut-in and cutoff settings too close.	Adjust settings, maintain minimum 20 psi (138 kPa or 1.4 kg/sq cm) differential.
	Waterlogged tank.	Add air to tank. Check air charging system and air release valve. Also check tank and connections for air leaks.
	Leaking foot valve.	Check for backflow into well; if excessive or if pump shaft is turning backward, correct problem as soon as possible.
	Time delay relay or pump start/stop timers are malfunctioning.	Check relay or timers for proper operation, replace defective components.

[26] *Meg.   A procedure used for checking the insulation resistance on motors, feeders, bus bar systems, grounds, and branch circuit wiring.*

TROUBLESHOOTING GUIDE (continued)

Symptom	Probable Cause	Corrective Action
1.413 *Fuses Blow, Circuit Breaker or Overload Relays Trip When Pump Is in Operation*	Switch box or control not properly vented, or in full sunshine or dead air location, overload relay may be tripping due to external heat.	Provide adequate ventilation (may require small fan). Provide shelter from sun. Paint box or panel with heat reflective paint, preferably white.
	Incorrect voltage.	Check incoming power source. If not within prescribed limits, notify power company.
	Overload relays tripped.	Check motor running amperage, verify that thermal relay components are correctly sized to operating conditions. Repeated tripping will weaken units, replace if necessary.
	Motor overloaded and running very hot.	Modern motors are designed to run hot and if the hand can be held on the motor for 10 seconds without extreme discomfort, the temperature is not damaging. Motor current should not exceed *NAMEPLATE*[27] rating. Fifteen percent overload reduces motor life by 50 percent.
1.414 *Pump Will Not Deliver Normal Amount of Water*	Pump breaking suction.	Check water level to be certain water is above pump bowls when operating. If not, lower bowls.
	Pump impeller improperly adjusted.	Check adjustment and lower impellers (qualified personnel only).
	Rotation incorrect.	Check rotation.
	Impellers worn.	If well pumps sand, impeller could be excessively worn thus reducing amount of water pump can deliver. Evaluate and re-condition pump bowls if required.
	Pump control valve malfunctioning.	Check limit switch for proper travel and contact. Adjust or re-place as required.
	Impeller or bowls partially plugged.	Wash down pump by forcing water back through discharge pipe. Evaluate sand production from well.
	DRAWDOWN[28] more than anticipated.	Check pumping water level. Reduce production from pump or lower bowls.
	Pump motor speed too slow.	Check speed and compare with performance curves. Also check lift and discharge pressure for power requirements.
1.415 *Pump Takes Too Much Power*	Impellers not properly adjusted.	Refer to manufacturer's bulletin for adjustment of open or closed impellers.
	Well is pumping sand.	Check water being pumped for presence of sand. Restrict discharge until water is clean. Care should be taken not to shut down pump if it is pumping very much sand.
	Crooked well, pump shaft binding.	Reshim between pump base and pump head to center shaft in motor quill. Never shim between pump head and motor.
	Worn bearings or bent shaft.	Check and replace as necessary.
1.416 *Excessive Operating Noise*	Motor bearings worn.	Replace as necessary.
	Bent line shaft or head shaft.	Check and replace.
	Line shaft bearings not receiving oil.	Make sure there is oil in the oil reservoir and the oiler solenoid is opening. Check sight gage drip rate, adjust drip feed oiler for 5 drops per minute plus 1 drop per minute for each 40 feet (12 m) of column.

---

[27] *Nameplate.   A durable metal plate found on equipment which lists critical operating conditions for the equipment.*
[28] *Drawdown.   The drop in the water table or level of water in the ground when water is being pumped from a well.*

WATER SYSTEMS OPERATION AND MAINTENANCE VIDEO TRAINING SERIES

CHAPTER (VIDEO) 2

HYPOCHLORINATION

VIDEO 2 SUMMARY

Video 2, HYPOCHLORINATION, provides operators with the knowledge, skills, and abilities they need to safely operate, maintain, and troubleshoot hypochlorination systems. Information is provided on how to inspect a hypochlorination system, calculate chlorine dosage, determine hypochlorinator settings, and also to operate, maintain, and troubleshoot hypochlorinators. Procedures are provided to safely prepare and mix chlorine solutions, measure chlorine residual, and safely handle and store hypochlorite compounds.

CONTENTS OF VIDEO 2

HYPOCHLORINATION VIDEO

INTRODUCTION

Description of Hypochlorination System

Reasons for Hypochlorination/Disinfection

Safe Drinking Water Act (SDWA)

Contents of This Video

TOUR OF TREATMENT PLANT

Surface Water Treatment Plant

Ozonation System

Chemical Injection

Coagulation/Flocculation

Sedimentation

Filtration

Disinfection

pH Adjustment

HYPOCHLORINATION PROCESS

Disinfection

Use of Sodium Hypochlorite

Hypochlorination Pump

Critical Spare Parts

MIXING THE HYPOCHLORITE SOLUTION

Safety

Add Hypochlorite Chemicals to Water or Solution

Add Water

Mix Solution

HYPOCHLORINATOR SETTINGS AND ADJUSTMENT

Stroke

Frequency

1. How much chlorine is needed?

2. How many pounds of chlorine solution are needed?

3. How many gallons of chlorine per hour are needed?

OPERATION, MAINTENANCE, AND TROUBLESHOOTING

      Routine Procedures

      Walk Through Procedures

      Detailed O & M Procedures

      Troubleshooting (processes, hypochlorinator pump, valves, be observant)

RECORDKEEPING

      Importance

      Daily Log

      Monthly Reports

      Chemical Inventory

      Vendors

MIKE'S TIP, CHLORINE HAZARDS

      Chemical Safety

      Calcium and Sodium Hypochlorite

      Refer to Material Safety Data Sheets (MSDSs)

      Use Proper Protection Equipment

      Store Chemicals Separately and Safely

      Clean Up Spills

SUMMARY OR TASKS

      Daily

      Weekly

      Monthly

      Preparation of Solutions

      Follow Safe Procedures

      Use NSF (National Sanitation Foundation) Approved Chemicals

      Develop a Good Operation Plan

      Handle Chemicals Safely

      Recordkeeping

CONTENTS OF CHAPTER 2

**HYPOCHLORINATION
LEARNING BOOKLET**

OBJECTIVES

Chapter (Video) 2.   HYPOCHLORINATION

Following completion of Video 2 and Chapter 2, you should be able to:

1. Describe reasons for drinking water disinfection,

2. Describe factors influencing disinfections,

3. Inspect a hypochlorination system,

4. Calculate chlorine dosage,

5. Determine hypochlorinator setting,

6. Safely operate and maintain hypochlorinators,

7. Clean hypochlorite feed pump (acid flushing, washing, and lubrication),

8. Review critical spare parts list,

9. Safely prepare and mix chlorine solutions (calcium and sodium hypochlorite),

10. Measure chlorine residual,

11. Troubleshoot hypochlorination systems,

12. Use hypochlorite safely,

13. Administer a hypochlorination safety program, and

14. Keep accurate hypochlorination records.

LEARNING BOOKLET STUDY MATERIAL

This section of the *LEARNING BOOKLET* contains important information. Read this section after watching the video and before attempting to take the Objective Test for this chapter.

Material covered in this section will help you better understand the material in the video. Also some critical information is easier to present in the *LEARNING BOOKLET*, such as illustrating forms and calculations.

Chapter (Video) 2.   HYPOCHLORINATION

2.0   PURPOSE OF DISINFECTION

2.00   Making Water Safe for Consumption

Our single most important natural resource is water. Without water we could not exist. Unfortunately, safe water is becoming very difficult to find. In the past, safe water could be found in remote areas, but with population growth and related pollution of waters, there are very few natural waters left that are safe to drink without treatment of some kind.

Water is the universal solvent and therefore carries all types of dissolved materials. Water also carries biological life forms which can cause diseases. These waterborne pathogenic organisms are listed in Table 2.1. Most of these organisms and the diseases they transmit are no longer a problem in the United States due to proper water protection, treatment, and monitoring. However, many developing regions of the world still experience serious outbreaks of various waterborne diseases.

TABLE 2.1   PATHOGENIC ORGANISMS (DISEASES) TRANSMITTED BY WATER

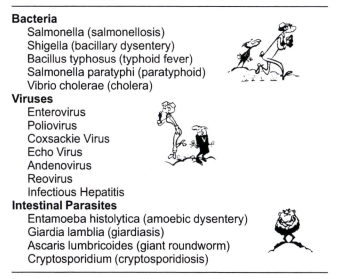

Bacteria
    Salmonella (salmonellosis)
    Shigella (bacillary dysentery)
    Bacillus typhosus (typhoid fever)
    Salmonella paratyphi (paratyphoid)
    Vibrio cholerae (cholera)
Viruses
    Enterovirus
    Poliovirus
    Coxsackie Virus
    Echo Virus
    Andenovirus
    Reovirus
    Infectious Hepatitis
Intestinal Parasites
    Entamoeba histolytica (amoebic dysentery)
    Giardia lamblia (giardiasis)
    Ascaris lumbricoides (giant roundworm)
    Cryptosporidium (cryptosporidiosis)

One of the cleansing processes in the production of safe water is called disinfection. Disinfection is the selective destruction or inactivation of pathogenic organisms. Don't confuse disinfection with sterilization. Sterilization is the complete destruction of all organisms. Sterilization is not necessary in water treatment and is also quite expensive. (Also note that disinfection does not remove toxic chemicals which could make the water unsafe to drink.)

2.01   Safe Drinking Water Act (SDWA)

In the United States, the U.S. Environmental Protection Agency is responsible for setting drinking water standards and for ensuring their enforcement. This agency sets federal regulations which all state and local agencies must enforce. The 1976 Primary Drinking Water Regulations contain specific maximum allowable levels of substances known to be hazardous to human health. In addition to describing maximum contaminant levels (MCLs), the 1976 Primary Drinking Water Regulations also give detailed instructions on what to do when you exceed the maximum contaminant level for a particular substance. In Table 2.2 you will find an example of the Primary Drinking Water Regulations for COLIFORM[1] bacteria which are supposed to be killed by disinfection. Table 2.3 lists the coliform samples required per population served.

The Safe Drinking Water Act (SDWA), originally enacted in 1974, was amended in 1980, 1986, and 1996 to expand and strengthen the protection of drinking water. The 1986 amendments, for example, authorized penalties for tampering with drinking water supplies and mandated complete elimination of lead from drinking water. The 1996 SDWA amendments require EPA to develop several new rules and regulations, including the Disinfectant/Disinfection By-Products (D/DBP) Rule, Enhanced Surface Water Treatment Rule (ESWTR), Ground Water Disinfection Rule (GWDR), Lead and Copper Rule revisions, and regulations for arsenic, radon, and sulfate.

In 1998, the Interim Enhanced Surface Water Treatment Rule (IESWTR) and the Disinfectant/Disinfection By-Products (D/DBP) Rule were signed into law, but further modifications of these two rules are still under development. The goal of the IESWTR is to reduce the occurrence of Cryptosporidium and other disease-causing organisms. The new D/DBP Rule was developed to protect the public from harmful concentrations of disinfectants and from trihalomethanes which could form when disinfection by-products combine with organic matter in drinking water. Water systems serving 10,000 or more people have three years (from December 16, 1998) to comply with both the D/DBP and the IESWTR regulations. Small systems (serving fewer than 10,000 people) have five years to comply.

Operators are urged to develop close working relationships with their state regulatory agencies to keep themselves informed of the expected future changes in regulations.

2.1   FACTORS INFLUENCING DISINFECTION

2.10   pH

The pH of water being treated can alter the efficiency of disinfectants. Chlorine, for example, disinfects water much faster at a pH around 7.0 than at a pH over 8.0.

---

[1] Coliform (COAL-i-form).   A group of bacteria found in the intestines of warm-blooded animals (including humans) and also in plants, soil, air and water. Fecal coliforms are a specific class of bacteria which only inhabit the intestines of warm-blooded animals. The presence of coliform bacteria is an indication that the water is polluted and may contain pathogenic (disease-causing) organisms.

TABLE 2.2   MICROBIOLOGICAL STANDARDS [a,b]

Maximum Contaminant Level Goal (MCLG): zero

Maximum Contaminant Level (MCL):

1. Compliance based on presence/absence of total coliforms in sample, rather than an estimate of coliform density.

2. MCL for system analyzing at least 40 samples per month: no more than 5.0 percent of the monthly samples may be total coliform-positive.

3. MCL for systems analyzing fewer than 40 samples per month: no more than 1 sample per month may be total coliform-positive.

[a] See Chapter 22, "Drinking Water Regulations," *WATER TREATMENT PLANT OPERATION*, Volume II, and the poster provided with this manual for more details.
[b] See Chapter 7, "Laboratory Procedures," *SMALL WATER SYSTEM OPERATION AND MAINTENANCE*, for details on how to do the coliform bacteria tests (membrane filter (MF), multiple tube fermentation (MPN), presence-absence, Colilert, and Colisure).

MONITORING AND REPEAT SAMPLE FREQUENCY AFTER A TOTAL COLIFORM-POSITIVE ROUTINE SAMPLE

No. Routine Samples/Month	No. Repeat Samples [a]	No. Routine Samples Next Month [b]
1/mo or fewer	4	5/mo
2/mo	3	5/mo
3/mo	3	5/mo
4/mo	3	5/mo
5/mo or more	3	Table 2.3

[a] Number of repeat samples in the same month for each total coliform-positive routine sample.
[b] Except where the state has invalidated the original routine sample, substitutes an on-site evaluation of the problem, or waives the requirement on a case-by-case basis.

2.11   Temperature

Temperature conditions also influence the effectiveness of the disinfectant. The higher the temperature of the water, the more efficiently it can be treated. Water near 70 to 85°F (21 to 29°C) is easier to disinfect than water at 40 to 60°F (4 to 16°C). Longer contact times are required to disinfect water at lower temperatures. To speed up the process, operators often simply use larger amounts of chemicals. Where water is exposed to the atmosphere, the warmer the water temperature the greater the dissipation rate of chlorine into the atmosphere.

2.12   Turbidity

Under normal operating conditions, the turbidity level of water being treated is very low by the time the water reaches the disinfection process. Excessive turbidity will greatly reduce the efficiency of the disinfecting chemical or process. Studies in water treatment plants have shown that when water is filtered to a turbidity of one unit or less, most of the bacteria have been removed.

The suspended matter itself may also change the chemical nature of the water when the disinfectant is added. Some types of suspended solids can create a continuing demand for the chemical, thus changing the effective germicidal (germ killing) properties of the disinfectant.

2.13   Organic Matter

Organics found in the water can consume great amounts of disinfectants while forming unwanted compounds. *TRIHALOMETHANES* [2] are an example of undesirable compounds formed by reactions between chlorine and certain organics. Disinfecting chemicals often react with organics and *REDUCING AGENTS* [3] (Section 2.15). Then, if any of the chemical remains available after this initial reaction, it can act as an effective disinfectant. The reactions with organics and reducing agents, however, will have significantly reduced the amount of chemical available for disinfection.

2.14   Inorganic Matter

Inorganic compounds such as ammonia (NH_3) in the water being treated can create special problems. In the presence of ammonia, some oxidizing chemicals form side compounds causing a partial loss of disinfecting power. Silt can also create a chemical demand. It is clear, then, that the chemical proper-

[2] *Trihalomethanes (THMs) (tri-HAL-o-METH-hanes).   Derivatives of methane, CH_4, in which three halogen atoms (chlorine or bromine) are substituted for three of the hydrogen atoms. Often formed during chlorination by reactions with natural organic materials in the water. The resulting compounds (THMs) are suspected of causing cancer.*
[3] *Reducing Agent.   Any substance, such as a base metal (iron) or the sulfide ion (S^{2-}), that will readily donate (give up) electrons. The opposite is an oxidizing agent.*

TABLE 2.3   TOTAL COLIFORM SAMPLING REQUIREMENTS
ACCORDING TO POPULATION SERVED

Population Served	Minimum Number of Routine Samples Per Month[a]	Population Served	Minimum Number of Routine Samples Per Month
25 to 1,000 [b]	1 [c]	59,001 to 70,000	70
1,001 to 2,500	2	70,001 to 83,000	80
2,501 to 3,300	3	83,001 to 96,000	90
3,301 to 4,100	4	96,001 to 130,000	100
4,101 to 4,900	5	130,001 to 220,000	120
4,901 to 5,800	6	220,001 to 320,000	150
5,801 to 6,700	7	320,001 to 450,000	180
6,701 to 7,600	8	450,001 to 600,000	210
7,601 to 8,500	9	600,001 to 780,000	240
8,501 to 12,900	10	780,001 to 970,000	270
12,901 to 17,200	15	970,001 to 1,230,000	300
17,201 to 21,500	20	1,230,001 to 1,520,000	330
21,501 to 25,000	25	1,520,001 to 1,850,000	360
25,001 to 33,000	30	1,850,001 to 2,270,000	390
33,001 to 41,000	40	2,270,001 to 3,020,000	420
41,001 to 50,000	50	3,020,001 to 3,960,000	450
50,001 to 59,000	60	3,960,001 or more	480

[a] A noncommunity water system using groundwater and serving 1,000 persons or fewer may monitor at a lesser frequency specified by the state until a sanitary survey is conducted and the state reviews the results. Thereafter, noncommunity water systems using groundwater and serving 1,000 persons or fewer must monitor in each calendar quarter during which the system provides water to the public, unless the state determines that some other frequency is more appropriate and notifies the system (in writing). In all cases, noncommunity water systems using groundwater and serving 1,000 persons or fewer must monitor at least once/year.

A noncommunity water system using surface water, or groundwater under the direct influence of surface water, regardless of the number of persons served, must monitor at the same frequency as a like-sized community public system. A noncommunity water system using groundwater and serving more than 1,000 persons during any month must monitor at the same frequency as a like-sized community water system, except that the state may reduce the monitoring frequency for any month the system serves 1,000 persons or fewer.

[b] Includes public water systems which have at least 15 service connections, but serve fewer than 25 persons.

[c] For a community water system serving 25 to 1,000 persons, the state may reduce this sampling frequency if a sanitary survey conducted in the last five years indicates that the water system is supplied solely by a protected groundwater source and is free of sanitary defects. However, in no case may the state reduce the sampling frequency to less than once/quarter.

ties of the water being treated can seriously interfere with the effectiveness of disinfecting chemicals.

2.15   Reducing Agents

Chlorine combines with a wide variety of materials, especially reducing agents. Most of the reactions are very rapid, while others are much slower. These side reactions complicate the use of chlorine for disinfection. The demand for chlorine by reducing agents must be satisfied before chlorine becomes available to accomplish disinfection. Examples of inorganic reducing agents present in water which will react with chlorine include hydrogen sulfide (H_2S), ferrous ion (Fe^{2+}), manganous ion (Mn^{2+}), and the nitrite ion (NO_2^-). Organic reducing agents in water also will react with chlorine and form chlorinated organic materials of potential health significance.

2.16   Microorganisms

2.160   Numbers and Types of Microorganisms

Microorganism concentration is important because the higher the number of microorganisms, the greater the demand for a disinfecting chemical. The resistance of microorganisms to specific disinfectants varies greatly. Non-spore-forming bacteria are generally less resistant than spore-forming bacteria. Cysts and viruses can be very resistant to certain types of disinfectants.

2.161   Removal Processes

Pathogenic organisms can be removed from water, killed, or inactivated by various physical and chemical water treatment processes. These processes are:

1. *COAGULATION.* Chemical coagulation followed by sedimentation and filtration will remove 90 to 95 percent of the pathogenic organisms, depending on which chemicals are used. Alum usage can increase virus removals up to 99 percent.

2. *SEDIMENTATION.* Properly designed sedimentation processes can effectively remove 20 to 70 percent of the pathogenic microorganisms. This removal is accomplished by allowing the pathogenic organisms (as well as non-pathogenic organisms) to settle out by gravity, assisted by chemical floc.

3. *FILTRATION.* Filtering water through granular filters is an effective means of removing pathogenic and other organisms from water. The removal rates vary from 20 to 99+ percent depending on the coarseness of the filter media and the type and effectiveness of pretreatment.

4. *DISINFECTION.* Disinfection chemicals such as chlorine are added to water to kill or inactivate pathogenic microorganisms.

2.17 Points of Application

Provisions should be made to feed chlorine at several different locations in the plant. The place of feed may vary from time to time depending on source water quality. If natural organics are not present in the source water, chlorination early in the treatment process can provide effective disinfection and reduce chlorine costs.

2.2 PROCESS OF DISINFECTION

2.20 Purpose of Process

The purpose of disinfection is to destroy harmful organisms. This can be accomplished either physically or chemically. Physical methods may (1) physically remove the organisms from the water, or (2) introduce motion that will disrupt the cells' biological activity and kill them.

Chemical methods alter the cell chemistry causing the microorganism to die. The most widely used disinfectant chemical is chlorine. Chlorine is easily obtained, relatively cheap, and most importantly, leaves a *RESIDUAL CHLORINE*[4] that can be measured. Other disinfectants are also used. There has been increased interest in disinfectants other than chlorine because of the *CARCINOGENIC*[5] compounds that chlorine may form (trihalomethanes or THMs).

2.3 CHLORINE RESIDUALS

2.30 Types of Chlorine Residuals

Operators must be acquainted with the three types of chlorine residuals that can be found in treated water.

1. *FREE*

Free available chlorine residual includes that chlorine in the form of hypochlorous acid (HOCl) and hypochlorite ion (OCl⁻). Hypochlorous acid is the most effective disinfectant form of chlorine. Hypochlorite ion is much less effective as

a disinfectant than hypochlorous acid. The pH determines whether the free chlorine is in the form of hypochlorous acid or hypochlorite ion. The lower the pH, the greater the percent of hypochlorous acid.

2. *COMBINED*

Combined available chlorine residual includes that chlorine in the three chloramine forms (monochloramine, dichloramine, and nitrogen trichloride) which are produced when chlorine reacts with ammonia. Combined chlorine requires up to 100 times the contact time or at least 25 times the chlorine concentration to achieve the same degree of disinfection as free available chlorine.

3. *TOTAL*

The total chlorine residual is the sum of the free residual and the combined residual.

Chlorine residual test kits measure the free available chlorine residual and the total chlorine residual. The combined available chlorine residual is the difference. For example, a test kit could measure the free chlorine residual as one mg/*L* and the total chlorine residual as three mg/*L*. The combined available chlorine residual would be two mg/*L* (3 mg/*L* − 1 mg/*L* = 2 mg/*L*).

Operators should strive to maintain a free chlorine residual to accomplish disinfection and to avoid depending on the much weaker combined chlorine residual. Thus, in performing a chlorine residual test, the small system operator should make sure that the test result indicates only the *FREE* chlorine residual concentration.

Operators of small treatment plants frequently ask, "What chlorine residual should I maintain to guarantee that the finished water is adequately disinfected?" This is a very important question and one that must be answered correctly. But it is impossible to give a simple answer covering all situations because, as already explained, the required chlorine concentration is related to the contact time, the pH, and the water temperature.

2.31 Measurement of Chlorine Residual

2.310 Methods of Measuring Chlorine Residual

AMPEROMETRIC TITRATION[6] provides for the most convenient and most repeatable chlorine residual results. However, amperometric titration equipment is more expensive than equipment for other methods. DPD tests can be used and are less expensive than other methods, but this method requires the operator to match the color of a sample with the colors on a comparator. See Chapter 7, "Laboratory Procedures," in *SMALL WATER SYSTEM OPERATION AND MAINTENANCE*, for detailed information on these tests.

Residual chlorine measurements of treated water should be taken at least three times per day on small systems and once every two hours on large systems to ensure that the treated water is being adequately disinfected. A free chlorine residual of at least 0.5 mg/*L* in the treated water at the point of application is usually recommended.

---

[4] *Residual Chlorine. The concentration of chlorine present in water after the chlorine demand has been satisfied. The concentration is expressed in terms of the total chlorine residual, which includes both the free and combined or chemically bound chlorine residuals.*

[5] *Carcinogen (CAR-sin-o-JEN). Any substance which tends to produce cancer in an organism.*

[6] *Amperometric (am-PURR-o-MET-rick) Titration. A means of measuring concentrations of certain substances in water (such as strong oxidizers) based on the electric current that flows during a chemical reaction.*

ALL surface water systems and groundwater systems under the influence of surface water must provide disinfection. Systems are required to monitor the disinfectant residual leaving the plant and at various points in the distribution system. The water leaving the plant must have at least 0.2 mg/L of the disinfectant, and the samples taken in the distribution system must have a detectable residual. Certain guidelines must be followed to ensure that there is enough contact time between the disinfectant and the water so that the microorganisms are inactivated.

If at any time the disinfectant residual leaving the plant is less than 0.2 mg/L, the system is allowed up to four hours to correct the problem. If the problem is corrected within this time, it is not considered a violation but the regulatory agency must be notified. The disinfectant residual must be measured continuously. For systems serving fewer than 3,300 people, this may be reduced to once per day.

The disinfectant in the distribution system must be measured at the same frequency and location as the total coliform samples. Measurements for heterotrophic plate count (HPC) bacteria may be substituted for disinfectant residual measurements. If the HPC is less than 500 colonies per mL, then the sample is considered equivalent to a detectable disinfectant residual. For systems serving fewer than 500 people, the regulatory agency may determine the adequacy of the disinfectant residual in place of monitoring.

2.311 Amperometric Titration for Free Chlorine Residual

1. Place a 200-mL sample of water in the titrator.

2. Start the agitator.

3. Add 1 mL of pH 7 buffer.

4. Titrate with 0.00564 *N* phenylarsene oxide solution.

5. End point is reached when further additions (drops) will not cause a deflection on the microammeter.

6. mL of phenylarsene oxide used in titration is equal to mg/L of free chlorine residual.

2.312 DPD Colorimetric Method for Free Chlorine Residual *(Figures 2.1 and 2.2)*

This procedure is for the use of prepared powder pillows.

1. Collect a 100-mL sample.

2. Add color reagent.

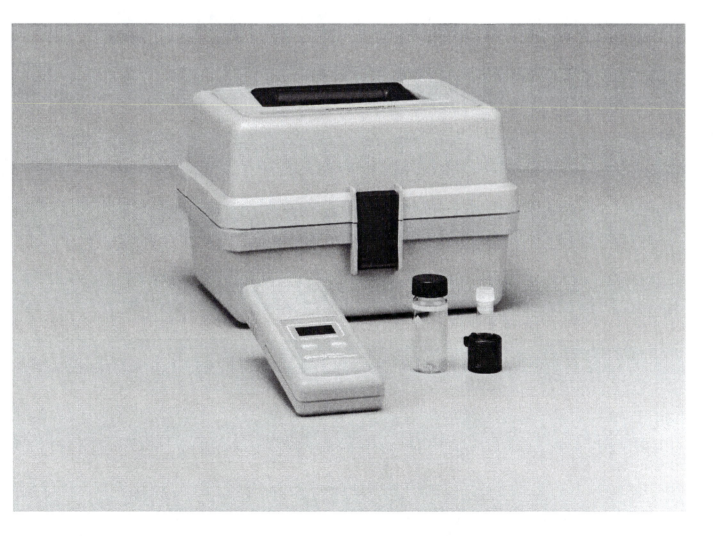

Fig. 2.1   Direct reading colorimeter for free chlorine residuals
(Permission of the HACH Company)

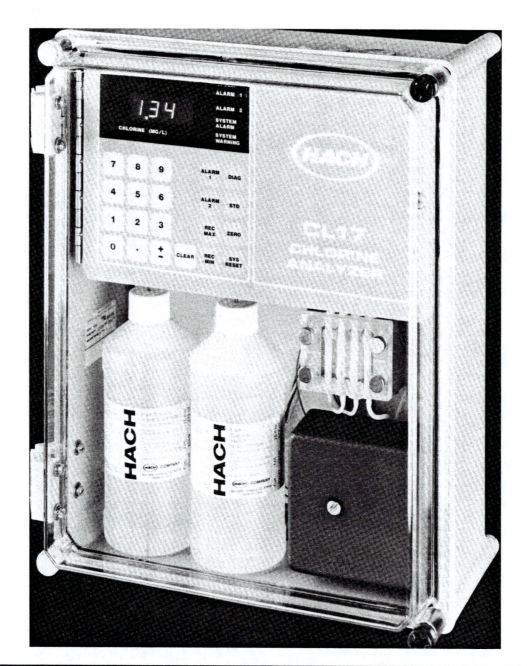

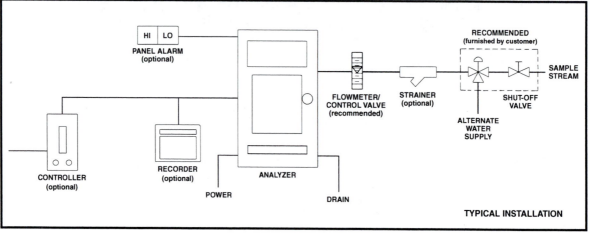

Fig. 2.2   Continuous on-line free chlorine residual analyzer

(Permission of the HACH Company)

3. Match color sample with a color on the comparator to obtain the chlorine residual in mg/L.

Operators using the DPD colorimetric method to test water for a free chlorine residual need to be aware of a potential error that may occur. If the DPD test is run on water containing a combined chlorine residual, a precipitate may form during the test. The particles of precipitated material will give the sample a turbid appearance or the appearance of having color. This turbidity can produce a positive test result for free chlorine residual when there is actually no chlorine present. Operators call this error a "false positive" chlorine residual reading.

2.4   HYPOCHLORINATORS

2.40   Typical Hypochlorinator Installation

A hypochlorinator is a piece of equipment used to feed liquid chlorine (bleach) solutions. Hypochlorinators used on small water systems are very simple and relatively easy to install. Typical installations are shown in Figures 2.3 and 2.4. Hypochlorinator systems usually consist of a chemical solution tank for the hypochlorite, diaphragm-type pump (Figure 2.5), power supply, water pump, pressure switch, and water storage tank.

There are two methods of feeding the hypochlorite solution into the water being disinfected. The hypochlorite solution may be pumped directly into the water (Figure 2.6). In the other method, the hypochlorite solution is pumped through an *EJECTOR*[7] (also called an eductor or injector) which draws in additional water for dilution of the hypochlorite solution (Figure 2.7).

2.41   Hypochlorinator Start-up

a. Solution. Chemical solutions have to be made up. Most agencies buy commercial or industrial hypochlorite at around 12 to 15 percent chlorine. This solution is usually

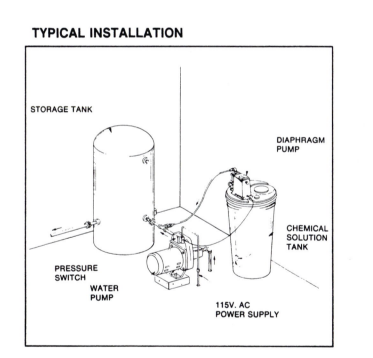

TYPICAL INSTALLATION

STORAGE TANK

DIAPHRAGM PUMP

CHEMICAL SOLUTION TANK

PRESSURE SWITCH

WATER PUMP

115V. AC POWER SUPPLY

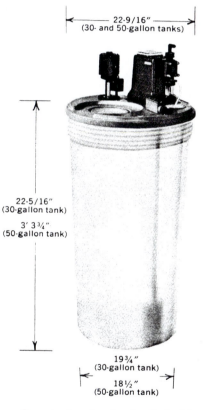

22-9/16"
(30- and 50-gallon tanks)

22-5/16"
(30-gallon tank)

3' 3¾"
(50-gallon tank)

19¾"
(30-gallon tank)

18½"
(50-gallon tank)

Pump-tank system for chemical mixing and metering. Cover supports pump, impeller-type mixer, and liquid-level switch.

Fig. 2.3   Typical hypochlorinator installation
(Permission of Wallace & Tiernan Division, Pennwalt Corporation)

---

[7] *Ejector.   A device used to disperse a chemical solution into water being treated.*

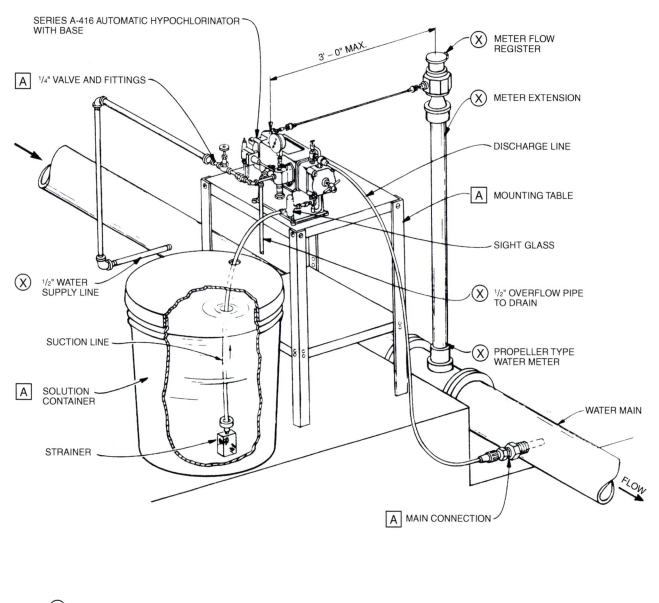

SERIES A-416 AUTOMATIC HYPOCHLORINATOR WITH BASE

3' – 0" MAX.

X METER FLOW REGISTER

A 1/4" VALVE AND FITTINGS

X METER EXTENSION

DISCHARGE LINE

A MOUNTING TABLE

SIGHT GLASS

X 1/2" WATER SUPPLY LINE

X 1/2" OVERFLOW PIPE TO DRAIN

SUCTION LINE

X PROPELLER TYPE WATER METER

A SOLUTION CONTAINER

WATER MAIN

STRAINER

FLOW

A MAIN CONNECTION

X NOT FURNISHED BY W & T.

A ACCESSORY ITEM FURNISHED ONLY IF SPECIFICALLY LISTED IN QUOTATION AND AS CHECKED ON THIS DRAWING.

NOTE: Hypochlorinator paced by a propeller-type water meter.

Fig. 2.4 Typical hypochlorinator installation
(Permission of Wallace & Tiernan Division, Pennwalt Corporation)

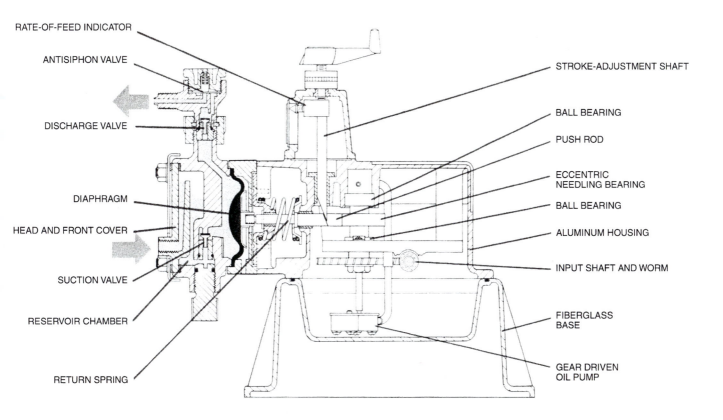

RATE-OF-FEED INDICATOR

ANTISIPHON VALVE

DISCHARGE VALVE

DIAPHRAGM

HEAD AND FRONT COVER

SUCTION VALVE

RESERVOIR CHAMBER

RETURN SPRING

STROKE-ADJUSTMENT SHAFT

BALL BEARING

PUSH ROD

ECCENTRIC
NEEDLING BEARING

BALL BEARING

ALUMINUM HOUSING

INPUT SHAFT AND WORM

FIBERGLASS
BASE

GEAR DRIVEN
OIL PUMP

Belt guard
removed
to show
step pulley

Fig. 2.5   Diaphragm-type pump
(Permission of Wallace & Tiernan Division, Pennwalt Corporation)

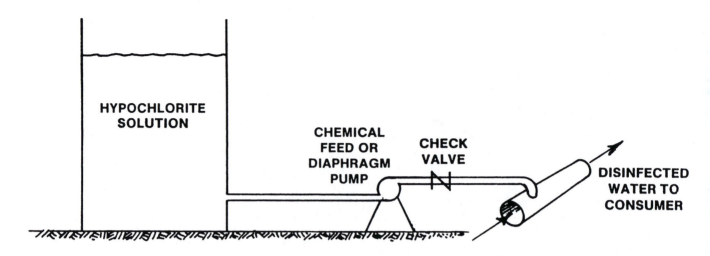

Fig. 2.6   Hypochlorinator direct pumping system

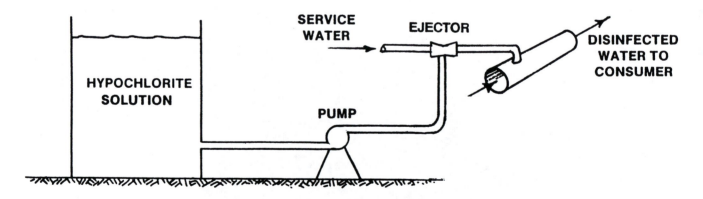

NOTE: Pump is chemical feed or diaphragm pump.

Fig. 2.7   Hypochlorinator injector feed system

diluted down to a two percent solution. If using commercially prepared solutions, dosage rates will have to be calculated.

b. Electrical. Lock out the circuit while making an inspection of an electrical circuit. Normally no adjustments are needed. Look for frayed wires. Turn the power back on. Leave the solution switch off.

c. Turn the chemical pump on. Make any necessary adjustments while the pump is running. Never adjust the pump while it is off because damage to the pump will occur.

d. Make sure solution is being fed into the system. Measure the chlorine residual just downstream from where solution is being fed into the system. You may have a target residual you wish to maintain at the beginning of the system, such as 2.0 mg/L.

e. Check the chlorine residual in the system. The residual should be measured at the most remote test location within the distribution system and should be at least 0.2 mg/L free residual chlorine. This chlorine residual is necessary to protect the treated water from any recontamination. Adjust the chemical feed as needed.

2.42 Hypochlorinator Shutdown

a. Short Duration

  (1) Turn the water supply pump off. You do not want to pump any unchlorinated water and possibly contaminate the rest of the system.

  (2) Turn the hypochlorinator off.

  (3) When making any repairs, lock out the circuit or pull the plug from an electric socket.

b. Long Duration

  (1) Obtain another hypochlorinator as a replacement.

2.43 Normal Operation of Hypochlorinator

Normal operation of the hypochlorination process requires routine observation and preventive maintenance.

DAILY

a. Inspect the building to make sure only authorized personnel have been there.

b. Read and record the level of the solution tank at the same time every day.

c. Read the meters and record the amount of water pumped.

d. Check the chlorine residual (0.2 mg/L) in the system and adjust the chlorine feed rate as necessary. Try to maintain a chlorine residual of 0.2 mg/L at the most remote point in the distribution system. The suggested free chlorine residual for treated water or well water is 0.5 mg/L at the point of chlorine application provided the 0.2 mg/L residual is maintained throughout the distribution system and coliform test results are negative.

e. Check the chemical feed pump operation. Most hypochlorinators have a dial with a range from 0 to 10 which indicates the chlorine feed rate. Initially set the pointer on the dial to approximately 6 or 7 on the dial and use a two percent hypochlorite solution. The pump should be operated in the upper ranges of the dial. This will require the frequency of the strokes or pulses from the pump to be frequent enough so that the chlorine will

be fed continuously to the water being treated. Adjust the feed rate after testing chlorine residual levels.

WEEKLY

a. Clean the building.

b. Replace the chemicals and wash the chemical storage tank. Try to have a 15- to 30-day supply of chlorine in storage for future needs. When preparing hypochlorite solutions, prepare only enough for a two- or three-day supply.

MONTHLY

a. Check the operation of the check valve.

b. Perform any required preventive maintenance.

c. Cleaning

  Commercial sodium hypochlorite solutions (such as Clorox) contain an excess of caustic (sodium hydroxide or NaOH). When this solution is diluted with water containing calcium and also carbonate alkalinity, the resulting solution becomes supersaturated with calcium carbonate. This calcium carbonate tends to form a coating on the poppet valves in the solution feeder. The coated valves will not seal properly and the feeder will fail to feed properly.

  Use the following procedure to remove the carbonate scale:

  (1) Fill a one-quart (one-liter) Mason jar half-full of tap water.

  (2) Place one fluid ounce (20 mL) of 30 to 37 percent hydrochloric acid (swimming pool acid) in the jar. *ALWAYS ADD ACID TO WATER, NEVER THE REVERSE.*

  (3) Fill the jar with tap water.

  (4) Place the suction hose of the hypochlorinator in the jar and pump the entire contents of the jar through the system.

  (5) Return the suction hose to the hypochlorite solution tank and resume normal operation.

    You can prevent the formation of the calcium carbonate coatings by obtaining the dilution water from an ordinary home water softener.

NORMAL OPERATION CHECKLIST

a. Check chemical usage. Record solution level and the water pump meter reading or number of hours of pump operation. Calculate the amount of chemical solution used and compare with the desired feed rate. See Example 1.

b. Determine if every piece of equipment is operating.

c. Inspect the lubrication of the equipment.

d. Check the building for any possible problems.

e. Clean up the area.

FORMULAS

To determine the actual chlorine dose of water being treated by either a chlorinator or a hypochlorinator, we need to know the gallons of water treated and the pounds of chlorine used to disinfect the water.

1. Calculate the pounds of water disinfected.

   Water, lbs = (Water Pumped, gallons)(8.34 lbs/gal)

2. To calculate the volume of hypochlorite used from a container, we need to know the dimensions of the container.

   $$\frac{\text{Volume,}}{\text{gallons}} = \frac{(0.785)(\text{Diameter, in})^2(\text{Depth, ft})(7.48 \text{ gal/cu ft})}{144 \text{ sq in/sq ft}}$$

3. To calculate the pounds of chlorine used to disinfect water, we need to know the gallons of hypochlorite used and the percent available chlorine in the hypochlorite solution.

   $$\frac{\text{Chlorine,}}{\text{lbs}} = (\text{Hypochlorite, gal})(8.34 \text{ lbs/gal})\left(\frac{\text{Hypochlorite, \%}}{100\%}\right)$$

4. To determine the actual chlorine dose in milligrams per liter, we divide the pounds of chlorine used by the millions of pounds of water treated. Pounds of chlorine per million pounds of water is the same as parts per million or milligrams per liter.

   $$\text{Chlorine Dose, mg/}L = \frac{\text{Chlorine Used, lbs}}{\text{Water Treated, Million lbs}}$$

EXAMPLE 1

Water pumped from a well is disinfected by a hypochlorinator. A chlorine dosage of 1.2 mg/L is necessary to maintain an adequate chlorine residual throughout the system. During a one-week time period, the water meter indicated that 2,289,000 gallons of water were pumped. A two-percent sodium hypochlorite solution is stored in a three-foot diameter plastic tank. During this one-week period, the level of hypochlorite in the tank dropped 2 feet, 8 inches (2.67 feet). Does the chlorine feed rate appear to be too high, too low, or about right?

Known	**Unknown**
Desired Chlorine Dose, mg/L = 1.2 mg/L	1. Actual Chlorine Dose, mg/L
	2. Is Actual Dose OK?
Water Pumped, gal = 2,289,000 gal	
Hypochlorite, % = 2%	
Chemical Tank Diameter, ft = 3 ft	
Chemical Drop in Tank, ft = 2.67 ft	

1. Calculate the pounds of water disinfected.

   Water, lbs = (Water Pumped, gallons)(8.34 lbs/gal)

   = (2,289,000 gal)(8.34 lbs/gal)

   = 19,090,000 lbs

   or = 19.09 Million lbs

2. Calculate the volume of 2 percent sodium hypochlorite used in gallons.

   $$\frac{\text{Hypochlorite,}}{\text{gallons}} = (0.785)(\text{Diameter, ft})^2(\text{Depth, ft})(7.48 \text{ gal/cu ft})$$

   $$= (0.785)(3 \text{ ft})^2(2.67 \text{ ft})(7.48 \text{ gal/cu ft})$$

   = 141.1 gallons

3. Determine the pounds of chlorine used to disinfect the water.

   $$\frac{\text{Chlorine,}}{\text{lbs}} = (\text{Hypochlorite, gal})(8.34 \text{ lbs/gal})\left(\frac{\text{Hypochlorite, \%}}{100\%}\right)$$

   $$= (141.1 \text{ gal})(8.34 \text{ lbs/gal})\left(\frac{2\%}{100\%}\right)$$

   = 23.5 lbs Chlorine

4. Calculate the chlorine dosage in mg/L.

   $$\text{Chlorine Dose, mg/}L = \frac{\text{Chlorine Used, lbs}}{\text{Water Treated, Million lbs}}$$

   $$= \frac{23.5 \text{ lbs chlorine}}{19.09 \text{ Million lbs water}}$$

   $$= 1.23 \text{ mg/}L$$

Since the actual chlorine dose (1.23 mg/L) was slightly greater than the desired dose of 1.2 mg/L, the chlorine feed rate appears OK.

2.44 Abnormal Operation (Troubleshooting) of Hypochlorinator

a. Inform your supervisor of the problem.

b. If the hypochlorinator malfunctions, it should be repaired immediately. See the shutdown operation (see Section 2.42).

c. Solution tank level.

   (1) If too low: Check the adjustment of the pump.

   Check the hour meter of the water pump.

   (2) If too high: Check the chemical pump.

   Check the hour meter of the water pump.

d. Determine if the chemical pump is not operating.

   TROUBLESHOOTING GUIDELINES

   (1) Check the electrical connection.

   (2) Check the circuit breaker.

   (3) Check for stoppages in the flow lines.

CORRECTIVE MEASURES

(1) Shut off the water pump so that no contaminated water is pumped into the system.

(2) Check for a blockage in the solution tank.

(3) Check the operation of the check valve.

(4) Check the electrical circuits.

(5) Replace the chemical feed pump with another pump while repairing the defective unit.

e. The solution is not being pumped into the water line.

TROUBLESHOOTING GUIDELINES

(1) Check the solution level.

(2) Check for blockages in the solution line.

2.45 Maintenance of Hypochlorinators

Hypochlorinators on small systems are normally small, sealed systems that cannot be repaired so replacement of the entire unit is the only solution. Maintenance requirements are normally minor such as changing the oil and lubricating the moving parts. Review the manufacturer's specifications for maintenance requirements.

2.5 LABORATORY TESTS

1. Chlorine Residual in System

a. Chlorine residual tests using the *DPD*[8] *METHOD*[9] should be taken daily at various locations in the system. A remote tap is ideal for one sampling location. Take the test sample from a tap as close to the main as possible. Allow the water to run at least 5 minutes before sampling to ensure a representative sample from the main.

Operators using the DPD colorimetric method to test water for a free chlorine residual need to be aware of a potential error that may occur. If the DPD test is run on water containing a combined chlorine residual, a precip-

itate may form during the test. The particles of precipitated material will give the sample a turbid appearance or the appearance of having color. This turbidity can produce a positive test result for free chlorine residual when there is actually no chlorine present. Operators call this error a "false positive" chlorine residual reading.

b. Chlorine residual test kits are available for small systems.

2. Bacteriological Analysis (Coliform Tests)

Samples should be taken routinely in accordance with health department requirements. Take samples according to approved procedures.[10] Be sure to use a sterile plastic or glass bottle. If the sample contains any chlorine residual, sufficient sodium thiosulfate should be added to neutralize all of the chlorine residual. Usually 0.1 milliliter of 10 percent sodium thiosulfate in a 120-mL (4 oz) bottle is sufficient for distribution systems. The "thio" should be added to the sample bottle before sterilization.

2.6 TROUBLESHOOTING HYPOCHLORINATORS

2.60 Disinfection Troubleshooting

TABLE 2.4 DISINFECTION TROUBLESHOOTING GUIDE

Operating Symptoms	Probable Cause	Remedy
1. Increase in coliform level	Low chlorine residual	Raise chlorine dose
2. Drop in chlorine level	a. Increase in chlorine demand	Raise chlorine dose and find out why chlorine demand increased or chlorine feed rate dropped
	b. Drop in chlorine feed rate	

2.61 Hypochlorination System Failure

IF YOUR CHLORINATION SYSTEM FAILS, DO NOT ALLOW UNCHLORINATED WATER TO ENTER THE DISTRIBUTION SYSTEM. Never allow unchlorinated water to be delivered to your consumers. If your chlorination system fails and cannot be repaired within a reasonable time period, notify your supervisor and officials of the health department. To pre-

---

[8] *DPD (pronounce as separate letters). A method of measuring the chlorine residual in water. The residual may be determined by either titrating or comparing a developed color with color standards. DPD stands for N,N-diethyl-p-phenylene-diamine.*

[9] *See Section 2.31, "Measurement of Chlorine Residual," for details on how to perform the DPD test for measuring chlorine residual.*

[10] *See SMALL WATER SYSTEM OPERATION AND MAINTENANCE, Chapter 7, "Laboratory Procedures," for proper procedures for collecting and analyzing samples for chlorine residuals and coliform tests.*

vent this problem from occurring, your plant should have backup or standby chlorination facilities.

2.62   Emergency Disinfection Plan

All water treatment plants should have an emergency disinfection plan. The plan must be ready to be implemented any time a disinfection failure occurs in order to prevent the delivery to the distribution system of any water that is not disinfected or is inadequately disinfected. The plan should be posted in the plant or at a place that is readily available to the plant operator or an emergency crew.

The emergency disinfection plan should include information outlining the corrective actions that must be taken until the disinfection problem is properly corrected. The plan should include a description of the existing disinfection facilities and the operating and monitoring procedures of these facilities. Emergency telephone numbers must be listed for the appropriate health department officials and also of the operators available and the equipment suppliers needed to make the repairs. Review your emergency disinfection plan at least once a year and check to be sure all phone numbers are still current.

Procedures should be outlined for the emergency response if the disinfection system failed, but no inadequately disinfected water entered the water distribution system. These procedures should include how to immediately shut down the water treatment plant if possible. Use of alternative water sources, if available, should be explained and procedures for implementation of water conservation measures should be outlined. If a backup chlorinator or a chemical feeder from a less critical treatment process is available, this equipment should be used. If no backup equipment is available, procedures for manual disinfection at the plant and also the distribution reservoirs need to be outlined. Also increased monitoring of bacteriological quality and chlorine residual levels of the water being delivered to and within the distribution system must be performed.

If inadequately disinfected water entered the water distribution system, additional procedures must be implemented. Health department officials must be notified immediately. The distribution system must be flushed to remove inadequately disinfected water using properly disinfected water and properly disinfected water must be distributed within the system as quickly as possible.

2.7   CT VALUES

Operators of small treatment plants frequently ask, "What chlorine residual should I maintain to guarantee that the finished water is adequately disinfected?" This is a very important question and one that must be answered correctly. But it is impossible to give a simple answer covering all situations because, as already explained, the required chlorine concentration is related to the contact time, the pH, and the water temperature.

A workable method for calculating the required chlorine concentration under various conditions is described in this section. The calculation uses the following formula:

$$C \times T = A$$

where C = the free available chlorine residual concentration in milligrams per liter,

   T = the chlorine contact time in minutes, and

   A = a number which varies with the pH as shown in Table 2.5

TABLE 2.5   RELATIONSHIP BETWEEN pH AND A

pH range	A (for cold water, 0° to 5°C)
7.0 – 7.5	12
7.5 – 8.0	20
8.0 – 8.5	30
8.5 – 9.0	35

For example, suppose in a particular small water plant that the minimum chlorine contact time from the point of chlorine injection to the entrance of the distribution system is 30 minutes. Then for the formula, T = 30. The pH of the water was found to be 7.2 and the water temperature during the winter months is usually just above freezing, say 1° or 2° Celsius. Then from Table 2.5, the value of A in this case is 12. Substituting these values in the formula we obtain:

$$C \times T = A$$
$$C \times 30 = 12$$

Solving for C,

$$C = \frac{A}{T}$$

$$C, \text{mg}/L = \frac{12}{30}$$

$$= \frac{4}{10}$$

$$= 0.4 \text{ mg}/L \text{ free chlorine residual}$$

This calculation tells us that good disinfection of the water supply will be accomplished under the existing conditions by maintaining a free chlorine residual of at least 0.4 mg/L for the 30-minute contact time. Notice that a stronger chlorine residual would be required if the pH were increased, say to 8.3. Then, A = 30.

$$C \times T = A$$
$$C \times 30 = 30$$

Or

$$C = \frac{30}{30}$$

$$= 1.0 \text{ mg}/L \text{ free chlorine residual}$$

The efficiency of the disinfectant is measured by the time "T" in minutes of the disinfectant's contact in the water and the concentration "C" in mg/L of the disinfectant residual measured at the end of the contact time. The product of these two parameters (C × T) provides a measure of the degree of pathogenic inactivation. The required CT value to achieve inactivation depends on the organism in question, pH, and temperature of the water supply. Table 2.6 shows the combinations of disinfectant, pH, and temperature that will produce 99.9 percent *Giardia lamblia* (a disease-causing organism) inactivation.

TABLE 2.6   CT VALUES REQUIRED FOR 99.9% *GIARDIA LAMBLIA* INACTIVATION

Disinfectant	pH	10 °C	15 °C	20 °C	25 °C
Free Chlorine[a]	6	79	53	39	26
	7	112	75	56	37
	8	162	108	81	54
Ozone	6 – 9	1.4	0.95	0.72	0.48
Chloramines	6 – 9	1,850	1,500	1,100	750

[a] with 1 mg/L free chlorine residual

Time or "T" is measured from the point of application to the point where "C" is determined. "T" must be based on peak hour flow rate conditions. In pipelines, "T" is calculated by dividing the volume of the pipeline in gallons by the flow rate in gallons per minute (GPM). In reservoirs and basins, dye tracer tests must be used to determine "T." In this case, "T" is the time it takes for 10 percent of the tracer to pass the measuring point.

Sometimes you may increase the chlorine dose setting on your chlorinator and *THE CHLORINE RESIDUAL MAY ACTUALLY DROP* (Figure 2.8, *BREAKPOINT CHLORINATION*)![11] This can happen when ammonia is present. Also under these conditions you may receive complaints that your water tastes like chlorine. The solution to this problem is to increase the chlorine dose even more! For additional information on breakpoint chlorination, see *SMALL WATER SYSTEM OPERATION AND MAINTENANCE*, Chapter 5, "Disinfection." You are at the proper setting if:

1. You are maintaining the chlorine residual from the above calculations,

2. An increase in the hypochlorinator feed setting will produce a calculated chlorine dose increase of 0.1 mg/L and the resulting actual chlorine residual increases by 0.1 mg/L,

3. Chlorine residual tests at the far end of the distribution system produce chlorine residuals of at least 0.2 mg/L, and

4. Coliform test results from throughout the distribution system are negative.

2.8 HYPOCHLORINATION SAFETY PROGRAM

2.80 Cooperation

Every good safety program begins with cooperation between the employee and the employer. The employee must take an active part in the overall program. The employee must be responsible and should take all necessary steps to prevent accidents. This begins with the attitude that as good an effort as possible must be made by everyone. Safety is everyone's priority. The employer also must take an active part by supporting safety programs. There must be funding to purchase equipment and to enforce safety regulations required by OSHA and state industrial safety programs. The following items should be included in all safety programs.

1. Establishment of a formal safety program.

2. Written rules.

3. Periodic hands-on training using safety equipment.
   a. Leak-detection equipment
   b. Self-contained breathing apparatus (Figure 2.9)
   c. Atmospheric monitoring devices

4. Establishment of emergency procedures for chlorine leaks and first aid.

5. Establishment of a maintenance and calibration program for safety devices and equipment.

6. Provide police and fire departments with tours of facilities to locate hazardous areas and provide chlorine safety information.

All persons handling chlorine should be thoroughly aware of its hazardous properties. Personnel should know the location and use of the various pieces of protective equipment and be instructed in safety procedures. In addition, an emergency procedure should be established and each individual should be instructed how to follow the procedures. An emergency checklist also should be developed and available. For additional information on this topic, see the Chlorine Institute's *CHLORINE MANUAL*.[12]

2.81 Hypochlorite Safety

Hypochlorite does not present the hazards that gaseous chlorine does and therefore is safer to handle. When spills occur, wash with large volumes of water. The solution is messy to handle. Hypochlorite causes damage to your eyes and skin upon contact. Immediately wash affected areas thoroughly with water. Consult a physician if the area appears burned. Hypochlorite solutions are very corrosive. Hypochlorite compounds are nonflammable; however, they can cause fires when they come in contact with organics or other easily oxidizable substances.

2.82 Operator Safety Training

Training is a concern to everyone, especially when your safety and perhaps your life is involved. Every utility agency should have an operator chlorine safety training program that introduces new operators to the program and updates previously trained operators. As soon as a training session ends, obsolescence begins. People will forget what they have learned if they don't use and practice their knowledge and skills. Operator turnover can dilute a well-trained staff. New equipment and also new techniques and procedures can dilute the readiness of trained operators. An ongoing training program could include a monthly luncheon seminar, a monthly

---

[11] *Breakpoint Chlorination.   Addition of chlorine to water until the chlorine demand has been satisfied. At this point, further additions of chlorine will result in a free chlorine residual that is directly proportional to the amount of chlorine added beyond the breakpoint.*

[12] *Write to: The Chlorine Institute, Inc., 1300 Wilson Boulevard, Arlington, VA 22209. Pamphlet 1. Price to members, $28.00; nonmembers, $70.00; plus $6.95 shipping and handling.*

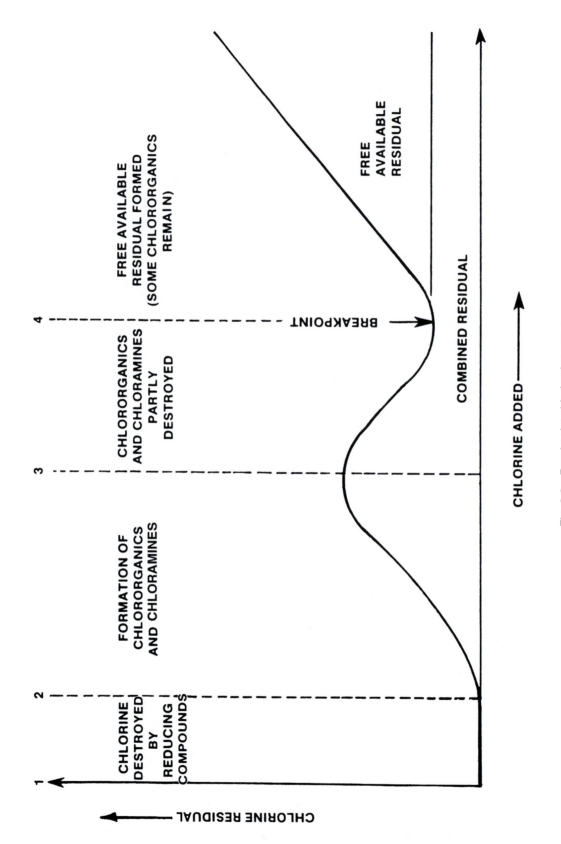

Fig. 2.8   Breakpoint chlorination curve

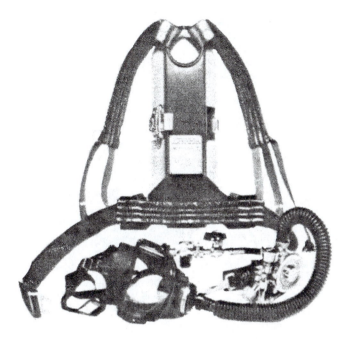

Fig. 2.9   Self-contained breathing apparatus
(Courtesy of PPG Industries)

safety bulletin that is to be read by every operator, and outside speakers who reinforce and refresh specific elements of safety training.

2.83   CHEMTREC (800) 424-9300

Safely handling chemicals used in daily water treatment is an operator's responsibility. However, if the situation ever gets out of hand, there are emergency teams that will respond with help anywhere there is an emergency. If an emergency does develop in your plant and you need assistance, call CHEMTREC (Chemical Transportation Emergency Center) for assistance. CHEMTREC will provide immediate advice for those at the scene of an emergency and then quickly alert experts whose products are involved for more detailed assistance and appropriate follow-up.

CHEMTREC'S EMERGENCY TOLL-FREE TELEPHONE NUMBER IS (800) 424-9300.

2.9   RECORDS

An important part of hypochlorinator operation is keeping adequate records. The records must be legible and kept in an organized format. They should be written down in a permanent manner that can be preserved indefinitely for future reference. Records scribbled with a dull pencil on assorted scraps of paper are worthless and suggest incompetence.

The records should show the date and time the hypochlorinator was inspected, the flow rate of the water being treated, the total gallons of water treated, the feed rate of the hypochlorinator, the pounds of chlorine used, the calculated chlorine dosage, the chlorine residual concentration in the water as measured with the test kit, and the operator's name. The operator can conveniently tabulate this information on a standard record sheet similar to the one in Tables 2.7 and 2.8.

Hypochlorinators not in service require more maintenance than those in service. The operator must be alert to spot failures and repair the equipment quickly because lack of disinfection is not, of course, acceptable. If possible, the operator should have a spare hypochlorinator on hand that can replace the failing unit. If not, the treatment plant must be shut down until the hypochlorinator is repaired. If the plant must operate without a hypochlorinator, consumers must be notified to boil all drinking water. The operator should save the manufacturer's operation manual for reference and keep repair parts in stock at all times. Contacts should be established with the hypochlorinator supplier or manufacturer so that service and parts can be obtained quickly. A program of periodic maintenance on hypochlorination equipment will prevent the vast majority of hypochlorinator failures. Regular disassembly and cleaning of the hypochlorinator and replacement of critical parts is recommended insurance against a breakdown.

2.10   CHLORINATION ARITHMETIC

All calculations in this section can be performed by addition, subtraction, multiplication and division on a pocket electronic calculator.

FORMULAS

There are two approaches to calculating chlorine doses in milligrams per liter. They both give the same results, but have a slightly different form. From the basic equation,

$$\text{Chlorine, lbs} = (\text{Volume, M Gal})(\text{Dose, mg/}L)(8.34\text{ lbs/gal}),$$

we can rearrange the equation and solve for the dose in milligrams per liter.

$$\text{Chlorine Dose,}\atop \text{mg/}L = \frac{\text{Chlorine, lbs}}{(\text{Volume, M Gal})(8.34\text{ lbs/day})}$$

If the basic equation is expressed as a chemical feeder setting in pounds per day, then the flow would be in million gallons per day (MGD).

$$\text{Chlorine Dose,}\atop \text{mg/}L = \frac{\text{Chlorine, lbs/day}}{(\text{Flow, MGD})(8.34\text{ lbs/gal})}$$

Both of the above equations are also expressed in terms of pounds or pounds per day of chlorine per million pounds or million pounds per day of water.

$$\text{Chlorine Dose,}\atop \text{mg/}L = \frac{\text{Chlorine, lbs/day}}{\text{Water, Million lbs/day}}$$

2.100   Disinfection of Facilities

2.1000   Wells and Pumps

EXAMPLE 2

How many gallons of 5.25 percent sodium hypochlorite will be needed to disinfect a well with an 18-inch diameter casing and well screen? The well is 300 feet deep and there is 200 feet of water in the well. Use an initial chlorine dose of 100 mg/L.

Known		Unknown
Hypochlorite, %	= 5.25%	5.25% Hypochlorite, gal
Chlorine Dose, mg/L	= 100 mg/L	
Diameter, in	= 18 in	
Water Depth, ft	= 200 ft	

1. Find the volume of water in the well in gallons.

$$\text{Water Vol,}\atop \text{gal} = \frac{(0.785)(\text{Diameter, in})^2(\text{Water Depth, ft})(7.48\text{ gal/cu ft})}{144\text{ sq in/sq ft}}$$

$$= \frac{(0.785)(18\text{ in})^2(200\text{ ft})(7.48\text{ gal/cu ft})}{144\text{ sq in/sq ft}}$$

$$= 2{,}642\text{ gal}$$

2. Determine the pounds of chlorine needed.

$$\text{Chlorine, lbs} = (\text{Volume, M Gal})(\text{Dose, mg/}L)(8.34\text{ lbs/gal})$$

$$= (0.002642\text{ M Gal})(100\text{ mg/}L)(8.34\text{ lbs/gal})$$

$$= 2.2\text{ lbs chlorine}$$

3. Calculate the gallons of 5.25 percent sodium hypochlorite solution needed.

$$\text{Sodium Hypochlorite}\atop \text{Solution, gallons} = \frac{(\text{Chlorine, lbs})(100\%)}{(8.34\text{ lbs/gal})(\text{Hypochlorite, }\%)}$$

$$= \frac{(2.2\text{ lbs})(100\%)}{(8.34\text{ lbs/gal})(5.25\%)}$$

$$= 5.0\text{ gallons}$$

Five gallons of 5.25 percent sodium hypochlorite should do the job.

TABLE 2.7 OPERATION RECORD FOR SODIUM HYPOCHLORINATOR

OPERATION RECORD FOR SODIUM HYPOCHLORINATOR

REPORT NO. _____

WATER SUPPLIER _____

SYSTEM NAME _____ SYSTEM NO. _____

FOR WEEK OF _____ THRU _____ 19 ____

ITEM A.	STRENGTH OF BLEACH USED	5.25%	12.5%	1.0%
ITEM B.	POUNDS OF CHLORINE PER GALLON	0.44 LBS.	1.04 LBS.	0.083 LBS.

ITEM C. SIZE OF CHLORINE SOLUTION TANK: _____ GALLONS

ITEM D. SIDEWALL DEPTH OF SOLUTION TANK: _____ INCHES

ITEM E. STRENGTH OF SOLUTION: EACH GALLON OF BLEACH IS ADDED TO _____ GALLONS OF WATER.

ITEM F. GALLONS OF BLEACH IN A FULL TANK OF SOLUTION: _____ GALLONS.

ITEM G. POUNDS OF CHLORINE IN ONE INCH OF SOLUTION DEPTH: _____ POUNDS PER INCH DEPTH.

$$\frac{\text{(GAL. BLEACH IN FULL TANK) (POUNDS CHLORINE/GALLON)}}{\text{(SIDEWALL DEPTH OF SOLUTION TANK)}} = \frac{\text{(ITEM F) X (ITEM B)}}{\text{(ITEM D)}}$$

DAY	DATE	TIME	CHLORINE RESIDUALS mg/l			WATER PRODUCTION			CHLORINATION TREATMENT					
			#1	#2	#3	PLANT OPERATING RATE G.P.M.	WATER METER READING (GALLONS)	GALLONS OF WATER TREATED	FEEDER SETTING	INCHES OF SOLUTION IN TANK	INCHES OF SOLUTION USED	POUNDS OF CHLORINE USED (ITEM G) TIMES (COLUMN 8)	AVERAGE CHLORINE DOSE mg/l (NOTE 1)	QUARTS OF BLEACH TO BE ADDED (NOTE 2)
COLUMN NUMBER	1	2	3			4	5	6	7		8	9	10	11
SUN.														
SAT.														
FRI.														
THUR.														
WED.														
TUE.														
MON.														
READINGS FORWARD														
WEEKLY TOTALS ———————→														

REPORT SUBMITTED BY:

NOTE 1: AVG. CHLORINE DOSE (mg/l) $= \dfrac{\text{(LBS. OF CHLORINE USED) X (120,000)}}{\text{(GAL OF WATER TREATED)}} = \dfrac{\text{(COL 9) X (120,000)}}{\text{(COL 6)}}$

_____
SIGNATURE

NOTE 2: QUARTS OF BLEACH TO BE ADDED $= \dfrac{\text{(INCHES SOLN. USED) X (4) X}\ \substack{\text{(GALLONS OF BLEACH}\\\text{IN A FULL TANK)}}}{\text{(SIDEWALL DEPTH OF SOLUTION TANK)}} = \dfrac{\text{(COL 8) X (4) X (ITEM F)}}{\text{(ITEM D)}}$

TABLE 2.8 INSTRUCTIONS FOR COMPLETING TABLE 2.7, "OPERATION RECORD FOR SODIUM HYPOCHLORINATOR"

ITEM A and ITEM B — Circle the strength of chlorine bleach and the corresponding value for pounds of chlorine per gallon that is purchased for mixing the chlorine solution.

ITEM C — Record the capacity of the chlorine solution tank in gallons.

ITEM D — Record the sidewall depth of the solution tank when it is full.

ITEM E — Record the number of gallons of water that are added to each gallon of bleach for preparing chlorine solution.

ITEM F — Using the information in Item E, calculate the gallons of bleach in a full tank of solution.

ITEM G — Calculate the pounds of chlorine in one inch of solution depth in the tank. For example, assume that a 30-gallon solution tank is used and that the chlorine solution is made by mixing 4 gallons of water with each gallon of 5.25% household bleach (Clorox or Purex). Therefore, the full 30-gallon tank will contain 6 gallons of bleach. Since each gallon of 5.25% bleach contains 0.44 pounds of chlorine, 6 gallons of bleach contain (6) × (0.44) = 2.64 pounds of chlorine. If the tank has a sidewall depth of 36 inches, there are (2.64) ÷ (36) = 0.073 pounds of chlorine in each inch of solution depth in the tank.

Columns 1 through 7 in the daily record form are self-explanatory.

COLUMN 8 — Measure the inches of chlorine solution used from the tank and record it in Column 8.

COLUMN 9 — Calculate the pounds of chlorine used by multiplying the inches of chlorine solution used (Column 8) times the pounds of chlorine in one inch of solution depth (Item G). Record the answer in Column 9.

COLUMN 10 — Calculate the average chlorine dose by multiplying the pounds of chlorine used (Column 9) times 120,000 and divide by the gallons of water treated (Column 6). Record the answer in Column 10.

COLUMN 11 — To refill the solution tank proceed as follows. Multiply the inches of solution used from the tank (Column 8) times four. Then multiply that answer times the gallons of bleach that are in the tank when it is full, in this example, 6 gallons. Divide this answer by the total sidewall depth of the solution tank (36") to obtain the number of *QUARTS* of bleach that should be added to the tank. Enter the answer in Column 11. After the bleach is added, fill the tank to the top with clean water. This procedure will maintain the chlorine solution in the tank at a uniform strength.

$$\frac{\text{Inches of Solution Used} \times 4 \times \text{Gallons of Bleach in a Full Tank}}{\text{Sidewall Depth of Solution Tank}} = \frac{\text{Column 8} \times 4 \times \text{Item F}}{\text{Item D}}$$

2.1001 Mains

EXAMPLE 3

A section of an old 8-inch water main has been replaced and a 350-foot section of pipe needs to be disinfected. An initial chlorine dose of 400 mg/L is expected to maintain a chlorine residual of over 300 mg/L during the three-hour disinfection period. How many gallons of 5.25 percent sodium hypochlorite solution will be needed?

Known	Unknown
Diameter of Pipe, in = 8 in	5.25% Hypochlorite, gallons
or 8 in/12 in/ft = 0.67 ft	
Length of Pipe, ft = 350 ft	
Chlorine Dose, mg/L = 400 mg/L	
Hypochlorite, % = 5.25%	

1. Calculate the volume of water in the pipe in gallons.

Pipe Volume, gallons = (0.785)(Diameter, ft)²(Length, ft)(7.48 gal/cu ft)

= (0.785)(0.67 ft)²(350 ft)(7.48 gal/cu ft)

= 923 gallons of water

2. Determine the pounds of chlorine needed.

Chlorine, lbs = (Volume, M Gal)(Dose, mg/L)(8.34 lbs/gal)

= (0.000923 M Gal)(400 mg/L)(8.34 lbs/gal)

= 3.08 lbs chlorine

3. Calculate the gallons of 5.25 percent sodium hypochlorite solution needed.

$$\frac{\text{Sodium Hypochlorite}}{\text{Solution, gallons}} = \frac{(\text{Chlorine, lbs})(100\%)}{(8.34 \text{ lbs/gal})(\text{Hypochlorite, \%})}$$

$$= \frac{(3.08 \text{ lbs})(100\%)}{(8.34 \text{ lbs/gal})(5.25\%)}$$

= 7.0 gallons

Seven gallons of 5.25 percent solution of sodium hypochlorite should do the job.

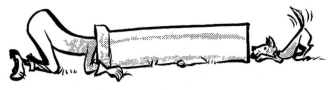

2.1002   Tanks

EXAMPLE 4

An existing service storage reservoir has been taken out of service for inspection, maintenance and repairs. The reservoir needs to be disinfected before being placed back on line. The reservoir is 6 feet deep, 10 feet wide, and 25 feet long. An initial chlorine dose of 100 mg/*L* is expected to maintain a chlorine residual of over 50 mg/*L* during the 24-hour disinfection period. How many gallons of 5.25 percent sodium hypochlorite solution will be needed?

Known		Unknown
Tank Depth, ft	= 6 ft	5.25% Hypochlorite, gal
Tank Width, ft	= 10 ft	
Tank Length, ft	= 25 ft	
Chlorine Dose, mg/*L*	= 100 mg/*L*	
Hypochlorite, %	= 5.25%	

1. Calculate the volume of water in the tank in gallons.

$$\text{Tank Volume, gallons} = \text{(Length, ft)(Width, ft)(Depth, ft)(7.48 gal/cu ft)}$$
$$= \text{(25 ft)(10 ft)(6 ft)(7.48 gal/cu ft)}$$
$$= 11,220 \text{ gallons}$$

2. Determine the pounds of chlorine needed.

$$\text{Chlorine, lbs} = \text{(Vol water, M Gal)(Chlorine Dose, mg/}L\text{)(8.34 lbs/gal)}$$
$$= \text{(0.01122 M Gal)(100 mg/}L\text{)(8.34 lbs/gal)}$$
$$= 9.36 \text{ lbs chlorine}$$

3. Calculate the gallons of 5.25 percent sodium hypochlorite solution needed.

$$\text{Sodium Hypochlorite Solution, gallons} = \frac{\text{(Chlorine, lbs)(100\%)}}{\text{(8.34 lbs/gal)(Hypochlorite, \%)}}$$
$$= \frac{\text{(9.36 lbs)(100\%)}}{\text{(8.34 lbs/gal)(5.25\%)}}$$
$$= 21.4 \text{ gallons}$$

Twenty-two gallons of 5.25 percent sodium hypochlorite solution should do the job.

2.101   Disinfection of Water From Wells

2.1010   Chlorine Dose

EXAMPLE 5

A chlorine demand test from a well water sample produced a result of 1.2 mg/*L*. The water supplier would like to maintain a chlorine residual of 0.2 mg/*L* throughout the system. What should be the chlorine dose in mg/*L* from either a chlorinator or hypochlorinator?

Known		Unknown
Chlorine Demand, mg/*L*	= 1.2 mg/*L*	Chlorine Dose, mg/*L*
Chlorine Residual, mg/*L*	= 0.2 mg/*L*	

Calculate the chlorine dose in mg/*L*.

$$\text{Chlorine Dose, mg/}L = \text{Chlorine Demand, mg/}L + \text{Chlorine Residual, mg/}L$$
$$= 1.2 \text{ mg/}L + 0.2 \text{ mg/}L$$
$$= 1.4 \text{ mg/}L$$

NOTE: Be sure to check the chlorine residual regularly throughout the system. If the residual is low or there are coliforms present in the test results, then the residual should be increased.

2.1011   Chlorinator

EXAMPLE 6

A deep well turbine pump is connected to a hydropneumatic tank. Under normal operating heads, the pump delivers 500 GPM. If the desired chlorine dosage is 3.5 mg/*L*, what should be the setting on the rotameter for the chlorinator (lbs chlorine per 24 hours)?

Known		Unknown
Pump Flow, GPM	= 500 GPM	Rotameter Setting, lbs chlorine/24 hours
Chlorine Dose, mg/*L*	= 3.5 mg/*L*	

1. Convert pump flow to million gallons per day (MGD).

$$\text{Flow, MGD} = \frac{\text{(500 GPM)(60 min/hr)(24 hr/day)}}{1,000,000/\text{Million}}$$
$$= 0.72 \text{ MGD}$$

2. Calculate the rotameter setting in pounds of chlorine per 24 hours.

$$\text{Rotameter Setting, lbs/day} = \text{(Flow, MGD)(Dose, mg/}L\text{)(8.34 lbs/gal)}$$
$$= \text{(0.72 MGD)(3.5 mg/}L\text{)(8.34 lbs/gal)}$$
$$= 21.0 \text{ lbs chlorine/day}$$
$$= 21.0 \text{ lbs chlorine/24 hours}$$

EXAMPLE 7

Using the results from Example 6 (a chlorinator setting of 21 lbs per 24 hours), how many pounds of chlorine would be used in one month if the pump hour meter shows the pump operates an average of 20 hours per day? The chlorinator operates only when the pump operates. How many 150-pound cylinders will be needed per month?

Known		Unknown
Chlorinator Setting, lbs/day	= 21 lbs/day	1. Chlorine Used, lbs/mo
Pump Operation, hr/day	= 20 hr/day	2. Cylinders Needed, no/mo
Chlorine Cylinders, lbs/cyl	= 150 lbs/cyl	

1. Calculate the chlorine used in pounds per month.

$$\text{Chlorine Used, lbs/mo} = \frac{\text{(Cl Setting, lbs/day)(Operation, hr/day)(30 days/mo)}}{24 \text{ hr/day}}$$
$$= \frac{\text{(21 lbs/day)(20 hr/day)(30 days/mo)}}{24 \text{ hr/day}}$$
$$= 525 \text{ lbs/mo}$$

2. Determine the number of 150-pound cylinders needed per month.

$$\text{Cylinders Needed,} \atop \text{no/mo} = \frac{\text{Chlorine Used, lbs/mo}}{\text{Chlorine Cylinders, lbs/cyl}}$$

$$= \frac{525 \text{ lbs Cl/mo}}{150 \text{ lbs Cl/cylinder}}$$

$$= 3.5 \text{ Cylinders/month}$$

EXAMPLE 8

A deep well turbine pump delivers 400 GPM throughout a 24-hour period. The weight of chlorine in a 150-pound cylinder was 123 pounds at the start of the time period and 109 pounds at the end of the 24 hours. What was the chlorine dose rate in mg/L?

Known	Unknown
Pump Flow, GPM = 400 GPM	Chlorine Dose, mg/L
Time Period, hr = 24 hr	
Chlorine Wt at Start, lbs = 123 lbs	
Chlorine Wt at End, lbs = 109 lbs	

1. Convert flow of 400 GPM to MGD.

$$\text{Flow, MGD} = \frac{(400 \text{ gal/min})(60 \text{ min/hr})(24 \text{ hr/day})}{1,000,000/\text{Million}}$$

$$= 0.576 \text{ MGD}$$

2. Calculate the chlorine dose rate in mg/L.

$$\text{Chlorine Dose,} \atop \text{mg/L} = \frac{\text{Chlorine Used, lbs/day}}{(\text{Flow, MGD})(8.34 \text{ lbs/gal})}$$

$$= \frac{(123 \text{ lbs} - 109 \text{ lbs})/1 \text{ day}}{(0.576 \text{ MGD})(8.34 \text{ lbs/gal})}$$

$$= \frac{14 \text{ lbs chlorine/day}}{(0.576 \text{ MGD})(8.34 \text{ lbs/gal})}$$

$$= \frac{2.9 \text{ lbs Chlorine}}{1 \text{ M lbs Water}}$$

$$= 2.9 \text{ mg/L}$$

2.1012 Hypochlorinator

EXAMPLE 9

Water from a well is being treated by a hypochlorinator. If the hypochlorinator is set at a pumping rate of 50 gallons per day (GPD) and uses a 3 percent available hypochlorite solution, what is the chlorine dose rate in mg/L if the pump delivers 350 GPM?

Known	Unknown
Hypochlorinator, GPD = 50 GPD	Chlorine Dose, mg/L
Hypochlorite, % = 3%	
Pump, GPM = 350 GPM	

1. Convert the pumping rate to MGD.

$$\text{Pumping Rate,} \atop \text{MGD} = \frac{(350 \text{ GPM})(60 \text{ min/hr})(24 \text{ hr/day})}{1,000,000/\text{Million}}$$

$$= 0.50 \text{ MGD}$$

2. Calculate the chlorine dose rate in pounds per day.

$$\text{Chlorine Dose,} \atop \text{lbs/day} = \frac{(\text{Flow, gal/day})(\text{Hypochlorite, \%})(8.34 \text{ lbs/gal})}{100\%}$$

$$= \frac{(50 \text{ gal/day})(3\%)(8.34 \text{ lbs/gal})}{100\%}$$

$$= 12.5 \text{ lbs/day}$$

3. Calculate the chlorine dose in mg/L.

$$\text{Chlorine Dose,} \atop \text{mg/L} = \frac{\text{Chlorine Dose, lbs/day}}{(\text{Flow, MGD})(8.34 \text{ lbs/gal})}$$

$$= \frac{12.5 \text{ lbs chlorine/day}}{(0.50 \text{ M Gal/day})(8.34 \text{ lbs/gal})}$$

$$= 3 \text{ lbs chlorine/M lbs water}$$

$$= 3 \text{ mg/L}$$

EXAMPLE 10

Water pumped from a well is disinfected by a hypochlorinator. During a one-week time period, the water meter indicated that 1,098,000 gallons of water were pumped. A 2.0 percent sodium hypochlorite solution is stored in a 2.5-foot diameter plastic tank. During this one-week time period, the level of hypochlorite in the tank dropped 18 inches (1.50 ft). What was the chlorine dose in mg/L?

Known	Unknown
Water Treated, M Gal = 1.098 M Gal	Chlorine Dose, mg/L
Hypochlorite, % = 2.0%	
Hypochlorite Tank D, ft = 2.5 ft	
Hypochlorite Used, ft = 1.5 ft	

1. Calculate the pounds of water disinfected.

$$\text{Water, lbs} = (\text{Water Treated, M Gal})(8.34 \text{ lbs/gal})$$

$$= (1.098 \text{ M Gal})(8.34 \text{ lbs/gal})$$

$$= 9.16 \text{ M lbs water}$$

2. Calculate the volume of hypochlorite solution used in gallons.

$$\text{Hypochlorite,} \atop \text{gal} = (0.785)(\text{Diameter, ft})^2(\text{Drop, ft})(7.48 \text{ gal/cu ft})$$

$$= (0.785)(2.5 \text{ ft})^2(1.5 \text{ ft})(7.48 \text{ gal/cu ft})$$

$$= 55.0 \text{ gallons}$$

3. Determine the pounds of chlorine used to treat the water.

$$\text{Chlorine,} \atop \text{lbs} = (\text{Hypochlorite, gal})\left(\frac{\text{Hypochlorite, \%}}{100\%}\right)(8.34 \text{ lbs/gal})$$

$$= (55.0 \text{ gal})\left(\frac{2.0\%}{100\%}\right)(8.34 \text{ lbs/gal})$$

$$= 9.17 \text{ lbs chlorine}$$

4. Calculate the chlorine dose in mg/L.

$$\text{Chlorine Dose, mg/}L = \frac{\text{Chlorine Used, lbs}}{\text{Water Treated, Million lbs}}$$

$$= \frac{9.17 \text{ lbs Chlorine}}{9.16 \text{ M lbs Water}}$$

$$= \frac{1.0 \text{ lbs Chlorine}}{1 \text{ M lbs Water}}$$

$$= 1.0 \text{ mg/}L$$

EXAMPLE 11

Estimate the required concentration of a hypochlorite solution (%) if a pump delivers 600 GPM from a well. The hypochlorinator can deliver a maximum of 120 GPD and the desired chlorine dose is 1.8 mg/L.

Known	Unknown
Pump Flow, GPM = 600 GPM	Hypochlorite Strength, %
Hypochl Flow, GPD = 120 GPD	
Chlorine Dose, mg/L = 1.8 mg/L	

1. Calculate the flow of water treated in million gallons per day.

$$\text{Water Treated, M Gal/day} = \frac{(600 \text{ GPM})(60 \text{ min/hr})(24 \text{ hr/day})}{1,000,000/\text{Million}}$$

$$= 0.864 \text{ MGD}$$

2. Determine the pounds of chlorine required per day.

$$\text{Chlorine Required, lbs/day} = (\text{Flow, MGD})(\text{Dose, mg/}L)(8.34 \text{ lbs/gal})$$

$$= (0.864 \text{ MGD})(1.8 \text{ mg/}L)(8.34 \text{ lbs/gal})$$

$$= 13.0 \text{ lbs chlorine/day}$$

3. Calculate the hypochlorite solution strength as a percent.

$$\text{Hypochlorite Strength, \%} = \frac{(\text{Chlorine Required, lbs/day})(100\%)}{(\text{Hypochlorinator Flow, GPD})(8.34 \text{ lbs/gal})}$$

$$= \frac{(13.0 \text{ lbs/day})(100\%)}{(120 \text{ GPD})(8.34 \text{ lbs/gal})}$$

$$= 1.3\%$$

EXAMPLE 12

A hypochlorite solution for a hypochlorinator is being prepared in a 55-gallon drum. If 10 gallons of 5 percent hypochlorite is added to the drum, how much water should be added to the drum to produce a 1.3 percent hypochlorite solution?

Known	Unknown
Drum Capacity, gal = 55 gal	Water Added, gal
Hypochlorite, gal = 10 gal	
Actual Hypo, % = 5%	
Desired Hypo, % = 1.3%	

or

$$\text{Desired Hypo, \%} = \frac{(\text{Hypo, gal})(\text{Hypo, \%})}{\text{Hypo, gal + Water Added, gal}}$$

Rearrange the terms in the equation.

(Desired Hypo, %)(Hypo, gal + Water Added, gal) = (Hypo, gal)(Hypo, %)

(Desired Hypo, %)(Hypo, gal) + (Desired Hypo, %)(Water Added, gal) = (Hypo, gal)(Hypo, %)

(Desired Hypo, %)(Water Added, gal) = (Hypo, gal)(Hypo, %) − (Desired Hypo, %)(Hypo, gal)

Calculate the volume of water to be added in gallons.

$$\text{Water Added, gal} = \frac{(\text{Hypo, gal})(\text{Actual Hypo, \%}) - (\text{Desired Hypo, \%})(\text{Hypo, gal})}{\text{Desired Hypo, \%}}$$

$$= \frac{(10 \text{ gal})(5\%) - (1.3\%)(10 \text{ gal})}{1.3\%}$$

$$= \frac{50 - 13}{1.3}$$

$$= 28.5 \text{ gallons of water}$$

Add 28.5 gallons of water to the 10 gallons of 5 percent hypochlorite in the drum.

2.102   Video Hypochlorination Problem

EXAMPLE 13

Hypochlorinator Settings and Adjustment

Determine hypochlorinator stroke and frequency settings.

1. How much chlorine do we need?

Flow to be treated, 30,000 gallons or 0.03 Million Gallons
Desired chlorine dose, 1.3 mg/L

$$\text{Chlorine, lbs} = (\text{Water Volume, MG})(\text{Dose, mg/}L)(8.34 \text{ lbs/gal})$$

$$= (0.03 \text{ MG})(1.3 \text{ mg/}L)(8.34 \text{ lbs/gal})$$

$$= 0.375 \text{ lb Chlorine Needed}$$

2. How many pounds of 1.5 percent chlorine solution are needed to obtain 0.375 pound of chlorine?

$$\text{Chlorine Solution, lbs} = \frac{\text{Chlorine Needed, lbs}}{\text{Portion Chlorine in Chlorine Solution}}$$

$$= \frac{0.375 \text{ lb Chlorine Needed}}{0.015 \text{ Portion Chlorine in Solution}}$$

$$= 25 \text{ lbs Chlorine Solution Needed}$$

3. How many gallons of chlorine solution are needed?

$$\text{Chlorine Solution, gallons} = \frac{\text{Chlorine Solution, lbs}}{8.34 \text{ lbs/gal}}$$

$$= \frac{25 \text{ lbs Chlorine Solution Needed}}{8.34 \text{ lbs/gal}}$$

$$= 3 \text{ gallons of Chlorine Solution Needed}$$

4. How many gallons of chlorine solution are needed per hour from a hypochlorinator (chemical feed pump) operating 8 hours per day?

$$\text{Pump Feed Rate, gal/hr} = \frac{\text{Chlorine Solution Needed, gallons}}{\text{Time Feed Pump Operators, hours}}$$

$$= \frac{3 \text{ gallons Chlorine Solution Needed}}{8 \text{ hours of operation per day}}$$

$$= 0.375 \text{ gal/hr}$$

5. Determine the hypochlorinator stroke and frequency settings if the pump capacity is one gallon per hour.

a. At what percent capacity must the pump operate?

$$\text{Capacity, \%} = \frac{(\text{Required Feed Rate, gal/hr})(100\%)}{\text{Pump Capacity, gal/hr}}$$

$$= \frac{(0.375 \text{ gal/hr})(100\%)}{1 \text{ gal/hr}}$$

$$= 37.5\%$$

b. Assume a stroke setting of 50 percent.

c. Calculate the frequency setting.

$$\text{Frequency, \%} = \frac{\text{Capacity, \%}}{\text{Stroke, \%}}$$

$$= \frac{(37.5\%)(100\%)}{50\%}$$

$$= 75\%$$

If we exceed the pump capacity to pump the chlorine needed, we should use a stronger chlorine solution.

2.11   ADDITIONAL READING

To obtain information regarding the topics in this chapter, review the appropriate chapters and sections in the following operator training manual:

SMALL WATER SYSTEM OPERATION AND MAINTE-NANCE. Obtain from the Office of Water Programs, California State University, Sacramento, 6000 J Street, Sacramento, CA 95819-6025, phone (916) 278-6142 or visit the website at www.owp.csus.edu. Price, $45.00.

2.12   ACKNOWLEDGMENT

Material contained in this chapter is copyrighted by the California State University, Sacramento Foundation and is reproduced by permission.

WATER SYSTEMS OPERATION AND MAINTENANCE VIDEO TRAINING SERIES

CHAPTER (VIDEO) 3

WATER STORAGE TANKS

VIDEO 3 SUMMARY

Video 3, WATER STORAGE TANKS, provides operators with the knowledge, skills, and abilities they need to inspect, protect, operate, and maintain water storage tanks. Information is provided on the purpose of water storage facilities, the tank materials, and the types of water storage tanks. Emphasis is placed on how to operate, maintain, and disinfect water storage tanks. An important topic is how to protect tanks from contamination. Other topics include how to perform duties safely and the importance of good records.

CONTENTS OF VIDEO 3

WATER STORAGE TANKS VIDEO

INTRODUCTION

   Purpose of Storage Facilities

   Description of Types of Tanks

   Topics Covered in Video

PERSONAL SAFETY/ENVIRONMENT

   Safety Issues

   Environment

OPERATION/CONTAMINATION

   Control of Water Levels

   Collecting Samples

   Indicators of Contamination

   Avenues of Contamination

   Water Quality Degradation

INSPECTION/MAINTENANCE/RECORDS

   Inspection

   Maintenance

   Records

TANK INSPECTION

SUMMARY

CONTENTS OF CHAPTER 3

WATER STORAGE TANKS
LEARNING BOOKLET

OBJECTIVES

Chapter (Video) 3.   WATER STORAGE TANKS

Following completion of Video 3 and Chapter 3, you should be able to:

1. Identify various types of water storage tanks,

2. Inspect storage tanks,

3. Safely operate and maintain a storage tank,

4. Collect samples from a storage tank,

5. Troubleshoot storage tank problems,

6. Protect a storage tank from corrosion,

7. Disinfect a storage tank, and

8. Develop a storage tank recordkeeping system and keep accurate records.

LEARNING BOOKLET STUDY MATERIAL

This section of the *LEARNING BOOKLET* contains important information. Read this section after watching the video and before attempting to take the Objective Test for this chapter.

Material in this section will help you to better understand the material presented in the video. Also some critical information is easier to present in the *LEARNING BOOKLET*, such as illustrating forms and calculations.

CHAPTER 3.   WATER STORAGE TANKS

3.0   PURPOSE OF STORAGE FACILITIES[1]

The main purpose of a water storage facility is to provide a sufficient amount of water to average or equalize the daily demands on the water supply system. The storage facility should be able to provide water for *AVERAGE*[2] and *PEAK DEMANDS*.[3] Also, the storage facility helps maintain adequate pressures throughout the entire system.

Other purposes of water storage include meeting the needs for fire protection, industrial requirements, and reserve storage. During a fire or other type of emergency, sufficient storage should be available to meet fire demands, as well as other demands, and also maintain system pressures. In some areas the water supply system may serve some type of industry.

Storage requirements will depend on the type of industry and the flow and pressure demands of the industrial activities of each industrial facility served by the water supply system. Reserve storage requirements depend on standby power requirements and alternate sources of water supply. Reserve requirements may be specified by fire insurance regulations. Reserve storage capacity may be provided to meet future growth and development demands of the area being served.

Reservoirs are storage facilities and may be of several different types. We often think of a reservoir as an open body of water contained by an earth-fill dam or a concrete dam. This chapter, however, will discuss various types of steel and concrete tanks (Figures 3.1 and 3.2) which are basically covered

2,000,000-Gallon Standpipe—Brown Deer, Wis.

1,700,000-Gallon Reservoir—Pleasant Hill, Calif.

500,000-Gallon Pedestal Spheroid—Warwick, R.I.

2,000,000-Gallon Turbospherical—Denton, Texas

Fig. 3.1   Photos of typical storage facilities
(Permission of Pittsburgh-Des Moines Corporation)

---

[1] *For additional information on storage facilities, see Chapter 3, "Reservoir Management and Intake Structures," in WATER TREATMENT PLANT OPERATION, Volume I, in this series of manuals.*

[2] *Average Demand.   The total demand for water during a period of time divided by the number of days in that time period. This is also called the average daily demand.*

[3] *Peak Demand.   The maximum momentary load placed on a water treatment plant, pumping station or distribution system. This demand is usually the maximum average load in one hour or less, but may be specified as the instantaneous load or the load during some other short time period.*

distribution system reservoirs for the storage of treated water and are commonly used in most water systems, especially small water systems.

The requirements for a specific storage facility will depend upon a system's individual needs. To select a suitable type of storage facility, the answers to the following questions must be known:

1. What is the maximum-day use?

2. What is the maximum-hourly use?

3. What type of pressure will the facility be required to provide and maintain throughout the system?

4. What size will be necessary to fulfill the requirements for emergencies such as fire flow?

Water storage facilities are used to store water from wells or water treatment facilities at times when demands for water are low and to distribute the water during periods of high demand. Water storage facilities are found at one or more locations in areas closest to the ultimate users, where higher pressures

are needed, and where land is available. The benefits of distribution system storage are:

1. Demands on the source of water, the pumping facilities, and the transmission and distribution mains are more nearly equalized and also the capacities of the tanks and other treatment facilities in the system need not be so large.

2. System flows and pressures are improved and stabilized, thus providing better service to the customers in the area.

3. Reserve water supplies are provided in the distribution system for emergencies such as firefighting and power outages.

3.1 TYPES AND MATERIALS OF STORAGE FACILITIES

The following types of storage facilities are common to a water system: clear wells (Figure 3.3), elevated tanks (Figure 3.4), standpipes (Figure 3.5), ground-level storage tanks (Figure 3.6), hydropneumatic or pressure tanks (Figure 3.7), and surge tanks (Figure 3.8). Let's study the definition of each tank and the differences among the tanks.

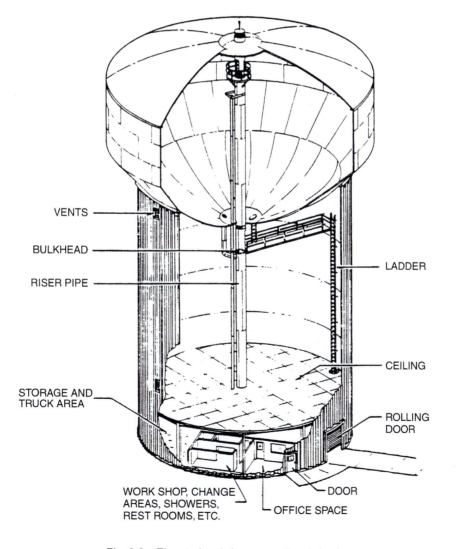

Fig. 3.2   Elevated tank (cross-sectional view)
(Permission of Pittsburgh-Des Moines Corporation)

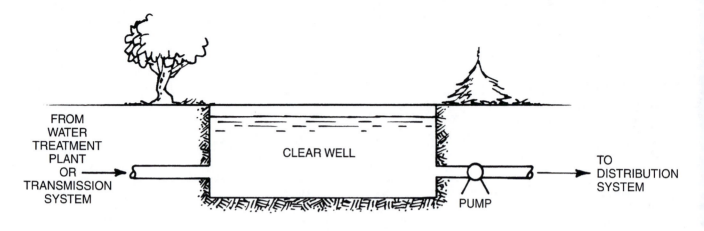

FROM
WATER
TREATMENT
PLANT
OR →
TRANSMISSION
SYSTEM

CLEAR WELL

PUMP

TO
DISTRIBUTION
SYSTEM

Fig. 3.3   Clear well

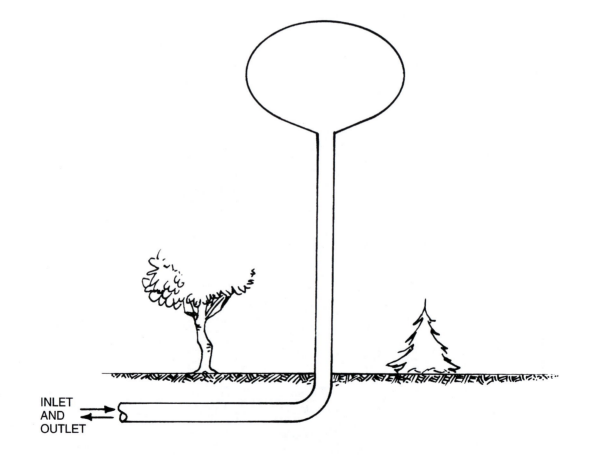

INLET
AND
OUTLET

Fig. 3.4   Elevated storage tank

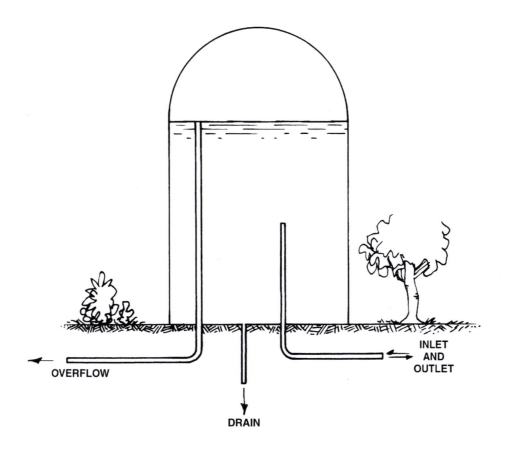

Fig. 3.5   Standpipe

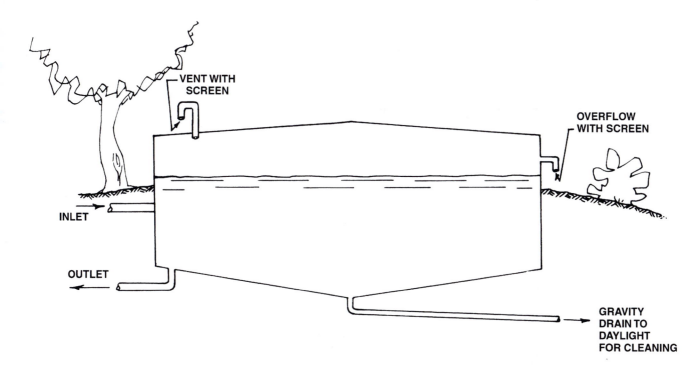

Fig. 3.6   Ground-level service storage reservoir

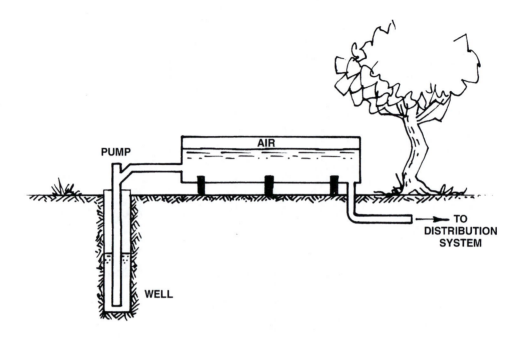

Fig. 3.7   Hydropneumatic or pressure tank

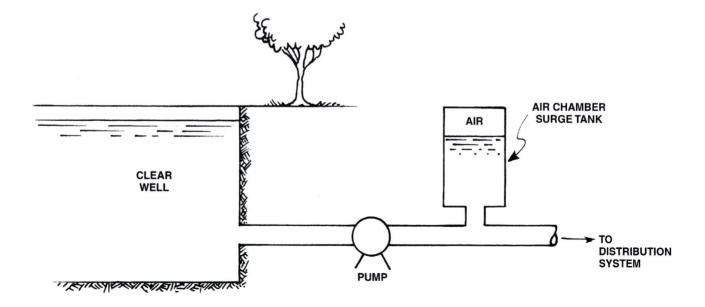

Fig. 3.8   Surge tank

3.10   Clear Wells

Clear wells are used for the storage of filtered water from a treatment plant. These storage tanks are of sufficient capacity to allow fairly constant filtration rates. This type of storage facility will allow a filter plant to operate continuously at an average flow rate and place neither fluctuating nor excessive demands on the filters. Clear wells store excess water when the demand for water is low and supply additional water when the demand is high.

Clear wells may be located below the ground surface and are often made of concrete. They must be protected from contamination and unauthorized entry. Periodically they must be inspected for leaks.

3.11   Elevated Tanks

Elevated tanks are elevated above the service zone and are used primarily to maintain an adequate and fairly uniform pressure to that service zone. They are often installed where the land is flat. Elevated tanks are used to:

1. Eliminate the need for continuous pumping,

2. Minimize variations in distribution system water pressures due to short-term shutdowns of power or pumps,

3. Equalize the water pressure in the distribution system by the proper location of the tanks,

4. Provide a small amount of water for storage (especially to meet demands such as fires), and

5. Reduce auxiliary power requirements.

One limitation of elevated tanks is that the pressure in the distribution system may vary with the water level in the tank.

3.12   Standpipes

Standpipes are tanks that stand on the ground and have a height greater than their diameter. For example, a tank that has the following dimensions is a standpipe—a 10-foot (3-m) diameter and a height of 20 feet (6 m). The bottom of a standpipe is on the ground, whereas the bottom of an elevated tank is above the ground.

Standpipes may be constructed of steel or concrete. They are usually located on high ground at or near a well field or at a point in the distribution system where equalizing storage is needed. Standpipes are used to lower fire insurance costs of consumers. When compared with elevated storage tanks, standpipes are preferred because they are:

1. Easier to maintain,

2. More accessible for observation and sampling to determine the quality of the stored water,

3. Safer to work around, and

4. Less objectionable from an aesthetic viewpoint.

Standpipes constructed of steel require more maintenance than those built of concrete.

Standpipes can provide large volumes of water at low pressures. This storage is available for fire protection if fire pumpers are used. When operating under these conditions, you may create a vacuum on the distribution system. This may result in the introduction of contamination to the mains. If this happens, you must issue boil-water orders to your consumers, flush the system, and sample for COLIFORMS[4] to be sure the water is safe to drink.

3.13   Ground-Level Reservoirs

Most ground-level reservoirs are constructed of concrete and are either circular or rectangular in shape. They may be buried in the ground or located on the ground surface. All reservoirs should be covered to reduce the possibility of contamination. Some concrete reservoirs are built with parks, parking lots, or tennis courts on top of them. These reservoirs are located above the service area to maintain the required pressures.

All storage facilities should be located above drainage areas and locations subject to flooding. Care must be taken to ensure that runoff water and debris cannot enter the reservoir and contaminate the water. Overflow and air vents should be screened so that birds, rodents, and debris cannot enter the reservoir. Vents must be adequate and never be blocked so air can flow freely without any obstruction. Properly functioning vents are essential to prevent a pressure developing in the reservoir when it fills or a vacuum when it empties or is drained. Reservoirs must be fenced to prevent access by vandals or other unauthorized persons.

3.14   Hydropneumatic or Pressure Tanks

A hydropneumatic tank contains a system in which a water pump is controlled by the air pressure in a tank partially filled with water. This type of facility is usually found in smaller water systems. Hydropneumatic tanks are used with a well or a booster pump in water supply systems that do not have a storage reservoir. The tank is used to maintain water pressures in the system and to control the operation of the pump. CAUTION: Hydropneumatic tanks are pressure vessels. Because of the high pressure in the tank, care must be used when operating and maintaining these facilities, especially the pressure relief valves.

---

[4] Coliform (COAL-i-form).   A group of bacteria found in the intestines of warm-blooded animals (including humans) and also in plants, soil, air and water. Fecal coliforms are a specific class of bacteria which only inhabit the intestines of warm-blooded animals. The presence of coliform bacteria is an indication that the water is polluted and may contain pathogenic (disease-causing) organisms.

Hydropneumatic tanks must contain the proper amount of air to be effective. The recommended water to air ratio is approximately two-thirds water to one-third air. If there is not enough air in a hydropneumatic tank, the pump may operate continuously. An automatically operated air pump should be available to maintain the proper amount of air. The tank should have a sight glass so the water-air ratio in the tank can be observed.

A limitation of hydropneumatic or pressure tanks is that they do not provide much storage to meet demands during power outages. Also a very limited amount of time is available to do maintenance or repair work on wells, pumps, or water treatment equipment. If a pressure filter must be washed using water from a pressure tank, the amount of water remaining in storage and pressure in the system may become fairly low by the time the backwash job is completed. For additional information on hydropneumatic and pressure tanks, see Chapter 3, "Wells," Section 3.29, "Hydropneumatic Pressure Tank Systems," and Section 3.15, "Determination of Working Pressure," in *SMALL WATER SYSTEM OPERATION AND MAINTENANCE*.

3.15   Surge Tanks

Surge tanks are not necessarily storage facilities, but are used mainly to control *WATER HAMMER*[5] or to regulate the flow of water. Their primary purpose is to protect pipelines against destruction due to excess surge pressure (water hammer). Surge tanks are filled with air and allow the pressure surge to flow into the air space instead of stressing the pipeline. Surge tanks do not absorb energy. Their function is simply to absorb the sudden surge (pressure of water) in the air space thus eliminating possible breaks in the distribution system pipelines. An insufficient amount of air in a surge tank will defeat its intended purpose and will allow surge problems in the distribution system.

3.2   STORAGE SYSTEM SURVEILLANCE AND INSPECTION

3.20   Purpose of System Surveillance and Inspection

Surveillance and inspection of storage systems is done for three reasons. First, to detect and correct any problems that are sanitary hazards; second, to detect and correct any significant deterioration of facilities or equipment used for the storage and transportation of the water supply; and third, to detect the encroachment of other utilities (sewer, power, gas, phone, cable TV). Some types of surveillance, such as checking for vandalism, are performed routinely, while others are done only under special circumstances, such as checking for damage after a storm. Generally, routine surveillance in a storage system would only involve above-ground facilities such as reservoirs, pump stations, and valves. However, some less frequent surveillance can also be made of underground facilities as described later in this section.

Critical areas of the storage system should be patrolled routinely so that the water utility will have an early warning of any adverse conditions that might appear. Any activity or situation that might endanger a water facility or the quality of the water must be investigated and reported without delay. Possible damage from floods, earthquakes, tornadoes, or fires needs to be looked into promptly.

Just as important as routine patrolling is having the field crews watch for actual or potential problems as they attend to their duties. The sooner corrective action is taken after a problem is found, the easier it usually is to make the correction. The longer water quality or facilities deteriorate, the more difficult the situation becomes.

3.21   Treated Water Storage Facilities

Storage facilities in the distribution system are the most obvious facilities needing surveillance. They are generally not under a positive pressure (except for pressure tanks) and are usually above or at ground level. They are, therefore, the most susceptible part of the distribution system to quality degradation from external sources. Open reservoirs are the most critical type of reservoir in this regard, with below-ground reservoirs next in line. Just about anything that one could think of has been found during inspections of reservoirs. For example, cans, bottles, papers, and even a pile of human fecal matter were found on a reservoir ledge inside a covered, 10 million gallon (38,000 cu m) reservoir. Finding small animals, dead or alive, in reservoirs is not uncommon.

Daily surveillance is recommended for trespassing, vandalism, dumping of trash, or swimming. Pay particular attention to fence and screen openings, roof damage, intact locks on reservoirs, and to manholes or doors. In one case, repeated high bacterial counts occurred and an inspection revealed that a roof manhole was open and several pigeons had entered and drowned in the water. If these daily inspections reveal any change in water color, odor, or turbidity or if any other evidence indicates the water may have been tampered with, take the facility out of service and contact the health department immediately to determine what further action should be taken. Some tests that can be quickly made are chlorine residual, conductance (for TDS), pH, and alkalinity. Bacteriological tests take longer to complete, but should also be made (for example, 24-hour coliform tests by the membrane filter method).

---

[5] *Water Hammer.   The sound like someone hammering on a pipe that occurs when a valve is opened or closed very rapidly. When a valve position is changed quickly, the water pressure in a pipe will increase and decrease back and forth very quickly. This rise and fall in pressures can cause serious damage to the system.*

Inspect reservoir covers frequently to determine if they are watertight. If a roof develops leaks, any contaminants on the roof, such as bird droppings, will be washed into the reservoir. Even concrete roofs may develop cracks in time and permit leakage. Vent screens should be inspected to ensure they are in good condition. If the screens on the vents are torn or rust away, it is obvious that small animals can gain entry to the reservoir. Vent areas must be protected to prevent rain, wind-blown items (leaves, paper), roof drainage, debris and, to the extent possible, dust and dirt from entering the reservoir. Also check the screening on the vertical overflow pipes. In one case, the decomposed remains of two rodents were found in a tank which the rodents apparently had crawled into through an unscreened vertical overflow pipe some 20 ft (6 m) high.

Other reservoir inspections may be made at less frequent intervals. Weekly or more frequent inspections are advisable to note any algae, slime and/or worm growths, floating or settled materials, or deterioration (corrosion or dry rot) of roofing and wooden trusses.

After a heavy rain, inspect the reservoir for damage. If a below-ground reservoir is located where it could be affected by floods, an inspection should be made during such periods to determine whether or not storm waters are getting into the facility or erosion is undermining the structure.

At least once a year, the interior of each storage tank should be inspected to determine the condition of the interior coating and whether the tank needs to be washed out, completely cleaned, or recoated. Interior inspections may also reveal the presence of animals, birds, or debris in the tank. The condition of the vents can be seen quite well from the interior of the tank. Preferably every year, but certainly at least every other year, each reservoir should be drained and thoroughly inspected to determine if there is any significant leakage or corrosion and to observe the nature and amount of sediments on the floor or bottom. Cleaning of the reservoir usually takes place at this time. Divers are being used to inspect, clean, and repair tanks without draining them.

Routinely inspect any sewers located near below-ground reservoirs to determine if there is any noticeable leakage around them. The possibility exists that leaking wastewater could seep through (infiltrate) the ground and cracks in reservoir walls and reach the stored water. As part of the surveillance made after storms, be alert to possible overflow of wastewater from damaged or overloaded sewers to a reservoir area.

3.22 Vandalism

The normal security measures taken to prevent vandalism include locks on doors and gates, fences, lighting, posting signs, and patrolling. These measures will not stop vandalism, but should reduce it. These protective measures must not be ignored and allowed to deteriorate into uselessness (such as a fence with a hole in it).

If vandalism or illegal entry is found, make a thorough investigation to determine what damage might have been done and whether there is any possibility of a threat to the quality of the water supply. Check the appearance and odor of the water supply in the area. Record the condition of all locks, any questionable conditions in the areas where unauthorized entry apparently took place, the presence of hazardous material containers, missing items, and damaged equipment. Contact any neighbors in the area for additional information and request assistance to watch the facility. Then promptly report any damage or questionable conditions you have found to responsible supervisory personnel. If water quality may be affected, the health department should be called immediately. If the questionable part of the system can be isolated, this should be done. Notify customers and the health department if a decision is made to shut down part of the system.

As already noted, if there is any detectable change in color, odor, or turbidity of the water, or any other evidence that the water has been tampered with, the facility should be *IMMEDIATELY TAKEN OUT OF SERVICE.* Water quality tests that can be done promptly and would be indicative of suspected contamination should be promptly run. Tests that can be quickly made are turbidity, chlorine residual, conductance (for TDS), pH, and alkalinity. Bacteriological tests take longer to complete, but should also be made (for example, 24-hour coliform tests by the membrane filter method).

Fortunately, most acts of vandalism cause only superficial damage and do no serious harm. Water quality safeguards against minor vandalism are built into most systems and their operation. Existing chlorine residuals will assist in minimizing any threat from disease organisms. A large dilution factor is normally present which will also minimize any contamination threat. Routine sampling and continuous water quality monitoring assist in revealing any possible threat to water quality. For example, telemetering of chlorine residuals and turbidity can indicate water quality problems. Similarly, telemetering of pressures, flows, and reservoir levels can help detect operational problems early.

Automatic controls will often compensate for or minimize certain acts of vandalism. The fact that most of the distribution system is underground and relatively inaccessible makes only a small portion of the system actually vulnerable. Reservoirs that may have been contaminated can usually be readily isolated as reserve supplies of water are often available from other sources. "Looped" distribution lines will allow the isolation of problem areas. Finally, the consumer can be counted upon to quickly report any perceived change in water appearance, taste, or odor.

If the vandal is still present and does not leave, notify the authorities (supervisor, police) immediately. *DO NOT ATTEMPT TO USE FORCE* on a vandal, even a child, because you or the vandal could be injured. After the episode is over, make a complete written report describing the vandalism (including photos) and its actual and potential effects on the physical system and water quality.

3.3 OPERATION[6]

3.30 Storage Tanks

Procedures for operating storage tanks will vary depending on the design of the facilities and the demands for water. Typical procedures could include (1) filling all storage tanks during periods of off-peak electrical demands, and/or (2) maintaining specified minimum pressures at certain critical points in the distribution system.

Normally, storage tanks are installed to supply water during periods of high water demand. Therefore, during periods of

---

[6] *For additional information on operation, see Chapter 5, "Distribution System Operation and Maintenance," in WATER DISTRIBUTION SYSTEM OPERATION AND MAINTENANCE.*

low water demand, the excess pumping capacity is used to fill the tanks before the next period of high water demand occurs. If off-peak electrical energy is available at reduced rates, the pumps can be operated during this period to fill the storage tanks.

All storage tanks should be operated according to the design engineer's and manufacturer's instructions. We must remember that in the design stages of any water system, there usually is a valid reason for the type of storage tank that was selected. Small changes in the distribution system, such as pipeline extensions or the addition of a few new services, usually will not change the requirements of the storage facility. Major system changes, such as larger size main lines or the installation of multiple services, can change storage requirements and may require more tank storage.

Frequently the water supplier tries to maintain specified minimum target water pressures throughout the distribution system. Under these circumstances, the pump or pumps are operated whenever needed to maintain the desired pressures. Sometimes there may be several pumps available and they may be variable-speed pumps. The operator maintains pressures throughout the system by regulating the number of pumps operating and/or controlling the pump speed.

Many water supply systems are instrumented and automated. Instruments are used to measure water pressures automatically throughout the distribution system and to measure water levels in service storage tanks. Whenever water pressures or water levels drop below minimum target levels, pumps will automatically be started. These pumps will stay on until pressures or water levels reach maximum levels and then the pumps will stop. In some systems there may be more than one minimum level. For example, pump number one may come on at one pressure or water level and pump number two may start at a lower level.

Operators of automated systems must inspect the measuring instruments (pressure gages and water levels) for proper measurement and must also be sure the pumps start and stop at the proper levels. (Sections 2.50, "Booster Pumps," and 2.52, "Gages," in *WATER DISTRIBUTION SYSTEM OPERATION AND MAINTENANCE*, discuss the maintenance and troubleshooting of pumps and gages.)

A modification of normal operating procedures that can reduce costs is the "time-of-day" pumping concept. With this method, pumps are used only during the off-peak hours of electrical usage—namely during the hours between 10 p.m. and 6 a.m. Many electrical utilities offer a special lower rate for usage of electricity during off-peak hours.

Abnormal operating conditions include (1) excessive water demands, such as fire demands, (2) broken or out-of-service pumps, mains, or tanks, and (3) *STALE WATER*[7] in tanks creating tastes and odors in systems before design demand flows develop. Emergency plans must be developed in cooperation with the fire department that specify how operators should respond when a fire occurs. A serious fire will require that all pumps operate at full capacity. When all pumps are operating at full capacity, there is a significant danger of *BACKSIPHONAGE*[8] into the water supply. Whenever large pumps are put on line or taken off line, care must be exercised so that surges (water hammer) do not burst pipes due to excessive pressure or collapse pipes due to negative pressures caused by pressure surge waves. These pumping conditions can also create electrical power surges which may cause pump motors to trip out (stop working) and produce even more serious problems.

Failures of pumps, mains, and tanks create serious problems. Emergency response plans must be developed *IN ANTICIPATION* of these events. Such planning could reveal the need for backup or alternative systems. Many water utility agencies have standby pumps and generators for use during emergencies. Know where you can obtain additional pumps, pipes, fittings, and other necessary supplies and equipment during emergencies. The purchase and storage of essential items *IN ADVANCE* may be appropriate. Temporary (and then permanent) repairs should be made as quickly as possible to avoid overloading the remaining facilities and to prevent additional breakdowns.

An emergency public relations program may be helpful to encourage consumers to reduce water usage during periods when facilities are overloaded. If the public understands the nature and seriousness of a crisis, they will usually cooperate.

New facilities are sometimes constructed and placed on line before a significant demand for water has developed. Under these circumstances, large quantities of water may remain in storage facilities for excessive time periods allowing tastes and odors to develop in the water. To avoid this problem, periodically allow a storage tank to empty and then refill. The tank could be emptied into the system and used by consumers. If this is not possible, the tank could be drained and the water donated for some use beneficial to the community. As a last resort, the water may simply have to be wasted.

---

[7] *Stale Water.   Water which has not flowed recently and may have picked up tastes and odors from distribution lines or storage facilities.*
[8] *Backsiphonage.   A form of backflow caused by a negative or below atmospheric pressure within a water system.*

3.31 Storage Levels

The main function of a distribution storage facility is to take care of daily demands and especially peak demands. Operators must be concerned with the amount of water in the storage facility at particular times of the day. Water levels drop during peak demands and rise during low demands. Most distribution systems establish a pattern which the operator should study in order to better anticipate system demands. Figure 3.9 shows a typical water usage flow curve over a 24-hour period. Ideally, extra water is supplied from storage during the hours that consumption is above average and water is delivered to fill the storage facility during the hours consumption is below average flows. The pattern for any particular system not only varies during the day as shown in Figure 3.9, but varies during different days of the week, especially on weekends and holidays. Demands for water also change during different times of the year because of varying weather conditions. Knowing these patterns, the operator can better anticipate and be ready for expected high-demand periods. The operator should know how high the water level should be each morning so that the system's demands will be met during the rest of the day.

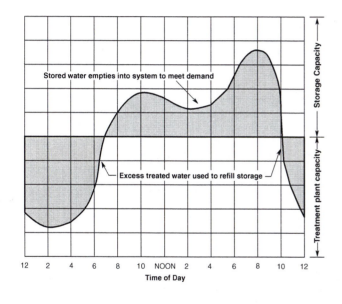

Fig. 3.9 Typical daily use (summer) flow curve
(Reprinted from *OPFLOW*, July 1978, by permission.
Copyright 1978, the American Water Works Association)

The volume of water in a reservoir can be readily determined if you know the water level. Water level indicators are, therefore, essential to successful reservoir operation. Devices range from a simple float connected to an indicator that goes up and down on a staff gage and which can be directly read (Figure 3.10), to telemetry equipment that transmits information concerning water levels to any distance and does it continuously or on demand. Recorders might also be used. Staff gages normally have water level readings in feet (or centimeters) and the level noted can be readily converted to the volume of water stored in the reservoir (see Example 1). Each water level should be read at approximately the same time each day and the readings recorded. Checks should be made at other times of the day to determine whether any unusual

demand conditions have occurred. If any significant increase in demand over that anticipated is noted, the operator should initiate an earlier increase of flow to the reservoir. Automatic water level regulation can be achieved using *ALTITUDE-CONTROL VALVES.*[9] These valves are designed to (1) prevent overflows from the storage tank or reservoir, or to (2) maintain a constant water level as long as water pressure in the distribution system is adequate. The simplest form of level control is a pressure-activated switch which turns a pump on and off. This switch is often sufficient for small water systems. The use of advance warning alarms to signal when water levels are too low or too high is recommended.

A number of routine checks need to be made at reservoirs depending on the type of equipment available. If advance warning alarms are used, they should be tested to ensure they will work when needed. In many reservoirs the water level is controlled automatically. Provisions should be made to allow the operator to test the system to be sure it is working properly. Time clocks are often used to operate valves or pumps that control water coming into the reservoir. They should occasionally be checked and reset if necessary. If they malfunction, the water level could vary too widely. Problems can also be caused by sticking or non-seating valves. The operator must be certain that all altitude and overflow valves in use are in good working condition.

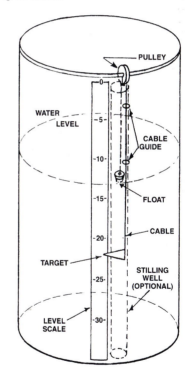

Fig. 3.10 Measuring water level in a tank

FORMULAS

To determine the volume of a storage facility, we need to know the dimensions of the facility. If the tank is rectangular, we need to know the length, width, and depth of water.

Volume, cu ft = (Length, ft)(Width, ft)(Depth, ft)

[9] *Altitude Valve. A valve that automatically shuts off the flow into an elevated tank when the water level in the tank reaches a predetermined level. The valve automatically opens when the pressure in the distribution system drops below the pressure in the tank.*

If the tank is circular, we need to know the diameter and depth of water.

Volume, cu ft = (0.785)(Diameter, ft)^2(Depth, ft)

To convert a volume from cubic feet to gallons, we multiply the volume in cubic feet by 7.48 gallons per cubic foot.

Volume, gal = (Volume, cu ft)(7.48 gal/cu ft)

EXAMPLE 1

Estimate the volume of water (cubic feet and gallons) in the tank shown in Figure 3.10. The tank is 20 feet in diameter and 35 feet deep. The target indicates that the depth of water is 22 feet and the water level indicates that the water is 13 feet from the top of the tank.

Known	**Unknown**
Diameter, ft = 20 ft	1. Volume, cubic feet
Depth, ft = 22 ft	2. Volume, gallons

1. Calculate the volume of water in the tank in cubic feet.

$$\text{Volume, cu ft} = (0.785)(\text{Diameter, ft})^2(\text{Depth, ft})$$
$$= (0.785)(20 \text{ ft})^2(22 \text{ ft})$$
$$= 6{,}908 \text{ cu ft}$$

2. Calculate the volume of water in the tank in gallons.

$$\text{Volume, gal} = (\text{Volume, cu ft})(7.48 \text{ gal/cu ft})$$
$$= (6{,}908 \text{ cu ft})(7.48 \text{ gal/cu ft})$$
$$= 51{,}672 \text{ gallons}$$

Many operators prepare tables or charts that contain the volume in a tank for each foot in depth. These tables and charts could be prepared for the tank in Example 1 by reworking the problem for depths other than 22 feet. With these tables and charts, the operator records the depth in the tank, refers to the table or chart, and obtains the volume of water in the tank.

3.32   Storage Level Controls

Several different types of control systems are used to monitor water levels in storage facilities and also to start and stop pumps. One of the simplest types of control systems uses electrodes mounted at various levels in the storage facility. These electrodes sense the rise and fall of the water level and start and stop the pumps as necessary.

Two problems may be encountered by operators of this type of control system. When the electrodes need replacement or repair, they can be difficult to reach. This problem can be solved by placing the electrodes at a location where access is easy. Another problem with probes is that they may corrode or become contaminated, thus requiring replacement.

Another method of sensing water levels in a storage facility is the use of ultrasonic signals. A transmitter sends a continuous high-frequency sound wave to a receiver. When the receiver is covered with water, the signal is broken. Once the signal is broken, a pump can be started or stopped depending on the desired situation in the storage tank.

Pressure switches are also placed in storage facilities to start or stop water pumps. These switches can be set to respond to changes in water pressure. Pressure switches are easy to install, inexpensive, and very easy to calibrate. Switches must be calibrated to respond at the proper water surface level. If a switch must be replaced, the calibration procedure must be repeated.

Solid-state electronic sensors are available that can measure the actual water surface level and start or stop a pump. Calibration of solid-state electronic sensors consists of dialing the set point to the desired start or stop water surface level for a pump.

Differential-pressure altitude valves are also used to regulate water surface levels in a storage facility. These valves shut off flow into a storage facility when it becomes full and reopen when the tank level drops to a predetermined level or the pressure in the distribution system drops to a predetermined pressure.

Pump stations are not always located in the same place as the storage facility. Under these conditions a signal must be transmitted from the storage facility to the pump or pumps. Also some type of indicator showing the level of water in the storage facility is desirable at the pump station. The transmission cable may be buried underground or an overhead wire may be used to transmit signals from a tank to a pump. Underground cable should be of the armored variety to protect it from rodents.

Radio frequencies are also used to transmit signals from sensors to pumps. Problems may develop if lightning or excessive voltage interferes or disrupts the signals. These improper signals may cause a pump to start or stop at the wrong time. Lightning protectors can be installed to prevent the disruption of signals.

Usually when a pump receives a signal to start, a light will come on in the control panel indicating that the pump is running. However, even when the pump running light is on, the pump may not be pumping water. To ensure that the pump is actually pumping water, a positive flow report-back signal should be installed on the control panel. This report-back signal may be a flowmeter, an ultrasonic flow switch, a pressure switch, or a check valve with an arm-actuated mercury switch.

Most water utilities need only a small amount of instrumentation and controls. The best approach is to purchase high-quality instruments that will require little maintenance and operate for many years. If at all possible, the simple maintenance should be performed by the utility's operators.[10] *REMEMBER*, though, that only *TRAINED* and *QUALIFIED* operators should be permitted to repair electrical equipment. See Chapter 7, Section 7.37, "Working Around Electrical Units," in *WATER DISTRIBUTION SYSTEM OPERATION AND MAINTENANCE*, for additional safety precautions.

3.33   Pumps

CENTRIFUGAL PUMPS[11] (Figure 3.11) cannot operate unless the impeller is submerged in water; *NEVER ATTEMPT*

---

[10] *For additional information on instrumentation and controls, see Chapter 19, "Instrumentation," in WATER TREATMENT PLANT OPERATION, Volume II, in this series of manuals.*

[11] *Centrifugal (sen-TRIF-uh-gull) Pump.   A pump consisting of an impeller fixed on a rotating shaft that is enclosed in a casing, and having an inlet and discharge connection. As the rotating impeller whirls the liquid around, centrifugal force builds up enough pressure to force the water through the discharge outlet.*

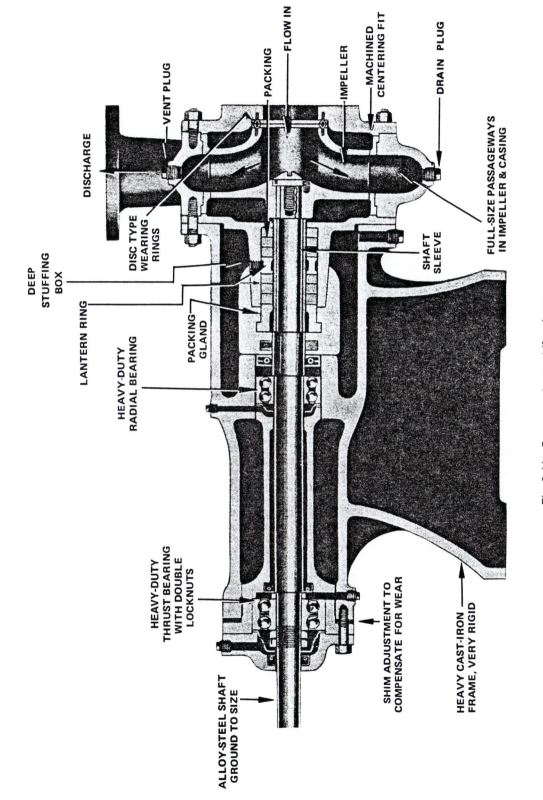

Fig. 3.11   Source water centrifugal pump

TO START A CENTRIFUGAL PUMP UNTIL YOU KNOW THAT THE PUMP IS PROPERLY PRIMED[12] (Figure 3.12). There are several ways to prime a pump so the impeller is submerged in water. A special primer pump may be used to pump water into the pump casing and submerge the impeller. A priming water tank or an auxiliary water supply may be used to prime the pump by adding water to the pump casing and bleeding off the air in the casing. Air may be removed from the pump casing by the use of an electric or hand-operated vacuum pump which causes water to flow into the suction pipe and pump casing. *FOOT VALVES*[13] (Figure 3.12) may be installed on the inlet of the pump suction pipe to keep the pump and suction line full of water. However, if the foot valve develops a leak, the pump will lose its prime. If the pump impeller is located below the surface of the water being pumped (such as a booster pump), the pump will not need to be primed.

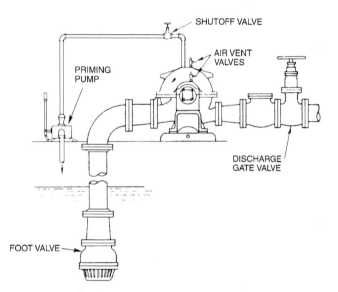

Fig. 3.12   Pump priming installation

(Reprinted from *WATER DISTRIBUTION OPERATOR TRAINING HANDBOOK*, by permission. Copyright 1976, the American Water Works Association)

When starting an electric motor-driven centrifugal pump, the following procedure is recommended:

1. Check the lubrication (use only "food-grade" lubricants),

2. Prime the pump and make sure that the pump and suction piping are free of air,

3. Reduce electric current and water surge on start-up by starting the pump with the discharge valve closed or throttled,

4. Open the discharge valve slowly as soon as the pump is running,

5. Inspect the packing glands to see that water seals are functioning properly, and

6. Measure the running amperage and investigate any abnormal demands or changes from the usual readings.

Continuously operating pumps should be inspected on a regular basis. Inspection should include observing and recording pump suction and discharge pressures, output flow, and electric current demands. Also check for excessive or abnormal noises, vibrations, heat, and odors. If the packing glands are leaking excessively, they should be tightened so that there is only a small amount of leakage. This small amount of leakage helps cool the pump shaft and reduce premature packing wear and scored shaft sleeves. Do not tighten too much and cause an increase in heating and/or damage to the pump. If a centrifugal pump does not operate as expected, refer to Section 2.50, "Booster Pumps," Table 2.2, Centrifugal Pump Troubleshooting Chart, in *WATER DISTRIBUTION SYSTEM OPERATION AND MAINTENANCE.*

3.34   Sampling

All storage facilities should be regularly sampled to determine the quality of water that enters and leaves the facility. Sampling data and visual observations can help you establish a routine for the periodic cleaning of the tank. Indicators that may help you decide when the tank will need cleaning are turbidities over an accepted standard (such as 1.0 *TURBIDITY UNITS*[14]), excessive color, tastes and odors, and *POSITIVE BACTERIOLOGICAL SAMPLES*[15] (which indicate the presence of bacterial contamination). Samples should be collected at the inlet and outlet to the storage facility as well as at various depths and cross sections to ensure measurement of water quality throughout the facility.

3.35   Troubleshooting

Water quality problems may be of the microbiological type, which could be caused by loss of chlorine residual, growth of bacteria, and direct entry of birds, rodents, snakes, and debris. Chemical water quality problems may be caused by leaching of chemicals from tank linings or coatings. Leaching of chemicals could cause taste and odor problems, and the

---

[12] *Prime.   The action of filling a pump casing with water to remove the air. Most pumps must be primed before start-up or they will not pump any water.*

[13] *Foot Valve.   A special type of check valve located at the bottom end of the suction pipe on a pump. This valve opens when the pump operates to allow water to enter the suction pipe but closes when the pump shuts off to prevent water from flowing out of the suction pipe.*

[14] *Turbidity Units (TU).   Turbidity units are a measure of the cloudiness of water. If measured by a nephelometric (deflected light) instrumental procedure, turbidity units are expressed in nephelometric turbidity units (NTU) or simply TU. Those turbidity units obtained by visual methods are expressed in Jackson Turbidity Units (JTU) which are a measure of the cloudiness of water; they are used to indicate the clarity of water. There is no real connection between NTUs and JTUs. The Jackson turbidimeter is a visual method and the nephelometer is an instrumental method based on deflected light.*

[15] *Positive Bacteriological Sample.   A water sample in which gas is produced by coliform organisms during incubation in the multiple tube fermentation test. See Chapter 11, Laboratory Procedures, "Coliform Bacteria," in WATER TREATMENT PLANT OPERATION, Volume I, for details.*

quantity of disinfection by-products in the treated water could increase during storage. Common causes of physical water quality problems include settling and collection of sediment, rust, and chemical precipitates. Also dust, dirt, birds, snakes, and other animals could enter the storage facility.

Water quality in a storage facility could degrade due to excessive water age caused by low demands for water and short-circuiting within the distribution storage reservoir. Other causes of water quality degradation in the storage reservoir include poor design, inadequate maintenance, and improperly applied and/or cured coatings and linings.

If water quality problems develop, you must determine where the problem is coming from and what action will be taken to solve the problem. Table 3.1 is a summary of water quality problems that may develop in storage tanks and distribution systems. The table lists the problems, identifies possible causes, and proposes potential solutions. You will learn more about how to solve water quality problems as you continue through this video series and LEARNING BOOKLET.

For additional information, see Chapter 4, "Water Quality Considerations in Distribution Systems," Section 4.52, "Quality Degradation in Storage Facilities," in WATER DISTRIBUTION SYSTEM OPERATION AND MAINTENANCE.

In some areas where seasonal demands become very low, the chlorine residual may become depleted in the storage tank due to excessive detention time. If this is a problem, auxiliary chlorination stations may be needed in the distribution system or at secondary or booster pump stations to maintain desired chlorine residuals.

In addition to troubleshooting water quality problems, you should regularly inspect the storage facility. Be sure the gate to the facility is locked to keep out vandals and unauthorized persons. The access opening to the facility must be locked and provide a seal to keep out rain and debris. All vent, overflow, and drain screens must be in good condition. Carefully inspect the tank cover for any defects. Look at the water surface for debris and dead birds and rodents.

TABLE 3.1   TROUBLESHOOTING WATER QUALITY PROBLEMS IN STORAGE TANKS AND DISTRIBUTION SYSTEMS

Problem	Possible Cause	Potential Solution
1. Tastes and Odors	High chlorine residual	Use BREAKPOINT CHLORINATION[a] or lower chlorine dosage
	Biological (algal) growth or microorganisms	Chlorinate
	Dead end in main or tank	Flushing or eliminate dead end
2. Turbidity	Silt or clay in suspension	Flushing of mains or proper operation of water treatment plant (proper coagulant, dosage, and operation of coagulation, flocculation, and filtration processes)
	Calcium carbonate	
	Aluminum hydrate, precipitated iron oxide	
	Microscopic organisms	
	Floc carryover	
3. Color	Decay of vegetable matter	Chlorination
	Microscopic organisms	Chlorination
4. Positive Coliform Results	Contaminated distribution system	Locate and remove source
	CROSS CONNECTION[b]	Install backflow prevention or AIR GAP[c] devices, flush, and temporarily increase chlorine dosage
	Negative pressure in main	Repair main, increase chlorine feed rate, flush system, and SAMPLE. Maintain a positive pressure in main (at least 5 psi, 0.35 kg/sq cm or 34.5 kPa)
	No or improper disinfection of new or repaired wells, reservoirs, or mains	Use proper disinfection procedures

[a] Breakpoint Chlorination.   Addition of chlorine to water until the chlorine demand has been satisfied. At this point, further additions of chlorine will result in a free chlorine residual that is directly proportional to the amount of chlorine added beyond the breakpoint.
[b] Cross Connection.   A connection between a drinking (potable) water system and an unapproved water supply. For example, if you have a pump moving nonpotable water and hook into the drinking water system to supply water for the pump seal, a cross connection or mixing between the two water systems can occur. This mixing may lead to contamination of the drinking water.
[c] Air Gap.   An open vertical drop, or vertical empty space, that separates a drinking (potable) water supply to be protected from another water system in a water treatment plant or other location. This open gap prevents the contamination of drinking water by backsiphonage or backflow because there is no way raw water or any other water can reach the drinking water supply.

3.4 MAINTENANCE[16]

3.40 Preventive and Corrective Maintenance

Maintenance is the necessary key in the efficient operation of any water system. Webster says that "maintenance is the upkeep of property or equipment." There are two types of maintenance—preventive and corrective. Preventive maintenance is something that is done before some type of deterioration takes place. Painting puts a protective covering on the tank thus protecting it from deterioration (rust formation).

Corrective maintenance or repair is maintenance that is necessary when a problem already exists. An example is the replacing of deteriorated overflow and vent screens on a tank that have failed and do not serve the purpose of keeping birds or rodents out of the tank.

Problems will not disappear—they only get worse. For that reason alone, maintenance is important.

3.41 Painting

Several factors must be considered before painting the outside of a storage tank. Many water utility agencies try to paint the outside of their steel tanks once every five years. The time a coating lasts depends on: (1) *PROPER SURFACE PREPARATION*, (2) a good, durable paint, (3) good workmanship, (4) adequate drying and aging, and (5) proper maintenance (through periodic inspection and spot, partial, or complete removal of old paint and repainting as necessary).

A tank's interior coating will generally protect the interior for three to five years, depending on local conditions. Routine inspection is the best way to determine when a tank requires maintenance. New tanks or newly painted tanks should be inspected after one year of use. Otherwise, a tank should be drained, cleaned, and inspected once a year, depending on local conditions. Three types of inspections can be made:

1. A visual inspection, which is made from the roof hatch with the water level lowered to about half-full or less;

2. A detailed inspection, accomplished by draining the tank, washing it, and then inspecting the interior coating; and

3. A detailed inspection using divers and video cameras and then cleaning the tank with a device similar to a vacuum cleaner.

A visual inspection may be made in the odd numbered years and a detailed cleaning and inspection may be made in the even numbered years. For example, first anniversary (after painting)—visual inspection, and second anniversary—complete cleaning and inspection.

The best time of year to take a storage facility out of service for complete cleaning and inspection is during the period of lowest water consumption. For most water utilities in warmer climates, this will be during the period from October to April. However, this time period will vary depending on the climate and seasonal water demands. In very cold climates storage facilities are not taken out of service and painted in the winter.

When a tank is to be taken out of service, coordination and planning are necessary so that the distribution system will be able to meet the water demands of its customers. Here are some steps that may be followed for the draining of a storage facility for complete cleaning and inspection:

1. Make sure provisions are made to supply adequate water to the distribution system during shutdown. Be sure that customers who are most affected by the loss of available water from the tank in question will not experience shortages of water or inadequate pressures;

2. Secure (block) inlet line so that no water may enter while the tank is out of service for maintenance;

3. Draw the tank down until there is about 1 foot (0.3 m) of water left covering the bottom of the tank;

4. Secure (block) the discharge line so that no water will be used from the tank while it is being cleaned;

5. Collect a sample of the water remaining in the tank. Also collect a sample of silt/mud from the tank bottom for biological analysis. Analyze the mud/silt for snails and worms. If snails and/or worms are present, try to determine the source and eliminate it;

6. Drain and dispose of the remaining water and silt/mud;

7. Wash the interior tank walls with a water hose and brushes;

8. Inspect interior coating. Look for flaking, peeling, and rust.

The tank's interior inspection should be done by you or by a representative of a professional tank cleaning and painting service company. If you plan to hire someone to clean and recoat your tank, the following suggestions are recommended:

1. Verify the potential contractor's credentials, experience, license, and liability insurance,

2. Ask for references, and

3. Contact the references for their recommendations.

If substantial flaking, peeling, or rust are noted during inspection, the tank's interior should be prepared for repainting.

Preparing a tank's interior for repainting is a very important step if the new coat is to be of any value. Sandblasting is recommended. A brush-off blast (SSPC-SP 7/NACE No. 4)[17] may be used when minor deterioration has occurred. Where extensive deterioration is present, the near-white blast (SSPC-SP 14/NACE No.8)[17] is recommended. Clean up the sand and wash down the interior of the tank to remove any particles of sand. The tank is now ready for painting. If the paint removed is a lead-base paint, special precautions must be taken during

---

[16] For additional information on maintenance, especially equipment maintenance, see Chapter 18, "Maintenance," in WATER TREATMENT PLANT OPERATION, Volume II, in this series of manuals.

[17] SSPC: The Society for Protective Coatings, 40 24th Street, 6th Floor, Pittsburgh, PA 15222-4656.

the sandblasting procedures and also for the collection and removal of sand and paint. Contact the appropriate regulatory agency in your area for details regarding the required procedures.

There are many interior paint and coating systems that can be used in water storage tanks. They are divided into two basic categories: (1) long-life coatings, and (2) short-life coatings. A short-life coating is any paint or material that will protect the interior surface of a tank up to approximately six years. A long-life coating is a coating or material that can protect the interior surface for up to ten years and possibly longer. Long-life coatings will cost from 30 to 50 percent more than a short-life coating. Since a long-life coating may last up to three times longer than a short-life coating, a long-life coat-

---

SAFETY NOTICE

Before anyone ever enters a tank for any reason, these safety procedures must be followed:

1. First test the atmosphere in the tank for oxygen (should be 19.5 to 23.5 percent); then test for combustible and toxic gases. Contact your local safety equipment supplier for the proper types of atmospheric testing devices. These devices should have alarms that are activated whenever an unsafe atmosphere is encountered.

2. Provide adequate ventilation, especially when painting. A self-contained breathing apparatus may be necessary.

3. All persons entering a tank must wear a safety harness.

4. One person trained in tank rescue procedures, safety, and first aid must remain at the tank entrance observing the actions of all people in the tank. An additional person must be readily available to help the person at the tank entrance with any rescue operation.

Additional confined space safety procedures may also be required. Check with your local regulatory agency and see Chapter 7, "Safety," Section 7.63, "Confined Spaces," in *WATER DISTRIBUTION SYSTEM OPERATION AND MAINTENANCE*, for information about permits and a description of some other confined space hazards and procedures.

---

ing can reduce your maintenance cost over a period of 10 to 20 years.

Care must be used in the selection of the tank's interior coating. Coatings fall into the category of *INDIRECT ADDITIVES* to the potable water supply and must be of an appropriate quality for this use. Accordingly, they must be nontoxic, must not release organic or inorganic compounds to the surrounding water in toxicologically (poisonous) significant amounts, and must not impart objectionable tastes or odors to the water.

Many states require that paints and coatings used in potable water systems be approved by the state. The U.S. Environmental Protection Agency (EPA) provides guidance to states regarding the acceptability of paints and coatings for use in potable water service through the Office of Ground Water and Drinking Water (OGWDW) additives advisory program. Information on whether particular products have been successfully evaluated by EPA or a state can be obtained from your state health department, the EPA regional office or the EPA-OGWDW. Additionally, paints and coatings approved for use by the Food and Drug Administration (FDA) for continuous contact with aqueous (watery) foods as defined in the Code of Federal Regulations (21 CFR) are generally acceptable for use in potable water systems.

The paint or coating should also meet AWWA Specifications[18] or *NSF STANDARDS 60 AND 61*.[19] Products that contain lead or *PCBs*[20] are not recommended for potable water use according to recommendations from the Additives Evaluation Branch of EPA's Office of Ground Water and Drinking Water. Coatings using trichloroethylene and tetrachloroethylene should also be avoided.

The best method of applying a coat of paint is by spraying. The cross-spraying method should be used. Spray an area to be painted with horizontal strokes. After the first area has been painted (a 6-foot (2-m) wide section) with one coat, move to one side of the first area. Spray another 6-foot (2-m) wide section. Spray half of the original section and three feet (one meter) of a new, unpainted area. Continue this procedure all the way around the tank. Repeat this procedure using vertical strokes and again overlapping half a section every time. This method not only provides an adequate film thickness, but also reduces the chances of holidays (unpainted spots).

---

[18] *AWWA STANDARD FOR COATING STEEL WATER-STORAGE TANKS, D102-03.* Obtain from American Water Works Association (AWWA), Bookstore, 6666 West Quincy Avenue, Denver, CO 80235. Order No. 44102. Price to members, $42.00; nonmembers, $61.00; price includes cost of shipping and handling.

[19] NSF (National Sanitation Foundation) STANDARDS 60 (Drinking Water Treatment Chemicals) AND 61 (Drinking Water System Components). Obtain from Techstreet, 777 East Eisenhower Parkway, Ann Arbor, MI 48108. Phone (800) 699-9277 or visit the NSF website: www.nsf.org.

[20] PCBs or **P**oly**c**hlorinated **B**iphenyls. A class of organic compounds that cause adverse health effects in domestic water supplies.

Drying time is of prime importance, especially if the paint job is going to be effective. *ALWAYS* assume that a tank's interior does not have sufficient ventilation. A forced-draft ventilation procedure should be used to dry (cure) the coating on a tank's interior. This ventilation will help speed up the drying time. Thorough drying is critical if the paint is to adhere (stick) properly to the tank's interior walls. If drying time is insufficient, problems with tastes and odors or the leaching of potentially toxic materials may occur. To be on the safe side, you may wish to double the drying (curing) time recommended by the paint manufacturer.

Paint manufacturers have developed paints for the exteriors of water storage tanks that allow for the removal of graffiti. A typical anti-graffiti paint is a protective urethane coating that resists graffiti penetration and corrosion. A manufacturer-recommended cleaning agent is used to remove graffiti and other potential stains.[21]

3.42 Corrosion Control[22]

Corrosion may occur either on the inside or outside of the metal surface of a storage facility. Many factors influence the rate of corrosion. The warmer the water, the faster the chemical corrosion reactions. If a water is corrosive, high water velocities will cause rapid pipe deterioration but with little metal pickup. When water velocities are low, there is a longer contact time between the water and the pipe and there could be a higher metal pickup (consumer complaints of red or dirty water). When two different metals come in contact, the difference in electrical potential causes a flow of current (electrons) which results in corrosion.

Substances in the water also influence the rate of corrosion. Dissolved oxygen in the water can increase corrosion rates. Carbon dioxide lowers the pH of a water which makes it more corrosive. Dissolved minerals (salts) in a water increase the rate of corrosion. Sulfate-reducing bacteria can cause increased corrosion.

When waters from different sources and of considerably different chemical content are mixed, the formation of a scale or coating may result. However, when a hard water is replaced with a soft water, corrosion will often result because the scale (protective coating) is dissolved by the soft water.

Painting either the outside or inside of a tank is a form of corrosion control. Usually when one thinks of corrosion control, interior corrosion or metal corrosion comes to mind. A coat of paint is the least expensive type of corrosion control; it is the most important part of any corrosion-control program.

Methods of corrosion control include:

1. Metallic coatings such as zinc or aluminum to protect tank metals such as steel or aluminum (outside coating);

2. Nonmetallic coatings to protect tank metals. Appropriate coatings include coal tar enamels (bituminous), asphaltics, cement mortar, epoxy resins, vinyl resins and paints, coal tar-epoxy enamels, inorganic zinc, silicate paints, and organic zinc metals (be sure that any coating you use has been approved for use in potable water);

3. Chemicals could be added during the treatment of water which would deposit a protective coating or film on the tank's metal (calcium hydroxide (lime), sodium carbonate (soda ash), zinc orthophosphate, and silicate compounds, for example); and

4. Electrical control (*CATHODIC PROTECTION*[23]).

Rarely is one of these methods used by itself as a means of controlling corrosion. The addition of chemicals to water in order to deposit a protective coating is an excellent method of controlling corrosion. Any substance which promotes film formation on the surface to be protected when added to water is known as a corrosion inhibitor. Lime, soda ash, and caustic soda (sodium hydroxide) are chemicals that are used to help control corrosion. When added to water these chemicals will increase the pH. At a certain pH, depending on the temperature, total dissolved solids, calcium concentration, and alkalinity level of the water, the calcium carbonate equilibrium will be reached. For any pH above the equilibrium level, a thick coating of calcium carbonate will form on surfaces exposed to the water. This coating will protect the surfaces from corrosion. As long as the pH remains above the equilibrium level, the coating will not dissolve and will provide protection against corrosion.

Chemical inhibitors reduce the rate of corrosion by preventing dissolved oxygen from reaching the cathodic areas, thus inhibiting the rate-controlling cathodic reactions. Chemical inhibitors are applied to water entering a tank or pipeline by means of a continuously operated pump. The chemicals added to the water deposit a chemical film on the insides of the pipe or tank, thus protecting the interior. Sodium hexametaphosphate (polyphosphate) compounds are commonly used because they combine with (tie up) a variety of *IONS*[24] including iron, manganese, and calcium, thus preventing their build-up as rust or scale. Polyphosphate is available either in a dry or liquid form. The liquid form is becoming more widely used because less equipment is needed for its application than for the dry form.

---

[21] For information about a product specially formulated to provide anti-graffiti protection, contact American Polymer Corporation, 9176 South 300 West, Suite 4, Sandy, UT 84070, or call (800) 676-5963.

[22] For additional information on the causes of corrosion and methods of corrosion control, see Chapter 8, "Corrosion Control," in WATER TREATMENT PLANT OPERATION, Volume I, in this series of manuals.

[23] Cathodic (ca-THOD-ick) Protection.   An electrical system for prevention of rust, corrosion, and pitting of metal surfaces which are in contact with water or soil. A low-voltage current is made to flow through a liquid (water) or a soil in contact with the metal in such a manner that the external electromotive force renders the metal structure cathodic. This concentrates corrosion on auxiliary anodic parts which are deliberately allowed to corrode instead of letting the structure corrode.

[24] Ion.   An electrically charged atom, radical (such as SO_4^{2-}), or molecule formed by the loss or gain of one or more electrons.

While polyphosphate compounds are commonly used, special pumps and safety equipment must be used for safe and proper application. Phosphate is usually fed at a rate of not more than 5 mg/*L*. This chemical is costly and monitoring the feed rate and resulting concentration in the potable water is essential. Chemical control methods should be used as a supplement to the proper choice of metals and metallic and non-metallic coatings.

Cathodic protection (Figure 3.13) must not be regarded as a substitute for the use of a proper interior coating or the application of inhibitors, but should be used if necessary to supplement the other methods. Cathodic protection uses an electrical system for the prevention of corrosion and pitting of steel and iron surfaces in contact with water. A low-voltage current is made to flow through a liquid or soil in contact with the metal in such a manner that the external *ELECTROMOTIVE FORCE*[25] renders the metal structure *CATHODIC*[26] and transfers the corrosion to auxiliary sacrificial *ANODIC*[27] parts which are deliberately allowed to corrode instead of letting the water storage facility corrode. The key to successful use of cathodic protection is the replacement of the sacrificial anodes (usually made of magnesium or zinc) when they have been corroded away. These anodes (sacrificial) should be inspected (weighed to determine loss in weight due to corrosion) at least yearly and replaced when necessary.

Cathodic protection systems not only prevent corrosion, but can reduce time and money spent cleaning and painting. Also the time required for a storage facility to be out of service for maintenance can be reduced. Cathodic protection of a water storage facility is effective only for those areas that are covered by water. The need for a high-quality coating is not eliminated by the installation of a cathodic protection system.

3.43 Concrete Storage Facilities

Maintenance of concrete water storage facilities is very similar to steel tanks. Vents and overflows must be properly screened to keep out birds, rodents, and insects. After the first year in service and every other year thereafter, the facility should be drained, cleaned, and inspected. Special attention must be given to cracks which may allow either leakage or the inflow of contaminated water. Any material used for painting, coating, or repairs must be approved for use in potable water systems. New facilities and old facilities after inspection and repair must be properly disinfected. *ALWAYS FOLLOW SAFE PROCEDURES BEFORE ENTERING AND WHENEVER YOU MUST ENTER A CONCRETE STORAGE FACILITY (CONFINED SPACE).*

Whenever you inspect a concrete storage facility, be sure the facility is secure from vandals and unauthorized persons. Inspect the access to the facility and cover to be sure contaminated water cannot get inside. Look at the surface of the water to be sure there is no floating debris or dead birds or rodents.

WARNING: Never attempt to empty any underground tank when the water table is high. If the water table is high, an empty tank could float to the water surface like a cork. When this happens the tank could crack and inlet and outlet pipes could be damaged.

3.44 Inspection and Cleaning of Tanks

Commercial divers are being used by many water agencies to maintain the interior of water storage tanks. Divers are hired to inspect, clean, and do repairs under water, so the water storage tanks don't have to be drained (and consequently taken out of service) while the work is being done.

Commercial divers can videotape their inspection while in a water tank so operators will be able to see any problems discovered by divers during an underwater inspection. Other services provided by divers include underwater still photography, corrosion severity estimates, and corrosion and pit depths. Divers also clean the insides of tanks without having to drain a tank. Operators need to maintain a higher chlorine residual in the tank during the inspection and cleaning process to protect against bacterial contamination. Divers and equipment need to be disinfected with a solution containing a minimum of 200 mg/*L* chlorine before entering a tank.

When hiring a commercial diver, use only qualified divers who have completed an Association of Commercial Diving Educators (ACDE) approved commercial dive training program. Do not use SCUBA-equipped or sport-trained divers in your potable water tank. Commercial divers are outfitted with a "dry" suit and surface-supplied diving equipment (an external air source that provides the lifeline of both air and information to and from the surface). The diver's "umbilical cord" includes the capability for voice communication between operators and the diver. Live video images can also be transmitted by this line, so that operators above water can see everything the diver sees. The American Water Works Association's (AWWA) current diving standard for potable water diving specifies surface-supplied diving equipment as well as the use of dry diving suits.

Safety must always be the ultimate concern. Commercial diving crews must be trained to assess onsite conditions and be equipped with all necessary equipment to perform routine jobs safely. A major concern is ladder safety and personal fall protection. Elevated tanks require special equipment and techniques to complete an inspection and cleaning job without incident.

Hiring a commercial diving contractor can save your water utility a lot of time, water, and money. The process can be simple, but requires some planning to be sure safety issues are resolved beforehand. If a tank has water in it, and there is safe access for a diver, cost-saving inspection, cleaning, and preventive maintenance can be performed by a commercial dive team.

3.45 Grounds

Storage facility grounds should be landscaped and kept clean. Well-kept landscaping is not only aesthetically desirable, but gives everyone the impression of a well-run operation.

---

[25] *Electromotive Force (E.M.F.).*   The electrical pressure available to cause a flow of current (amperage) when an electric circuit is closed. Also called voltage.
[26] *Cathode (KA-thow-d).*   The negative pole or electrode of an electrolytic cell or system. The cathode attracts positively charged particles or ions (cations).
[27] *Anode (an-O-d).*   The positive pole or electrode of an electrolytic system, such as a battery. The anode attracts negatively charged particles or ions (anions).

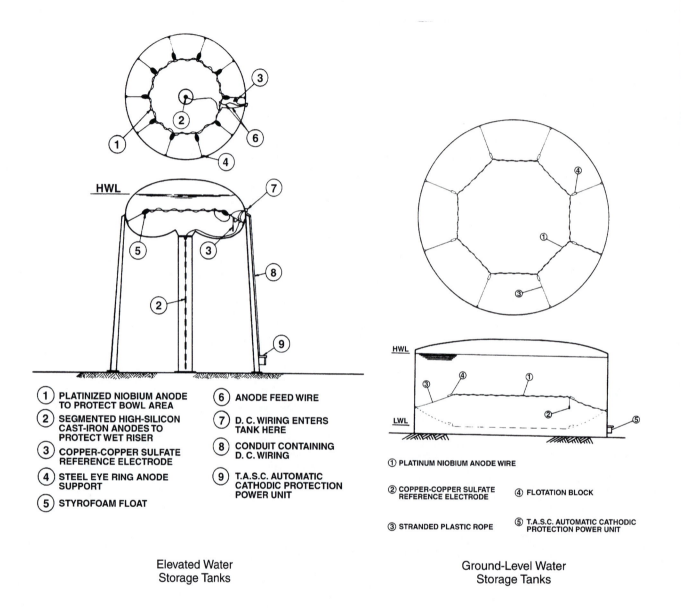

Elevated Water Storage Tanks

1. PLATINIZED NIOBIUM ANODE TO PROTECT BOWL AREA
2. SEGMENTED HIGH-SILICON CAST-IRON ANODES TO PROTECT WET RISER
3. COPPER-COPPER SULFATE REFERENCE ELECTRODE
4. STEEL EYE RING ANODE SUPPORT
5. STYROFOAM FLOAT
6. ANODE FEED WIRE
7. D. C. WIRING ENTERS TANK HERE
8. CONDUIT CONTAINING D. C. WIRING
9. T.A.S.C. AUTOMATIC CATHODIC PROTECTION POWER UNIT

Ground-Level Water Storage Tanks

1. PLATINUM NIOBIUM ANODE WIRE
2. COPPER-COPPER SULFATE REFERENCE ELECTRODE
3. STRANDED PLASTIC ROPE
4. FLOTATION BLOCK
5. T.A.S.C. AUTOMATIC CATHODIC PROTECTION POWER UNIT

PERMANODE ANODE SYSTEM

The only proven permanent anode system for water tanks subject to winter icing conditions. Ten or more years of continuous cathodic protection can be expected instead of the 9-10 months previously provided by aluminum anode systems. This provides even greater economics to water tank owners in Northern climates.

Fig. 3.13   Cathodic protection systems
(Courtesy of Harco Corporation, Medina, Ohio)

3.46 Inspections

Inspections are a very important element of a preventive maintenance program. Inspections are conducted to determine the structural conditions of the storage reservoir, to identify any sanitary defects in the storage system, to evaluate the need for cleaning the storage facility, to determine maintenance needs and the effectiveness of the maintenance program, and also to identify any existing or potential water quality problems.

Inspections may be routine, periodic, or comprehensive. Routine inspections are part of the normal, daily routine and include a check of security items. Periodic inspections are more detailed than routine inspections and may require climbing the facility and looking inside. During these sanitary inspections, check the security at the site, site drainage, penetrations into the system from such sources as vents, hatches, taps, cathodic protection systems, and overflows. Also look for evidence of entrance into the storage tank by birds, animals, and snakes. Measure the depth of any sediment inside the tank. Inspect structural and coating systems to determine the condition of the exterior coating, concrete foundations and visible footings, structural components such as stiffeners and wind rods, ladders, vents, safety devices, interior coating or liner, cathodic protection system, overflow pipe, weir boxes, and bug screens. Wet inspections are conducted by divers or remotely operated equipment.

Routine inspections should be conducted daily or weekly, periodic inspections should be performed monthly or quarterly. Comprehensive inspections should be scheduled every three to five years maximum and possibly more often as indicated by water quality needs.

3.47 Emergency Maintenance

Examples of emergency maintenance include penetration of the storage facility due to vandalism, localized corrosion, or splits due to extensive metal loss. Stress failure in a plate or weld or structural collapse due to vacuum pressure will require an emergency response. Emergencies also are caused by high turbidity and/or bacteria from excessive sediment, animal contamination due to screen failure, or human contamination. Other emergencies include major rips or tears in floating covers, separation of the reservoir from inlet or outlet piping, and catastrophic failure of a concrete or steel reservoir caused by undermining of the foundation. Many of these emergency conditions are the direct result of having neglected to perform routine maintenance and inspections of water storage tanks.

Natural disasters such as earthquakes, floods, fires, and tornadoes also may create conditions requiring emergency maintenance of water storage facilities.

3.48 Cleaning Storage Tanks

Storage tanks may be cleaned by either out-of-service cleaning methods or in-service cleaning methods. Out-of-service cleaning consists of draining, washing, and disinfecting the tank before returning it to service. In-service cleaning uses divers or remotely operated equipment. This equipment is similar to a vacuum cleaner and it removes soft material from the bottom of the tank.

Frequency of cleaning storage tanks depends on sediment buildup, development of biofilms, and results from water quality monitoring. Covered facilities are cleaned every three to five years, but possibly more often based on the results of water quality monitoring and inspections. Uncovered storage facilities should be cleaned annually or possibly twice a year, if needed. Uncovered facilities should be covered or replaced by covered facilities as soon as possible.

3.5 DISINFECTION OF TANKS[28]

Disinfection is the inactivation or destruction of disease-producing organisms. New storage facilities and facilities that have been repaired, cleaned, or had cathodic protection installed must be disinfected. Always disinfect water storage facilities whenever there has been any opportunity for contamination.

Liquid chlorine (or gas), calcium hypochlorite, and sodium hypochlorite are commonly used as disinfectants. There are several methods used to disinfect a water storage facility. *NOTICE:* Before anyone enters a water storage facility for any reason, follow the safety procedures listed under the *SAFETY NOTICE* on page 85.

WARNING

BEFORE attempting to spray the interior of a tank, be sure there is adequate ventilation. If adequate ventilation is not available, the person doing the spraying must use a self-contained breathing apparatus.

ALWAYS wear protective clothing when spraying a tank interior. Protective clothing should consist of a rubberized suit (rain gear—rubber pants and coat), rubber boots, gloves, hat, and a face shield.

Whenever anyone enters a tank, they must wear a safety harness for rescue purposes. Someone must be at the tank entrance to observe the person in the tank and also to hold the safety rope attached to the harness being worn by the person in the tank. A method of communication using tugs on the safety rope must be established *BEFORE* anyone enters a tank. For example, one tug may mean help and two tugs means everything is OK.

In addition to the backup person at the tank entrance, a third person must be readily available to assist the person at the tank entrance.

NO ONE should enter a tank for any reason or under any circumstances without two people standing by for rescue purposes. Too often someone has entered a tank to rescue a friend and died also.

Spray or brush the interior of the storage facility with 200 mg/L (200 ppm) chlorine solution. The chlorine solution can be mixed in a crock or small tank. The application can be accomplished by using garden hoses with nozzles and pressure can be provided by a gasoline-driven pump. (Be sure to station the gasoline engine outside the tank to prevent the buildup of dangerous exhaust vapors.) A 200-mg/L chlorine concentration can be uncomfortable to work with inside of a storage facility. *ALWAYS PROVIDE ADEQUATE VENTILATION WHENEVER ANYONE IS INSIDE A TANK FOR ANY REASON.* The amount and type of ventilation depends on the situation.

To prepare a 200-mg/L solution using sodium hypochlorite, let's use a 100-gallon (380-L) crock of water and assume that the sodium hypochlorite has five percent *AVAILABLE CHLORINE.*[29] Sodium hypochlorite usually is available in the range from 5 to 15 percent available chlorine. The sodium hypochlorite must be thoroughly mixed with water to produce the chlorine solution.

FORMULAS

To determine the amount of sodium hypochlorite needed in pounds, you may use the following formula:

$$\text{Hypochlorite, lbs} = \frac{\left(\dfrac{\text{Volume of Water,}}{\text{Million Gallons}}\right)\left(\dfrac{\text{Chlorine Conc,}}{\text{mg/L}}\right)\left(8.34 \text{ lbs/gal}\right)100\%}{\text{Available Chlorine, \%}}$$

Also, you should know that

100 gal of water = 0.0001 MG of water, and

1 gal of water = 8.34 lbs.

These are constants you should remember.

EXAMPLE 2

Prepare a 200-mg/L solution of chlorine using a 100-gallon crock (0.0001 million gallons) and a sodium hypochlorite solution containing five percent available chlorine. How many gallons of hypochlorite should be added to the 100 gallons of water in the crock?

Known	**Unknown**
Chlorine Conc, mg/L = 200 mg/L	Hypochlorite, gallons
Vol of Water, MG = 0.0001 MG	
Available Cl, % = 5%	

1. Calculate the pounds of hypochlorite needed to produce a chlorine concentration of 200 mg/L.

$$\text{Hypochlorite, lbs} = \frac{\left(\dfrac{\text{Volume of Water,}}{\text{Million Gallons}}\right)\left(\dfrac{\text{Chlorine Conc,}}{\text{mg/L}}\right)\left(8.34 \text{ lbs/gal}\right)100\%}{\text{Available Chlorine, \%}}$$

$$= \frac{(0.0001 \text{ MG})(200 \text{ mg/L})(8.34 \text{ lbs/gal})(100\%)}{5\%}$$

$$= 3.34 \text{ lbs}$$

2. Determine the gallons of 5 percent sodium hypochlorite to be added to the 100 gallons of water.

$$\frac{\text{Hypochlorite,}}{\text{gallons}} = \frac{\text{Hypochlorite, lbs}}{8.34 \text{ lbs/gal}}$$

$$= \frac{3.34 \text{ lbs}}{8.34 \text{ lbs/gal}}$$

$$= 0.40 \text{ gallon}$$

After the tank has been sprayed with the hypochlorite solution, allow it to stand unused for at least 30 minutes before filling. Fill the tank with distribution system water that has been treated with chlorine to provide a chlorine residual of 3 mg/L. Let the water in the tank stand for 3 to 6 hours. Take a bacterial sample of tank water in a sterile container and test for coliform bacteria (see Chapter 11, "Laboratory Procedures," "Coliform Bacteria," in *WATER TREATMENT PLANT OPERATION,* Volume I). Be sure to add enough sodium thiosulfate to the sampling bottle before it is sterilized to neutralize all chlorine in the water. After a sample is collected, shake the bottle and test to be sure there is no chlorine residual. After bacteriological tests prove negative (no coliforms), steps can be taken to put the tank back into service.

Another method of disinfecting a water storage tank is to fill the tank with water with a high enough chlorine concentration to produce a chlorine residual of 3 mg/L. This method of disinfection is used after the tank has been cleaned and the cathodic protection device has been serviced as necessary. The tank is inspected to be sure that all equipment and tools have been removed. Sufficient chlorine is then applied to the water entering the tank to end up with 3.0 mg/L of chlorine residual. The water in the tank is sampled for bacteriological tests 24 hours after the tank has been filled. After bacteriological tests prove negative (no coliforms), the tank is put back in service.

EXAMPLE 3

How many pounds of chlorine gas are needed to disinfect a one million-gallon water storage tank if the desired chlorine dose is 3.0 mg/L? Assume that there is no chlorine demand in the water used to fill the tank. Therefore, we will end up with a 3.0 mg/L chlorine residual.

Known	**Unknown**
Chlorine Conc, mg/L = 3.0 mg/L	Chlorine Gas, lbs
Vol of Water, MG = 1.0 MG	

Calculate the pounds of chlorine gas needed to produce a 3 mg/L chlorine residual in a one million-gallon storage tank.

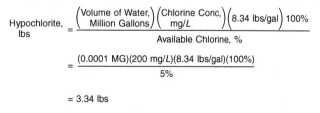

$$\frac{\text{Chlorine}}{\text{Gas, lbs}} = \left(\frac{\text{Vol of Water,}}{\text{Mil Gallons}}\right)\left(\frac{\text{Chlorine Conc,}}{\text{mg/L}}\right)\left(8.34 \text{ lbs/gal}\right)$$

$$= (1.0 \text{ MG})(3.0 \text{ mg/L})(8.34 \text{ lbs/gal})$$

$$= 25.0 \text{ lbs Chlorine Gas}$$

---

[29] *Available Chlorine. A measure of the amount of chlorine available in chlorinated lime, hypochlorite compounds, and other materials that are used as a source of chlorine when compared with that of elemental (liquid or gaseous) chlorine.*

A chlorinator can be installed to add chlorine to the water entering the storage tank or a separate chlorine solution feed line can be used to convey the chlorine solution to the one million-gallon storage tank. Weigh the 150-pound (68-kg) chlorine cylinder at the start. After the chlorine cylinder weight has dropped by 25 pounds (11.5 kg), you will know you have added enough chlorine. Be sure to mix the chlorine solution with the water filling the tank so the chlorine solution will be evenly mixed throughout the tank.

Another acceptable method of disinfecting a water storage tank is to fill the tank with potable water that has been treated to provide a chlorine residual of at least 10 mg/L after a six-hour contact period. This six-hour period is sufficient when chlorine or sodium hypochlorite has been applied to the water entering the tank at a uniform rate by the use of a portable chlorinator or a chemical feed pump (hypochlorinator). When sodium hypochlorite (a liquid) or calcium hypochlorite (a tablet) has been used either by pouring the liquid into the storage facility or by use of tablets that are dissolved by the water flowing into the tank, the water should have a 10-mg/L chlorine residual after a 24-hour contact period.

The last acceptable method described here requires that enough chlorine be added to the water to produce 50 mg/L of available chlorine when the storage tank is approximately five percent full. This solution of chlorine and water must be held in the tank for at least six hours. After six hours the storage tank is filled to the overflow level with potable water and held at this level for at least 24 hours.

After a water storage tank has been disinfected, the remaining mixture of chlorine and water must be properly disposed of. Any water with a chlorine residual of 2 mg/L or more either must be diluted with additional water or the chlorine must be properly neutralized before being discharged. Chlorine neutralization chemicals include sulfur dioxide (SO_2), sodium bisulfite ($NaHSO_3$), sodium sulfite (Na_2SO_3), or sodium thiosulfate ($Na_2S_2O_3 \cdot 5\ H_2O$). The amount of neutralizing chemical will depend on the chlorine residual and the type of neutralizing chemical. By mixing various amounts of a neutralizing chemical with the water in the tank, you can determine the amount of chemical that will just neutralize all of the chlorine residual.

A highly chlorinated water MAY be discharged to a sanitary sewer provided PERMISSION IS OBTAINED from the local agency that operates the wastewater collection system and treatment facilities. If the chlorinated water is discharged slowly and there is no opportunity for BACKFLOW[30] or BACK-SIPHONAGE[31] between the wastewater collection system and the water storage tank, this method MAY be approved.

Chlorinated waters should not be discharged to any surface waters (storm drains, rivers, lakes) without obtaining approval of the appropriate water pollution control agencies.

NOTES:

1. When disinfecting a water storage facility for the first time (a newly purchased or constructed tank), the chlorine residual should be 50 mg/L (instead of 3 mg/L when placing a tank back in service) for 24 hours.

2. Small water storage tanks are commonly disinfected with a chlorine dosage of 50 mg/L. A chlorine residual of at least 10 mg/L must remain at the end of the 24-hour disinfection period. Large clear wells are usually disinfected with chlorine residuals of 3 mg/L. AWWA's standards for disinfection of tanks[32] list three disinfection methods. The important point is, IF YOU RECEIVE NEGATIVE COLIFORM TEST RESULTS (NO COLIFORMS PRESENT), YOU HAVE ADEQUATELY DISINFECTED THE STORAGE FACILITY.

3. Whenever you collect a sample for a bacteriological test (coliforms), be sure to use a sterile plastic or glass bottle that contains sufficient sodium thiosulfate to neutralize all of the chlorine residual.[33] The amount of sodium thiosulfate depends on whether the sample contains a chlorine residual of 3 mg/L or 50 mg/L. Add sufficient sodium thiosulfate to the sample bottle, sterilize the bottle, and then collect the sample for the coliform test. After the sample has been collected, shake the sample and measure the chlorine residual. If there is a chlorine residual, carefully add more sterilized sodium thiosulfate, shake sample, measure the chlorine residual, and continue repeating the procedures until there is no chlorine residual. A good practice is to discuss the project you are working on with your lab and have the lab sterilize sufficient sodium thiosulfate in the sample bottle when the bottle is sterilized.

Chlorine gas is used with large-capacity storage tanks because of the relatively low price of chlorine. Small storage tanks are treated with sodium hypochlorite or calcium hypochlorite. The guideline for use of chlorine gas versus sodium hypochlorite is: for any tank over 100,000 gallons (380 cu m) capacity, use chlorine gas; for any tank below 100,000 gallons (380 cu m) capacity, sodium hypochlorite may be easier to use.

After water in a storage tank has negative bacteriological results (no coliforms), it may be returned to service. To return a storage tank to service:

1. Empty the tank of chlorinated water. Discharge to a storm drainage system may be acceptable if you have a small

---

[30] Backflow.   A reverse flow condition, created by a difference in water pressures, which causes water to flow back into the distribution pipes or storage tank of a potable water supply from any source or sources other than the intended source. Also see BACKSIPHONAGE.

[31] Backsiphonage.   A form of backflow caused by a negative or below atmospheric pressure within a water system. Also see BACKFLOW.

[32] AWWA STANDARD FOR DISINFECTION OF WATER-STORAGE FACILITIES, C652-02. Obtain from American Water Works Association (AWWA), Bookstore, 6666 West Quincy Avenue, Denver, CO 80235. Order No. 43652. Price to members, $42.00; nonmembers, $61.00; price includes cost of shipping and handling.

[33] A 120-mL sample bottle requires 0.1 mL of ten percent sodium thiosulfate ($Na_2S_2O_3 \cdot 5\ H_2O$) to neutralize about a 15 mg/L chlorine residual.

volume of water with a high chlorine residual and there is sufficient dilution water in the drainage system. If you have a large volume of water with a low chlorine residual, gradually release this water into the distribution system, being careful not to produce too high a chlorine residual at a consumer's tap. Other alternatives include allowing the tank to sit while chlorine dissipates or adding sodium bisulfite to reduce the residual.

2. Open outlet valve from tank to the distribution system.

3. Make sure inlet valve to tank is open so that tank will *FLOAT ON SYSTEM*[34] (draw down and fill as needed).

4. If appropriate, remove interim method of providing water to distribution system (no longer needed because tank is back in service).

MIKE'S TIP

One gallon of sodium hypochlorite contains six percent chlorine. The addition of one gallon of six percent chlorine to 60,000 gallons of water will produce an increase in the chlorine concentration of 1 ppm (1 part chlorine per million parts water or 1 milligram chlorine per liter of water—1mg Cl/L). How many gallons of six percent chlorine must be added to 300,000 gallons of water to produce a 1 ppm concentration of chlorine?

Known	**Unknown**
Tank Volume, gal = 300,000 gal	Chlorine, gallons

$$\text{Chlorine dose, ppm} = \frac{60{,}000 \text{ gal water}}{1 \text{ gal 6\% Cl}}$$

Calculate the gallons of hypochlorite needed to produce 1 ppm in 300,000 gallons of water.

$$\begin{aligned}
\text{Chlorine, gallons} &= \frac{\text{Tank Volume, gal}}{60{,}000 \text{ gal/1gal 6\% Cl}} \\
&= \frac{300{,}000 \text{ gallons}}{60{,}000 \text{ gal/gal 6\% Cl}} \\
&= 5 \text{ gal of 6\% hypochlorite}
\end{aligned}$$

3.6 RECORDS

Records provide necessary data for the effective operation of a water system. Records of equipment should include the *NAMEPLATE*[35] data, date of installation, start-up data, failures, and any type of service performed on the equipment. Results of tank inspections, condition of tank, maintenance performed, and all repairs or corrective action must be recorded. These records should be kept for at least five years. A list available to all involved operators of particular problems and the means used to resolve each problem is an essential part of any recordkeeping system. Performance data must be kept on your corrosion-control program. Also, the engineering plans and specifications of each type of tank structure in your system are part of your permanent records.

3.7 SAFETY

SAFETY IS EVERYONE'S RESPONSIBILITY FROM THE HEAD OF THE WATER UTILITY AGENCY TO EVERY WATER SUPPLY SYSTEM OPERATOR. However, you are the most important person when the subject of safety comes up. You have a dual responsibility. You are required to use safety equipment provided by your agency and you should be watchful for unsafe conditions and report them to your supervisor.

In working around water storage facilities, the following safety hazards should be of personal concern to you:

1. Make sure the area around the storage facility is clean and clear of debris.

2. Use care when climbing storage facility ladders or stairways. When using ladders, use a ladder safety belt. Remember: only one person at a time on a ladder. When a ladder is not in use, have the ladder guard in place so that unauthorized persons will not be able to use it. Be very careful using safety climbing devices that are equipped with a cable because cables can fail due to vibrations caused by winds.

   If a stairway is used to climb up to the storage facility, safety treads should be placed on stairs and a handrail should be used.

3. When entering a storage facility for inspection, test the atmosphere and make sure you have sufficient ventilation. Monitor the facility before entering to verify that you are not entering an oxygen-deficient atmosphere and that there are no toxic or explosive gases present (especially when applying coatings).

   Make sure adequate ventilation is available during inspection or maintenance in the facility. Use forced-draft ventilation where necessary for safety of personnel.

   Be sure to wear a safety harness. One person must be at the entrance watching you at all times. A third must be readily available to help with rescue operations. For additional information on how to safely enter a storage tank, see Section 7.63, "Confined Spaces," in *WATER DISTRIBUTION SYSTEM OPERATION AND MAINTENANCE.*

Safety should be made part of your routine operation. Safety is a way of thinking that can help you operate and maintain your facilities more effectively.

---

[34] *Float On System.   A method of operating a water storage facility. Daily flow into the facility is approximately equal to the average daily demand for water. When consumer demands for water are low, the storage facility will be filling. During periods of high demand, the facility will be emptying.*

[35] *Nameplate.   A durable metal plate found on equipment which lists critical operating conditions for the equipment.*

3.8 ADDITIONAL READING

To obtain information regarding the topics in this chapter, review the appropriate chapters and sections in the following operator training manuals:

1. *WATER DISTRIBUTION SYSTEM OPERATION AND MAINTENANCE*, price $45.00,

2. *SMALL WATER SYSTEM OPERATION AND MAINTENANCE*, price $45.00,

3. *WATER TREATMENT PLANT OPERATION*, Volume I, price $45.00, and

4. *WATER TREATMENT PLANT OPERATION*, Volume II, price $45.00.

All of these operator training manuals can be obtained from the Office of Water Programs, California State University, Sacramento, 6000 J Street, Sacramento, CA 95819-6025, phone (916) 278-6142 or visit the website at www.owp.csus.edu.

3.9 ACKNOWLEDGMENT

Material contained in this chapter is copyrighted by the California State University, Sacramento Foundation and is reproduced by permission.

WATER SYSTEMS OPERATION AND MAINTENANCE VIDEO TRAINING SERIES

CHAPTER (VIDEO) 4

SAMPLING AND TESTING

VIDEO 4 SUMMARY

Video 4, SAMPLING AND TESTING, provides operators with the knowledge, skills, and abilities they need to conduct sampling and testing. Information is provided on how to collect samples for BACT, chlorine residual, and also lead and copper. Also procedures are provided on how to measure pH and chlorine residuals.

CONTENTS OF VIDEO 4

SAMPLING AND TESTING VIDEO

INTRODUCTION

    Importance of Sampling

    Representative Sampling/Observations

    BACT Samples

    Chlorine Residual Samples

    Lead and Copper Samples

    Recordkeeping

REPRESENTATIVE SAMPLING/OBSERVATIONS

    When and Where To Collect Samples

    Physical Quality Observations

    Grab and Composite Samples

BACT SAMPLES

    Why Take Samples

    Sampling Schedule

    Demonstration of Procedure

CHLORINE RESIDUAL SAMPLES

    Why, Where, and When

    Demonstration of Procedure

LEAD AND COPPER SAMPLES

    Why, Where, and When

    Consumer Assistance, Sampling Kit, Procedures

    Information Recorded

    Thank Consumer and Provide Results

RECORDKEEPING

    Why

    Importance

    Storage—Hard Copy and Computer

    Construction and As-Built (Record) Drawings

    Lab Results

    Insurance

SUMMARY

CONTENTS OF CHAPTER 4

SAMPLING AND TESTING
LEARNING BOOKLET

OBJECTIVES

Chapter (Video) 4.   SAMPLING AND TESTING

Following completion of Video 4 and Chapter 4, you should be able to:

1. Collect representative samples and also preserve and transport the samples to a laboratory,

2. Complete a chain-of-custody form for samples transported to a laboratory,

3. Collect BACT samples and transport the samples to a laboratory,

4. Collect chlorine residual samples and measure chlorine residuals in the field,

5. Instruct consumers on how to collect lead and copper samples,

6. Collect samples for lead and copper analysis and transport samples to the laboratory, and

7. Properly store records.

LEARNING BOOKLET STUDY MATERIAL

This section of the *LEARNING BOOKLET* contains important information. Read this section after watching the video and before attempting to take the Objective Test for this chapter.

Material covered in this section will help you better understand the material in the video. Also some critical information is easier to present in the *LEARNING BOOKLET*, such as information on CT calculations.

Chapter (Video) 4.   SAMPLING AND TESTING

IMPORTANCE OF SAMPLING AND TESTING FOR COMPLIANCE

A clean, safe supply of drinking water that is free from harmful microorganisms is essential for life and the protection of public health. Many regulatory agencies control drinking water quality by setting standards for relevant water quality indicators. Water suppliers meet these standards by providing an appropriate level of water treatment, including disinfection. The local circumstances and resources of a small water utility should determine the standards that are relevant and the treatment that is appropriate to provide an adequate margin of safety.

When standards have been set there needs to be a system for measuring for compliance with those standards, otherwise there is no point in having standards. This video provides guidance to water utilities on how to monitor compliance with standards. It covers the following aspects of sampling:

- Sampling—including sampling points, frequencies, methods, and logging;

- Analysis—including training and management of analysts, analytical methods, analytical quality control, and analyst's work sheets; and

- Reporting—including analyst's reports and validation, release of results, and recording of results.

Video 4 and Chapter 4 also discuss the differences between operational monitoring and compliance monitoring.

4.0   STANDARDS FOR DRINKING WATER QUALITY

Standards for drinking water quality have been created for various kinds of guidelines or characteristics of water. There are several very important water quality guidelines.

MICROBIOLOGICAL water quality indicators include the usual organisms such as coliforms, specifically fecal coliforms (*E. coli*), which are not harmful themselves but when found indicate that the water supply may have been contaminated by harmful organisms. When they are detected, immediate investigation should be initiated and, if contamination is confirmed, remedial action should be taken.

AESTHETIC water quality indicators—these affect the color, taste, odor, or appearance of water. If any are found at levels above the standards, it is likely to mean that consumers will find the water *UNPALATABLE*[1] but it is unlikely to mean that the water is not safe to drink.

NATURAL SUBSTANCES that are present in water, such as arsenic, fluoride, and boron, must be controlled because they may pose a risk to health at high concentrations.

POLLUTANTS—these are substances such as nitrate, pesticides, and heavy metals which can contaminate water sources as a consequence of agricultural or industrial activity in the watershed and which, at high concentrations, pose a risk to health.

PIPE MATERIALS—these are substances such as lead and copper which can contaminate water after it has left a treatment plant as a result of leaching from pipes in the distribution system or pipes belonging to the consumer. High concentrations of these contaminants may pose a risk to health.

DISINFECTION BY-PRODUCTS—these are substances formed by the chemical reaction between organic (and sometimes inorganic) substances present in the source water and the disinfectant used, often chlorine. Common by-products are the *TRIHALOMETHANES*,[2] such as chloroform. It is much more important to ensure adequately disinfected water supplies than to focus too heavily on controlling disinfection by-products. The health risk from microorganisms is *ACUTE*[3] and severe compared to a relatively low risk from long-term exposure to disinfection by-products.

OPERATIONAL WATER QUALITY INDICATORS—these provide a good indication of the efficiency of operation of key treatment processes. Operational water quality indicators include pH value, turbidity, coagulant residual, and disinfectant residual. They are particularly useful quality indicators for small water supplies in rural communities.

---

[1] *Palatable (PAL-uh-tuh-bull).   Water at a desirable temperature that is free from objectionable tastes, odors, colors, and turbidity. Pleasing to the senses.*

[2] *Trihalomethanes (THMs) (tri-HAL-o-METH-hanes).   Derivatives of methane, CH_4, in which three halogen atoms (chlorine or bromine) are substituted for three of the hydrogen atoms. Often formed during chlorination by reactions with natural organic materials in the water. The resulting compounds (THMs) are suspected of causing cancer.*

[3] *Acute Health Effect.   An adverse effect on a human or animal body, with symptoms developing rapidly.*

4.00   Goals of Plant Operation

In the operation of small water treatment plants, competent and responsible operators try to achieve three basic objectives:

1. Production of a safe drinking water,

2. Production of an aesthetically pleasing drinking water, and

3. Production of drinking water at a reasonable cost.

From a public health perspective, production of a safe drinking water, one that is free of harmful bacteria and toxic materials, is the first priority. Federal, state, and local regulations (drinking water standards) control all aspects of treatment of public water supplies to ensure the delivery of safe water to consumers.

In addition to providing safe water, it is also important to produce a high-quality water that appeals to the consumer. Generally, this means that the water must be clear (free of turbidity), colorless, and free of objectionable tastes and odors. Consumers also want water supplies that do not stain plumbing fixtures and clothes, do not corrode plumbing fixtures and piping, and do not leave scale deposits or spot glassware.

4.01   Drinking Water Regulations

For centuries people have judged water quality on the basis of taste, smell, and sight. To a large degree, this is still true. However, many consumers today are demanding water that is not only free of objectionable tastes and odors, but also free of harmful bacteria, organic and inorganic chemical contaminants, turbidity, and color.

Current water quality standards include both federal and state regulations. Primary regulations establish maximum contaminant levels (MCLs) based on the health significance of the contaminants; the secondary standards are established based on *AESTHETIC*[4] considerations. Primary standards are federally enforceable, but secondary standards may or may not be enforced at the option of each state.

Under the Safe Drinking Water Act (SDWA), each state was given the option of assuming primary enforcement responsibility for public water systems on the condition that the state would adopt regulations at least as stringent as the EPA regulations and would implement adequate monitoring and enforcement procedures. Most states have agreed to these terms and have been delegated primary responsibility by the EPA.

Operators are urged to stay in close contact with their regulatory agencies and become thoroughly familiar with their requirements. The major provisions of the Safe Drinking Water Act (SDWA) are summarized on the poster that came with this *LEARNING BOOKLET.*

4.02   Safe Drinking Water Act (SDWA)

The Safe Drinking Water Act (SDWA) and its amendments contain specific maximum allowable levels of substances known to be hazardous to human health. In addition to describing maximum contaminant levels (MCLs), these federal drinking water regulations also give detailed instructions on what to do when the MCL for a particular substance is exceed-

ed. For example, the SDWA regulations specify that repeat samples are required for each coliform-positive sample. All samples must be collected the same day. At least one sample must be taken from the same tap as the original sample, another from an upstream connection, and one from downstream. All coliform positives must be tested for the presence of fecal coliform or *E. coli*. If the repeat sample is fecal coliform positive, or if the original fecal coliform or *E. coli* positive is followed by a total coliform positive, the state must be notified on the same business day.

4.1   SAMPLING

Operators perform a variety of laboratory tests on source water samples, process water samples, and finished water samples to monitor overall water quality and to evaluate process performance. The sampling location and type of water sample used for a particular analysis will vary depending on the purpose of the analysis. Compliance with the maximum contaminant levels (MCLs) is usually measured at the point where water enters the distribution system. However, operators must realize that water can degrade in the distribution or delivery system. In all cases, it is important to stress that the water sample must be representative of actual conditions of the entire flow being sampled.

4.10   Importance of Sampling

Sampling is a vital part of studying the quality of water in a water treatment process, distribution system, or source of water supply. A major source of error in the whole process of obtaining water quality information often occurs during sampling. Proper sampling procedures are essential to obtain an accurate description of the material or water being sampled and tested. This fact is not well enough recognized and cannot be overemphasized.

In any type of testing program where only small samples (a liter or two) are withdrawn from perhaps millions of gallons of water under examination, there is potential uncertainty because of possible sampling errors. Water treatment decisions based upon incorrect data may be made if sampling is performed in a careless and thoughtless manner. Obtaining good results will depend to a great extent upon the following factors:

1. Ensuring that the sample taken is truly representative of the water under consideration,

2. Using proper sampling techniques, and

3. Protecting and preserving the samples until they are analyzed.

---

[4] *Aesthetic (es-THET-ick). Attractive or appealing.*

4.11 Importance of Representative Sampling

A *REPRESENTATIVE SAMPLE*[5] must be collected in order for test results to have any significant meaning. Without a representative sample, the test results will not reflect actual water conditions.

The sampling of a tank or a lake that is completely mixed is a simple matter. Unfortunately, most bodies of water are not well mixed and obtaining samples that are truly representative of the whole body depends to a great degree on sampling technique. A sample that is properly mixed (integrated) by taking small portions of the water at points distributed over the whole body represents the material better than a sample collected from a single point. The more portions taken, the more nearly the sample represents the original. The sample error would reach zero when the size of the sample became equal to the original volume of material being sampled but, for obvious reasons, this method of decreasing sample error is not practical. The size of sample depends on how many and which specific water quality indicators are being tested. Every precaution must be taken to ensure that the sample collected is as representative of the water source or process being examined as is feasible.

4.12 Source Water Sampling

RIVERS

To adequately determine the composition of a flowing stream, each sample (or set of samples taken at the same time) must be representative of the entire flow at the sampling point at that instant. Furthermore, the sampling process must be repeated frequently enough to show significant changes of water quality that may occur over time in the water passing the sampling point.

On small or medium-sized streams, it is usually possible to find a sampling point at which the composition of the water is presumably uniform at all depths and across the stream. Obtaining representative samples in these streams is relatively simple. For larger streams, more than one sample may be required. A portable *CONDUCTIVITY*[6] meter is very useful in selecting good sampling sites.

RESERVOIRS AND LAKES

Water stored in reservoirs and lakes is usually poorly mixed. *THERMAL STRATIFICATION*[7] and associated depth changes in water composition (such as dissolved oxygen) are among the most frequently observed effects. Single samples can therefore be assumed to represent only the spot of water from which the sample came. Therefore, a number of samples must be collected at different depths and from different areas of the impoundment to accurately sample reservoirs and lakes.

GROUNDWATER

Most of the physical factors that promote mixing in surface waters are absent or much less effective in groundwater systems. Wells usually draw water from a considerable thickness of saturated rock and often from several different strata (layers). These water components are mixed by the turbulent flow of water in the well before they reach the surface and become

available for sampling. Most techniques for well sampling and exploration are usable only in unfinished or nonoperating wells. Usually the only means of sampling the water tapped by a well is the collection of a pumped sample. The operator is cautioned to remember that well pumps and casings can contribute to sample contamination. If a pump has not run for an extended period of time prior to sampling, the water collected may not be representative of the normal water quality.

4.13 In-Plant Sampling

Collection of representative samples within the water treatment plant is really no different from sample collection in a stream or river. The operator simply wants to be sure the water sampled is representative of the water passing that sample point. In many water plants, money is spent to purchase sample pumps and piping only to sample from a point that is not representative of the passing water. A sample tap in a dead area of a reservoir or on the floor of a process basin serves no purpose in helping the plant operator with control of water quality. The operator is urged to find each and every sample point and ensure that it is located where it will provide a useful and representative sample. If the sampling point is not properly located, plan to move the piping to a better location.

4.14 Distribution System Sampling

Representative sampling in the distribution system is a true indication of system water quality. Results of sampling should show if there are quality changes in the system, or some parts of the system, and may point to the source of a problem (such as tastes and/or odors). Sampling points should be selected, in part, to trace the course from the finished water source (at the well or plant), through the transmission mains, and then through the major and minor arteries of the system. A sampling point on a major artery, or on an active main directly connected to it, would be representative of the water quality being furnished to a subdivision of this network. Generally, these primary points are used as "official" sampling points to evaluate actual water quality.

Obtaining a representative sample from the distribution system is not as easy as it might seem. One would think almost any faucet would do, but experience has shown otherwise. Local conditions at the tap and in its connection to the main can easily make the point unrepresentative of water being furnished to your customers. The truest evaluation of water in a distribution system can be obtained from samples drawn directly from the main. You might think that samples taken from a fire hydrant would prove satisfactory, but this is usually not the case. The problem with fire hydrants as sampling points is that they give erratic (uneven) results due to the way they are constructed and their lack of use. In general, an ideal sampling station is one that has a short, direct connection with the main and is made of corrosion-resistant material.

In most smaller water systems, special sampling taps are not available; therefore, customers' faucets must be used to collect samples. The best sampling points are front yard faucets on homes supplied by short service lines (homes with short service lines are located on the same side of the street as the water main).

---

[5] *Representative Sample.* A sample portion of material or water that is as nearly identical in content and consistency as possible to that in the larger body of material or water being sampled.

[6] *Conductivity.* A measure of the ability of a solution (water) to carry an electric current.

[7] *Thermal Stratification (STRAT-uh-fuh-KAY-shun).* The formation of layers of different temperatures in a lake or reservoir.

If possible, you should contact the person in the home and obtain permission to collect the sample. Disconnect the hose from the faucet if one is attached and don't forget to reconnect the hose when finished collecting the sample. Open the faucet to a convenient flow for sampling (usually about half a gallon per minute). Allow the water to flow until the water in the service line has been replaced twice. Since 50 feet (15 m) of three-quarter inch (18-mm) pipe contains over one gallon (3.8 liters), four or five minutes will be required to replace the water in the line twice. Collect the sample. Be sure the sample container does not touch the faucet. Do not try to save time by turning the faucet handle to wide open to flush the service line. This will disturb sediment and incrustations in the line which must be flushed out before the sample can be collected.

4.2 TYPES OF SAMPLES

There are generally two types of samples collected by waterworks operators, and either type may be obtained manually or automatically. The two types are grab samples and composite samples.

4.20 Grab Samples

A grab sample is a single water sample collected at no specific time. Grab samples will show the water characteristics at the time the sample was taken. A grab sample may be preferred over a composite sample when:

1. The water to be sampled does not flow continuously,

2. The water's characteristics are relatively constant, and

3. The water is to be analyzed for water quality indicators that may change with time, such as dissolved gases, coliform bacteria, residual chlorine, temperature, and pH.

4.21 Composite Samples

In many processes, the water quality is changing from moment to moment or hour to hour. A continuous sampleranalyzer would give the most accurate results in these cases. However, since operators themselves are often the sampleranalyzer, continuous analysis would leave little time for anything but sampling and testing. Except for tests that cannot wait due to rapid physical, chemical, or biological changes of the sample (such as tests for dissolved oxygen, pH, and temperature), a fair compromise may be reached by taking samples throughout the day at hourly or two-hour intervals. Each

sample should be refrigerated immediately after it is collected. At the end of 24 hours, a portion of each sample is mixed with the other samples. The size of the portion is in direct proportion to the flow when the sample was collected and the total size of sample needed for testing. For example, if hourly samples were collected when the flow was 1.2 MGD, use a 12-mL portion sample, and when the flow was 1.5 MGD, use a 15-mL portion sample. The resulting mixture of portions of samples is called a COMPOSITE SAMPLE.[8] In no case, however, should a composite sample be collected for bacteriological examination.

When the samples are taken, they can either be set aside to be combined later or combined as they are collected. In both cases, they should be stored at a temperature of 4°C until they are analyzed.

4.3 MEASURING FOR COMPLIANCE

There is no point in setting standards for drinking water quality unless there is also a system for measuring compliance with those standards. Compliance may be measured at one or more points in the water supply system depending on where standards apply, the properties of the water quality indicators, and the nature of the water supply system.

Standards for drinking water quality may apply at various points in the water supply system. These points are:

- At the exit from a water treatment works—this is appropriate for operational parameters and for those parameters whose concentration is unlikely to change as the water travels through the distribution system;

- At a point in the water supplier's distribution system (such as a service reservoir)—this may be particularly important for microbiological parameters and disinfectant residual as a measure of the integrity of the system;

- Where the water leaves the water supplier's distribution system and enters the customer's pipe system (it is usually difficult to monitor water quality at this point); and

- At a customer's tap.

Some standards may apply at more than one point.

Ideally, to protect public health, standards should apply at the customer's tap. If there is a failure to meet a standard at a customer's tap, it may be due to the quality of the water supplied by the water supplier or it may be due to contamination arising from the condition of the customer's piping system or the presence of water conditioning and other devices installed by the customer.

Measuring for compliance essentially consists of three elements: sampling, analysis, and reporting. It is important that each one of these is carried out properly and accurately; otherwise, there is no point in taking the sample and making and reporting on the measurement.

There are a number of very important considerations in specifying sampling requirements. Ideally full details of sampling procedures, including the points below, should be contained in a sampling manual held by all samplers and other appropriate personnel, such as sampling system planners and

---

[8] Composite (come-PAH-zit) (Proportional) Sample.   A composite sample is a collection of individual samples obtained at regular intervals, usually every one or two hours during a 24-hour time span. Each individual sample is combined with the others in proportion to the rate of flow when the sample was collected. The resulting mixture (composite sample) forms a representative sample and is analyzed to determine the average conditions during the sampling period.

managers. The Appendix at the end of this chapter contains some examples of the types of monitoring data sheets that could be included in a sampling manual.

4.30   Sampling Points

Sampling points should be appropriate for determining compliance with the standards. This means that samples should be taken at the point or points where the standards apply.

The sampling point or points should be representative of the body of water being sampled. For example, if you are monitoring the quality of water in a service reservoir, the sampling point should allow you to collect a representative sample of the water leaving the service reservoir.

The selection of sampling points is more complicated when samples are required from customers' taps. In a particular water supply system, there are basically three options:

- The taps could be chosen at random from all the taps in the system.

- The taps could be located at fixed points in the system, with these points being sampled on a regular basis. (If this option is used, it is important that some points be located close to the treatment works and other points near the extremities of the distribution system to ensure that the samples collected are representative of water quality throughout the system.)

- The taps could be a mixture of fixed points and randomly chosen points.

4.31   Sampling Frequencies

There should be a defined frequency of sampling for each water quality indicator. The frequency will depend on the importance of the water quality indicators, the expected variation in the indicator concentration or value, how close the indicator concentration or value is to the standard, where the standard applies, and where the sample is to be taken.

4.32   Sampling Methods

It is essential that the sampling method selected enables the operator to obtain a representative sample of the water, avoids contamination of the sample when it is being collected, and avoids contamination or change in the composition of the sample during transport to the laboratory.

The type of sample to be collected will depend on the way in which the standard is applied. Typically, standards are applied as absolute maximums; in this case a "spot" or "grab" sample is required. However, if a standard is applied as an average, particularly over a short time, it may be appropriate to take a composite sample of the water supplied during that time.

4.4   SAMPLING DEVICES AND TECHNIQUES

4.40   Sampling Devices

Automatic sampling devices are wonderful timesavers but they are expensive. As with anything automatic, problems do arise and the operator should be on the lookout for potential difficulties.

Manual sampling equipment includes dippers, weighted bottles, hand-operated pumps, and cross-section samplers. Dippers consist of wide-mouth, corrosion-resistant containers (such as cans or jars) on long handles that collect a sample for

testing. A weighted bottle is a collection container that is lowered to a desired depth. At this depth a cord or wire removes the bottle stopper so the bottle can be filled (see Figure 4.1).

Some water treatment facilities use sample pumps to collect the sample and transport it to a central location. The pump and its associated piping should be corrosion-resistant and sized to deliver the sample at a high enough velocity to prevent sedimentation in the sample line.

Many water agencies have designed and installed special sampling stations throughout their distribution systems (see Figure 4.2). These stations provide an excellent location to sample the actual quality of water in your distribution system.

4.41   Surface Sampling

A surface sample is obtained by grasping the sample container at the base with one hand and plunging the bottle into the water with the mouth down to avoid collecting any material floating on the surface. Position the mouth of the bottle into the current and away from the hand of the collector (see Figure 4.3). If the water is not flowing, an artificial current can be created by moving the bottle horizontally in the direction it is pointed and away from the sampler. Tip the bottle slightly upward to allow air to exit so the bottle can fill. Tightly stopper and label the bottle.

Another technique for collecting a surface sample is to place the bottle in a weighted frame that holds the bottle securely when sampling from a walkway or other structure above the body of water. Remove the stopper or lid and lower the device to the water surface. A nylon rope, which does not absorb water and will not rot, is recommended. Face the bottle mouth upstream by swinging the sampling device downstream and then allow it to drop into the water without slack in the rope. Pull the sample device rapidly upstream and out of the water simulating (imitating) the scooping motion of the hand sampling described previously. Take care not to dislodge dirt or other debris that might fall into the open sample container from above. Be sure to label the container when sampling is completed.

4.42   Depth Sampling

Several additional pieces of equipment are needed for collection of depth samples from basins, tanks, lakes, and reservoirs. These depth samplers require lowering the sampling device and container to the desired water depth, then opening, filling, and closing the container and returning the device to the surface. Although depth measurements are best made with a pre-marked steel cable, the sample depths can be determined by pre-measuring and marking a nylon rope at intervals with a non-smearing ink, paint, or fingernail polish. One of

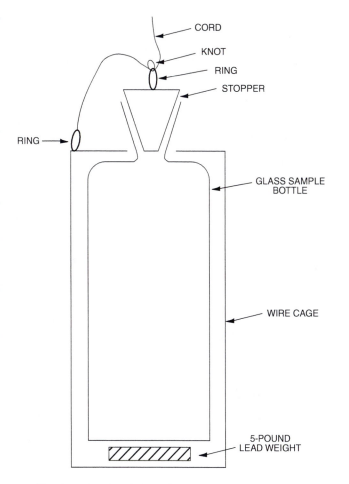

CORD
KNOT
RING
STOPPER
RING
GLASS SAMPLE BOTTLE
WIRE CAGE
5-POUND LEAD WEIGHT

Fig. 4.1   Sectional view of homemade depth sampler

Fig. 4.2   Distribution system sampling station

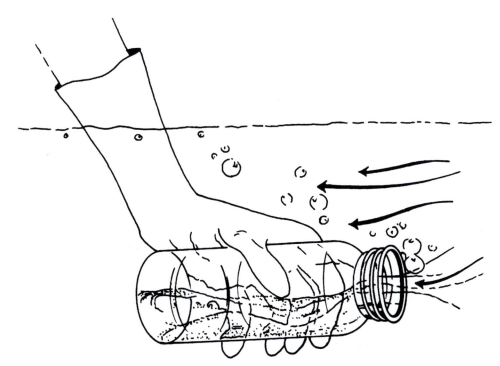

Fig. 4.3   Demonstration of technique used in grab sampling of surface waters
(Source: US EPA "Microbiological Methods For Monitoring the Environment," December 1978)

the most common commercial devices is called a Kemmerer sampler (see Figure 4.4). This type of depth sampler consists of a cylindrical tube that contains a rubber stopper or valve at each end. The device is lowered into the water in the open position and the water sample is trapped in the cylinder when the valves are closed by the dropped messenger.

Figures 4.1 and 4.5 show typical depth samplers. These samplers are lowered to the desired depth. A jerk on the cord will remove the stopper and allow the bottle in the depth sampler to fill. Good samples can be collected in depths of water up to 40 feet (12 m).

4.43   Water Tap Sampling

To collect samples from water main connections, first flush the service line for a brief period of time. Samples should not be taken from drinking fountains, restrooms, or taps that have aerators. Aerators can change water quality indicators such as pH and dissolved oxygen, and can harbor bacteria under some conditions. Do not sample from taps surrounded by excessive foliage (leaves, flowers) or from taps that are dirty, corroded, or are leaking. Never collect a sample from a hose or any other attachment fastened to a faucet. Care must be taken to be sure that the sample collector does not come in contact with the faucet.

4.44   First-Draw Sampling

The Lead and Copper Rule calls for first-draw or first-flush samples. These are water samples taken at the customer's tap after the water stands motionless in the plumbing pipes for at least six hours. This usually means taking a sample early in the day before water is used in the kitchen or bathroom.

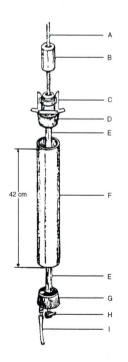

Fig. 4.4   Kemmerer depth sampler. (A) nylon line, (B) messenger, (C) catch set so that the sampler is open, (D) top rubber valve, (E) connecting rod between the valves, (F) tube body, (G) bottom rubber valve, (H) knot at the bottom of the suspension line, and (I) rubber tubing attached to the spring-loaded check valve.

(Source: US EPA "Microbiological Methods For Monitoring the Environment," December 1978)

Fig. 4.5   Depth sampler
(Courtesy of HACH Company)

4.45   Sampling Containers and Preservation of Samples

The shorter the time that elapses between the actual collection of the sample and the analysis, the more reliable your results will be. Samples should be preserved if they are not going to be analyzed immediately due to remoteness of the laboratory or workload. Preservation of some types of samples is essential to prevent deterioration of the sample. Some water quality indicators, such as residual chlorine and temperature, require immediate analysis, while samples for other water quality indicators can be preserved and transported to the laboratory. A summary of acceptable sample containers, preservative, and maximum time between sampling and analysis is shown on Table 4.1.

Whatever type of container you use, clearly identify the sample location, date and time of collection, name of collector, and any other pertinent information.

4.5   IMPORTANCE OF LABORATORY PROCEDURES

Water treatment processes cannot be controlled effectively unless the operator has some means to check and evaluate the quality of water being treated and produced. Laboratory quality control tests provide the necessary information to monitor the treatment processes and to ensure a safe and pleasant-tasting drinking water for all who use it. By relating laboratory results to treatment operations, the water treatment or supply system operator can first select the most effective operational procedures, then determine the efficiency of the treatment processes, and identify potential problems before they affect finished water quality. For these reasons, a clear understanding of laboratory procedures is a must for every waterworks operator.

TABLE 4.1   RECOMMENDATION FOR SAMPLING AND PRESERVATION OF SAMPLES ACCORDING TO MEASUREMENT[a]

Measurement	Vol. Req. (mL)	Container[b]	Preservative	Max. Holding Time[c]
PHYSICAL PROPERTIES				
Color	500	P,G	Cool, 4°C	48 hours
Conductance	500	P,G	Cool, 4°C	28 days
Hardness[d]	100	P,G	HNO_3 to pH <2, H_2SO_4 to pH <2	6 months
pH[d]	25	P,G	Det. on site	Immediately
Residue, Filterable	100	P,G	Cool, 4°C	7 days
Temperature	1,000	P,G	Det. on site	Immediately
Turbidity	100	P,G	Cool, 4°C	48 hours
METALS (Fe, Mn)				
Dissolved or Suspended	200	P,G	Filter on site, HNO_3 to pH <2	6 months
Total	100	P,G	Filter on site, HNO_3 to pH <2	6 months
INORGANICS, NONMETALLICS				
Acidity	100	P,G	Cool, 4°C	14 days
Alkalinity	200	P,G	Cool, 4°C	14 days
Bromide	100	P,G	None Req.	28 days
Chloride	50	P,G	None Req.	28 days
Chlorine, Total Residual	500	P,G	None Req.	Immediately
Cyanide, Total and Amenable to Chlorination	500	P,G	Cool, 4°C, NaOH to pH >12, 0.6 gm ascorbic acid[e]	14 days
Fluoride	300	P	None Req.	28 days
Nitrogen				
Ammonia	500	P,G	Cool, 4°C, H_2SO_4 to pH <2	28 days
Kjeldahl and Organic	500	P,G	Cool, 4°C, H_2SO_4 to pH <2	28 days
Nitrate-Nitrite	200	P,G	Cool, 4°C, H_2SO_4 to pH <2	28 days
Nitrate	100	P,G	Cool, 4°C	48 hours
Nitrite	100	P,G	Cool, 4°C	48 hours
Dissolved Oxygen				
Probe	300	G with top	Det. on site	Immediately
Winkler	300	G with top	Fix on site, store in dark	8 hours
Phosphorus				
Orthophosphate	50	P,G	Filter on site, Cool, 4°C	48 hours
Elemental	50	G	Cool, 4°C	48 hours
Total	50	P,G	Cool, 4°C, H_2SO_4 to pH <2	28 days
Silica	50	P	Cool, 4°C	28 days
Sulfate	100	P,G	Cool, 4°C	28 days
Sulfide	100	P,G	Cool, 4°C, add zinc acetate plus H_2SO_4 to pH >9	7 days
Sulfite	50	P,G	Det. on site	Immediately

[a] "Required Containers, Preservation Techniques, and Holding Times." Code of Federal Regulations, Protection of Environment, CFR 40, Part 136.3, revised as of July 1, 2004. Obtain from the U.S. Government Printing Office, Superintendent of Documents, PO Box 371954, Pittsburgh, PA 15250-7954. Stock Number 869-052-00157-1. Price, $61.00.

[b] Polyethylene (P) or Glass (G). For metals, polyethylene with a polypropylene cap (no liner) is preferred.

[c] Holding times listed above are recommended for properly preserved samples based on currently available data. It is recognized that for some sample types, extension of these times may be possible while for other types, these times may be too long. Where shipping regulations prevent the use of the proper preservation technique or the holding time is exceeded, such as the case of a 24-hour composite, the final reported data for these samples should indicate the specific variance.

[d] Hardness and pH are usually considered chemical properties of water rather than physical properties.

[e] Use ascorbic acid only if residual chlorine is present.

SPECIAL NOTE: Whenever you collect a sample for a bacteriological test (coliforms), be sure to use a sterile plastic or glass bottle. If the sample contains any chlorine residual, sufficient sodium thiosulfate should be added to neutralize all of the chlorine residual. Usually two drops (0.1 mL) of ten percent sodium thiosulfate for every 100 mL of sample is sufficient, unless you are disinfecting mains or storage tanks.

NOTICE

THE COLLECTION OF A BAD SAMPLE OR A BAD LABORATORY RESULT IS WORSE THAN NO RESULTS. TO PREVENT BAD RESULTS REQUIRES (1) CONSTANT MAINTENANCE AND CALIBRATION OF LABORATORY EQUIPMENT, AND (2) USE OF CORRECT LAB PROCEDURES. ALSO, RESULTS OF LAB TESTS ARE OF NO VALUE TO ANYONE UNLESS THEY ARE USED.

4.6 CHLORINE RESIDUAL TESTING

4.60 Importance

Many small water system operators attempt to maintain a chlorine residual throughout the distribution system. Chlorine is very effective in biological control and especially in elimination of coliform bacteria that might reach water in the distribution system through cross connections or leakage into the system. A chlorine residual also helps to control any microorganisms that could produce slimes, tastes, or odors in the water in the distribution system.

Adequate control of coliform "aftergrowth" is usually obtained only when chlorine residuals are carried to the farthest points of the distribution system. To ensure that this is taking place, make daily chlorine residual tests. A chlorine residual of about 0.2 mg/L measured at the extreme ends of the distribution system is usually a good indication that a free chlorine residual is present in all other parts of the system. This small residual can destroy a small amount of contamination, so a lack of chlorine residual could indicate the presence of heavy contamination. If routine checks at a given point show measurable residuals, any sudden absence of a residual at that point should alert the operator to the possibility that a potential problem has arisen which needs prompt investigation. Immediate action that can be taken includes retesting for chlorine residual, then checking chlorination equipment, and finally searching for a source of contamination that could cause an increase in the chlorine demand.

4.61 Chlorine Residual Curve

The chlorine residual curve procedure is a quick and easy way for an operator to estimate the proper chlorine dose, especially when surface water conditions are changing rapidly such as during a storm.

Fill a CLEAN five-gallon bucket from a sample tap located at least two 90-degree elbows (or where chlorine is completely mixed with the water in the pipe) AFTER the chlorine has been injected into the pipe. Immediately measure the chlorine residual and record this value on the "time zero" line of your record sheet (Figure 4.6). This is the initial chlorine residual. At 15-minute intervals, vigorously stir the bucket using an up and down motion. (A large plastic spoon works well for this purpose.) Collect a sample from one or two inches below the water surface and measure the chlorine residual. Record this chlorine residual value on the record sheet. For at least one hour, collect a sample every 15 minutes, measure the chlorine residual, and record the results to indicate the "chlorine demand" of the treated water. Plot these recorded values on a chart or graph paper as shown on Figure 4.6. Connect the plotted points to create a chlorine residual curve. If the chlorine residual after one hour is not correct (about 0.2 mg/L), increase or decrease the initial chlorine dose so the final chlorine residual will be approximately at the desired ultimate chlorine residual in the water distribution system. Repeat this

procedure until the desired TARGET initial chlorine residual will achieve the desired chlorine residual throughout the distribution system.

Precautions that must be taken when performing this test include being sure the five-gallon plastic test bucket is clean and only used for this purpose. A new bucket does not need to be used for every test, but the bucket should be new when the first test is performed. The stirrer should also be clean. DO NOT USE THE STIRRER FOR THE CHLORINE SOLUTION MIXING AND HOLDING TANK. During the test the bucket should be kept cool so that the chlorine gas does not escape from the water and give false chlorine residual values.

The chlorine demand for groundwater changes slowly, or not at all; therefore, the "initial" or "target" chlorine residual does not have to be checked more frequently than once a month. Always be sure to measure the chlorine residual in the distribution system on a daily basis. This is also a good check that the chlorination equipment is working properly and that the chlorine stock solution is the correct concentration.

The chlorine demand for surface water can change continuously, especially during storms and the snow melt season. Experience has proven that the required "initial" or "target" chlorine residual at time zero is directly related to the turbidity of the finished (treated) water. The higher the finished water turbidity, the higher the "initial" chlorine residual value will have to be to ensure the desired chlorine residual in the distribution system. Careful documentation of this information in your records will greatly reduce the lag time in chlorine addition changes to maintain the desired residual in the distribution system and the delivery of safe drinking water to your consumers. Experience and a review of your records will indicate that for a given turbidity value, you can estimate the desired "initial" chlorine residual, which will require a given chlorinator output level for a given water flow rate.

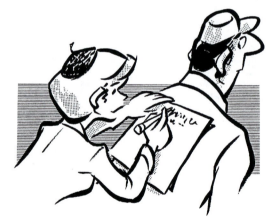

Acknowledgment

The information in Sections 4.60 and 4.61 was developed by Bill Stokes. His suggestions and procedures are greatly appreciated.

The monitoring data sheets reproduced in the Appendix of this chapter were provided by the Drinking Water Section of the Oregon Health Division. Permission to reprint the data sheets also is greatly appreciated.

4.62 Critical Factors

Both *CHLORINE RESIDUAL* and *CONTACT TIME* are essential for effective killing or inactivation of pathogenic microorganisms. Complete initial mixing is very important. Changes

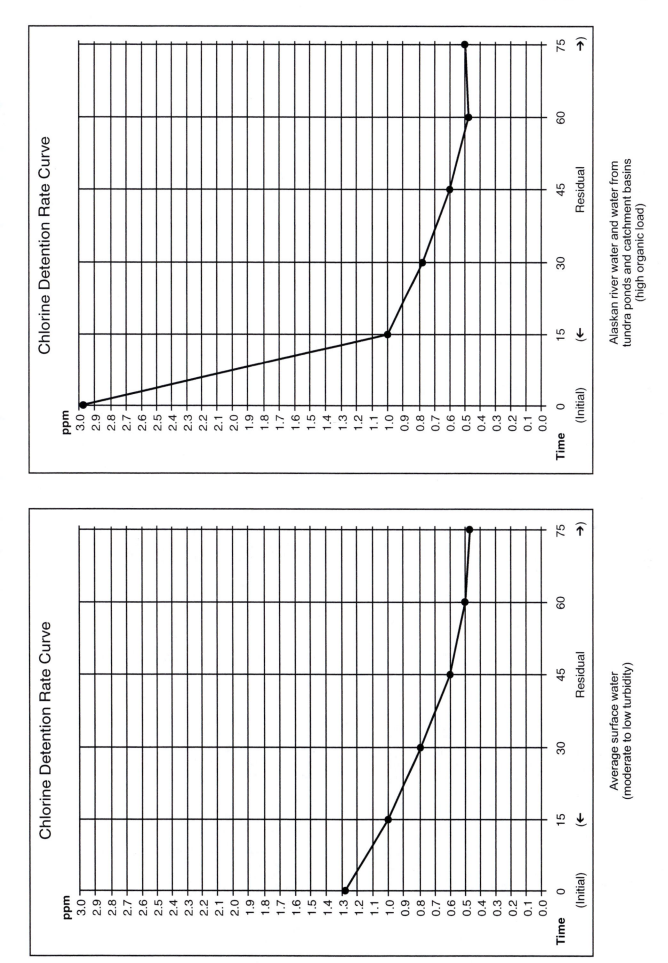

Fig. 4.6   Chlorine detention rate curves

in pH affect the disinfection ability of chlorine and you must re-examine the best combination of contact time and chlorine residual when the pH fluctuates. Critical factors influencing disinfection are summarized as follows:

1. Effectiveness of upstream treatment processes. The lower the turbidity (suspended solids, organic content, reducing agents) of the water, the better the disinfection.

2. Injection point and method of mixing to get disinfectant in contact with water being disinfected. Depends on whether using prechlorination or postchlorination.

3. Temperature. The higher the temperature, the more rapid the rate of disinfection.

4. Dosage and type of chemical. Usually the higher the dosage, the faster the disinfection rate. The form (chloramines or free chlorine residual) and type of chemical also influence the disinfection rate.

5. pH. The lower the pH, the better the disinfection.

6. Contact time. With good initial mixing, the longer the contact time, the better the disinfection.

7. Chlorine residual.

4.63 CT Values

The purpose of the Surface Water Treatment Rule (SWTR) is to ensure that pathogenic organisms are removed and/or inactivated by the treatment process. To meet this goal, all systems are required to disinfect their water supplies. For some water systems using very clean source water and meeting other criteria to avoid filtration, disinfection alone can achieve the 3-log (99.9%) *Giardia* and 4-log (99.99%) virus inactivation levels required by the SWTR. For extremely clean source waters there may be virtually no *Giardia* or viruses present and achieving 3-log or 4-log inactivation levels will be impossible and not necessary.

Several methods of disinfection are in common use, including free chlorination, chloramination, use of chlorine dioxide, and application of ozone. The concentration of chemical needed and the length of contact time needed to ensure disinfection are different for each disinfectant. Therefore, the efficiency of the disinfectant is measured by the time "T" in minutes of the disinfectant's contact in the water and the concentration "C" of the disinfectant residual in mg/L measured at the end of the contact time. The product of these two factors (C×T) provides a measure of the degree of pathogenic inactivation. The required CT value to achieve inactivation is dependent on the organism in question, type of disinfectant, pH, and temperature of the water supply.

Time or "T" is measured from point of application to the point where "C" is determined. "T" must be based on peak hour flow rate conditions. In pipelines, "T" is calculated by dividing the volume of the pipeline in gallons by the flow rate in gallons per minute (GPM). In reservoirs and basins, dye tracer tests must be used to determine "T." If a dye tracer is used, "T" is the time it takes for 10 percent of the tracer to pass the measuring point.

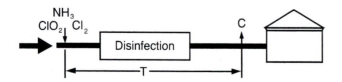

A properly operated filtration system can achieve limited removal or inactivation of microorganisms. Because of this, systems that are required to filter their water are permitted to apply a factor that represents the microorganism removal value of filtration when calculating CT values to meet the disinfection requirements. The factor (removal credit) varies with the type of filtration system. Its purpose is to take into account the combined effects of both disinfection and filtration in meeting the SWTR microbial standards.

Please refer to the Arithmetic Appendix at the end of *WATER TREATMENT PLANT OPERATION*, Volume I, Section A.16, "Calculation of CT Values," for instructions on how to perform these calculations for a water treatment plant.

For more detailed information about the requirements and application of the Surface Water Treatment Rule, you may wish to order a copy of the publication, *GUIDANCE MANUAL FOR COMPLIANCE WITH THE FILTRATION AND DISINFECTION REQUIREMENTS FOR PUBLIC WATER SYSTEMS USING SURFACE WATER SOURCES*. It is available from the American Water Works Association (AWWA), Bookstore, 6666 West Quincy Avenue, Denver, CO 80235. Order No. 20271. Price to members, $57.00; nonmembers, $84.00; price includes cost of shipping and handling.

4.7 THE LEAD AND COPPER RULE

4.70 Health Concerns

The health concerns about exposure to lead are best described by the EPA:

Lead is a common, natural, and often useful metal found throughout the environment in lead-based paint, air, soil, household dust, food, certain types of pottery, porcelain, pewter, and water. Lead can pose a significant risk to your health if too much of it enters your body. Lead builds up in the body over many years and can cause damage to the brain, red blood cells, and kidneys. The greatest risk is to young children and pregnant women. Amounts of lead that won't hurt adults can slow down normal mental and physical development of growing bodies. In addition, a child at play often comes into contact with sources of lead contamination—like dirt and dust—that rarely affect an adult.

Lead in drinking water, although rarely the sole cause of lead poisoning, can significantly increase a person's total lead exposure, particularly the exposure of infants who drink baby formulas and concentrated juices that are mixed with water. The EPA estimates that drinking water can make up 20 percent or more of a person's total exposure to lead.

Lead is unusual among drinking water contaminants in that it seldom occurs naturally in water supplies like rivers and lakes. Lead enters drinking water primarily as a result of the corrosion, or wearing away, of materials containing lead in the water distribution system and household plumbing. (See Figure 4.7.) These materials include lead-based solder used to join copper pipe, brass and chrome-plated brass faucets and, in some cases, pipes made of lead that connect your house to the water main (service lines).

When water stands in lead pipes or plumbing systems containing lead for several hours or more, the lead may dissolve into your drinking water. This means the first water drawn from the tap in the morning, or later in the afternoon after returning from work or school, can contain fairly high levels of lead.

Contaminant	Low Level Health Effects	Sources in Drinking Water
Lead	**Children:** Altered physical and mental development; interference with growth; deficits in IQ, attention span, and hearing. **Women:** Increased blood pressure; shorter gestational period **Men:** Increased blood pressure	Corrosion of: Lead solder and brass faucets and fixtures Lead service lines (20% of public water systems) Source water (1% of systems)
Copper	Stomach and intestinal distress; Wilson's Disease	Corrosion by-products: Interior household and building pipes Source water (1% of systems)

Public Water System (PWS) and Homeowner Plumbing

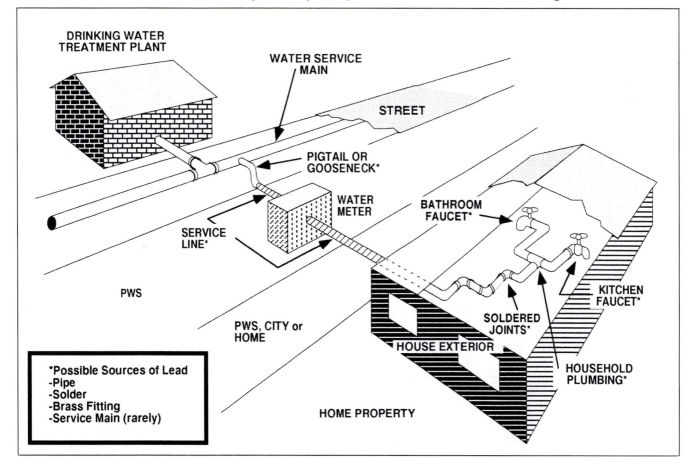

Fig. 4.7   *Health effects and sources of lead and copper*

Copper in drinking water usually results from the reaction of aggressive water on copper plumbing. Treatment of surface water in storage reservoirs to control algae may also cause high levels of copper. Copper is an essential nutrient, but excessive amounts of copper can be harmful to humans. The health effects of copper include stomach and intestinal distress. Prolonged doses result in liver damage. Excess intake of copper or the inability to metabolize copper is called Wilson's Disease.

4.71   Regulations

As part of the Safe Drinking Water Act Amendments of 1986, the U.S. Congress directed the Environmental Protection Agency to develop regulations for monitoring and control of lead and copper in drinking water. On June 7, 1991, EPA published the final Lead and Copper Rule. Revisions of the Rule were published January 12, 2000. The Rule and its implications are both complex and significant. Major features of the Rule are explained in this section. More detailed information can be obtained from the EPA or your state regulatory agency, or from the American Water Works Association, 6666 West Quincy Avenue, Denver, CO 80235, phone (303) 794-7711.

The issue of lead contamination in water supplies and in other environmental media (air, paint, food) continues to be a subject of considerable activity on the part of individual state governments, Congress, and the EPA. Further amendments to the rules or regulations governing lead contamination in water, monitoring requirements, and mitigation measures may be developed and may affect how the June 7, 1991, Lead and Copper Rule is implemented. You are encouraged to seek the most current status of lead contamination regulations from the regulatory agencies in your state before starting a monitoring or mitigation program to ensure that your program meets all applicable requirements. The information provided in this section applies to the final Lead and Copper Rule of June 7, 1991, published in the *FEDERAL REGISTER*.

The 1991 Lead and Copper Rule includes the following elements:

- Maximum Contaminant Level Goals (MCLGs), which are described as "nonenforceable health-based targets," and action levels are established for lead and copper;

- Monitoring requirements for lead, copper, and other corrosion analysis constituents, analytical methods, and laboratory certification requirements;

- Treatment techniques for lead and copper, required if the action levels are exceeded during monitoring, including optimal corrosion-control treatment, source water treatment, and lead service line replacement;

- Public notification and public education program requirements;

- Utility system recordkeeping and reporting requirements; and

- Variances and exemptions from the regulations and compliance schedules based on size of the population served by the utility system.

4.8   MONITORING REQUIREMENTS

4.80   Initial Requirements

The first requirement of the Lead and Copper Rule is for monitoring to determine if either of these metals exceeds the levels at which further action must be taken. An unusual provision of the Lead and Copper Rule is that the monitoring samples must be collected at the customers' taps, rather than only at the water treatment plant or in the distribution system. The samples must be taken from locations identified by the utility as "high-risk," including:

- Homes with lead solder installed after 1982,

- Homes with lead pipes, and

- Homes with lead service lines.

4.81   Monitoring Frequency

The number of samples to be collected for lead and copper analysis is based on the size of the distribution system; the sampling frequency is every six months for the initial monitoring program. There are two monitoring periods each year, January to June and July to December. If the system is in compliance, either as demonstrated by monitoring or after installation of corrosion control, a reduced monitoring frequency can be initiated. Table 4.2 lists the number of sampling sites required, based on system size, for initial and reduced monitoring.

TABLE 4.2 SAMPLING SITES REQUIRED FOR LEAD AND COPPER ANALYSIS		
System Size (Population)	Sampling Sites Required (Base Monitoring)	Sampling Sites Required (Reduced Monitoring)
>100,000	100	50
10,001 – 100,000	60	30
3,301 – 10,000	40	20
501– 3,300	20	10
101 – 500	10	5
≤100	5	5

Reduced Monitoring:

- All public water systems that meet the lead and copper action levels or maintain optimal corrosion-control treatment for two consecutive six-month monitoring periods may reduce the number of tap water sampling sites as shown in Table 4.2 and their collection frequency to once per year.

- All public water systems that meet the lead and copper action levels or maintain optimal corrosion-control treatment for three consecutive years may reduce the number of tap water sampling sites as shown in Table 4.2 and their collection frequency to once every three years.

4.82 Sampling Procedure

The samples are to be collected as "first-draw" samples from the cold water tap in either the kitchen or bathroom, or from a tap routinely used for consumption of water if in a building other than a home. A first-draw sample is defined as the first liter of water collected from a tap that has not been used for at least 6 hours, but preferably unused no more than twelve hours. Faucet aerators should be removed prior to sample collection. The Lead and Copper Rule allows homeowners to collect samples for the utility as long as the proper sample collection instructions have been provided. The EPA specifically prohibits the utility from disputing the accuracy of a sample collected by a resident.

4.9 ADDITIONAL READING

If you would like to learn more about monitoring, we recommend reading the following material from the operator training manual, *WATER TREATMENT PLANT OPERATION*, Volume I:

- Chapter 7, "Disinfection,"

- Chapter 8, "Corrosion Control" (includes Lead and Copper Rule),

- Chapter 10, "Plant Operation,"

- Chapter 11, "Laboratory Procedures," and

- Arithmetic Appendix, Section A.16, "Calculation of CT Values."

This training manual is available from the Office of Water Programs, California State University, Sacramento, 6000 J Street, Sacramento, CA 95819-6025. Price, $45.00.

4.10 ACKNOWLEDGMENTS

Portions of the material in Video 4 and this *LEARNING BOOKLET* were adapted from *MONITORING FOR COMPLIANCE, THE BLUE PAGES*, published by the International Water Services Association, 1998, London, United Kingdom.

The "Monitoring Data Sheets" in the Appendix were provided by Scott Curry, Drinking Water Section, Oregon Health Division.

To obtain an excellent training video, *GUIDE TO WATER SAMPLING*, contact Curtis Truss, Jr., Executive Director, Operator Training Committee of Ohio, Inc., 3972 Indianola Avenue, Columbus, OH 43214-3158. Phone, (614) 268-6826. Price, $25.00.

APPENDIX

Monitoring Data Sheets

Oregon Health Division, Drinking Water Section

COMMUNITY WATER SYSTEM
ROUTINE CHEMICAL MONITORING*

For Jan. 1999 to Dec. 2001 Compliance Period

Oregon Health Division
Drinking Water Section
731-4381

Chemicals		Surface Water	Ground Water
Inorganics		Yearly	One
Nitrate		Quarterly[1]	Yearly
Asbestos	AC Pipe	None[2]	
	Source	None[2]	
Synthetic Organics		One	
Volatile Organic		One	
Trihalomethane		Quarterly	
Radiological		Every 4 years	
Lead and Copper Rule		Yearly	

*This table describes the routine monitoring you must do. Waivers, reductions, wellhead protection programs, or detections will affect the sampling requirements. You will find details on number, location and timing of samples in the rule book.

Inorganics: testing may be reduced to one sample every 9 years if three rounds of sampling are completed and there are no MCL violations.

Nitrate: goes to quarterly sampling whenever a sample exceeds 5.0 mg/l.

SOC, VOC: testing may be reduced to one sample every 6 years if the system has a state approved wellhead protection program or a waiver.

Trihalomethanes: Trihalomethanes are monitored only by systems with a population of 10,000 or more.

[1] Nitrate: testing for surface systems can be reduced to annually after 4 quarters of sampling and a reduction is requested in writing.
[2] Asbestos: routine monitoring is one sample every nine years. Monitoring will go to one sample every 3 years if the system exceeds Lead or Copper action levels.

This table supersedes previous editions. Rev April 6, 1999

Contaminants and Maximum Levels

Inorganic	mg/l
Antimony Total	0.006
Arsenic	0.05
Asbestos	7 MFL[1]
Barium	2
Beryllium Total	0.004
Cadmium	0.005
Chromium	0.1
Cyanide	0.2
Fluoride	4.0
Mercury	0.002
Nickel	0.1
Nitrate	10
Nitrate-Nitrite	10
Nitrite	1
Selenium	0.05
Sodium	20[2]
Thallium Total	0.002

Lead and Copper

Copper	1.3*
Lead	.015*

Volatile Organics

1,1-Dichloroethylene	0.007
1,1,1-Trichloroethane	0.2
1,1,2-Trichloroethane	0.005
1,2-Dichloropropane	0.005
1,2-Dichloroethane	0.005
1,2,4-Trichlorobenzene	0.07
Benzene	0.005
Carbon Tetrachloride	0.005
Cis-1,2-Dichloroethylene	0.07
Dichloromethane	0.005
Ethylbenzene	0.7
Monochlorobenzene	0.1

O-Dichlorobenzene	0.6
P-Dichlorobenzene	0.075
Styrene	0.1
Tetrachloroethylene	0.005
Toluene	1.0
Total Xylenes	10.0
Trans-1,2-Dichloroethylene	0.1
Trichloroethylene	0.005
Vinyl Chloride	0.002

Synthetic Organics

	mg/l
2,4-D	0.07
2,4,5-TP Silvex	0.05
Adipates	0.4
Alachlor (Lasso)	0.002
Atrazine	0.003
Benzo(A)Pyrene	0.0002
BHC-gamma (Lindane)	0.0002
Carbofuran	0.04
Chlordane	0.002
Dalapon	0.2
Dibromochloropropane	0.0002
Dinoseb	0.007
Dioxin	3×10^{-8}
Diquat	0.02
Endothall	0.1
Endrin	0.002
Ethylene Dibromide (EDB)	0.00005
Glyphosate	0.7
Heptachlor Epoxide	0.0002
Heptachlor	0.0004
Hexachlorobenzene (HCB)	0.001
Hexachlorocyclopentadiene	0.05
Methoxychlor	0.04
Pentachlorophenol	0.001
Phthalates	0.006
Picloram	0.5
Polychlorinated Biphenyls (PCB)	0.0005
Simazine	0.004
Toxaphene	0.003
Vydate	0.2

[1] Million Fibers per Liter
[2] Advisory only
* Action Level

Noncommunity Water System
State Regulated Water System
Routine Chemical Monitoring*

Oregon Health Division
Drinking Water Section
731-4381

Chemicals	Sample
Inorganics (*Antimony, Arsenic, Barium, Beryllium, Cadmium, Chromium, Cyanide, Fluoride, Lead, Mercury, Nickel, Nitrite, Selenium, Thallium*)	Once
Nitrate	Yearly

Turbidity for Surface Water only	1 Reading Every 4 Hours[1]

	Source of Water		
Coliform Bacteria	Ground Water (well or spring)		Surface Water (stream, lake, etc)
	Average Daily Population Served		Monthly Sampling
	≤1000	>1000	
	Quarterly Sampling	Monthly Sampling	

Quarterly Sampling	Collect Sample Between[2]:		
1st Quarter	January 1	and	March 31
2nd Quarter	April 1	and	June 30
3rd Quarter	July 1	and	September 30
4th Quarter	October 1	and	December 31

* This table reflects base line monitoring. Waivers, reductions, or detections will affect sampling requirements.

[1] A system using a Slow Sand Filter can reduce monitoring to once a day upon Division approval.

[2] Sample early in quarter to avoid problems with mail, lost samples, weather, and other difficulites.

This chart replaces editions prior to 4/2/96

Contaminants and Maximum Levels

Inorganic Chemicals . . . . mg/l
Antimony Total 0.006
Arsenic 0.05
Barium 2
Beryllium Total 0.004
Cadmium 0.005
Chromium 0.1
Cyanide 0.2
Fluoride 4.0
Lead 0.015
Mercury 0.002
Nickel 0.1
Nitrate-Nitrite 10
Nitrite 1
Selenium 0.05
Thallium Total 0.002

Nitrate . . . . 10 mg/l

Coliform Bacteria . . . . None Present

Turbidity . . . . **Maximum Level**
  Conventional / Direct Filtration . . . . 0.5 NTU
  Slow Sand or Cartridge Filter . . . . . 1.0 NTU
  Diatomaceous Earth Filter . . . . 1.0 NTU
    Can not exceed 5.0 NTU at any time, and no more 5% of readings can be over the maximum level.

Non Transient Water System Routine Chemical Monitoring*

For Jan. 1999 to Dec. 2001 Compliance Period

Oregon Health Division
Drinking Water Section
731-4381

Chemicals		Surface Water	Ground Water
Inorganics		Yearly	One
Nitrate		Quarterly[1]	Yearly
Asbestos	AC Pipe	None[2]	
	Source	None[2]	
Synthetic Organics		One	
Volatile Organic		One	
Lead and Copper Rule		Yearly	

*This table describes the routine monitoring you must do. Waivers, reductions, wellhead protection programs, or detections will affect the sampling requirements. You will find details on number, location and timing of samples in the rule book.

Inorganics: testing may be reduced to one sample every 9 years if three rounds of sampling are completed and there are no MCL violations.

Nitrate: goes to quarterly sampling whenever a sample exceeds 5.0 mg/l.

SOC, VOC: testing may be reduced to one sample every 6 years if the system has a state approved wellhead protection program or a waiver.

[1] Nitrate: testing for surface systems can be reduced to annually after 4 quarters of sampling and a reduction is requested in writing.
[2] Asbestos: routine monitoring is one sample every nine years. Monitoring will go to one sample every 3 years if the system exceeds Lead or Copper action levels.

This table supersedes previous editions. Rev April 6, 1999

Contaminants and Maximum Levels

Inorganic

	mg/l
Antimony Total	0.006
Arsenic	0.05
Asbestos	7 MFL[1]
Barium	2
Beryllium Total	0.004
Cadmium	0.005
Chromium	0.1
Cyanide	0.2
Fluoride	4.0
Mercury	0.002
Nickel	0.1
Nitrate	10
Nitrate-Nitrite	10
Nitrite	1
Selenium	0.05
Sodium	20[2]
Thallium Total	0.002

Lead and Copper

Copper	1.3*
Lead	.015*

Volatile Organics

1,1-Dichloroethylene	0.007
1,1,1-Trichloroethane	0.2
1,1,2-Trichloroethane	0.005
1,2-Dichloropropane	0.005
1,2-Dichloroethane	0.005
1,2,4-Trichlorobenzene	0.07
Benzene	0.005
Carbon Tetrachloride	0.005
Cis-1,2-Dichloroethylene	0.07
Dichloromethane	0.005
Ethylbenzene	0.7
Monochlorobenzene	0.1
O-Dichlorobenzene	0.6
P-Dichlorobenzene	0.075
Styrene	0.1
Tetrachloroethylene	0.005
Toluene	1.0
Total Xylenes	10.0
Trans-1,2-Dichloroethylene	0.1
Trichloroethylene	0.005
Vinyl Chloride	0.002

Synthetic Organics

	mg/l
2,4-D	0.07
2,4,5-TP Silvex	0.05
Adipates	0.4
Alachlor (Lasso)	0.002
Atrazine	0.003
Benzo(A)Pyrene	0.0002
BHC-gamma (Lindane)	0.0002
Carbofuran	0.04
Chlordane	0.002
Dalapon	0.2
Dibromochloropropane	0.0002
Dinoseb	0.007
Dioxin	3×10^{-8}
Diquat	0.02
Endothall	0.1
Endrin	0.002
Ethylene Dibromide (EDB)	0.00005
Glyphosate	0.7
Heptachlor Epoxide	0.0002
Heptachlor	0.0004
Hexachlorobenzene (HCB)	0.001
Hexachlorocyclopentadiene	0.05
Methoxychlor	0.04
Pentachlorophenol	0.001
Phthalates	0.006
Picloram	0.5
Polychlorinated Biphenyls (PCB)	0.0005
Simazine	0.004
Toxaphene	0.003
Vydate	0.2

[1] Million Fibers per Liter
[2] Advisory only
* Action Level

WATER SYSTEMS OPERATION AND MAINTENANCE VIDEO TRAINING SERIES

CHAPTER (VIDEO) 5

INSPECTING A PUMP STATION

VIDEO 5 SUMMARY

Video 5, INSPECTING A PUMP STATION, provides operators with the knowledge, skills, and abilities they need to safely inspect and troubleshoot pump station performance. Emphasis is placed on what operators need to know to safely inspect and troubleshoot pump control panels (breakers, relays, contacts), measure amperage and voltage (using a volt-ohm meter), and properly lock out and tag out a system before performing maintenance tasks. Information is provided on how to identify and describe the basic components of a pump station. The importance of keeping and using accurate records is emphasized.

CONTENTS OF VIDEO 5

INSPECTING A PUMP STATION VIDEO

INTRODUCTION

    Purposes of a Pump Station

        Distribution System

        Storage Tanks

        Provide Continuous Service

        Provide Constant Pressure

        Fire and Emergency

    Types of Pumps

    Pump Control Panel

    Measuring Amperage and Voltage

    Lockout and Tagout

    Recordkeeping

TOUR OF A SMALL, TYPICAL URBAN PUMP STATION

    Basic Components of a Pump Station

    Power Control Facility

    Water Treatment Facility

    Production Facility (Well Pump)

    Blend in With Neighborhood

WELL COMPONENTS

    Electrical Supply

    Submersible Pump

    Vertical Turbine Pump

    Well Vent

    Air Release Valve

    Flush/Waste Valve Used at Start-up

    Pump Control Valve (smooths out surges)

    Add Hypochlorite

    Flowmeter

    Pressure Controls

    Sample Tap

    Control Valve to Distribution System

CONTROL PANEL

    Reduced Voltage Starter

    Power

    Circuit Breakers

    SCADA System

    Alarm System

ROUTINE INSPECTION

    Initial Look for Cleanliness, Security, Leaks

    Check Control Panel and SCADA

    Record Readings in Station Binder

    Chlorination System

    Chlorine Residual

    Well Screens and Vents

    Leaks

MEASURING VOLTAGE AND AMPERAGE

    Voltage (consistency across all three legs)

    Amperage

    How To Safely Use Meter

LOCKOUT/TAGOUT PROCEDURE

    Purpose

    Deenergize Electrical Equipment

    Everyone Has Their Own Kit

    How To Use Kit

RECORDKEEPING

    Why

    Information Recorded

    Keep Good Records

SUMMARY

    Inspection Procedures

    Production Facility

    Daily Inspections

    Monthly Inspections

    Electrical Maintenance and Repair

    Measuring Amperage and Voltage

    Lockout/Tagout

    Recordkeeping

CONTENTS OF CHAPTER 5

INSPECTING A PUMP STATION
LEARNING BOOKLET

OBJECTIVES

Chapter (Video) 5.   INSPECTING A PUMP STATION

Following completion of Video 5 and Chapter 5, you should be able to:

1. Describe the purpose of distribution system pumps,

2. Describe the purpose of well pumps,

3. Describe the importance of maintaining pressure in the distribution system,

4. Describe the importance of cross-connection control,

5. Safely inspect and troubleshoot pump control panels,

6. Safely inspect and troubleshoot pump systems,

7. Safely measure amperage and voltage (using a volt-ohm meter), and

8. Properly lock out and tag out a system before maintenance.

LEARNING BOOKLET STUDY MATERIAL

This section of the *LEARNING BOOKLET* contains important information. Read this section after watching the video and before attempting to take the Objective Test for this chapter.

Material covered in this section will help you better understand the material in the video. Also some critical information is easier to present in the *LEARNING BOOKLET*, such as illustrating forms and troubleshooting checklists.

Chapter (Video) 5.   INSPECTING A PUMP STATION

5.0   DISTRIBUTION SYSTEM PUMPS

5.00   Purpose of Pumps

Distribution system pumps are the heart of the distribution system. They pump water from wells and treatment plants into storage tanks and the distribution system which delivers water to consumers. The main purpose of the pumps is to ensure that a sufficient quantity of water at an adequate pressure is available at all times to meet consumer demands and also to meet demands for fire control.

5.01   Inspection and Preventive Maintenance Procedures

Inspection of a pump station includes a review of preventive maintenance procedures and their effectiveness. A comprehensive preventive maintenance program is necessary for all pump installations. Without such a program, the continued satisfactory operation of the pumps will be threatened and may result in unsatisfactory system performance. In many systems, a lengthy pump outage will severely strain the ability of the system to continue to serve sufficient water. Written detailed inspection, operation, and maintenance procedures should be available at convenient locations for all operators responsible for these duties. The statement, "When all else fails, follow directions" was never more true than for pump operation. Manufacturers' directions should be closely followed.

Pumps must be firmly installed to prevent problems from operating noise levels and alignment during the life of the equipment. Alignment procedures for the pump and driver are critical. There should be no strain on the pump case from the suction and discharge piping connections.

The starting, stopping, and regulation of pumping equipment can be achieved manually, automatically, or semi-automatically. There has been an increasing use of sensing and automatic control devices. The variables sensed may be water elevation, water pressure, quantity of water pumped, or any combination of the three. Long distance (remote) sensing operations can be set up using leased telephone circuits, radio signals, or pressure communicated through the water in the pipelines to transmit control system signals. The entire pumping function in a complex distribution system can be operated and controlled from a single point or control station or from multiple points.

As pump operating conditions vary widely, it is impossible to provide a preventive maintenance schedule that would apply to all systems. Regular inspections must be planned and followed. Inspection schedules are often based on the number of expected pump operating hours since the last inspection. A record of the inspections and of the pump maintenance performed must be kept to ensure that the necessary scheduled procedures are being followed.

Inspection and preventive maintenance procedures will cover many types of operations. Some of the more important procedures are listed below.

1. Observe and record pump pressures and output (flow), and the pump's current (electricity) demands.

2. Regularly check for excessive or abnormal noise, vibration, heat, and odor.

3. Provide grease and oil lubrication in accordance with the manufacturer's instructions. Lubrication should never be overdone as the addition of too much grease will cause a bearing to overheat, and too much oil will result in foaming. Proper lubrication for pump bearings cannot be overemphasized. The conditions of operation will determine how often a bearing should be greased.

4. Check bearing temperatures once per month with a thermometer. If the bearings are found to be running too hot, it could be the result of too much lubricant. Every three months, check the lubricated bearings for "saponification." This is a soapy or foamy condition of the lubricant which usually results from water or other fluid infiltrating past the bearing shaft seals. If the grease appears as a white foamy substance, flush the bearings with kerosene or solvent, clean thoroughly, and repack with the type of lubricant recommended by the manufacturer.

5. Listen for any bearing noise. Usually a ball bearing will give audible notice of impending failure. This early warning will give you time to plan a shutdown for maintenance.

6. Tighten the packing glands if they are leaking excessively. The tightening should be sufficient to permit only a small amount of leakage, but not result in an increase in packing-follower heating. Packing glands should never be tightened to the point where there is no leakage since this will cause undue packing wear and even a scored shaft or sleeve. Check the leakage rate daily. When the packing wears or is compressed so that the gland cannot be tightened farther, install a new set of rings. While mechanical seals require higher initial cost than packing, long-term costs may be lower.

7. Inspect the pump *PRIMING*[1] system. A priming system must be used to prevent the pump from running dry if the

---

[1] *Prime. The action of filling a pump casing with water to remove the air. Most pumps must be primed before start-up or they will not pump any water.*

pump operates with a *SUCTION LIFT*.[2] To protect against loss of prime, check valves or foot valves on the intake or suction piping of a pump are a necessity. Use only clean water for the priming. To facilitate priming, ejectors or vacuum pumps are also available. As the pumps are also prone to air binding, they are usually provided with manual or automatic vent valves on top of the pump casing. One type of priming pump installation is shown in Figure 5.1.

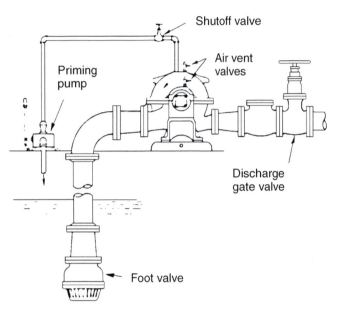

Fig. 5.1   Pump priming installation

(Reprinted from *WATER DISTRIBUTION OPERATOR TRAINING HANDBOOK*, by permission. Copyright 1976, the American Water Works Association)

8. Routinely operate internal combustion-driven pumps and generators on standby for 15 minutes once per week. Also check any automatic pump controls. If they fail during an emergency, the pumps must be operated with manual overrides.

9. Check pump alignment periodically to guard against premature bearing and coupling wear. Alignment should be checked when the pump is cold, and again when a unit has run long enough for it to reach the proper operating temperature. Alignment on new installations can change considerably in a short period of time. Daily checks should be made until a stable operation has been established.

Since pumps and controls are usually powered by electric energy, the operator should have some working knowledge of electric circuits and circuit testing instruments if effective maintenance is to be provided. Although the operator is usually not expected to be an expert in this field, an understanding of the basics of electricity is important if for no other reason than to learn how to avoid electric shock.

An electric motor failure can have serious consequences. The principal causes of such a failure are overheating caused by overloading, a locked rotor, rapid cycling, loss of cooling due to clogged or impeded ventilation, or low water level in a submersible pump casing. When overheating occurs, power is usually shut off by protective devices installed in motor circuits. Become familiar with these devices and learn where and how to reset them after finding the problem, if any, which caused the tripping of the circuit.

5.1   IMPORTANCE OF MAINTAINING PRESSURE IN SYSTEM

A main concern in operation of a water distribution system is the maintenance of a *CONTINUOUS POSITIVE PRESSURE* at all times to all consumers. This is necessary not only to meet the flow needs of the consumers, but to prevent contamination from backflow. The water supplier should try to maintain a minimum pressure of 35 psi (241 kPa or 2.45 kg/sq cm) at all points in the distribution system, with an absolute minimum of 20 psi (138 kPa or 1.4 kg/sq cm) even during fire flows. In commercial districts, pressures of 75 psi (517 kPa or 5.3 kg/sq cm) and higher are used, but the delivered pressure should not be more than 100 psi (690 kPa or 7.0 kg/sq cm). Pressures in this range (35 to 100 psi, 241 to 690 kPa, or 2.4 to 7.0 kg/sq cm) are sufficient for normal use without risk of damage to water-using facilities in the distribution system or on the consumer's premises. Excessive pressures could cause such damage as well as unintentional higher water usage. Where high main pressures cannot be avoided (on transmission mains), pressure-reducing valves are normally used.

Promptly investigate low-pressure complaints from consumers and make corrections where necessary. To determine the extent of a reported problem, use pressure gages or portable mechanical or battery-powered pressure recorders which can record data for a 24-hour period or longer by connecting to the consumer's system.

Pressure problems have many possible causes. A faulty pressure regulator might have a control water strainer that needs cleaning, or the regulator itself may be in need of repair. Sometimes, purposefully or otherwise, a line valve is left closed or partly closed causing loss of pressure, especially during higher flows. Low pressures can be caused by system lines being too small which will cause high velocities. High velocities occur when there is a large use of water due to unusually high consumer demands, firefighting, or a major leak. While these problems are out of the operator's control, they can be eased by maintaining adequate reserves in distribution

---

[2] *Suction Lift.   The NEGATIVE pressure [in feet (meters) of water or inches (centimeters) of mercury vacuum] on the suction side of the pump. The pressure can be measured from the centerline of the pump DOWN TO (lift) the elevation of the hydraulic grade line on the suction side of the pump.*

storage. Although about 35 percent or more of the storage capacity should normally be reserved for fire demand and emergency use, excessive peak hour or peak day demands can still seriously drain the available storage. Storage reservoirs should never be allowed to run too low. Activating a well or an interagency connection or increasing pumping to provide more water might help maintain adequate pressure. A potential source of an emergency water supply is older reservoirs that have been taken out of service when the physical growth of the service area has left them at too low an elevation to be useful; however, they have been kept available for emergency purposes. By slightly modifying the piping and using portable pumps, these older reservoirs can be used during emergencies.

Pressure problems can also be caused by pump failure. If automatic pump controls fail, the pumps must be operated with manual overrides during peak periods. If the pumps themselves fail or the power fails, the availability of self-powered pumps and generators is invaluable. Distribution system operators should have the basic knowledge to make prompt repairs on pumps that have failed and the necessary repair parts should be readily available. Operators should have access to emergency equipment and rental equipment with the authority to act.

5.2 POTENTIAL FOR CROSS CONNECTIONS AND BACKFLOW

5.20 Importance of Cross-Connection Control

BACKFLOW[3] of contaminated water through cross connections into community water systems is not just a theoretical problem. Contamination through cross connections has consistently caused more waterborne disease outbreaks in the United States than any other reported factor. Inspections have often disclosed numerous unprotected cross connections between public water systems and other piped systems on consumers' premises which might contain wastewater; stormwater; processed waters (containing a wide variety of chemicals); and untreated supplies from private wells, streams, and ocean waters. Therefore, an effective cross-connection control program is essential.

Backflow results from either BACK PRESSURE[4] or BACK-SIPHONAGE[5] situations in the distribution system. Back pressure occurs when the user's water supply is at a higher pressure than the public water supply system (Figure 5.2). Typical locations where back pressure problems could develop include services to premises where wastewater or toxic chemicals are handled under pressure or where there are unapproved auxiliary water supplies such as a private well or the use of surface water or seawater for firefighting. Backsiphonage is caused by the development of negative or below atmospheric pressures in the water supply piping (Figure 5.3). This condition can occur when there are extremely high water demands (firefighting), water main breaks, or the use of on-line booster pumps.

The best way to prevent backflow is to permanently eliminate the hazard. Back pressure hazards can be eliminated by severing (eliminating) any direct connection at the pump causing the back pressure with the domestic water supply system.

Another solution to the problem is to require an air gap separation device (Figure 5.6, page 137) where the water supply service line connects to the private system under pressure from the pump. To eliminate or minimize backsiphonage problems, proper enforcement of plumbing codes and improved water distribution and storage facilities will be helpful. As an additional safety factor for certain selected conditions, a double check valve (Figure 5.7, page 137) may be required at the meter.

5.21 Program Responsibilities

Responsibilities in the implementation of cross-connection control programs are shared by water suppliers, water users (businesses and industries), health agencies, and plumbing officials. The water supplier is responsible for preventing contamination of the public water system by backflow. This responsibility begins at the source, includes the entire distribution system, and ends at the user's connection. To meet this responsibility, the water supplier must issue (promulgate) and enforce needed laws, rules, regulations, and policies. Water service should not be provided to premises where the strong possibility of an unprotected cross connection exists. The essential elements of a water supplier cross-connection control program are discussed in the next section.

The water user is responsible for keeping contaminants out of the potable water system on the user's premises. When backflow prevention devices are required by the health agency or water supplier, the water user must pay for the installation, testing, and maintenance of the approved devices. The user is also responsible for preventing the creation of cross connections through modifications of the plumbing system on the premises. The health agency or water supplier may, when necessary, require a water user to designate a water supervisor or foreman to be responsible for the cross-connection control program within the water user's premises.

The local or state health agency is responsible for issuing and enforcing laws, rules, regulations, and policies needed to control cross connections. Also this agency must have a program that ensures maintenance of an adequate cross-connection control program. The protection of the system on the user's premises is provided where needed by the water utilities.

The plumbing agency (building inspectors) is responsible for the enforcement of building regulations relating to prevention of cross connections on the user's premises.

---

[3] Backflow.   A reverse flow condition, created by a difference in water pressures, which causes water to flow back into the distribution pipes of a potable water supply from any source or sources other than an intended source. Also see BACKSIPHONAGE.

[4] Back Pressure.   A pressure that can cause water to backflow into the water supply when a user's water system is at a higher pressure than the public water system.

[5] Backsiphonage.   A form of backflow caused by a negative or below atmospheric pressure within a water system. Also see BACKFLOW.

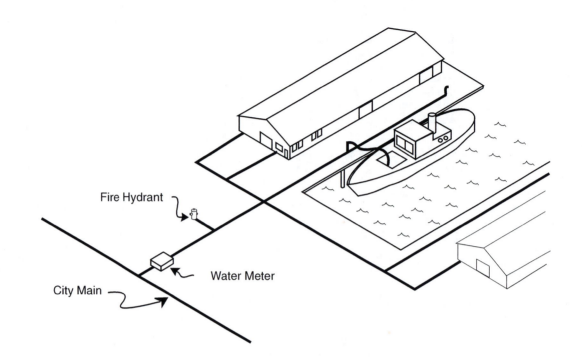

HYDRAULIC GRADIENT

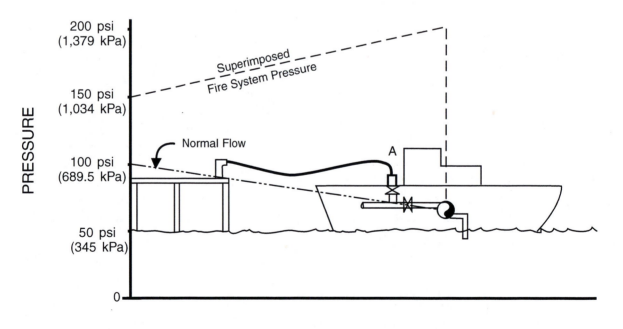

Fig. 5.2   Backflow due to back pressure

(Source: *MANUAL OF CROSS-CONNECTION CONTROL PROCEDURES AND PRACTICES*,
Sanitary Engineering Branch, California Department of Health Services, Berkeley, CA)

DISTRIBUTION SYSTEM

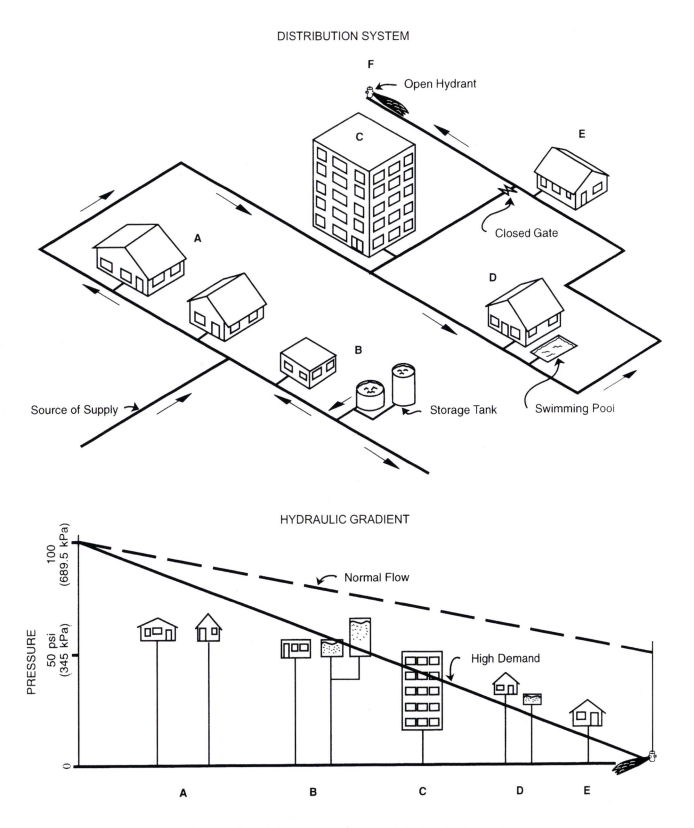

HYDRAULIC GRADIENT

Fig. 5.3   Backsiphonage due to extremely high water demand

(Source: *MANUAL OF CROSS-CONNECTION CONTROL PROCEDURES AND PRACTICES*,
Sanitary Engineering Branch, California Department of Health Services, Berkeley, CA)

5.22   Water Supplier Cross-Connection Control Program

The following elements should be included in each water supplier's cross-connection control program:

1. Enactment of an ordinance providing enforcement authority if the supplier is a governmental agency, or enactment of appropriate rules of service if the system is investor-owned.[6]

2. Training of personnel on the causes of and hazards from cross connections and procedures to follow for effective cross-connection control.

3. Listing and inspection or reinspection on a priority basis of all existing facilities where cross connections are of concern. A typical cross-connection survey form is shown in Figure 5.4.

4. Review and screening of all applications for new services or modification of existing services for cross-connection hazards to determine if backflow protection is needed.

5. Obtaining a list of approved backflow prevention devices and a list of certified testers, if available.

6. Acceptable installation of the proper type of device needed for the specific hazard on the premises.

7. Routine testing of installed backflow prevention devices as required by the health agency or the water supplier. Contact the health agency for approved procedures.

8. Maintenance of adequate records for each backflow prevention device installed, including records of inspection and testing. A typical form is shown in Figure 5.5.

9. Notification of each water user when a backflow prevention device has to be tested. This should be done after installation or repair of the device and at least once a year.

10. Maintenance of adequate pressures throughout the distribution system at all times to minimize the hazards from any undetected cross connections that may exist.

All field personnel should be constantly alert for situations where cross connections are likely to exist, whether protection has been installed or not. An example is a contractor using a fire hose from a hydrant to fill a tank truck for dust control or the jetting (for compaction) of pipe trenches. Operators should especially be on the lookout for illegal bypassing of installed backflow prevention devices.

5.23   Types of Backflow Prevention Devices

Different types of backflow prevention devices are available. The particular type of device most suitable for a given situation depends on the degree of health hazard, the probability of backflow occurring, the complexity of the piping on the premises, and the probability of the piping being modified. The higher the assessed risk due to these factors, the more reliable and positive the type of device needed. The types of devices normally approved are listed below according to the degree of assessed risk, with the type of device providing the greatest protection listed first. Only the first three devices are approved for use at service connections.

1. Air gap separation.

2. Reduced-pressure principle (RPP) device.

3. Double check valve.

4. Pressure vacuum breaker (only used for internal protection on the premises).

5. Atmospheric (non-pressure) vacuum breaker.

Figure 5.6 shows a typical air gap separation device and its recommended location. Figure 5.7 shows the installation of a typical double check valve backflow prevention device. These devices are normally installed on the water user's side of the connection to the utility's system and as close to the connection as practical. Figure 5.8 shows a typical installation of pressure vacuum breakers.

Only backflow prevention devices that have passed both laboratory and field evaluations by a recognized testing agency and that have been accepted by the health agency and the water supplier should be used.

5.24   Devices Required for Various Types of Situations

The state or local health agency should be contacted to determine the actual types of devices acceptable for various situations inside the consumer's premises. However, the types of devices generally acceptable for particular situations can be mentioned.

An air gap or a reduced-pressure principle (RPP) device is normally required at services to wastewater treatment plants, wastewater pumping stations, reclaimed water reuse areas, areas where toxic substances in toxic concentrations are handled under pressure, and premises having an auxiliary water supply that is or may be contaminated. The ultimate degree of protection is also needed in cases where fertilizer, herbicides, or pesticides are injected into a sprinkler system.

A double check valve device should be required when a moderate hazard exists on the premises or where an auxiliary supply exists, but adequate protection on the premises is provided.

Atmospheric and pressure vacuum breakers are usually required for irrigation systems; however, they are not adequate in situations where they may be subject to back pressure. If there is a possibility of back pressure, a reduced-pressure principle device is needed.

5.25   Typical Cross-Connection Hazards

5.250   Importance of Hazard Awareness

Water distribution system operators need to be aware of the types of hazardous chemicals that could enter the water distribution system as well as potential sources of these hazardous chemicals. Operators need to know the types of pollutants or contaminants that are used by consumers that could threaten the public health of consumers if they entered the distribution system. A knowledge of typical industries that have contaminated public water systems through cross connections will help operators protect the quality of the water delivered to consumers through the distribution system.

5.251   Hazardous Chemicals Used by Consumers

Chemicals used by industries may create a hazard to the public when the chemicals are used on site, enter the industry's water distribution system, and then may enter the public

---

[6] *A typical ordinance is available in CROSS-CONNECTION CONTROL MANUAL, available from National Technical Information Service (NTIS), 5285 Port Royal Road, Springfield, VA 22161. Order No. PB91-145490. EPA No. 570-9-89-007. Price, $33.50, plus $5.00 per order.*

CROSS-CONNECTION SURVEY FORM

Place:_____ Date:_____

Location:_____ Investigator(s)_____

Building Representative(s) and Title(s):

_____
_____

Water Source(s):_____
_____
_____

Piping System(s):_____
_____
_____

Points of Interconnection:_____
_____
_____
_____
_____

Special Equipment Supplied with Water and Source:

_____
_____
_____

Remarks or Recommendations:_____
_____
_____
_____
_____
_____

NOTE: Attach sketches of cross-connections found where necessary for
       clarity of description. Attach additional sheets for room-by-
       room survey under headings

                                      Description of
       Room Number   Cross-Connection(s)

Fig. 5.4   Typical cross-connection survey form

(From CROSS-CONNECTION CONTROL MANUAL, U.S. Environmental Protection Agency, Water Supply Division)

MAIL TO: Principal Sanitary Engineer
Department of Water and Power, City of Los Angeles
P.O. Box 111   Room A-18
Los Angeles, California 90051

CODE 03250
15M 7-77 P.O. 30582

RETURN NO LATER THAN:

MANUFACTURER	MODEL	SIZE	SERIAL NUMBER	SERVICE NUMBER

SERVICE ADDRESS:

LOCATION:

| 1 | 2 | 3 | 4 | 5 | 6 | 7 | 8 | 9 | 10 | 11 | 12 | 13 | 14 | 15 | 16 | 17 | 18 | 19 | 20 | 21 | 22 | 23 | 24 | 25 | 26 | 27 | 28 | 29 | 30 | 31 | 32 | 33 | 34 | 35 | 36 | 37 | 38 | 39 | 40 | 41 | 42 | 43 | 44 | 45 | 46 | 47 |

| 48 | 49 | 50 | 51 | 52 | 53 | 54 | 55 | 56 | 57 | 58 | 59 | 60 | 61 | 62 | 63 | 64 | 65 | 66 | 67 | 68 | 69 | 70 | 71 | 72 | 73 | 74 | 75 | 76 | 77 | 78 | 79 | 80 |

	CHECK VALVE #1	CHECK VALVE #2	CHECK VALVE #3	DIFFERENTIAL PRESSURE RELIEF VALVE
INITIAL TEST	1. LEAKED* ☐ 2. CLOSED TIGHT ☐	1. LEAKED ☐ 2. CLOSED TIGHT ☐	1. LEAKED ☐ 2. CLOSED TIGHT ☐	OPENED AT _____ LBS. REDUCED PRESSURE. ☐ DID NOT OPEN ☐

REPAIRS	CLEANED ☐
	REPLACED:
	DISC ☐
	SPRING ☐
	GUIDE ☐
	PIN RETAINER ☐
	HINGE PIN ☐
	SEAT ☐
	DIAPHRAGM ☐
	
	OTHER, DESCRIBE ☐
		CLEANED ☐
		REPLACED:
		DISC ☐
		SPRING ☐
		GUIDE ☐
		PIN RETAINER ☐
		HINGE PIN ☐
		SEAT ☐
		DIAPHRAGM ☐
		
		OTHER, DESCRIBE ☐
			CLEANED ☐
			REPLACED:
			DISC ☐
			SPRING ☐
			GUIDE ☐
			HINGE PIN ☐
			SEAT ☐
			DIAPHRAGM ☐
			
			OTHER, DESCRIBE ☐
				CLEANED ☐
				REPLACED:
				DISC:
				  UPPER ☐
				  LOWER ☐
				SPRING ☐
				DIAPHRAGM:
				LARGE:
				  UPPER ☐
				  LOWER ☐
				SMALL ☐
				SEAT:
				  UPPER ☐
				  LOWER ☐
				SPACER:
				  LOWER ☐
				OTHER DESCRIBE ☐

FINAL TEST	CLOSED TIGHT ☐	CLOSED TIGHT ☐	CLOSED TIGHT ☐	OPENED AT _____ LBS. REDUCED PRESSURE

The above report is certified to be true.

INITIAL TEST BY _____   CERTIFIED TESTER NO. ☐☐☐☐☐   DATE | MO. | DAY | YR. |

REPAIRED BY _____   DATE _____

FINAL TEST BY_____   CERTIFIED TESTER NO. ☐☐☐☐☐ | MO. | DAY | YR. |

Fig. 5.5   Typical backflow prevention device maintenance record form
(Permission of Department of Water and Power, City of Los Angeles)

TANK SHOULD BE OF SUBSTANTIAL CONSTRUCTION AND
OF A KIND AND SIZE TO SUIT CONSUMER'S NEEDS.
TANK MAY BE SITUATED AT GROUND LEVEL (WITH A
PUMP TO PROVIDE ADEQUATE PRESSURE HEAD) OR
BE ELEVATED ABOVE THE GROUND.

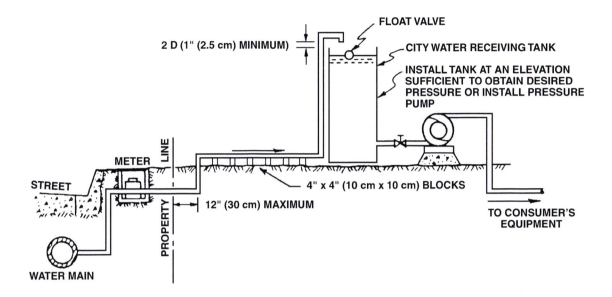

Fig. 5.6   Typical air gap separation

(From *MANUAL OF CROSS-CONNECTION CONTROL PRACTICES AND PROCEDURES*, Sanitary Engineering Branch, California Department of Health Services, Berkeley, CA)

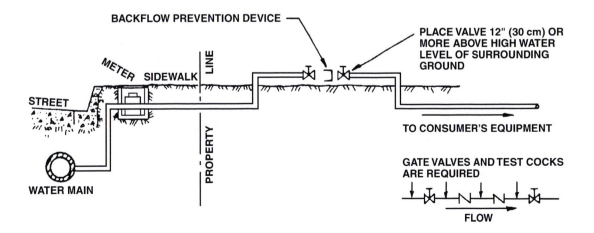

Fig. 5.7   Typical double check valve backflow prevention device

(From *MANUAL OF CROSS-CONNECTION CONTROL PRACTICES AND PROCEDURES*, Sanitary Engineering Branch, California Department of Health Services, Berkeley, CA)

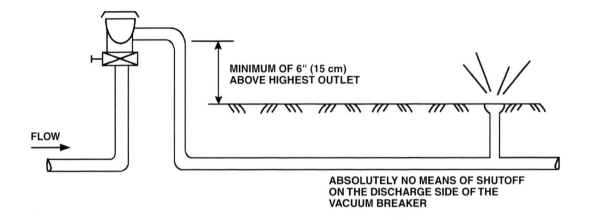

MINIMUM OF 6" (15 cm)
ABOVE HIGHEST OUTLET

FLOW

ABSOLUTELY NO MEANS OF SHUTOFF
ON THE DISCHARGE SIDE OF THE
VACUUM BREAKER

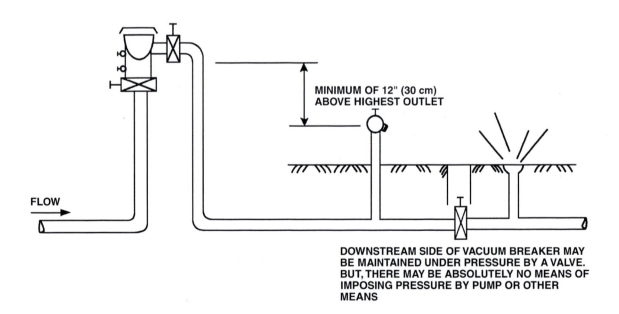

MINIMUM OF 12" (30 cm)
ABOVE HIGHEST OUTLET

FLOW

DOWNSTREAM SIDE OF VACUUM BREAKER MAY
BE MAINTAINED UNDER PRESSURE BY A VALVE.
BUT, THERE MAY BE ABSOLUTELY NO MEANS OF
IMPOSING PRESSURE BY PUMP OR OTHER
MEANS

Fig. 5.8   Typical installations of atmospheric (top) and pressure (bottom) vacuum breakers

(From *MANUAL OF CROSS-CONNECTION CONTROL PRACTICES AND PROCEDURES*, Sanitary Engineering Branch, California Department of Health Services, Berkeley, CA)

water distribution system through a cross connection. This section describes some typical industries and the protection recommended to protect public water distribution systems.

• Agriculture

Agriculture uses many different types of chemicals for different purposes. Toxic chemicals are used by agriculture in fertilizers, herbicides, and pesticides. *Protection recommended:* an air gap separation or a reduced-pressure principle backflow prevention assembly is recommended.

• Cooling Systems (Open or Closed)

Cooling systems, including cooling towers, usually require some treatment of the water for algae, slime, or corrosion control. *Protection recommended:* an air gap separation or a reduced-pressure principle backflow prevention assembly is recommended.

• Dye Plants

Most solutions used in dyeing are highly toxic. The toxicity depends on the chemicals used and their concentrations. *Protection recommended:* an air gap separation or a reduced-pressure principle backflow prevention assembly is recommended.

• Plating Plants

In plating work, materials are first cleaned in acid or caustic solutions at concentrations that are highly toxic. *Protection recommended:* an air gap separation or a reduced-pressure principle backflow prevention assembly is recommended.

• Steam Boiler Plants

Most boiler plants will use some form of boiler feedwater treatment. The chemicals typically used for this purpose include highly toxic compounds. *Protection recommended:* an air gap separation or a reduced-pressure principle backflow prevention assembly is recommended.

5.252 *Industries With Cross-Connection Potential*

A knowledge of industries that may have cross connections to a public water distribution system will help operators prevent the occurrence of cross connections. The following inspection guidelines list typical hazards and recommend cross-connection protection.

• Auxiliary Water Systems

An auxiliary water system is a water supply or source that is not under the control or the direct supervision of the water purveyor. An approved backflow prevention assembly must be installed at the service connection of the water purveyor to any premises where there is an auxiliary water supply or system, even though there is no connection between the auxiliary water supply and the public potable water system.

Typical auxiliary water systems include water used in industrialized water systems; water in reservoirs or tanks used for firefighting purposes; irrigation reservoirs; swimming pools; fish ponds; mirror pools; memorial and decorative fountains and cascades; cooling towers; and baptismal, quenching, washing, rinsing, and dipping tanks.

Protection recommended: an air gap separation or a reduced-pressure principle backflow prevention assembly is recommended where there is a health hazard. A double check valve assembly should be used where there is only a pollution hazard.

• Beverage Bottling and Breweries

An approved backflow prevention assembly must be installed on the service connection to any premises where a beverage bottling plant is operated or maintained and water is used for industrial purposes.

The hazards typically found in plants of this type include cross connections between the potable water system and steam-connected facilities; washers, cookers, tanks, lines, and flumes; can and bottle washing machines; lines in which caustic, acids, and detergents are used; reservoirs, cooling towers, and circulating systems; steam generating facilities and lines; industrial fluid systems and lines; water-cooled equipment; and firefighting systems, including storage reservoirs.

Protection recommended: an air gap separation or a reduced-pressure principle backflow prevention assembly is recommended where there is a health hazard. A double check valve assembly should be used where there is only a pollution hazard.

• Canneries, Packing Houses, and Reduction Plants

An approved backflow prevention assembly must be installed at the service connection to any premises where vegetable or animal matter is canned, concentrated, or processed.

The hazards typically found in plants of this type include cross connections between the potable water system and steam-connected facilities; washers, cookers, tanks, lines, and flumes; reservoirs, cooling towers, and circulating systems; steam generating facilities and lines; industrial fluid systems and lines; firefighting systems, including storage reservoirs; water-cooled equipment; and tanks, can and bottle washing machines, and lines.

Protection recommended: an air gap separation or reduced-pressure principle backflow prevention assembly is recommended.

• Chemical Plants—Manufacturing, Processing, or Treatment

An approved backflow prevention assembly shall be installed on the service connection to any premises where there is a facility requiring the use of water in the industrial process of manufacturing, storing, compounding, or processing chemicals. This will also include facilities where chemicals are used as additives to the water supply or in processing products. Cross connections may be numerous because of the intricate piping. The severity of these cross connections varies with the toxicity of the chemical used.

The hazards typically found in plants of this type include cross connections between the potable water system and formulating tanks and vats, decanter units, extractor/precipitators, and other processing units; reservoirs, cooling towers, and circulating systems; steam generating facilities and lines; firefighting systems, including storage reservoirs; water-cooled equipment; hydraulically operated equipment; equipment under hydraulic tests; pressure cookers, autoclaves, and retorts; and washers, cookers, tanks, flumes, and other equipment used for storing, washing, cleaning, blanching, cooking, flushing, or for the transmission of food, fertilizers, or wastes.

Protection recommended: an air gap separation or a reduced-pressure principle backflow prevention assembly is recommended where there is a health hazard.

• Dairies and Cold Storage Plants

An approved backflow prevention assembly shall be installed on the service connection to any premises on which a dairy, creamery, ice cream, cold storage, or ice manufacturing plant is operated or maintained, provided such a plant has on the premises an industrial fluid system, wastewater handling facilities, or other similar source of contamination that, if cross connected, would create a hazard to the public system.

The hazards typically found in these types of plants include cross connections between the potable water system and reservoirs, cooling towers, and circulation systems; steam generating facilities and lines; water-cooled equipment and tanks; can and bottle washing machines; and lines in which caustics, acids, detergents, and other compounds are circulated for cleaning, sterilizing, and flushing.

Protection recommended: an air gap separation or a reduced-pressure principle backflow prevention assembly is recommended where there is a health hazard. A double check valve assembly should be used where there is only a pollution hazard.

• Film Laboratories

An approved backflow prevention assembly must be installed on each service connection to any premises where a film laboratory, processing, or manufacturing plant is operated or maintained. This does not include darkroom facilities.

The hazards typically found in a plant of this type include cross connections between the potable water system and tanks, automatic film processing machines, and water-cooled equipment that may be connected to a sewer, such as compressors, heat exchangers, and air conditioning equipment.

Protection recommended: an air gap separation or a reduced-pressure principle backflow prevention assembly is recommended.

• Hospitals, Medical Buildings, Sanitariums, Morgues, Mortuaries, Autopsy Facilities, and Clinics

An approved backflow prevention assembly must be installed on the service connection to any hospital, medical buildings, and clinics. The hazards typically found in this type of facility include cross connections between the potable water system and contaminated or sewer-connected equipment; water-cooled equipment that may be sewer-connected; reservoirs, cooling towers, and circulating systems; and steam generating facilities and lines.

Protection recommended: an air gap separation or a reduced-pressure principle backflow assembly must be installed on the service connection to any hospital, mortuary, morgue, or autopsy facility, or to any multistoried medical building or clinic.

• Laundries and Dye Works (Commercial Laundries)

An approved backflow prevention assembly must be installed on each service connection to any premises where a laundry or dyeing plant is operated or maintained.

The hazards typically found in plants of this type include cross connections between the potable water system and laundry machines having under rim or bottom outlets; dye vats in which toxic chemicals and dyes are used; water storage tanks equipped with pumps and recirculating systems; shrinking, bluing, and dyeing machines with direct connections to circulating systems; retention and mixing tanks; wastewater pumps for priming, cleaning, flushing, or unclogging purposes; water-operated wastewater sump ejectors for operational purposes; sewer lines for the purpose of disposing of filter or softener backwash water from cooling systems; reservoirs, cooling towers, and circulating systems; and steam generating facilities and lines.

Protection recommended: an air gap separation or a reduced-pressure principle backflow prevention assembly is recommended.

• Marine Facilities and Dockside Watering Points

The actual or potential hazard to the utility's water system created by any marine facility or dockside watering point must be individually evaluated. The basic risk to a domestic water system is the possibility that contaminated water can be pumped into the domestic water system by the fire pumps or other pumps aboard a ship. The additional risk of dockside water facilities located on fresh water or diluted salt water is that if backflow occurs, it can be more easily digested because of the lack of salty taste.

Protection recommended: minimum system protection for marine installations may be accomplished in one of the following ways: (1) water connections directly to vessels for any purpose must have a reduced-pressure backflow prevention assembly installed at the pier hydrants; (2) where water is delivered to marine facilities for fire protection only, and no auxiliary water supply is present, all service connections should be protected by a reduced-pressure principle backflow prevention assembly; (3) water delivered to a marine repair facility should have a reduced-pressure principle backflow prevention assembly; (4) water delivered to small boat moorages that maintain hose bibbs on a dock or float should have a reduced-pressure principle backflow prevention assembly installed at the user connection and a hose connection vacuum breaker on all hose bibbs; and (5) water for fire protection aboard ship, connected to dockside fire hydrants, must not be taken aboard from fire hydrants unless the hydrants are on a fire system separated from the domestic system by an approved reduced-pressure principle backflow prevention assembly.

• Metal Manufacturing, Cleaning, Processing, and Fabricating Plants

An approved backflow prevention assembly must be installed on the service connection to any premises where metals are manufactured, cleaned, processed, or fabricated and the process involves used water and/or industrial fluids. This type of facility may be operated or maintained either as a separate function or other facility, such as an aircraft or automotive manufacturing plant.

The hazards typically found in a plant of this type include cross connections between the potable water and reservoirs, cooling towers, and circulating systems; steam generating facilities and lines; plating facilities involving the use of highly toxic chemicals; industrial fluid systems; tanks, vats, or other vessels; water-cooled equipment; tanks, can and bottle washing machines, and lines; hydraulically operated equipment; and equipment under hydraulic tests.

Protection recommended: an air gap separation or a reduced-pressure principle backflow prevention assembly is recommended where there is a health hazard. A double check valve assembly should be used where there is only a pollution hazard.

• Multistoried Buildings

Multistoried buildings may be broadly grouped into the following three categories in terms of their internal potable water systems:

1. Using only the service pressure to distribute the potable water throughout the structure, and with no internal potable water reservoir,

2. Using a booster pump to provide potable water directly to the upper floors, and

3. Using a booster pump to fill a covered roof reservoir from which there is a down-feed system for the upper floors.

Considerable care must be exercised to prevent the use of the suction-side line to these pumps from also being used as the takeoff for domestic, sanitary, laboratory, or industrial uses on the lower floors. Pollutants or contaminants from equipment supplied by takeoffs from the suction-side line may be easily pumped throughout the upper floors. In each of these systems it is probable that there is one or more takeoffs for industrial water within the building. Any loss of distribution main pressure will cause backflow from these buildings' systems unless approved backflow prevention assemblies are properly installed.

Protection recommended: an air gap separation or a reduced-pressure principle backflow prevention assembly where there is a health hazard; a reduced-pressure principle backflow prevention assembly when takeoffs for lower floor sanitary facilities are connected to the suction side of booster pump(s); and a double check valve assembly where there is a non-health hazard. The suction pressure on booster pumps should be limited to prevent drawing water from adjacent unprotected premises.

• Oil and Gas Production, Storage, or Transmission Properties

An approved backflow prevention assembly shall be installed at the service connection to any premises where animal, vegetable, or mineral oils and gases are produced, developed, processed, blended, stored, refined, or transmitted in a pipeline, or where oil or gas tanks are maintained. An approved backflow prevention assembly must be installed at the service connection where an oil well is being drilled, developed, operated, or maintained; or where an oxygen, acetylene, petroleum, or other manufactured gas production or bottling plant is operated or maintained.

The hazards typically found in plants of this type include cross connections between the potable water system and steam boiler lines; mud pumps and mud tanks; oil well casings; dehydration tanks and outlet lines from storage and dehydration tanks; oil and gas tanks; gas and oil lines; reservoirs, cooling towers, and circulating systems; steam generating facilities; industrial fluid systems; firefighting systems, including storage reservoirs; water-cooled equipment; hydraulically operated equipment and equipment under hydraulic tests.

Protection recommended: an air gap separation or a reduced-pressure principle backflow prevention assembly is recommended.

• Paper and Paper Product Plants

An approved backflow prevention assembly must be installed on the service connection to any premises where a paper or paper products plant (wet process) is operated or maintained.

The hazards typically found in a plant of this type include cross connections between the potable water system and pulp, bleaching, dyeing, and processing facilities that may be contaminated with toxic chemicals; reservoirs, cooling towers, and circulating systems; steam generating facilities and lines; industrial fluid systems and lines; water-cooled equipment; and firefighting systems, including storage reservoirs.

Protection recommended: an air gap separation or a reduced-pressure principle backflow prevention assembly is recommended.

• Plants or Facilities Handling Radioactive Material or Substances

An approved backflow prevention assembly must be installed at the service connection to any premises where radioactive materials or substances are processed in a laboratory or plant, or where they may be handled in such a manner as to create a potential hazard to the water system, or where there is a reactor plant.

Protection recommended: an air gap separation or a reduced-pressure principle backflow prevention assembly is recommended.

• Restricted, Classified, or Other Closed Facilities

An approved backflow prevention assembly must be installed on the service connection to any facility that is not readily accessible for inspection by the water purveyor because of military secrecy requirements or other prohibitions or restrictions.

Protection recommended: an air gap separation or a reduced-pressure principle backflow prevention assembly is recommended.

• Solar Domestic Hot Water Systems

An approved backflow prevention assembly must be installed on the service connection to any premises where there is a solar domestic hot water system.

The hazards typically found in a solar domestic system include cross connections between the potable water system and heat exchangers, tanks, and circulating pumps. Contamination can occur when the piping or tank walls of the heat exchanger between the potable hot water and the transfer medium begin to leak.

Protection recommended: the recommended protection depends on whether there is a possible health hazard or a non-health hazard. In either case a reduced-pressure principle backflow prevention assembly will always provide safe protection.

• Water Hauling Equipment

An approved backflow prevention assembly must be installed on any portable spraying or cleaning units that have the capability of connection to any potable water supply that does not contain a built-in approved air gap.

The hazards typically found in water hauling equipment include cross connections between the potable water system and tanks contaminated with toxic chemical compounds used in spraying fertilizers, herbicides, and pesticides; water hauling tanker trucks used in dust control; and other tanks on cleaning equipment.

Protection recommended: an air gap separation or a reduced-pressure principle backflow prevention assembly is recommended.

5.253   Maintenance and Testing Procedures

Backflow prevention programs must require the owners of buildings and facilities with backflow prevention devices to maintain the devices within their buildings and facilities in good working condition. Also, qualified persons must periodically test the backflow preventers for satisfactory performance.

5.254   Acknowledgment

Material in this section was obtained from *RECOMMENDED PRACTICE FOR BACKFLOW PREVENTION AND CROSS-CONNECTION CONTROL* (M14), available from American Water Works Association (AWWA), Bookstore, 6666 West Quincy Avenue, Denver, CO 80235. Order No. 30014. ISBN 1-58321-288-4. Price to members, $69.00; nonmembers, $99.00; price includes cost of shipping and handling.

5.3   WELL PUMPS AND SERVICE GUIDELINES

5.30   Purpose of Well Pumps

5.300   Well Pumps

Once a well is completed and water is available from an aquifer, some type of pump must be installed to lift the water from the well and deliver it to the point of use. The intent of this section is to discuss the general characteristics of well pumps operators are likely to encounter.

Well pumps are generally classified into two basic groups:

1. *POSITIVE DISPLACEMENT* pumps which deliver the same volume or flow of water against any *HEAD*[7] within their operating capacity. Typical types are piston (reciprocating) pumps, and screw or squeeze displacement (diaphragm) pumps; and

2. *VARIABLE DISPLACEMENT* pumps which deliver water with the volume or flow varying inversely with the head (the *GREATER* the head, the *LESS* the volume or flow) against which they are operating. The major types are centrifugal, jet, and air-lift pumps.

Either of these types of pumps can be used for pumping water from a well. However, centrifugal pumps are by far the most commonly used pump in the waterworks field because of their capability to deliver water in large quantities, against high as well as low heads, and with high efficiencies.

5.301   Shallow Well Pump

A pump installed above a well is often called a *SHALLOW WELL PUMP*; this pump takes water from the well by *SUCTION LIFT*.[8] Such a pump can be used for either a deep well or a shallow well providing the pumping level is within the suction lift capability of the pump (maximum of 20-feet (6-m) lift).

5.302   Deep Well Pump

A pump installed in the well with the *PUMP BOWL*[9] inlet submerged below the pumping level in the well is generally referred to as a *DEEP WELL PUMP*. This type of pump may be used for any well, regardless of depth, where the pumping level is below the limit of suction lift.

5.31   Types of Pumps

5.310   Centrifugal Pumps

A centrifugal pump raises the water by a centrifugal force which is created by a wheel, referred to as an *IMPELLER*, revolving inside a tight *CASING*. In operation, the water enters the pump at the center of the impeller, called the *EYE*. The impeller throws the water outward toward the inside wall of the casing by the centrifugal force resulting from the revolution of the impeller. The water passes through the channel or diffuser vanes between the rim of the impeller and the casing, and emerges at the discharge under pressure. Centrifugal pumps are used almost exclusively in the waterworks field. Advantages of centrifugal pumps include: (1) relatively small space needed for any given capacity, (2) rotary rather than reciprocating motion, (3) adaptability to high-speed driving mechanisms such as electric motors and gas engines, (4) low initial cost, (5) simple mechanism, (6) simple operation and repair, and (7) safety against damage from high pressure because of limited maximum pressure that can be developed. Centrifugal pumps are generally classed as *VOLUTE* or *TURBINE* pumps.

5.311   Volute-Type Pumps

This type of centrifugal pump has no diffusion vanes (see Figure 5.9). The impeller is housed in a spiral-shaped case in which the velocity of the water is reduced upon leaving the impeller, with a resultant increase in pressure. Ordinarily, the volute-type pump is of single-stage design and used in the water utility field for large-capacity, low-head application, and for low- to mid-range booster pump operations.

5.312   Turbine-Type Pumps

This type of centrifugal pump is the one most commonly used for well pump operations (see Figure 5.10). In the turbine-type pump, the impeller is surrounded by diffuser vanes which provide gradually enlarging passages in which the velocity of the water leaving the impeller is gradually reduced, thus transforming velocity head to pressure head.

Use of multi-stage pumps is standard practice in well pumping operations. The stages are bolted together to form a pump

---

[7] *Head.   The vertical distance (in feet) equal to the pressure (in psi) at a specific point. The pressure head is equal to the pressure in psi times 2.31 ft/psi.*

[8] *Suction Lift.   The NEGATIVE pressure [in feet (meters) of water or inches (centimeters) of mercury vacuum] on the suction side of a pump. The pressure can be measured from the centerline of the pump DOWN TO (lift) the elevation of the hydraulic grade line on the suction side of the pump.*

[9] *Pump Bowl.   The submerged pumping unit in a well, including the shaft, impellers and housing.*

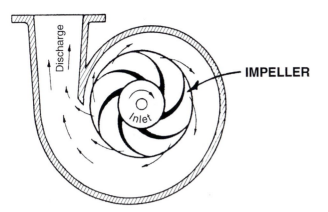

Volute-type centrifugal pump has no diffuser vanes or guides.

Fig. 5.9 Volute-type pump
(Source: *GROUNDWATER AND WELLS*,
permission of Johnson Division, UOP, St. Paul, Minn.)

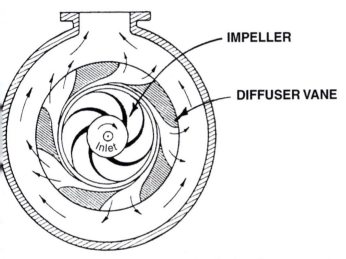

In turbine-type pump, water leaving the impeller moves out through the curved passages between diffuser vanes.

Fig. 5.10 Turbine-type pump
(Source: *GROUNDWATER AND WELLS*,
permission of Johnson Division, UOP, St. Paul, Minn.)

bowl assembly and it is not uncommon to assemble a pump bowl assembly with 10 or more stages. The function of each stage is to add pressure head capacity; the volume capacity and efficiency are almost identical for each stage. As an example, in the case of a 10-stage pump rated at 500 gallons per minute (32 liters/sec) at 250 feet (75 m) of required head, utilizing 40 *BRAKE HORSEPOWER*[10] (30 kW), the first stage would pump 500 gallons per minute (32 liters/sec) at 25 feet (7.5 m) of head, the next stage would not increase the GPM but would add 25 feet (7.5 m) more of head; each of the remaining eight stages would also add 25 feet (7.5 m) of head making the total 250 feet (75 m) of head. The capacity would remain at 500 GPM (32 L/sec). However, the brake horsepower for each stage is also additive (as is head). Therefore, if each stage requires 4 BHP (3 kilowatts), then the total for the 10 stages would amount to 40 BHP (30 kilowatts).

Well pumps for water utility operation are generally of the turbine design and often are referred to as variable-displacement deep well centrifugal pumps or more simply, *DEEP WELL TURBINE* pumps.

5.313 Deep Well Turbine Pumps

There are two classifications of deep well turbine pumps, depending upon the location of the prime mover (electric motor or engine).

1. *STANDARD DEEP WELL TURBINE* pumps are driven through a rotating shaft (lineshaft) connected to an electric motor or engine mounted on top of the well (see Figure 5.11). This type of pump requires lubrication of the lineshaft connecting the motor and the pump. Manufacturers have incorporated both *OIL LUBRICATION* and *WATER LUBRICATION* into this design.

   a. In *WATER LUBRICATED* models, the lineshaft is supported in the center of the pump column pipe by means of stainless-steel lineshaft sleeves equipped with neoprene bearings which are lubricated by the water as it flows upward in the column pipe (see Figure 5.12).

      This type of pump is most commonly used for large capacity wells and is designed specifically for each well and for its intended function.

      Pumping capacities generally range from 200 to 2,000 gallons per minute (12.6 to 126 liters per second).

   b. *OIL LUBRICATED* models have a watertight oil tube surrounding the lineshaft and oil is fed from the surface (see Figure 5.13).

   Although both oil and water lubricated pumps are used in water utility operation, oil lubricated pumps are most often used.

2. *SUBMERSIBLE DEEP WELL TURBINE* pumps use a pumping bowl assembly similar to the standard deep well turbine except that the motor is mounted directly beneath the bowl assembly. This eliminates the need for the lineshaft and oil tube (see Figure 5.14). Unit efficiency approaches that of a lineshaft turbine pump.

   Submersible pumps are available in a wide range of capacities from 5 to 2,000 gallons per minute (0.3 to 126 liters/sec), and are used by individual well owners as well as by small and large water system operators.

[10] *Brake Horsepower. (1) The horsepower required at the top or end of a pump shaft (input to a pump). (2) The energy provided by a motor or other power source.*

Submersible pumps are ideally suited to small water system operation where source capacities range from 25 to 1,000 gallons per minute (1.5 to 63 liters/sec). Maintenance is minimal, the noise level is very low, and they are suited to installations that have limited building areas.

5.32 Column Pipe

Operators should be aware of the functions of the pump column pipe in a deep well turbine pumping installation. The column pipe is an integral part of the pump assembly and serves three basic purposes: (1) the column pipe connects to the bottom of the surface discharge head, extends down into the well and connects to the top of the well pump (bowl unit) thereby supporting the pump in the well, (2) the column pipe delivers water under pressure from the well pump to the surface, and (3) keeps the lineshaft and shaft enclosing (oil) tube assembly in straight alignment. Column pipe assemblies for both water and oil lubricated pumps are shown in Figures 5.15 and 5.16.

5.33 Right-Angle Gear Drives (Figures 5.17 and 5.18)

Right-angle gear drives for water utility operations have two distinct applications and provide an economical, efficient, and positive power transmission from a horizontal prime mover (electric motor or engine) to a vertical shaft.

In one application, the right-angle gear drive replaces the electric motor on top of the well and is used on either a full-time or part-time basis.

In a second application, the right-angle gear drive is used with the electric motor. The gear drive is mounted on top of the well discharge head and the electric motor is connected to the right-angle gear drive. An extra long headshaft (an extension of the lineshaft) connects both prime movers to the bowl unit in the well. In most applications, the electric motor is the lead prime mover and the right-angle gear drive unit is used for standby or emergency purposes only. The unit is usually set up for automatic operation.

In either application, the prime mover could be in the form of a gasoline, natural gas, diesel, or propane-powered engine connected to the gear head by means of a flexible drive shaft.

5.34 Service Guidelines

DEEP WELL TURBINE, OIL LUBRICATED pumps are usually equipped with an automatic electric oiler system that is activated by means of an electric solenoid valve when the well pump starts. An adjusting needle and sight glass are part of this assembly. The needle valve is adjusted to feed approximately five drops per minute plus one drop of oil per minute for each 20 feet (6 m) of column during the first week of operation. The drip rate may thereafter be reduced to one drop per minute for each 40 feet (12 m) of column. Under no circumstances should the drip rate be less than five drops per minute, regardless of the length of column.

A good grade of turbine oil (mineral base) SAE 10 is used as the lubricant. Automotive or diesel engine lubricating oils cannot be used as a lineshaft lubricant. The oils listed in Table 5.1 (on page 146) are recommended for lubricating the lineshaft bearings. This list does not include all acceptable oils.

DEEP WELL TURBINE, WATER LUBRICATED pumps are self-lubricating and normally require little or no lineshaft maintenance. In a few cases where the static water level is over 100 feet (30 m) and the pump is operated on an intermittent basis, a special small-diameter, pressurized water line may be used to keep the bearings above the water level lubricated.

Fig. 5.11 Standard deep well turbine pump
(Permission of Jacuzzi Brothers, Inc.)

Water Lubricated

Oil Lubricated

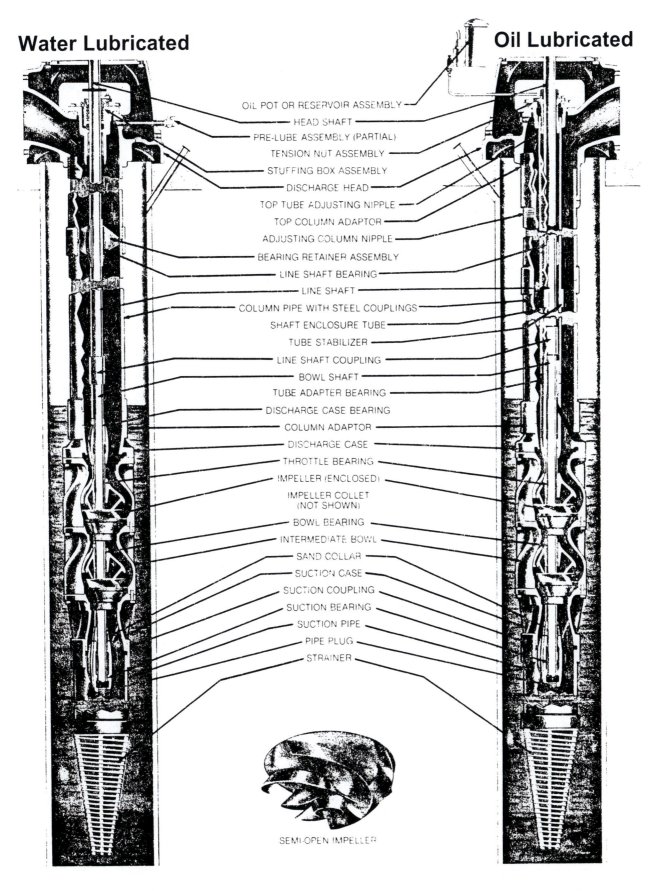

OIL POT OR RESERVOIR ASSEMBLY
HEAD SHAFT
PRE-LUBE ASSEMBLY (PARTIAL)
TENSION NUT ASSEMBLY
STUFFING BOX ASSEMBLY
DISCHARGE HEAD
TOP TUBE ADJUSTING NIPPLE
TOP COLUMN ADAPTOR
ADJUSTING COLUMN NIPPLE
BEARING RETAINER ASSEMBLY
LINE SHAFT BEARING
LINE SHAFT
COLUMN PIPE WITH STEEL COUPLINGS
SHAFT ENCLOSURE TUBE
TUBE STABILIZER
LINE SHAFT COUPLING
BOWL SHAFT
TUBE ADAPTER BEARING
DISCHARGE CASE BEARING
COLUMN ADAPTOR
DISCHARGE CASE
THROTTLE BEARING
IMPELLER (ENCLOSED)
IMPELLER COLLET
(NOT SHOWN)
BOWL BEARING
INTERMEDIATE BOWL
SAND COLLAR
SUCTION CASE
SUCTION COUPLING
SUCTION BEARING
SUCTION PIPE
PIPE PLUG
STRAINER

SEMI-OPEN IMPELLER

Fig. 5.12   Water lubricated pump

Fig. 5.13   Oil lubricated pump

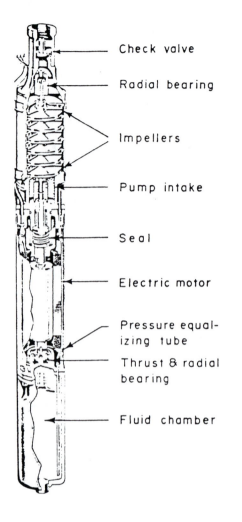

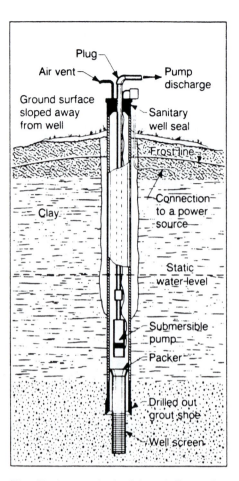

This well has been vented and sealed properly. The groundwater surface around the top of the casing has been graded to slope away in all directions. (After U.S. Environmental Protection Agency, 1973)

Fig. 5.14   Submersible pump
(Source: GROUNDWATER AND WELLS,
Johnson Division, UOP, Inc., St. Paul, Minn.)

TABLE 5.1   OILS RECOMMENDED FOR LUBRICATING THE LINESHAFT BEARINGS [a]

OIL	SOURCE
Turbine Oil, Light	Atlantic Refining
Teresso, #43	ESSO Standard
Gulfcrest, #44	Gulf
Turbo, #27	Shell
DTE, #797	Socony Mobil
Chevron OC Turbine, #9	Standard Oil of California
Nonpareil, Medium L5803	Standard Oil of Indiana
Sunvise, #916	Sun Oil
Regal, R & O	The Texas Company
Pacemaker, #1	Cities Service

[a]   JOHNSTON VERTICAL TURBINE PUMPS, INSTALLATION, OPERATION AND MAINTENANCE MANUAL, Glendora, CA.

5.35   Motors

Vertical, hollow-shaft motors for deep well turbine pumps (motor on top of well) require some degree of routine mainte-nance. The motor bearings at the top and bottom of the motor are enclosed within a weatherproof oil bath container. The oil in this container should be changed annually. Most motors are equipped with a lubrication instruction plate attached to the motor that specifies the proper type and viscosity of oil required for various operating temperatures.

On small motors, the bearings are generally grease lubricated and require weekly attention during the heavy pumping season. Do not use excess grease because the bearings will overheat. The motor manufacturer's instruction manual should specify the type of grease recommended for various applications.

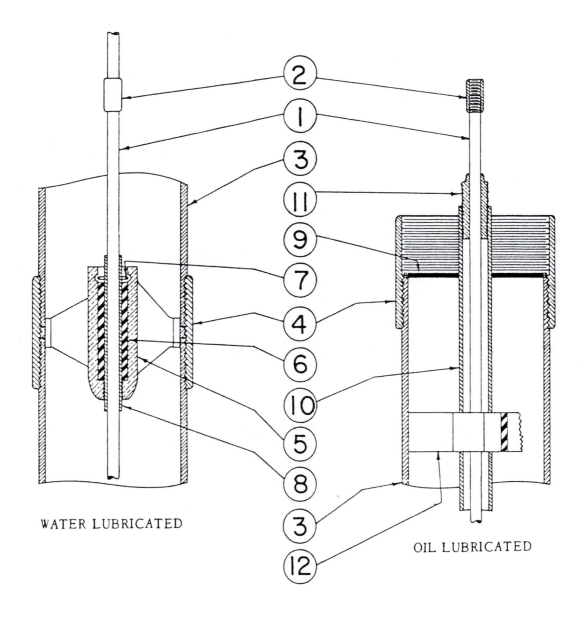

WATER LUBRICATED

OIL LUBRICATED

1 LINESHAFT	7 SNAP RING
2 SHAFT COUPLING	8 SHAFT SLEEVE
3 COLUMN PIPE	9 COLUMN PIPE SPACER RING (OPTIONAL)
4 COLUMN PIPE COUPLING	10 OIL TUBE
5 BEARING CAGE	11 LINESHAFT BEARING
6 RUBBER SHAFT BEARING	12 TUBE STABILIZER

Fig. 5.15   Column pipe assembly for
water lubricated pumps

Fig. 5.16   Column pipe assembly for
oil lubricated pumps

(Permission of Peabody Floway, Inc., Fresno, CA)

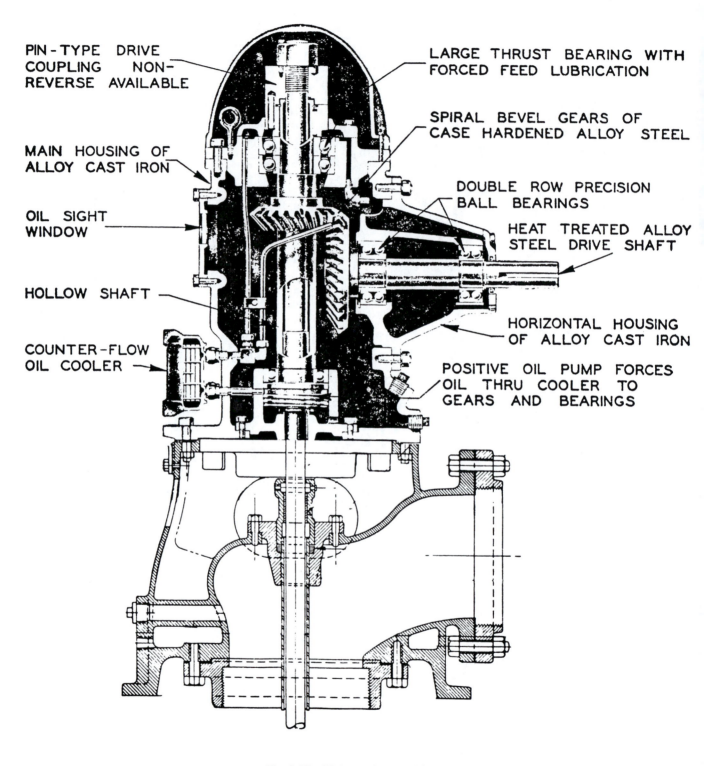

PIN-TYPE DRIVE COUPLING NON-REVERSE AVAILABLE

MAIN HOUSING OF ALLOY CAST IRON

OIL SIGHT WINDOW

HOLLOW SHAFT

COUNTER-FLOW OIL COOLER

LARGE THRUST BEARING WITH FORCED FEED LUBRICATION

SPIRAL BEVEL GEARS OF CASE HARDENED ALLOY STEEL

DOUBLE ROW PRECISION BALL BEARINGS

HEAT TREATED ALLOY STEEL DRIVE SHAFT

HORIZONTAL HOUSING OF ALLOY CAST IRON

POSITIVE OIL PUMP FORCES OIL THRU COOLER TO GEARS AND BEARINGS

Fig. 5.17   Right-angle gear drive

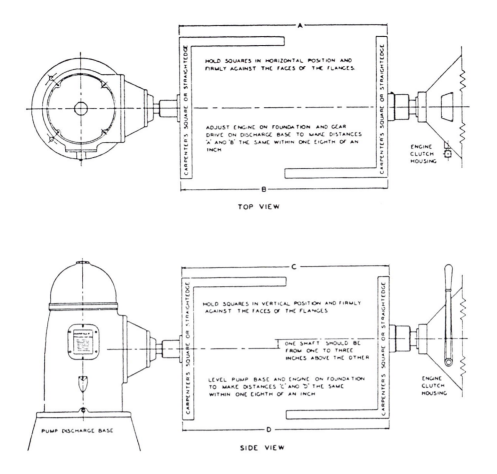

Fig. 5.18   Alignment of right-angle gear drive
(Source: Amarillo Right Angle Pump Drive, Amarillo, Texas)

5.4   ELECTRICAL SUPPLY AND CONTROLS

5.40   Purpose of Electrical Supply and Controls

Control, reduced to its basic definition, is the influence over the action of a device resulting from the measurement and decision of another device or control.

Many options are available for electrical and electronic control of well production. These range from a simple manual start/stop system to automated facilities complete with recorded drawdown and water quality analysis. In this section, we will limit our discussion to the most common and useful types of controls and automation.

5.41   Electrical Supply

5.410   Electricity

Electricity is normally supplied as an alternating current (A.C.) at 120, 240, or 480 volts. The voltage is considered the driving force and quite often the amount of voltage available depends on the location of the well installation and the ability of the utility company to provide power. The voltage required is related to the size of the pump; larger motors require higher voltages. High horsepower (HP) motors may require large surges of power at start-up.

5.411   Motor Starters

Motor starters are basically controls for starting and stopping motors used with large pumps. Upon receiving a signal to start, current is fed into the motor causing the pump to run. Starters can be direct, across-the-line types or what is referred to as step starters. In step starters power to the motor is increased slowly (in steps) allowing the pump to come up to speed gradually. This prevents pump damage and disturbances along electrical lines. A typical across-the-line starter arrangement for a three-phase pump is shown in Figure 5.19.

5.412   Auxiliary Power

Auxiliary power is an important consideration to many water districts. If a water supply system depends on wells and hy-

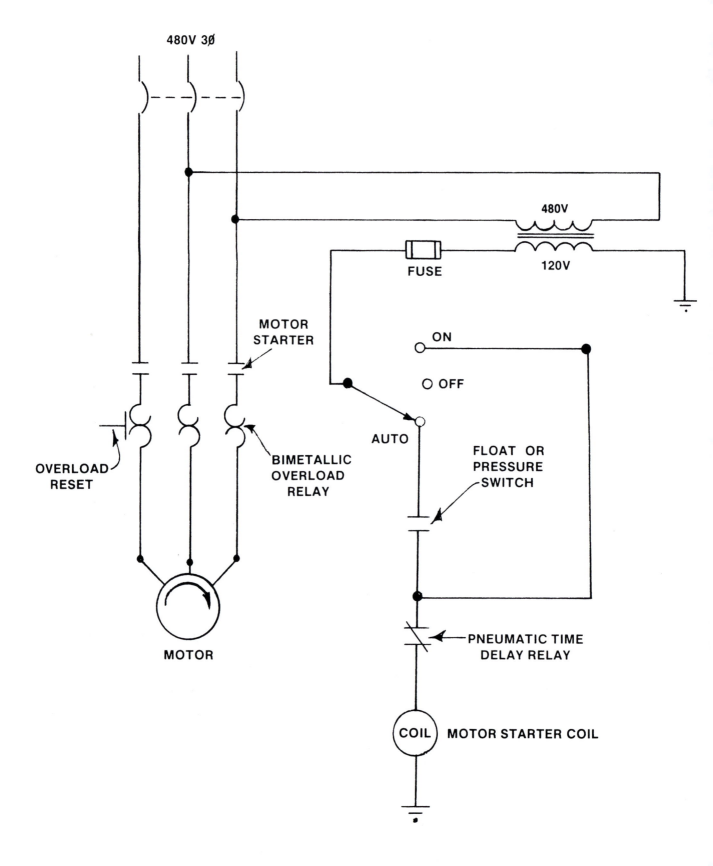

480V 3∅

480V

120V

FUSE

MOTOR
STARTER

ON

○ OFF

AUTO

FLOAT OR
PRESSURE
SWITCH

OVERLOAD
RESET

BIMETALLIC
OVERLOAD
RELAY

MOTOR

PNEUMATIC TIME
DELAY RELAY

COIL   MOTOR STARTER COIL

Fig. 5.19   Schematic of typical 3-phase pump control starter circuit

dropneumatic pressure tanks for both supply and storage, a power outage could create very severe water shortages. Auxiliary power is not difficult to provide at well sites, but it is expensive. These systems can be installed to start and stop automatically and are quite dependable. A typical gasoline-driven engine generator is shown in Figure 5.20. There are numerous manufacturers of diesel or gasoline-powered generators and they can be obtained in almost any size.

The manufacturers of auxiliary generators also produce automated control packages, but the most commonly used control device is a time delay starter. If a power failure occurs, a relay will sense the loss of power and drop out. A timer then measures a definite time delay that power is off and, after a predetermined period, the auxiliary engine is activated. Shutdown usually occurs in the same manner.

Although we are not going to describe auxiliary power systems in detail here, they should be an important consideration for any water district. These systems can be a real asset under very adverse conditions.

5.42   Pump Controls

5.420   Types of Controls

There are three major types of pump controls, (1) ON/OFF, (2) proportional, and (3) derivative (sometimes called "reset" or "rate"). Electrical controls fall mostly into the first category. ON/OFF, the simplest form, consists of a measured variable such as the level in a pond, or the pressure in a tank, which upon falling to some preset level, closes a switch contact. This engages a motor which drives a pump to increase the level until it reaches a preset cutoff point. For most applications, the use of the simple ON/OFF set of controls is quite acceptable, and it has the advantages of being low in cost, having few parts, and performing reliably.

As drinking water regulations become more stringent, some form of proportional control will be needed. Proportional control provides more corrective effort as the measured variable gets farther from the *SET POINT.*[11] In the case of the reservoir level, this might mean that as the level gets low, and then lower, several additional pumps may be called upon to pump into it. As the level approaches the desired level, the extra pumps are turned off, and eventually, as it arrives at the set point, all pumps stop. Figure 5.21 shows the typical start/stop arrangement for both ON/OFF and proportional controls.

The derivative or rate controls are used to maintain water levels or pressures within very close tolerances. This type of control is normally coupled with variable-speed motor drives. As the need arises, the controller can cause the pump to increase or decrease its speed to keep water levels or pressures within closely confined limits. Unless the system is highly sophisticated or is restricted by critical operating guidelines, rate controls are seldom used.

5.421   Control Systems

Control systems vary but practically all pumping facilities have some kind of automatic start/stop arrangement. Various pump start/stop sequences are associated with one or more of the following: pressure, water level, time sequences, heat protection, backspin protection, flow, and water quality. The control system is quite often coupled with recordings of flow, bearing temperatures, pressure, water levels, and alarms. The two most common pump control elements are pressure and water level.

5.422   Pressure

Pressure is a necessary element of a water system and can easily be monitored at various locations in the system. The most common such pressure regulation system is that associated with hydropneumatic tanks. As a pressure reduction is sensed, a signal is sent to the pumps to start. The subsequent pump start-up pushes water into the system which results in an increase in pressure. Once the desired pressure is reached and sustained for a predetermined length of time, a signal is sent to the pump ordering a shutdown. High or low pressure cutoffs (signals to shut off the pumps if pressure is too high or too low) are common safety features built into the system. These are often coupled with alarms which alert the operator to unusual conditions at the pump. High pressure might indicate valve failure or blockage in the discharge lines. Low pressure would be an indicator of excessive water use or a broken water line. In either case, the automatic pressure controls provide a mechanism for shutting down the pumps until the problem is located and corrected.

5.423   Water Level

The most frequently used pump control system is the water level controller in reservoirs and storage tanks. A sensor measures the water level and signals the pump to start or stop. As the water level is lowered in the tank, the pump is instructed to start. Once the tank has filled, the pump will be ordered to stop. A typical pump control system from a reservoir is shown in Figure 5.22. However, well pump starts/stops can also be controlled by the water level in a well.

In the case of wells, water level operation would only be implemented in the case of low-yield wells that had to be protected from overdraft. Damage to the pumps can occur if the water level is allowed to be drawn below the pump bowls. If low water level appears to be a real problem associated with a particular well, then some provision for low level shutdown must be made.

Other items that are often monitored or controlled automatically at pump installations are excessive power demand by the pump, bearing heat on the motor and/or pump, turbidity measurements, and flow. Backspin protection[12] is provided for with time delays built into the automatic controls. High head or high volume pumps are sometimes shut down through the use of automatic pump control valves. The total number and combination of controls of pumps is extremely large but automation can provide a high measure of reliability along with lower cost for operation and maintenance.

5.43   Equipment

Control equipment ranges from direct, connected units from tanks to pumps joined by signal wires, to units separated by several miles from the pumps which transmit signals through telephone lines or by radio. Definitions of equipment commonly used in control systems are listed in Section 5.44. Figure 5.23 shows a typical pump control operation.

---

[11] *Set Point.   The position at which the control or controller is set. This is the same as the desired value of the process variable. For example, a thermostat is set to maintain a desired temperature.*

[12] *If pump and motor are restarted while backspinning (water driving pump in reverse), the shaft may break causing expensive repairs. Provision must be made to prevent this from occurring.*

Fig. 5.20   Gasoline-powered auxiliary power generator
(Photo courtesy of Onan Corporation, Minneapolis, Minnesota)

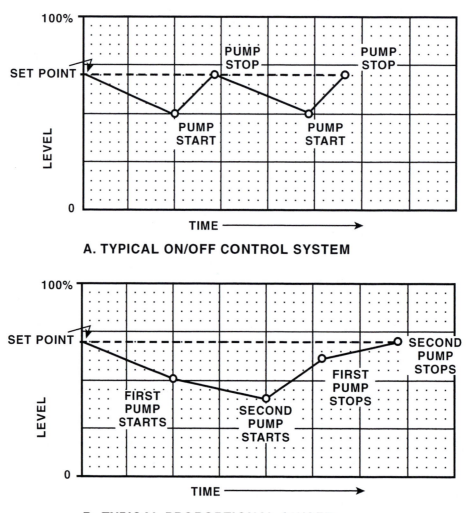

A. TYPICAL ON/OFF CONTROL SYSTEM

B. TYPICAL PROPORTIONAL ON/OFF
CONTROL SYSTEM

Fig. 5.21   Typical pump start/stop control systems

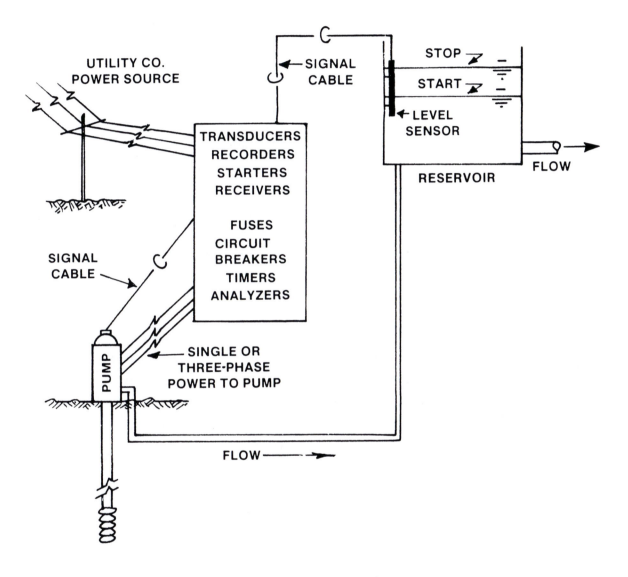

Fig. 5.22   Typical pump control system

APPLICATION EXAMPLE

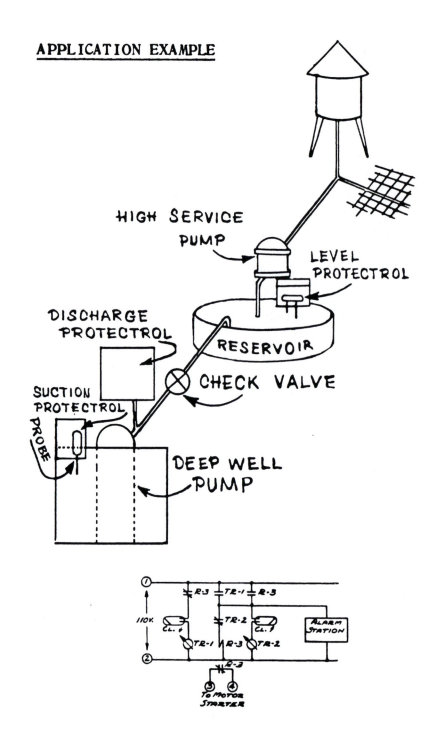

Two pressure elements are manifolded and tapped directly into the suction main. If pressure falls to a danger point, the "cutout" element will close its switch, completing the circuit to the timer (TR-1), which begins to time out. If pressure remains low long enough for timer to time out, its contact will close, energizing the relay (R-3). A normally closed relay contact then opens, stopping the pump. When the pressure rises, the "restore" switch closes, energizing the second timer (TR-2). After it has timed out, its normally closed contact will open, de-energizing the relay, allowing the pump to restart if required by primary control.

Fig. 5.23　Typical pump control operation

(Permission of Automatic Control Company)

5.44 Common Electrical Control Definitions

1. *ALARM CONTACT.* A switch that operates when some preset low, high or abnormal condition exists.

2. *ANALYZER.* A device which conducts periodic or continuous measurement of some factor such as chlorine, fluoride or turbidity. Analyzers operate by any of several methods including photocells, conductivity or complex instrumentation. A pH meter is a type of analyzer.

3. *CONTACTOR.* An electric switch, usually magnetically operated.

4. *CONTROLLER.* A device which controls the starting, stopping, or operation of a piece of equipment.

5. *HEAT SENSOR.* A device that opens and closes a switch in response to changes in the temperature. This device might be a metal contact, or a thermocouple which generates a minute electric current proportional to the difference in heat, or a variable resistor whose value changes in response to changes in temperature. Also called a temperature sensor.

6. *INTERLOCK.* An electric switch, usually magnetically operated. Used to interrupt all (local) power to a panel or device when the door is opened or the circuit is exposed to service.

7. *LEVEL CONTROL.* A float device (or pressure switch) which senses changes in a measured variable and opens or closes a switch in response to that change. In its simplest form, this control might be a floating ball connected mechanically to a switch or valve such as is used to stop water flow into a toilet when the tank is full.

8. *MEASURED VARIABLE.* A characteristic or component part that is sensed and quantified (reduced to a reading of some kind) by a primary element or sensor.

9. *PRESSURE CONTROL.* A switch which operates on changes in pressure. Usually this is a diaphragm pressing against a spring. When the force on the diaphragm overcomes the spring pressure, the switch is actuated (activated).

10. *PRIMARY ELEMENT.* A device that measures (senses) a physical condition or variable of interest. Floats and thermocouples are examples of primary elements. Also called a sensor.

11. *RECEIVER.* A device which indicates the result of a measurement. Most receivers in the water utility field use either a fixed scale and movable indicator (pointer) such as a pressure gage or a movable scale and movable indicator like those used on a circular flow-recording chart. Also called an indicator.

12. *RECORDER.* A device that creates a permanent record, on a paper chart or magnetic tape, of the changes in a measured variable.

13. *SENSOR.* A device that measures (senses) a physical condition or variable of interest. Floats and thermocouples are examples of sensors. Also called a primary element.

14. *SET POINT.* The position at which the control or controller is set. This is the same as the desired value of the process variable or level in a tank.

15. *SOLENOID.* A magnetically (electric coil) operated mechanical device. Solenoids can operate small valves or electric switches.

16. *STARTERS.* Most starters for small motors are "across-the-line" which means that they simply connect the motor terminals to the incoming line. Large motors would impose severe mechanical shock to the driven machine if started this way, as well as creating a severe disturbance to the electrical lines, causing dimming and flickering lights. Therefore, motors over 100 HP (75 kW) are usually started by "reduced voltage" starters or two-step starters. The voltage reduction can be accomplished by the use of an auto-transformer with taps that provide 50 percent voltage until the motor and load are moving, then go to full voltage "across-the-line." These can be operated manually, in response to a pair of switches, or automatically in response to motor current or a definite time delay which allows the assembly time to come up to speed.

17. *TIME LAG.* The time required for processes and control systems to respond to a signal or reach a desired level.

18. *TIMER.* A device for automatically starting or stopping a machine or other device at a given time.

19. *TRANSDUCER.* A device which senses some varying condition measured by a primary sensor and converts it to an electrical or other signal for transmission to some other device (a receiver) for processing or decision making. Flowmeters and heat sensors are examples of transducers.

20. *VARIABLE FREQUENCY DRIVE (V.F.D.).* A control system which allows the frequency of the current applied to the motor to be varied. The motor is connected to a low frequency source while standing still, and the frequency is increased gradually until the motor and pump, or other driven machine, is at the desired speed. This system offers the additional advantage of continuous control of speed, in accord with some measurement.

5.45 Instrumentation

For additional information on controls and instrumentation, see Chapter 19, "Instrumentation," in Volume II, *WATER TREATMENT PLANT OPERATION*, of this series of operator training manuals.

5.5 ELECTRICAL CIRCUITS AND CIRCUIT TESTING INSTRUMENTS

A common problem found in pump stations with a high rate of motor failure is voltage imbalance or unbalance. Unlike a single-phase condition, all three phases are present but the phase-to-phase voltage is not equal in each phase.

Voltage imbalance can occur in either the utility side or the pump station electrical system. For example, the utility company may have large single-phase loads (such as residential services) which reduce the voltage on a single phase. This same condition can occur in the pump station if a large number of 120/220 volt loads are present. Slight differences in voltage can cause disproportional current imbalance; this may be six to ten times as large as the voltage imbalance. For example, a two percent voltage imbalance can result in a 20 percent current imbalance. A 4.5 percent voltage imbalance will reduce the insulation life to 50 percent of the normal life. This is the reason a dependable voltage supply at the motor terminals is critical. Even relatively slight variations can greatly increase the motor operating temperatures and burn out the insulation.

It is common practice for electrical utility companies to furnish power to three-phase customers in open delta or wye configurations. An open delta or wye system is a two-transformer bank that is a suitable configuration where *LIGHTING LOADS ARE LARGE AND THREE-PHASE LOADS ARE LIGHT.* This is the exact opposite of the configuration needed by most pumping facilities where *THREE-PHASE LOADS ARE LARGE.* (Examples of three-transformer banks include Y-delta, delta-Y, and Y-Y.) In most cases, three-phase motors should be fed from three-transformer banks for proper balance. The capacity of a two-transformer bank is only 57 percent of the capacity of a three-transformer bank. The two-transformer configuration can cause one leg of the three-phase current to furnish higher amperage to one leg of the motor, which will greatly shorten its life.

Operators should acquaint themselves with the configuration of their electric power supply. When an open delta or wye configuration is used, operators should calculate the degree of current imbalance existing between legs of their polyphase motors. If you are unsure about how to determine the configuration of your system or how to calculate the percentage of current imbalance, *ALWAYS* consult a qualified electrician. *CURRENT IMBALANCE BETWEEN LEGS SHOULD NEVER EXCEED 5 PERCENT UNDER NORMAL OPERATING CONDITIONS* (NEMA Standards MGI-14.35).

Loose connections will also cause voltage imbalance as will high-resistance contacts, circuit breakers, or motor starters. Motor connections at the circuit box should be checked frequently (semiannually or annually) to ensure that the connections are tight and that vibrating wires have not rubbed through the insulation on the conductors. Measure the voltage at the motor terminals and calculate the percentage imbalance (if any) using the procedures below.

Another serious consideration for operators is voltage fluctuation caused by neighborhood demands. A pump motor in near perfect balance (for example, 3 percent unbalance) at 9:00 AM could be as much as 17 percent unbalanced by 4:00 PM on a hot day due to the use of air conditioners by customers on the same grid. Also, the hookup of a small market or a new home to the power grid can cause a significant change in the degree of current unbalance in other parts of the power grid. Because energy demands are constantly changing, water system operators should have a qualified electrician check the current balances between legs of their three-phase motors at least once a year.

Do not rely entirely on the power company to detect unbalanced current. Complaints of suspected power problems are frequently met with the explanation that all voltages are within the percentages allowed by law and no mention is made of the percentage of current unbalance which can be a major source of problems with three-phase motors. A little research of your own can pay large benefits. For example, a small water company in Central California configured with an Open Delta system (and running three-phase unbalances as high as 17 percent as a result) was routinely spending $14,000 a year for energy and burning out a 10-HP motor on the average of every 1.5 years (six 10-HP motors in 9 years). After consultation, the local power utility agreed to add a third transformer to each power board to bring the system into better balance.

Pump drop leads were then rotated, bringing overall current unbalances down to an average of 3 percent, heavy-duty three-phase capacitors were added to absorb the prevalent voltage surges in the area, and computerized controls were added to the pumps to shut them off when pumping volumes got too low. These modifications resulted in a saving in energy costs the first year alone of $5,500.00.

FORMULAS

Percentage of current unbalance can be calculated by using the following formulas and procedures:

$$\text{Average Current} = \frac{\text{Total of Current Value Measured on Each Leg}}{3}$$

$$\% \text{ Current Unbalance} = \frac{\text{Greatest Amp Difference from the Average}}{\text{Average Current}} \times 100\%$$

PROCEDURES

A. Measure and record current readings in amps for each leg. (Hookup 1.) Disconnect power.

B. Shift or roll the motor leads from left to right so the drop cable lead that was on terminal 1 is now on 2, lead on 2 is now on 3, and lead on 3 is now on 1. (Hookup 2.) Rolling the motor leads in this manner will not reverse the motor rotation. Start the motor, measure and record current reading on each leg. Disconnect power.

C. Again shift drop cable leads from left to right so the lead on terminal 1 goes to 2, 2 goes to 3, and 3 to 1. (Hookup 3.) Start pump, measure and record current reading on each leg. Disconnect power.

D. Add the values for each hookup.

E. Divide the total by 3 to obtain the average.

F. Compare each single leg reading to the average current amount to obtain the greatest amp difference from the average.

G. Divide this difference by the average to obtain the percentage of unbalance.

H. Use the wiring hookup that provides the lowest percentage of unbalance.

CORRECTING THE THREE-PHASE POWER UNBALANCE

Example: Check for current unbalance for a 230-volt, 3-phase 60-Hz submersible pump motor, 18.6 full load amps.

Solution: Steps 1 to 3 measure and record amps on each motor drop lead for Hookups 1, 2, and 3 (Figure 5.24).

		Step 1 (Hookup 1)	Step 2 (Hookup 2)	Step 3 (Hookup 3)
(T_1)		DL_1 = 25.5 amps	DL_3 = 25 amps	DL_2 = 25.0 amps
(T_2)		DL_2 = 23.0 amps	DL_1 = 24 amps	DL_3 = 24.5 amps
(T_3)		DL_3 = 26.5 amps	DL_2 = 26 amps	DL_1 = 25.5 amps
Step 4	Total = 75 amps		Total = 75 amps	Total = 75 amps
Step 5	Average Current =	Total Current =	$\dfrac{75}{3}$ = 25 amps	
			3 readings	
Step 6	Greatest amp difference from the average:		(Hookup 1) = 25 − 23 = 2	
			(Hookup 2) = 26 − 25 = 1	
			(Hookup 3) = 25.5 − 25 = 0.5	
Step 7	% Unbalance		(Hookup 1) = 2/25 x 100 = 8	
			(Hookup 2) = 1/25 x 100 = 4	
			(Hookup 3) = 0.5/25 x 100 = 2	

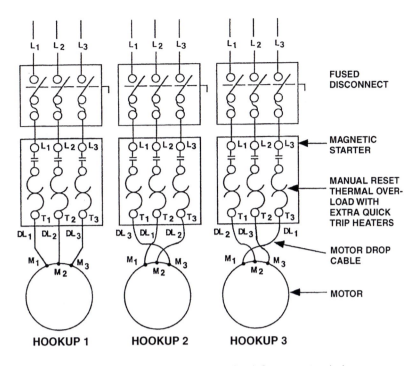

Fig. 5.24   Three hookups used to check for current unbalance

As can be seen, Hookup 3 should be used since it shows the least amount of current unbalance. Therefore, the motor will operate at maximum efficiency and reliability on Hookup 3.

By comparing the current values recorded on each leg, you will note the highest value was always on the same leg, L_3. This indicates the unbalance is in the power source. If the high current values were on a different leg each time the leads were changed, the unbalance would be caused by the motor or a poor connection.

If the current unbalance is greater than 5 percent, contact your power company for help.

ACKNOWLEDGMENT

Material on unbalanced current was provided by James W. Cannell, President, Canyon Meadows Mutual Water Company, Inc., Bodfish, CA. His contribution is greatly appreciated.

For an excellent summary of pump troubleshooting procedures, see *WATER DISTRIBUTION SYSTEM OPERATION AND MAINTENANCE*, Chapter 2, Table 2.2, "Centrifugal Pump Troubleshooting Chart," page 47. For additional information on pump maintenance, see Chapter 18, Section 18.2, "Mechanical Equipment," in *WATER TREATMENT PLANT OPERATION*, Volume II, in this series of manuals.

5.6   WORKING AROUND ELECTRICAL UNITS

Electricity is supplied as an alternating current (A.C.) at 120, 240, or 480 volts. Most wells or large pumps will be energized by 240 or 480 volts. Extremely large pumps may be energized by even higher voltages. Place nonconducting rubber mats on the floor in front of all power panels and motor control centers.

Care and caution should be used when working around equipment that is hooked up to any electric current. Water dis-

tribution system operators often work in damp and wet places using electric hand tools for routine maintenance work. The risk of shock or electrocution in such environments can be reduced substantially by the use of a device called a ground-fault circuit interrupter (GFCI).

A ground-fault circuit interrupter is NOT an over-current device. A GFCI is used to open a circuit if the current flowing to the load does not return by the prescribed route. In a simple 120-volt circuit, we usually think of the current flowing through the black (ungrounded) wire to the load and returning to the source through the white (grounded) wire. If it does not return through the grounded wire, then it must have gone somewhere else, usually to ground. The GFCI is designed to limit electric shock to a current level and time duration value below that which can produce serious injury. Several types of GFCIs are available, with some variations between types. Although all types will provide ground-fault protection, the specific application may dictate one type over another.

Ground-fault circuit interrupters are divided into two classes, Class A and Class B. The Class A device is designed to trip when current flow in other than the normal path is 6 milliamperes or greater. The Class B device will trip when current flow in other than the normal path is 20 milliamperes or greater. Class B devices are approved for use on underwater swimming pool lighting installed prior to the adoption of the 1996 National Electrical Code. The most commonly used types of GFCIs are circuit-breaker, receptacle, permanently mounted, portable, and cord-connected.

Ground fault receptacles should be installed in convenience receptacles where it is wet or damp, and a portable GFCI should be carried on your work vehicle and used whenever you are using portable electric tools in the field.

When maintenance is to be done on wells or pumps, lock out the electric current to the equipment. Open the breakers so that electric current is turned off.[13] Place a tag (Figure 5.25) with your name on it on opened breakers and locks to indicate that you turned off the breakers and locks. No one should remove the tag or close the breakers or locks but you. This will allow the equipment to be pulled and worked on without the fear of being shocked or burned. Personnel working around high-voltage equipment should be trained and have respect for electric current.

After work is completed on the equipment, personnel should stand clear when the equipment is energized (electric current turned on). Make sure that the equipment is properly grounded. Personnel working with electrical equipment should have a good knowledge of electric circuits and circuit testing and should be qualified to do this work. They should get clearance (approval) to work on the equipment before starting any repairs. If no one is knowledgeable about electric circuits, the water utility should contact an electrician from a local electrical firm.

Safe procedures that must be used when working around electrical equipment include:

1. Only permit qualified persons to work on electrical equipment,

2. Maintain electrical installations in a safe condition,

3. Protect electrical equipment and wiring from mechanical damage and environmental deterioration,

4. Install covers or barriers on boxes, fittings, and enclosures to prevent accidental contact with live parts,

5. Use an acceptable service pole,

6. Ground all electrical equipment,

7. Provide suitable overcurrent protection,

8. Lock out machinery during cleaning, servicing, or adjusting,

9. De-energize, lock out, and/or block all machinery to prevent movement if exposed parts are dangerous to personnel, and

10. If a switch or circuit breaker is tagged and locked out, do not remove the tag unless you are the person who locked out the device.

Whenever major replacement, repair, renovation, or modification of equipment is performed, OSHA regulations require that all equipment that could unexpectedly start up or release stored energy must be locked or tagged out to protect against accidental injury to personnel. Some of the most common forms of stored energy are electrical and hydraulic energy.

The energy isolating devices (switches, valves) for the equipment must be designed to accept a lockout device. A lockout device uses a positive means such as a lock, either key or combination type, to hold the switch in the safe position and prevent the equipment from becoming energized. In addition, prominent warnings, such as the tag illustrated in Figure 5.25, should be securely fastened to the energy isolating device and the equipment (in accordance with an established procedure) to indicate that both it and the equipment being controlled may not be operated until the tag and lockout device are removed by the person who installed them.

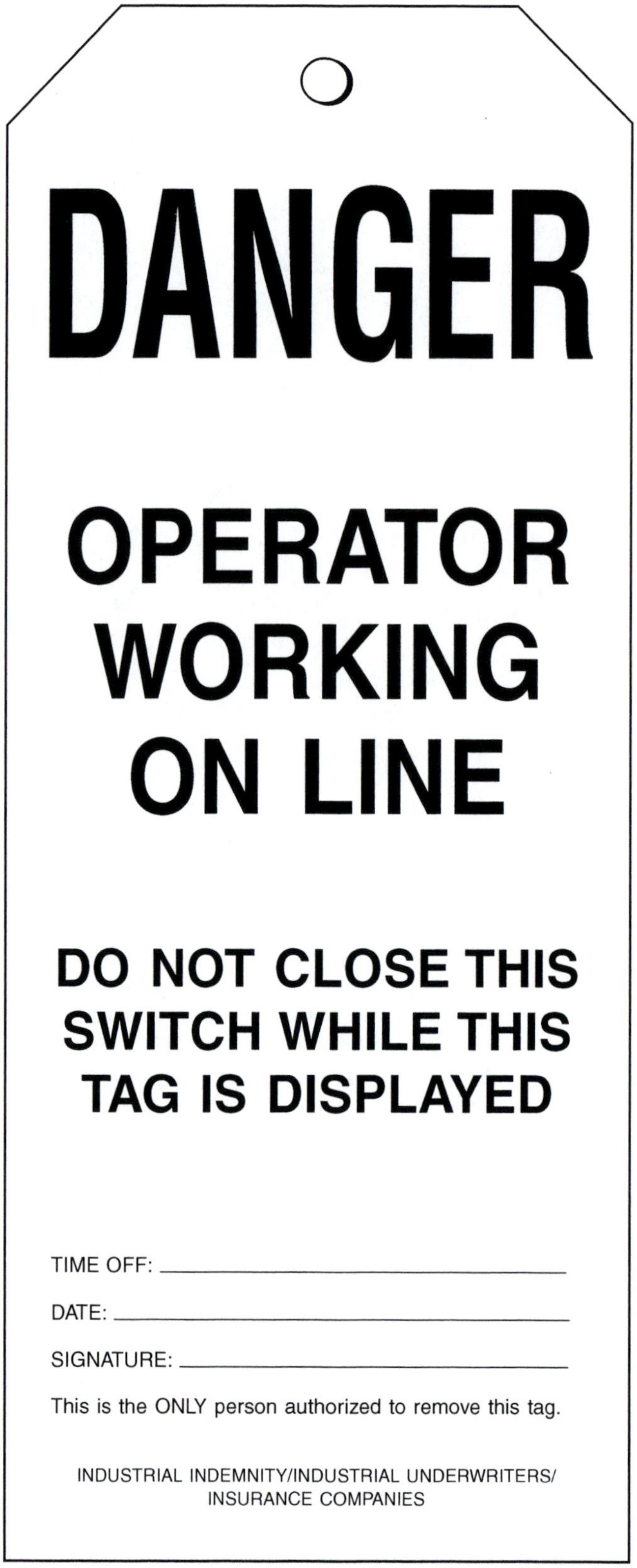

DANGER

OPERATOR WORKING ON LINE

DO NOT CLOSE THIS SWITCH WHILE THIS TAG IS DISPLAYED

TIME OFF: _____

DATE: _____

SIGNATURE: _____

This is the ONLY person authorized to remove this tag.

INDUSTRIAL INDEMNITY/INDUSTRIAL UNDERWRITERS/
INSURANCE COMPANIES

Fig. 5.25   Typical lockout warning tag
(Source: Industrial Indemnity/Industrial Underwriters Insurance Companies.)

---

[13] When an electrician "closes" an electrical circuit, the circuit is connected together and electricity will flow. Closing a circuit is similar to opening a valve in a pipeline. The reverse is also true. Opening an electrical circuit is similar to closing a valve on a pipeline.

For the safety of all personnel, each plant should develop a standard operating procedure that must be followed whenever equipment must be shut down or turned off for repairs. If every operator follows the same procedures, the chances of an accidental start-up injuring someone will be greatly reduced. The following procedures, prepared by the State of Oklahoma, can be used as a model for developing your own standard operating procedure for lockouts.

BASIC LOCKOUT/TAGOUT PROCEDURES

1. Notify all affected employees that a lockout or tagged system is going to be utilized and the reason why. The authorized employee shall know the type and magnitude of energy that the equipment utilizes and shall understand the hazard thereof.

2. If the equipment is operating, shut it down by the normal stopping procedure.

3. Operate the switch, valve, or other energy isolating device(s) so that the equipment is isolated from its energy source(s). Stored energy such as that in springs; elevated machine members; rotating flywheels; hydraulic systems; and air, gas, steam, or water pressure must be dissipated or restrained by methods such as repositioning, blocking, or bleeding down.

4. Lock out and/or tag out the energy isolating device with assigned individual lock or tag.

5. After ensuring that no personnel are exposed, and as a check that the energy source is disconnected, operate the pushbutton or other normal operating controls to make certain the equipment will not operate. *CAUTION! RETURN OPERATING CONTROLS TO THE NEUTRAL OR OFF POSITION AFTER THE TEST.*

6. The equipment is now locked out or tagged out and work on the equipment may begin.

7. After the work on the equipment is complete, all tools have been removed, guards have been reinstalled, and employees are in the clear, remove all lockout or tagout devices. Operate the energy isolating devices to restore energy to the equipment.

8. Notify affected employees that the lockout or tagout device(s) has been removed before starting the equipment.

EMERGENCY PROCEDURES

In the event of electric shock, the following steps should be taken:

1. Survey the scene and see if it is safe to enter.

2. If necessary, free the victim from a live power source by shutting power off at a nearby disconnect, or by using a dry stick or some other nonconducting object to move the victim.

3. Send for help, calling 911 or other appropriate emergency number in your community. Check for breathing and pulse. Begin CPR (cardiopulmonary resuscitation) immediately if needed.

REMEMBER, only trained and qualified individuals working in pairs should be allowed to service, repair, or troubleshoot electrical equipment and systems.

5.7 TROUBLESHOOTING

5.70 Need for Troubleshooting

Approximately 75 percent of well pump and control problems are associated with electricity. The well pump operator should have a good working knowledge of electric circuits and circuit testing instruments before attempting to service or troubleshoot the electric circuits and components commonly used in well pump operations. The operator should not undertake any electrically related troubleshooting or repair job until instructions have been received on how to do it properly and until the operator has been authorized to perform that job.

Small water utilities that do not have a knowledgeable operator or electrician on their staff should arrange with a local electrical firm or pump service company to perform this service.

5.71 Troubleshooting Guide

The "Troubleshooting Guide" on the following pages is designed to assist the operator or service personnel in diagnosing and correcting the most common problems associated with well pumping facilities.

TO USE THE GUIDE:

1. Find the appropriate condition in the SYMPTOM column or section.

2. Find the cause in the PROBABLE CAUSE column.

3. Perform the CORRECTIVE ACTION listed in the third column. The remedy is listed briefly and the procedures may not be detailed enough to cover every possibility.

The operator should not proceed if there is any doubt as to what is meant or what course of action should be taken to correct a given problem.

5.8 ADDITIONAL READING

To obtain additional information regarding the topics in this chapter, review the appropriate chapters and sections in the following operator training manuals:

1. *SMALL WATER SYSTEM OPERATION AND MAINTENANCE*, and

2. *WATER DISTRIBUTION SYSTEM OPERATION AND MAINTENANCE*.

These manuals can be obtained from the Office of Water Programs, California State University, Sacramento, 6000 J Street, Sacramento, CA 95819-6025, phone (916) 278-6142 or visit the website at www.owp.csus.edu. Price, $45.00 each.

5.9 ACKNOWLEDGMENT

Material contained in this chapter is copyrighted by the California State University, Sacramento Foundation and is reproduced by permission.

TROUBLESHOOTING GUIDE

Symptom	Probable Cause	Corrective Action
5.710 *Pump Will Not Start*	Circuit breaker or overload relay tripped, motor cold.	Reset breaker or reset manual overload relay.
	Fuses burned out.	Check for cause and correct, replace fuses.
	No power to switch box.	Confirm with multimeter by checking incoming power source, notify power company.
	Motor is hot and overload relay has tripped.	Allow motor to cool. Check supply voltage. If low, notify power company. If normal, reset overload relay, start motor, check amperage; if above normal, call electrician.
	Loose or broken wire, or short.	Tighten wiring terminal, replace any broken wires, check for shorts and correct.
	Low line voltage.	Check incoming power, use multimeter; if low, notify power company.
	Defective motor.	MEG[14] out motor; if bad, replace.
	Defective pressure switch.	With contact points closed, check for voltage through switch; if no voltage, replace switch; if low voltage, clean contact points; if full voltage, proceed to next item.
	Line to pressure switch is plugged or valve in line has accidentally been shut off.	Open valve if closed. Clean or replace line.
	Pump control valve malfunctioning.	Check limit switch for proper travel and contact. Adjust or replace as required.
	Defective time delay relay or pump start timer.	Check for voltage through relay or timer — replace as necessary — check for loose linkage.
	Float switch or transducer malfunctioning.	If pump is activated by float switch or pressure transducer on storage tank, check for incoming signal; if no signal, check out switch or transducer with multimeter. If OK, look for broken cable between storage tank and pump station.
5.711 *Pump Will Not Shut Off*	Defective pressure switch.	Points in switch stuck or mechanical linkage broken, replace switch.
	Line to pressure switch is plugged or valve in line has been accidentally shut off.	Open valve if closed. Clean or replace plugged line.
	Cutoff pressure setting too high.	Adjust setting.
	Pump control valve malfunctioning.	Check limit switch for proper travel and contact. Adjust or replace as required.
	Float switch or transducer malfunctioning.	Defective incoming signal, check and replace components as required. Check cable.
	Defective timer in pump stop mode.	Check for voltage through pump stop timer, replace if defective.
5.712 *Pump Starts Too Frequently*	Pressure switch cut-in and cutoff settings too close.	Adjust settings, maintain minimum 20 psi (138 kPa or 1.4 kg/sq cm) differential.
	Waterlogged tank.	Add air to tank. Check air charging system and air release valve. Also check tank and connections for air leaks.
	Leaking foot valve.	Check for backflow into well; if excessive or if pump shaft is turning backward, correct problem as soon as possible.
	Time delay relay or pump start/stop timers are malfunctioning.	Check relay or timers for proper operation, replace defective components.

[14] *Meg. A procedure used for checking the insulation resistance on motors, feeders, bus bar systems, grounds, and branch circuit wiring.*

TROUBLESHOOTING GUIDE (continued)

Symptom	Probable Cause	Corrective Action
5.713 **Fuses Blow, Circuit Breaker or Overload Relays Trip When Pump Is in Operation**	Switch box or control not properly vented, or in full sunshine or dead air location, overload relay may be tripping due to external heat.	Provide adequate ventilation (may require small fan). Provide shelter from sun. Paint box or panel with heat reflective paint, preferably white.
	Incorrect voltage.	Check incoming power source. If not within prescribed limits, notify power company.
	Overload relays tripped.	Check motor running amperage, verify that thermal relay components are correctly sized to operating conditions. Repeated tripping will weaken units, replace if necessary.
	Motor overloaded and running very hot.	Modern motors are designed to run hot and if the hand can be held on the motor for 10 seconds without extreme discomfort, the temperature is not damaging. Motor current should not exceed NAMEPLATE[15] rating. Fifteen percent overload reduces motor life by 50 percent.
5.714 **Pump Will Not Deliver Normal Amount of Water**	Pump breaking suction.	Check water level to be certain water is above pump bowls when operating. If not, lower bowls.
	Pump impeller improperly adjusted.	Check adjustment and lower impellers (qualified personnel only).
	Rotation incorrect.	Check rotation.
	Impellers worn.	If well pumps sand, impeller could be excessively worn thus reducing amount of water pump can deliver. Evaluate and recondition pump bowls if required.
	Pump control valve malfunctioning.	Check limit switch for proper travel and contact. Adjust or replace as required.
	Impeller or bowls partially plugged.	Wash down pump by forcing water back through discharge pipe. Evaluate sand production from well.
	DRAWDOWN[16] more than anticipated.	Check pumping water level. Reduce production from pump or lower bowls.
	Pump motor speed too slow.	Check speed and compare with performance curves. Also check lift and discharge pressure for power requirements.
5.715 **Pump Takes Too Much Power**	Impellers not properly adjusted.	Refer to manufacturer's bulletin for adjustment of open or closed impellers.
	Well is pumping sand.	Check water being pumped for presence of sand. Restrict discharge until water is clean. Care should be taken not to shut down pump if it is pumping very much sand.
	Crooked well, pump shaft binding.	Reshim between pump base and pump head to center shaft in motor quill. Never shim between pump head and motor.
	Worn bearings or bent shaft.	Check and replace as necessary.
5.716 **Excessive Operating Noise**	Motor bearings worn.	Replace as necessary.
	Bent line shaft or head shaft.	Check and replace.
	Line shaft bearings not receiving oil.	Make sure there is oil in the oil reservoir and the oiler solenoid is opening. Check sight gage drip rate, adjust drip feed oiler for 5 drops per minute plus 1 drop per minute for each 40 feet (12 m) of column.

[15] *Nameplate. A durable metal plate found on equipment which lists critical operating conditions for the equipment.*
[16] *Drawdown. The drop in the water table or level of water in the ground when water is being pumped from a well.*

WATER SYSTEMS OPERATION AND MAINTENANCE VIDEO TRAINING SERIES

CHAPTER (VIDEO) 6

DISTRIBUTION SYSTEMS

VIDEO 6 SUMMARY

Video 6, DISTRIBUTION SYSTEMS, provides operators with the knowledge, skills, and abilities they need to inspect, protect, operate, and maintain water distribution systems. Information is provided on how to exercise valves and flush distribution system mains. Operators also will be able to disinfect mains after repairs or replacement and make or supervise repairs and fix leaks without jeopardizing water quality. Information also is provided on how to locate buried pipes and detect leaks. The importance of a cross-connection control program is stressed.

CONTENTS OF VIDEO 6

DISTRIBUTION SYSTEMS VIDEO

INTRODUCTION

    Description of Distribution System

    Key Concerns

    Distribution System Surveillance Program

    Topics Covered in Video

SYSTEM VALVES AND METERS

    Types of Valves

    Scheduling for Exercising Valves

    Demonstration of Exercising Valves

    Types of Meters

    Recordkeeping

FLUSHING

LOCATING BURIED PIPES

LOCATING LEAKS

MAKING REPAIRS WITH COUPLINGS

    When To Use Couplings

    PVC and Iron Pipe

    Demonstration of Applying Couplings

MAKING REPAIRS—CUTTING /DISINFECTING/GLUING

    When To Replace a Section

    Demonstrations of Cutting, Disinfecting, and Gluing

CROSS CONNECTIONS

    Used To Prevent Contamination

    Who Is Responsible?

    Recordkeeping

SUMMARY

CONTENTS OF CHAPTER 6

DISTRIBUTION SYSTEMS
LEARNING BOOKLET

OBJECTIVES

Chapter (Video) 6.   DISTRIBUTION SYSTEMS

Following completion of Video 6 and Chapter 6, you should be able to:

1. Identify various parts of a water distribution system,

2. Identify and exercise distribution system valves,

3. Determine when to use couplings and make repairs using couplings,

4. Make repairs by replacing a pipe section,

5. Repair pipes by cutting, disinfecting, and gluing,

6. Flush distribution system mains,

7. Locate buried pipes,

8. Detect leaking pipes, and

9. Explain the importance of a cross-connection control program.

LEARNING BOOKLET STUDY MATERIAL

This section of the *LEARNING BOOKLET* contains important information. Read this section after watching the video and before attempting to take the Objective Test for this chapter.

Material covered in this section will help you better understand the material in the video. Also some critical information is easier to present in the *LEARNING BOOKLET*, such as illustrating forms and calculations.

Chapter (Video) 6.   DISTRIBUTION SYSTEMS

6.0   DISTRIBUTION SYSTEM O & M

Water distribution typically consists of pipes, storage facilities, pumping stations, valves, fire hydrants, meters, and other appurtenances (Figure 6.1). Together they make up what can be considered a single operating unit working to achieve its intended purpose. That purpose is to deliver adequate quantities of water at sufficient pressures at all times under continually changing conditions while at the same time protecting water quality. Two major elements combine to accomplish this purpose. The first deals with the physical features of the system and relates to its ability to withstand the stresses imposed on it, to protect the quality of the water it carries, and to deliver the supply in sufficient quantity through adequately sized facilities. The second element is the operation and maintenance of the system in a manner that preserves its integrity and the quality of the water it delivers. Of special importance is the maintenance of a *CONTINUOUS POSITIVE WATER PRESSURE* in the system under all conditions so as to protect the distribution system from the entrance of toxic and other undesirable substances. To properly understand and operate a distribution system, the operator must be thoroughly knowledgeable about both its physical and hydraulic characteristics.

6.1   SYSTEM SURVEILLANCE

6.10   Purpose of System Surveillance

Surveillance of distribution systems is done for three reasons. First, to detect and correct any problems that are sanitary hazards; second, to detect and correct any significant deterioration of facilities or equipment used for the storage and transportation of the water supply; and third, to detect the encroachment of other utilities (sewer, power, gas, phone, cable TV). Some types of surveillance, such as checking for vandalism, are performed routinely, while others are done only under special circumstances, such as checking for damage after a storm. Generally, routine surveillance in a distribution system would only involve above-ground facilities such as reservoirs, pump stations, and valves. However, some less frequent surveillance can also be made of underground facilities as described later in this section.

Critical areas of the distribution system should be patrolled routinely so that the water utility will have an early warning of any adverse conditions that might appear. Any activity or situation that might endanger a water facility or the quality of the water must be investigated and reported without delay. Possible damage from floods, earthquakes, tornadoes, or fires needs to be looked into promptly.

Just as important as routine patrolling is having the field crews watch for actual or potential problems as they attend to their duties. The sooner corrective action is taken after a problem is found, the easier it usually is to make the correction. The longer water quality or facilities deteriorate, the more difficult the situation becomes.

6.11   Treated Water Storage Facilities

Storage facilities in the distribution system are the most obvious facilities needing surveillance. They are generally not under a positive pressure (except for pressure tanks) and are usually above or at ground level. They are, therefore, the most susceptible part of the distribution system to quality degrada-

tion from external sources. Open reservoirs are the most critical type of reservoir in this regard, with below-ground reservoirs next in line. Just about anything that one could think of has been found during inspections of reservoirs. For example, cans, bottles, papers, and even a pile of human fecal matter were found on a reservoir ledge inside a covered, 10 million gallon (38,000 cu m) reservoir. Finding small animals, dead or alive, in reservoirs is not uncommon.

Daily surveillance is recommended for trespassing, vandalism, dumping of trash, or swimming. Pay particular attention to fence and screen openings, roof damage, intact locks on reservoirs, and to manholes or doors. In one case, repeated high bacterial counts occurred and an inspection revealed that a roof manhole was open and several pigeons had entered and drowned in the water. If these daily inspections reveal any change in water color, odor, or turbidity or if any other evidence indicates the water may have been tampered with, take the facility out of service and contact the health department immediately to determine what further action should be taken. Some tests that can be quickly made are chlorine residual, conductance (for TDS), pH, and alkalinity. Bacteriological tests take longer to complete, but should also be made (for example, 24-hour coliform tests by the membrane filter method).

Inspect reservoir covers frequently to determine if they are watertight. If a roof develops leaks, any contaminants on the roof, such as bird droppings, will be washed into the reservoir. Even concrete roofs may develop cracks in time and permit leakage. Vent screens should be inspected to ensure they are in good condition. If the screens on the vents are torn or rust away, it is obvious that small animals can gain entry to the reservoir. Vent areas must be protected to prevent rain, wind-blown items (leaves, paper), roof drainage, debris and, to the extent possible, dust and dirt from entering the reservoir. Also check the screening on the vertical overflow pipes. In one case, the decomposed remains of two rodents were found in a

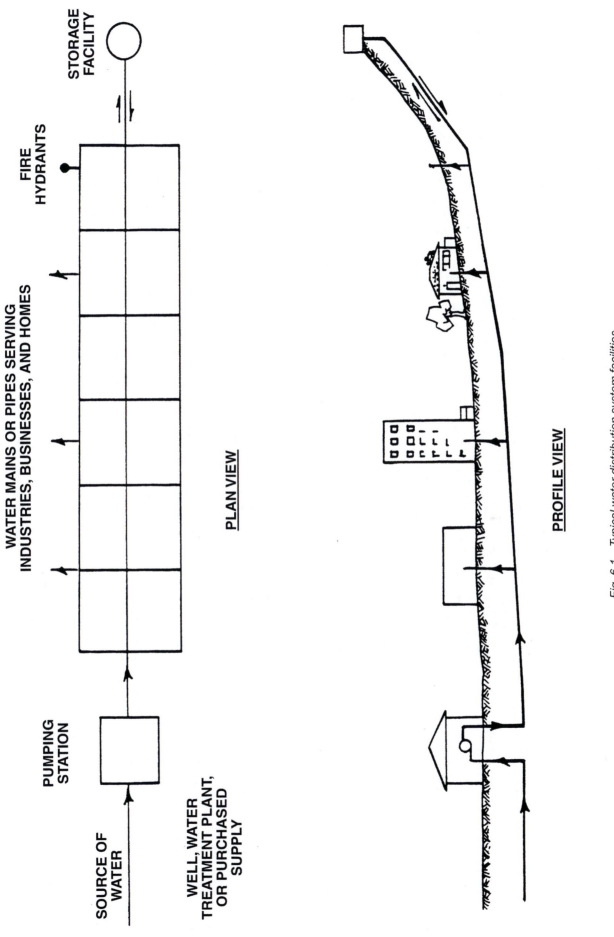

Fig. 6.1   Typical water distribution system facilities

tank which the rodents apparently had crawled into through an unscreened vertical overflow pipe some 20 ft (6 m) high.

Other reservoir inspections may be made at less frequent intervals. Weekly or more frequent inspections are advisable to note any algae, slime and/or worm growths, floating or settled materials, or deterioration (corrosion or dry rot) of roofing and wooden trusses.

After a heavy rain, inspect the reservoir for damage. If a below-ground reservoir is located where it could be affected by floods, an inspection should be made during such periods to determine whether or not storm waters are getting into the facility or erosion is undermining the structure.

At least once a year, the interior of each storage tank should be inspected to determine the condition of the interior coating and whether the tank needs to be washed out, completely cleaned, or recoated. Interior inspections may also reveal the presence of animals, birds, or debris in the tank. The condition of the vents can be seen quite well from the interior of the tank. Preferably every year, but certainly at least every other year, each reservoir should be drained and thoroughly inspected to determine if there is any significant leakage or corrosion and to observe the nature and amount of sediments on the floor or bottom. Cleaning of the reservoir usually takes place at this time. Divers are being used to inspect, clean, and repair tanks without draining them.

Routinely inspect any sewers located near below-ground reservoirs to determine if there is any noticeable leakage around them. The possibility exists that leaking wastewater could seep through (infiltrate) the ground and cracks in reservoir walls and reach the stored water. As part of the surveillance made after storms, be alert to possible overflow of wastewater from damaged or overloaded sewers to a reservoir area.

6.12   Mains

Water utility operators should be on the lookout for signs of unauthorized construction activity or soil erosion on or near the utility's pipelines which may pose a physical threat to the line. All wastewater facilities must be kept a proper distance from the mains or meet any special construction requirements. An observer from the utility should be present during any digging or excavation (especially blasting) near the mains. Reasonable access to the main must always be maintained, and there should be no construction on the piping right-of-way unless it is authorized by the utility. During the routine work of the field crews, operators should be on the lookout for possible main leaks and report any wet spots, sunken areas, or other unusual conditions.

Even though water mains are located in the ground and out of sight, they still need to be monitored. Valuable information can be obtained by inspecting the condition of the inside of mains when repairs or additions are made to the system, or even by examining pipe cut-outs from main tapping operations. When *TUBERCULATION*[1] or other deposition is found, take samples to the laboratory for analysis or further study to help determine the cause of their formation and to develop remedial treatment measures. Another method for checking pipe conditions is to place test pipe specimens (*COUPONS*[2]) in the distribution system where they can be periodically removed, examined, weighed, photographed, and put back.

6.13   Valves and Blowoffs

Valve boxes and other valve appurtenances should be checked at least annually to determine if they are damaged, filled with earth, or covered over by pavement. Vacuum or air relief valves ("air-vacs") and blowoffs should be inspected after rains or floods to ensure that they are not submerged in drainage waters and that they work properly.

6.14   Customer Services

Meter readers should be alert for any problems noted during their rounds. A periodic check should be made of the condition of the meter or curb box. If a box has been displaced and parts of it project out of the ground, there is a danger of injury resulting from tripping. This has been one of the most frequent sources of lawsuits against utilities. Leaking services should also be noted and reported.

6.15   Vandalism

The normal security measures taken to prevent vandalism include locks on doors and gates, fences, lighting, posting signs, and patrolling. These measures will not stop vandalism, but should reduce it. These protective measures must not be ignored and allowed to deteriorate into uselessness (such as a fence with a hole in it).

If vandalism or illegal entry is found, make a thorough investigation to determine what damage might have been done and whether there is any possibility of a threat to the quality of the water supply. Check the appearance and odor of the water supply in the area. Record the condition of all locks, any questionable conditions in the areas where unauthorized entry apparently took place, the presence of hazardous material containers, missing items, and damaged equipment. Contact any neighbors in the area for additional information and request assistance to watch the facility. Then promptly report any damage or questionable conditions you have found to responsible supervisory personnel. If water quality may be affected, the health department should be called immediately. If the

---

[1] *Tuberculation.   The development or formation of small mounds of corrosion products (rust) on the inside of iron pipe. These mounds (tubercles) increase the roughness of the inside of the pipe thus increasing resistance to water flow (decreases the C Factor).*

[2] *Coupon.   A steel specimen inserted into water to measure the corrosiveness of water. The rate of corrosion is measured as the loss of weight of the coupon (in milligrams) per surface area (in square decimeters) exposed to the water per day. 10 decimeters = 1 meter = 100 centimeters.*

questionable part of the system can be isolated, this should be done. Notify customers and the health department if a decision is made to shut down part of the system.

As already noted, if there is any detectable change in color, odor, or turbidity of the water, or any other evidence that the water has been tampered with, the facility should be *IMMEDIATELY TAKEN OUT OF SERVICE.* Water quality tests that can be done promptly and would be indicative of suspected contamination should be promptly run. Tests that can be quickly made are turbidity, chlorine residual, conductance (for TDS), pH, and alkalinity. Bacteriological tests take longer to complete, but should also be made (for example, 24-hour coliform tests by the membrane filter method).

Fortunately, most acts of vandalism cause only superficial damage and do no serious harm. Water quality safeguards against minor vandalism are built into most systems and their operation. Existing chlorine residuals will assist in minimizing any threat from disease organisms. A large dilution factor is normally present which will also minimize any contamination threat. Routine sampling and continuous water quality monitoring assist in revealing any possible threat to water quality. For example, telemetering of chlorine residuals and turbidity can indicate water quality problems. Similarly, telemetering of pressures, flows, and reservoir levels can help detect operational problems early.

Automatic controls will often compensate for or minimize certain acts of vandalism. The fact that most of the distribution system is underground and relatively inaccessible makes only a small portion of the system actually vulnerable. Reservoirs that may have been contaminated can usually be readily isolated as reserve supplies of water are often available from other sources. "Looped" distribution lines will allow the isolation of problem areas. Finally, the consumer can be counted upon to quickly report any perceived change in water appearance, taste, or odor.

If the vandal is still present and does not leave, notify the authorities (supervisor, police) immediately. *DO NOT ATTEMPT TO USE FORCE* on a vandal, even a child, because you or the vandal could be injured. After the episode is over, make a complete written report describing the vandalism (including photos) and its actual and potential effects on the physical system and water quality.

6.16   Telemetering

Some types of surveillance can also be accomplished by using remote indicating or recording systems. Remote control of a function usually involves telemetering. Quite simply, this involves the measuring, transmitting, and receiving of data at a distance by phone lines, radio, or microwave. Indicating or recording gages can be mounted at any convenient place, or a number of them can be put together on a central control panel and can show many different types of data, such as water elevations in reservoirs or tanks, rate of discharge of pumps, pressures in mains at any distant point, and rate of flow. Telemetered water quality data might also include residual chlorine, turbidity, and/or other water quality indicators. Strip charts or circular chart recorders may be used to record telemetered signals. Telemetering also can be used to start and stop pumps and open and close valves.

6.17   Other Surveillance

Water quality monitoring and cross-connection control can also be an important part of a utility's distribution system surveillance program.

6.2   SYSTEM VALVES

Distribution system shutoff valves are provided primarily to isolate small areas for emergency maintenance. Most of these valves, therefore, suffer from lack of operation rather than from wear. A comprehensive program of inspection, exercising, and maintenance of valves on a regular basis can help water utilities avoid potentially serious problems when the need to use a valve arises.

Operators should know *EXACTLY* where to go to shut off any valves at any time in case of a line break or other emergency. When breaks occur in water mains, crews often experience problems in *FINDING* valves whose locations are marked incorrectly on system maps. Other problems include valves that won't close or open after they are located. Time is often wasted looking for valves and after finding them getting them to work. The same devices used to locate mains are used to locate valves that may be lost or buried under earth or snow.

Routine valve inspections should be conducted and the following tasks performed:

1. Verify the accuracy of the location of the valve boxes on the system map (if incorrect, *CHANGE THE MAP*),

2. After removing the valve box cover, inspect the stem and nut for damage or obvious leakage,

3. Close the valve fully, if possible, and record the number of turns to the fully closed position,

4. Reopen the valve to reestablish system flows, and

5. Clean valve box cover seat. Sometimes covers on valve boxes will come off when traffic passes over them due to dirt in the seat.

Exercising (opening and closing a valve) should be done at the same time the valve inspection is made. Some manufacturers recommend that a valve stem never be left in a fully open position. They recommend that after fully opening a valve, back off the stem by one turn. Be careful closing valves because if some valves are closed too tight, damage to the valve or valve seat could result and cause the valve to leak.

Conditions of each system will determine how often the valves should be exercised, but in general it is recommended that all valves be exercised at least once a year. Planned exercising of valves verifies valve location, determines whether or not the valve works, and extends valve life by helping to clean encrustations from the valve seats and gates. Any valves that do not completely close or open should be replaced. Valves that leak around the stems should be repacked. To determine that a valve is closed, an aquaphone or other listening device can be used. Valves should be exercised in both directions (fully closed and fully opened) and the number of turns and direction of operation recorded. Valves operating in a direction opposite to that which is standard for the system need to be identified and this fact recorded. The condition of the valve packing, stem, stem nut, and gearing should be noted. A timely maintenance program should be initiated to correct any problems found during the inspection and exercising.

Two types of hydraulic problems can occur while operating a valve, cavitation (CAV-uh-TAY-shun) and water hammer. Cavitation results when a partial vacuum (voids) occurs on the downstream side of a valve and a small section of the pipe is filled with low-pressure vapor pockets. These pockets will collapse downstream (implode) and in doing so create a mechanical shock that causes small chips of metal to break away from the valve surfaces. A noisy or vibrating valve may be an indication that cavitation is occurring and the valve may eventually have to be replaced if cavitation is permitted to go on indefinitely. Water hammer is caused by closing a valve too quickly. The water flow is suddenly stopped, shock waves are generated, and the resulting large pressure increases throughout the system (even though very brief) can result in significant damage. Water hammer can be prevented by always closing the valves slowly, regardless of size or type.

Valves can be operated either manually or by a power actuator. Manual operation of large valves not only can be backbreaking labor, but is a slow process and, therefore, time consuming and costly. Power equipment (Figures 6.2 and 6.3) is available which will cut valve operating time considerably. Most types of power equipment are portable, fast, and efficient and can be powered by a portable air compressor, an electric generator, or a gas engine. A power valve operator can also be used to accurately count the number of turns to open or close a valve.

Two of the most important factors in maintaining distribution system valves are the availability of current and correct maps of the distribution system. A portion of a typical distribution system map for valves and hydrants is shown in Figure 6.4. Each utility should use this type of map, verify often that it is accurate, and keep the map up to date by immediately recording any changes such as replacements or additions. Some water departments equip their service trucks with "gate books" which carry all of the pertinent valve information including location, direction of turning to close, and number of turns required.

Maintaining current records is as important as maintaining current maps. A typical two-sided valve record form is shown in Figure 6.5. The location of a valve is obtained from a controlled survey bench mark or permanent reference point. The make of valve is important because different makes have different operating characteristics. The use of a simple valve

Fig. 6.2 How powered valve operators work
(Permission of E. H. Wachs Company)

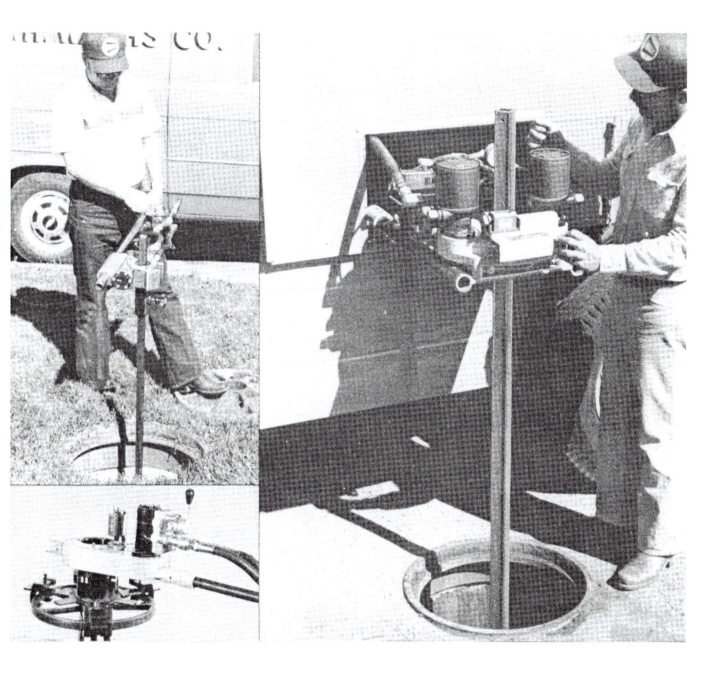

Fig. 6.3   Portable and truck-mounted powered valve operators

(Permission of E. H. Wachs Company)

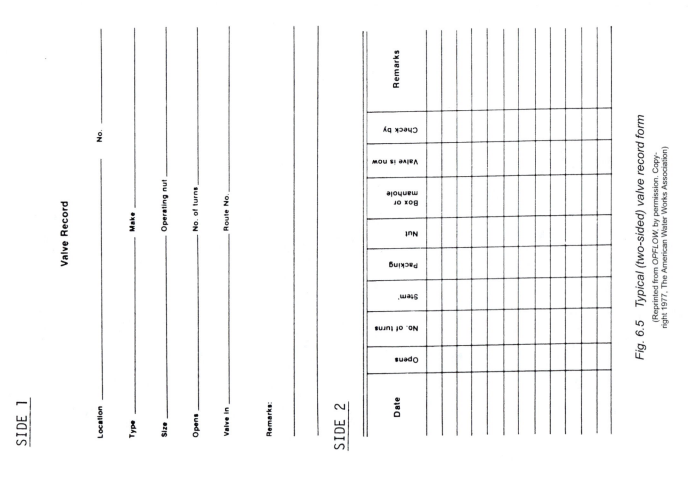

SIDE 1

Valve Record

No.

Location

Type   Make

Size   Operating nut

Opens   No. of turns

Valve In   Route No.

Remarks:

SIDE 2

Date	Opens	No. of turns	Stem	Packing	Nut	Box or manhole	Valve is now	Check by	Remarks

Fig. 6.5   Typical (two-sided) valve record form

(Reprinted from *OPFLOW*, by permission. Copyright 1977, The American Water Works Association)

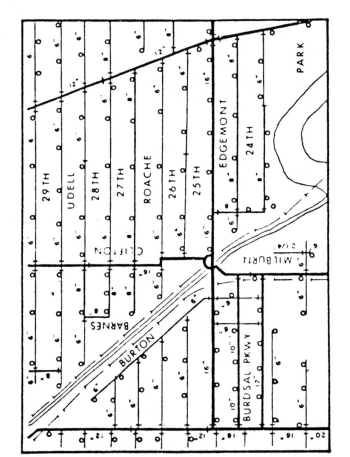

Fig. 6.4   Portion of a valve and hydrant map with street names and main sizes given

(Reprinted from *OPFLOW*, by permission. Copyright 1977, The American Water Works Association)

○ Hydrant
+ Valve

numbering system keyed to up-to-date maps is recommended. This procedure has proven to be quite helpful in locating valves rapidly and in communicating with others about particular valves.

Road improvements require constant attention from water distribution system operators to ensure that valves are not lost. Valve boxes can be graded out or covered with pavement. The center lines of roads, curb lines, and right-of-way lines used as reference points for locating valves can be changed. Changed measurements must be noted on valve record forms.

Corrosion is a problem for valves in some areas and can cause failure of bonnet and packing gland bolts. This is apparent when stem leakage occurs or when a valve is closed and the bonnet separates from the body. Stainless-steel bolts can be used for replacement, and the valve should be encased in polyethylene wrap.

Valves left closed in error can cause severe problems in a distribution system. Construction and maintenance crews operate valves as they do their work. Contractors and plumbers sometimes operate valves without permission. Separate pressure zones in distribution systems may be established by closing valves, thus increasing the possibility of problems related to the incorrect use of valves. Unexplained problems with pressure and excessive operation of pumps in a given area have been traced to valves left closed or open in error. When crews change shifts during a project, valve closures and openings information must be exchanged. Crew chiefs must be sure all valves are restored to proper positions whenever anyone discovers a valve in the wrong position.

Repairing in-line (installed) gate valves is a difficult task. If repairs are needed, proper advance planning is important. The valves needing repairs must be located. The valves that will be used to isolate a damaged valve must be in good operating condition. The necessary repair parts must be obtained in advance. When ordering repair parts, be sure to include the size, make, direction of opening, year of manufacture, and other pertinent information in order to ensure that the proper repair parts will be received.

Until the valve is isolated and opened up, it is difficult to determine what part of the valve is damaged. Therefore, make sure that all replacement parts are available before isolating the necessary section of the water main, excavating the valve, and making the repairs.

Most valves are located along roadways, and operators who locate, exercise, or dig up valves for repair are exposed to traffic hazards. Routine work is usually done during daylight, but traffic must be warned at all times. Motorists must be notified in advance of blocked lanes or work alongside of traveled lanes. This can be done by using high-level warning signs, barricades with lights for night work, traffic cones, warning flags, and flaggers. Repair crew vehicles with flashers can be positioned to alert traffic and to provide physical protection for the crew from oncoming traffic at the work site. Supervisors should hold a job-site meeting with operators to explain the task, the equipment to be used for the job, the hazards, the safety procedures to follow, and the safety equipment needed. See Chapter 7, Section 7.5, "Working in Streets," in *WATER DISTRIBUTION SYSTEM OPERATION AND MAINTENANCE*, for more safety information.

For additional information on valve maintenance, see Chapter 18, "Maintenance," Section 18.26, "Valves," in *WATER TREATMENT PLANT OPERATION*, Volume II, in this series of manuals.

6.3 METERS

6.30 Purpose of Meters

The primary function of a meter is to measure and display the amount of water passing through it. A metered water system is one in which meters are used at all strategic points: on main supply lines, pumping stations, reservoir outlets, connections to other utility systems, and at each customer's service. Metering provides many benefits. The customer can be billed for the exact amount of water used, the amount of water produced can be determined, losses of water can be detected by comparing service meter and hydrant use meter readings with production meter readings, and capacities of pipelines can be determined. By determining costs, metering prevents waste through excessive use of water and thereby reduces water consumption. Meters are also used to provide accurate blending of waters of different quality so that the mix in the reservoirs is of the same constant quality. The information obtained from metering can show how efficiently the water utility is operating and can provide for system control.

6.31 Meter Selection

In selecting meters, look for the ability to measure and register your anticipated flow levels, ability to meet required capacity with minimum head loss, durability, ruggedness, precision of workmanship, ease of repair, availability of spare parts, freedom from irritating noise, a reasonable price, and a manufacturer with a good reputation. When selecting a brand of water meter for your utility, be sure to consider the availability of replacement meters and spare parts. Also try to determine the delivery time for the manufacturer to respond to an order for a needed part. Check with other utilities to verify that the manufacturer has the kind of warranty you want and will stand behind its products.

Sufficient accuracy is needed so that small meters do not register less than 98.5 percent nor more than 101.5 percent of the water passing through them. Large meters should accurately measure between 97 and 103 percent. Certain large meters are accurate within 1 percent. Generally, meters of 1 inch (25 mm) and smaller should have a head loss not exceeding 15 psi (103 kPa or 1.0 kg/sq cm), while the head loss of larger meters should not exceed 20 psi (138 kPa or 1.4 kg/sq cm).

6.32 Meter Types

Basically, meters can be classified as small-flow meters, large-flow meters, and combination large/small-flow meters as shown below.

    I. Small-flow meters (displacement type)

        A. Nutating-disc
        B. Piston

    II. Large-flow meters (velocity type)

        A. Turbine
        B. Propeller
        C. Venturi
        D. Electronic
        E. Insertion

    III. Combination meters (compound type)

6.320 Displacement Meters

Displacement-type meters are small-diameter meters (up to 2 inches (50 mm)) commonly used for customer services. For commercial services, however, they may be as large as 6 inches (15 mm) (Figure 6.6). This type of meter measures the flow by registering the number of times the meter chamber, whose volume is known, is filled and emptied. In this chamber, which is usually cylindrical in shape, a piston or disc goes through a certain cycle of motion that corresponds to a single filling and emptying of the chamber. This movement is transferred to a register.

The advantages of displacement meters are that they can measure wide variations of flow rate within their rated capacity and, in sizes up to 2 inches (50 mm), are accurate in registering low flows. The principal limitations are that in sizes greater than 2 inches (50 mm), the sensitivity at the lower rate of flow decreases so much that it is advisable to use another type of meter. Their capacity is limited and at high flows there is a high head loss. Also, large quantities of foreign matter or corrosion will either stop the meter entirely or cause its accuracy to decrease because of friction.

The different ways in which the disc or piston in the displacement meter moves have been used to categorize the various types of displacement meters. The two types normally encountered are the nutating-disc and the piston meters.

The nutating-disc meter is the most commonly used meter on small-diameter domestic services (Figures 6.6 and 6.7). Nutating means nodding, which somewhat describes the action of the disc in the chamber of the meter. The disc may be flat or conical in shape and is made of hard rubber. When water flows, the tilted disc rotates. These meters are made with a bottom plate which breaks away automatically to prevent damage when the water freezes.

In the piston-type meter, water flows into a chamber and displaces a piston and the oscillatory circulating motion is transmitted to a register (Figure 6.8). Piston-type meters have a slightly greater head loss than nutating-disc meters.

6.321 Velocity-Type Meters

These meters are sometimes called current meters. They are found in sizes up to 36 inches (900 mm) and larger and actually measure the velocity of flow past a cross section of known area. Large quantities of water (within meter capacity) can be passed without any damage to their working parts and the meters are rugged and easy to maintain. Their rather low head loss is ideal for a meter that must pass high rates of flow; however, the meters become unreliable at low flow rates. Some low flows will pass through without being registered at all. This kind of meter is very satisfactory for main lines, pumps with continuous high flow rates and irrigation, golf course, industrial, and other high-flow uses.

Velocity meters include turbine (Figures 6.9 and 6.10) and propeller meters (Figure 6.11), as well as the Venturi, insertion type, and most electronic water meters.

In turbine or propeller meters, the rotors or propellers are turned by the flow of the water at a speed proportional to the velocity of water flow. This movement is then transmitted to a register. They are not designed for low flows or stop-and-go operation. Both types of meters are most useful in measuring continuously high flows, and both have low friction loss. The propeller meter may be installed within a section of pipe or it may be saddle mounted.

When main lines must be metered, it is desirable to have a meter that will not interfere with the flow of water if the meter fails. In case of fire, nothing must stop the effective flow of water. One principal type of meter that meets this requirement is the Venturi meter which is shown in Figure 6.12. A Venturi meter consists of an upstream reducer, a short throat piece, and a downstream expansion section which increases the diameter from the throat section to that of the downstream pipe. The amount of water passing through is metered by comparing the pressure at the throat and at a point upstream from the throat. Venturi meters are accurate over a large flow range and cause little friction loss.

An orifice plate can be used as an insertion-type meter. A thin plate with a circular hole in it is installed in the pipeline between a set of flanges (Figure 6.13). Flow is determined by comparing the upstream line pressure with the reduced pressure at the orifice restriction. Orifice plates are quite a bit less expensive than Venturi meters, occupy less space, but have more severe pressure losses and are somewhat less reliable.

6.322 Compound Meters

When water flow fluctuates widely, a compromise between the low- and high-flow meters is used. This compromise is a combination of the displacement and velocity-type meters and is called a compound meter. The displacement part of the meter records the low flows, and when the head loss through this part of the meter rises to a certain level, a compounding valve is actuated and permits the water to flow through the velocity portion of the meter. Compound meters are shown in Figures 6.14, 6.15, and 6.16.

Compound meters have special advantages in places where there are predominantly low or intermediate flows and only occasional high flows. This would include services to hotels, hospitals, factories, schools, apartment houses, commercial properties, and office buildings. They are best suited for locations with widely varying flows where accurate low-flow measurement is needed. However, where the majority of flows are moderate to high, a turbine meter is generally used.

The main advantage of compound meters, with the separate measuring chambers, is that they accurately measure flows from a fraction of a gallon up to the normal capacity of the pipeline. Even very small flows from leaks and individual faucets can be measured accurately. Compound meters can be subjected to high rates of flow for long time periods and are more rugged than displacement meters. Their limitations are that loss of head from friction is higher than in large-flow meters; during the changeover from low to high and high to low flows their accuracy drops; and they are large, cumbersome, and expensive.

6.323 Electronic Meters

Electronic meters include the magnetic and sonic types of meters. The magnetic meter is often called a "mag meter." Water flowing through a magnetic field induces a small electric current flow which is proportional to the water flow. The electric current produced is measured and mathematically changed to a measure of water flow.

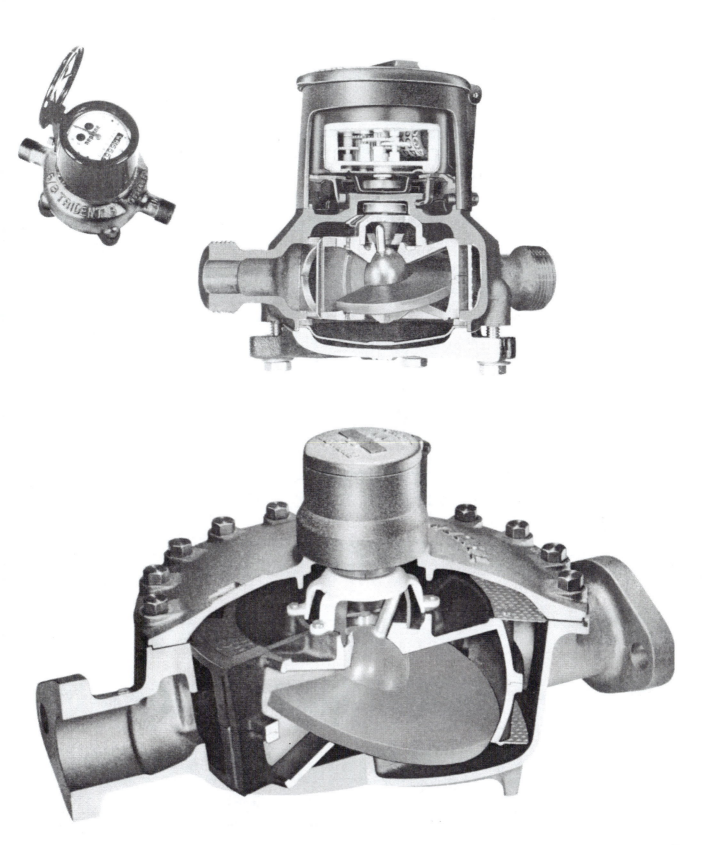

Fig. 6.6   Nutating-disc (nodding) water meters
(Permission of Neptune Water Meter Company)

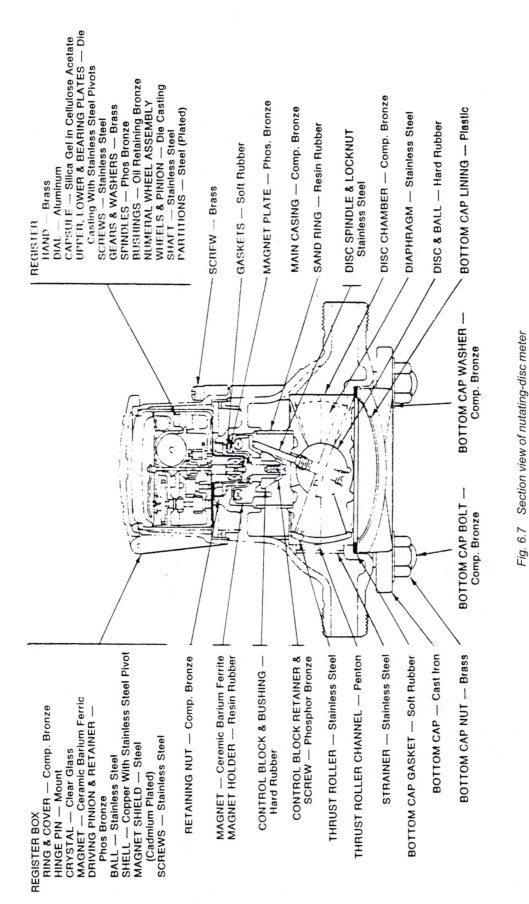

Fig. 6.7   Section view of nutating-disc meter

(Reprinted from WATER DISTRIBUTION OPERATOR TRAINING HANDBOOK, by permission.
Copyright 1976, the American Water Works Association)

Sonic meters contain sensors which are attached to the sides of a pipe. Sound pulses are sent alternately across the pipe in opposite diagonal directions. The frequency of the sound changes with the velocity of the water through which the sound waves must travel. An accurate measurement of water flow can be made using the difference between the frequency of the sound signal traveling with the flow of water and that traveling against the flow of water.

Electronic meters are generally highly accurate and there is no head loss. However, they are adversely affected by anything that distorts the velocity of the water flowing through the pipe such as elbows, pumps, and certain types of valves. This condition can make the meters so inaccurate as to be practically useless. The problem can be corrected, though, by leaving a distance of at least ten pipe diameters between an upstream obstruction or fitting and the flowmeter.

6.324 Proportional Meters

Another type of meter is the proportional meter in which a certain proportion of the total flow is diverted through a bypass meter and measured (Figure 6.17). The gears of the measuring bypass meter are adjusted to indicate on its register dial the total amount of water passing through the whole unit. The flows in the bypass line and the main pipe are proportional to the ratio of the areas of the bypass line and the main pipe. Therefore, a displacement or turbine meter which measures only the diverted flow can be calibrated to register the full amount of water in the main pipeline. The diversion of a portion of the flow through the bypass meter is accomplished by an orifice plate. This causes sufficient pressure differential to divert a portion of the water through the measuring meter. This type of meter is relatively accurate except for low flows. The meter is principally used to meter fire lines.

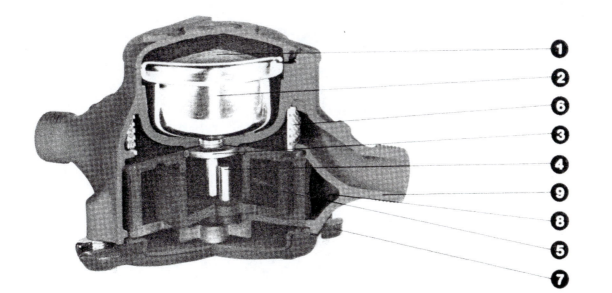

1. Heat-treated glass
2. Hermetically sealed register
3. Register retainer
4. Magnetic drive
5. Oscillating piston and piston roller
6. Cylindrical strainer
7. Interchangeable bottom plate
8. Measuring chamber
9. All cast bronze maincase

Fig. 6.8   Piston-type meter
(Courtesy of Rockwell International Corporation, Municipal & Utility Division)

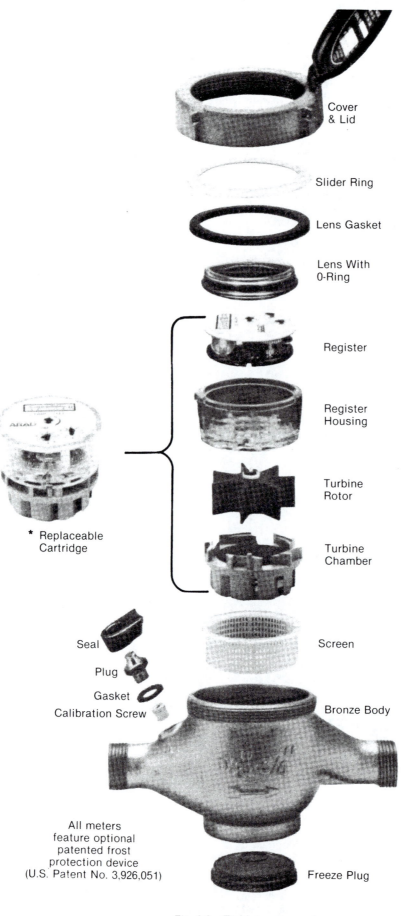

Cover & Lid

Slider Ring

Lens Gasket

Lens With 0-Ring

Register

Register Housing

Turbine Rotor

Turbine Chamber

Screen

Bronze Body

Freeze Plug

Seal

Plug

Gasket

Calibration Screw

* Replaceable Cartridge

All meters feature optional patented frost protection device (U.S. Patent No. 3,926,051)

Fig. 6.9   Turbine water meter

(Permission of Neptune Water Meter Company)

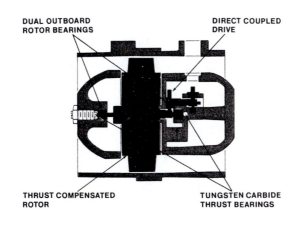

Fig. 6.10   Turbine water meter
(Permission of Western Water Meter)

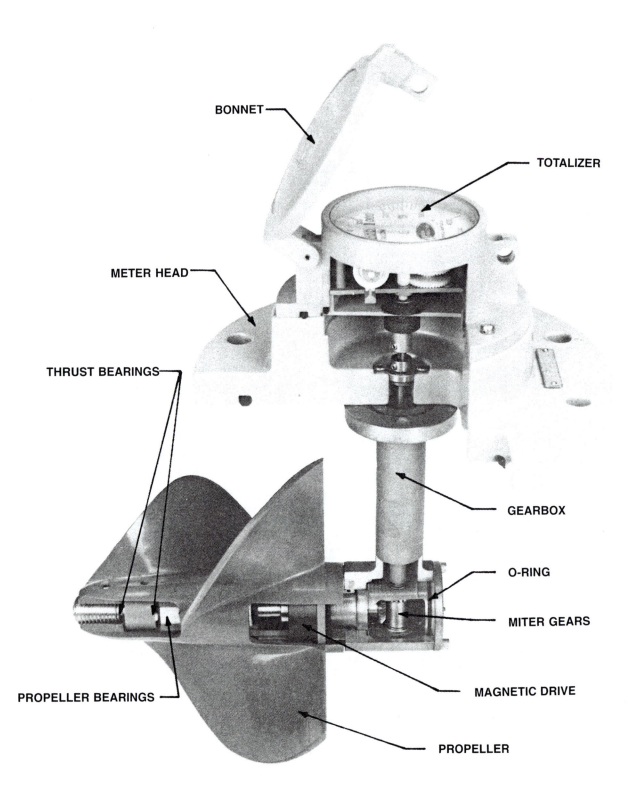

Fig. 6.11　Propeller meter
(Permission of Water Specialties Corporation)

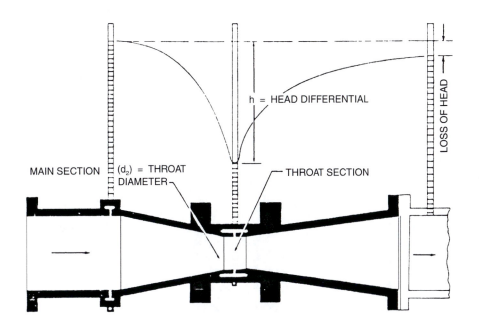

Fig. 6.12   Venturi meter

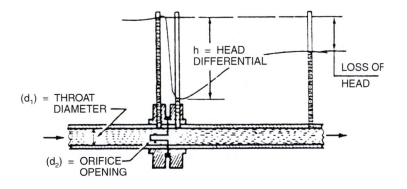

Fig. 6.13   Orifice plate meter

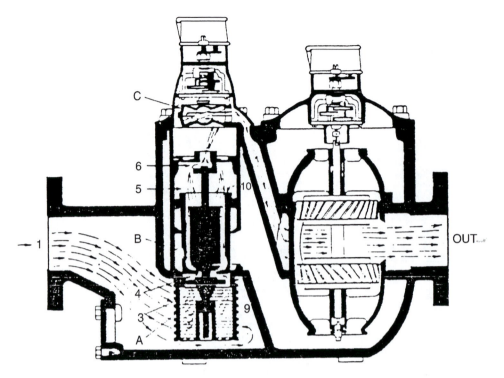

Low Flow

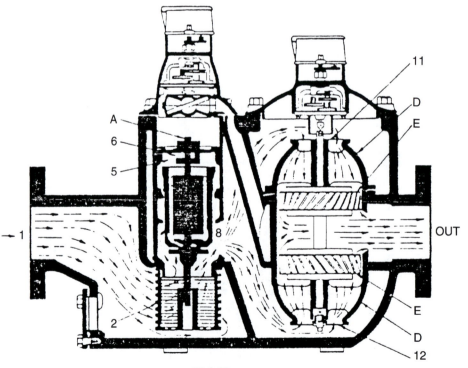

High Flow

Fig. 6.14   Flows through a compound meter

(Reprinted from *WATER DISTRIBUTION OPERATOR TRAINING HANDBOOK*, by permission.
Copyright 1976, the American Water Works Association)

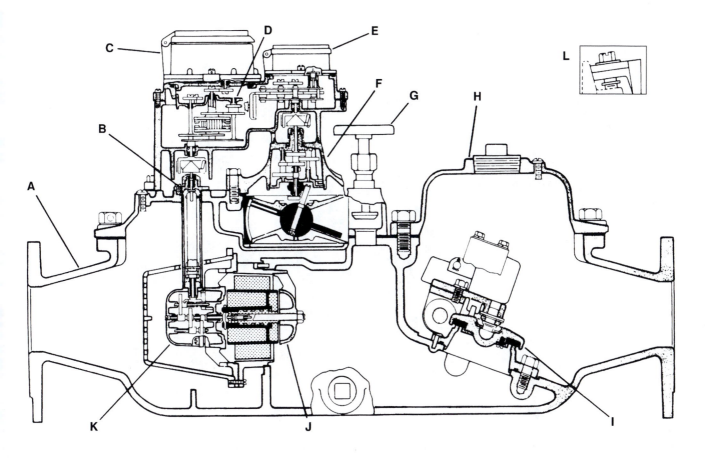

A. Main case
B. Stuffing box plate
C. Register and box
D. Combining drive

E. Test register and box
F. Disc section
G. Valve
H. Cover

I. Valve
J. Measure wheel and cage
K. Gear train
L. Clamps

Fig. 6.15   Sectional view of a compound meter
(Permission of Neptune Water Meter Company)

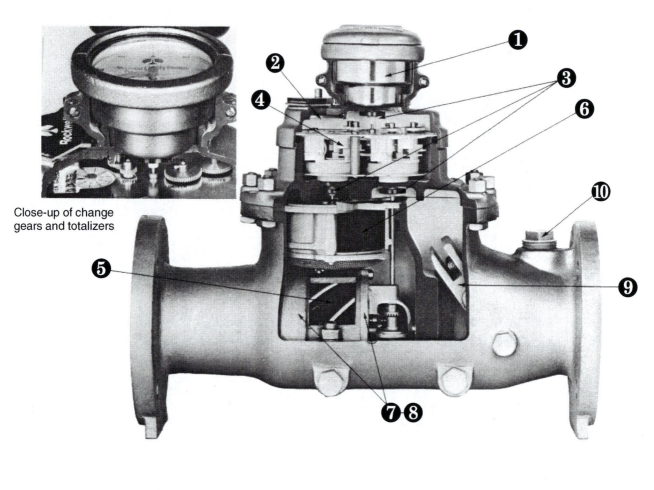

Close-up of change
gears and totalizers

1. Totalizing register	6. Turbine chamber
2. Bypass chamber register	7. Magnetic suspension
3. Magnetic couplings	8. Roller bearings
4. Sealed coordinator module	9. Automatic swing check valve
5. Bypass chamber	10. Test plug

Fig. 6.16   Cutaway views of a compound meter
(Permission of Rockwell International)

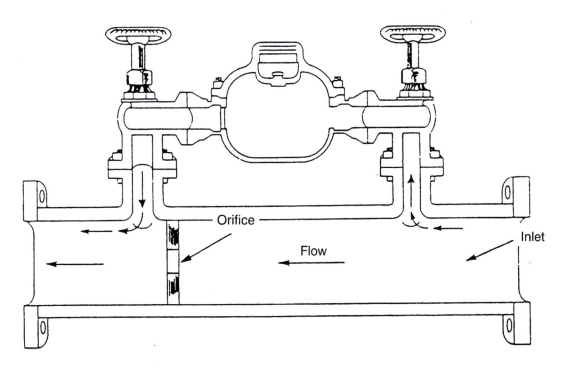

Fig. 6.17   Proportional meter

6.4   SYSTEM PIPES

6.40   Pipe Maintenance

Pipe maintenance is performed to prevent leakage, maintain or restore the pipe's carrying capacity, maintain proper water quality conditions in the pipe, and prolong the effective life of the pipe. A pipe's useful life can be greatly extended if it is properly maintained and rehabilitated. The type of maintenance carried out includes repairing leaks and breaks, flushing, cleaning, disinfecting, and relining.

Pipes deteriorate on the inside because of water corrosion and erosion and on the outside because of corrosion from aggressive soil moisture. Even under the best of conditions, pipe can be weakened and damaged with time. All types of metal, concrete, and asbestos-cement pipe are subject to some deterioration. This deterioration may be revealed as a loss of water carrying capacity, leaks, or degradation of water quality. Loss of water carrying capacity can result from corrosion, pitting, tuberculation, deposition of sediment, and slime growth.

6.41   Locating Leaks

Leak detection programs are an effective means for some water utilities to reduce operating and maintenance costs. If a leak detection crew can reduce the flow of leaks and produce cost savings greater than the cost of maintaining the field crew, then the leak detection program is economically justified. Leak detection programs can also be justified in terms of the early detection and repair of leaks while they are small, before serious failure occurs with resulting property damage, crew overtime, delays of other projects, and similar problems. Also a water shortage may require an effective leak detection program.

Leaks may originate from any weakened joint or fitting connection or from a damaged or corroded part of the pipe. Leaks are undesirable not only because they waste water, but because they can undermine pavements and other structures. Another undesirable effect of leaks is that the leak soaks the ground surrounding the pipe and, in the event that pressure is lost in the pipe, the water, combined now with dirt and other contaminants, may backflow into the pipe.

The total amount of leakage in a distribution system is affected by a number of factors. Improper pipe installation (bedding, backfill, misalignment) can result not only in weakened joint and fitting connections, but also in damage to the pipe itself and to any corrosion-protection measures that have been provided. The pipe's durability, strength, and corrosion resistance will vary with the type of pipe material used. Protection against corrosion is an important maintenance activity which will minimize leakage. The older the pipe, the more time there has been for corrosion to act and for the pipe system to be weakened, especially at joints and fittings. The longer the pipe system, the more "opportunity" (joints) there is for leaks to occur. Aggressive water and soil will accelerate corrosion in susceptible pipe. Systems with higher pressures produce more leakage. The vibration caused by traffic loading may cause damage to buried pipes. Soil movement due to changes in moisture, frost heave, and earthquakes causes damage to pipes. In all of these cases, the total amount of leakage is also affected by the type of soil surrounding the leaking pipes. In coarse soils (sands) the leakage may continue for a long time without detection, whereas in finer soils (clays) the leaks show up sooner on the surface, which means they may be detected sooner.

The process of locating a leak is often not easy and sometimes becomes a troublesome and frustrating experience.

Methods used to locate leaks include direct observation as well as use of sounding rods, listening devices, and data from a waste control study. The checklist in Figure 6.18 identifies a variety of steps that can be taken to determine whether leaks are occurring and to locate the sources of leaks.

Checklist for Leak Detection

1. Using sound-intensifying instruments, listen on fire hydrants, valves, meters, mains, and services. Do this periodically.

2. If leak sounds are heard, conduct a detailed investigation by listening on each meter in the area of the leak sound. Meters are convenient points for making contact with the underground piping system. Listening on the meter allows you to check the meter coupling and curb stop for leakage. Sounds heard at a meter may be a leak on the service or on the street main.

3. If meters are widely spaced, listen over the main at closely spaced intervals with sound-intensifying instruments to locate leaks in the main.

4. Have meter readers listen on services. Develop incentive programs to encourage meter readers to report leaks.

5. Inspect sewer manholes and catch basins for unusual amounts of clear water running in the sewer or coming through joints in the manhole.

6. Check all stream crossings for water bubbling up through the streambed or for the stream to be carrying a much larger volume of water than normal.

7. Check out sudden increases in metered consumption. This could indicate a service line leak.

8. Investigate complaints from customers who report hearing water running in their house piping. This may be caused by a service leak, by a leak in the neighbor's service, or by a leak in the main.

9. Investigate complaints of low pressure in the distribution system. This could indicate that a large leak has occurred. This condition may be reported by customers or by the fire department.

10. Check for commercial, industrial, and residential unmetered use.

11. Check for use from unmetered fire services and private yard hydrants.

12. Review policy on unmetered use: Is public use (for parks, street cleaning, and so forth) unmetered? Review policy on allowing contractors and others to fill tank trucks from hydrants without the water being metered.

13. Install meters in public buildings, churches, hospitals, schools, parks, municipal golf courses, pollution control plants, fire service, or anywhere unmetered water is used.

14. Meter all blowoffs of water from the distribution system.

15. Monitor the metered ratios. (Compare readings from the master meter at the plant, which measures all water entering the distribution system, to all metered readings from customers for the same period of time.)

Fig. 6.18   Checklist for leak detection

(Source: Pitotmeter Associates, Consulting Engineers.
Reprinted from *PACIFIC MOUNTAIN NETWORK NEWS*)

The simplest method of leak detection is to search for and locate wet spots which might indicate the presence of a leak. Sometimes these are reported by the system's customers. However, even if a damp spot is found, it does not necessarily mean that the leak can be easily found. The leak may be located directly below the damp area or it may be 50 yards (46 m) or more away. Often the leak is someplace other than where it would be expected because water will follow the path of least resistance to the ground surface.

After the general location of the leak has been determined, a probe may be used to find it exactly. This probe is a sharp-pointed metal rod that is thrust into the ground and then pulled up for inspection. If the rod is moist or muddy, the line of the leak is being followed. *BE CAREFUL YOU DON'T PROBE INTO AN ELECTRICAL CABLE.*

Listening devices are made up of sound-intensifying equipment that is used in a systematic fashion to locate leaks. The simplest listening device is a steel bar held against the pipe or valve. The device is moved in the direction of increasing sound until the leak is found. Patented leak detectors use audiophones to pick up the sound of escaping water. Some types of test rods can be driven into the ground and held against the pipe or held against above-ground hydrants and valves. Listening sticks are sometimes equipped with electronic controls giving the operator the ability to select different frequencies to reduce background noise. Different types of leak detection equipment are shown in Figures 6.19, 6.20, and 6.21.

Another method for locating leaks is the use of a leak noise correlator. This type of instrument locates leaks by noise intensity and the time it takes for the leak sound to travel to a pair of microphones placed on fittings (fire hydrants or stop valves) on each side of a suspected leak. Leak correlators are fairly accurate in locating a leak. However, they are of limited use in systems with reduced noise levels such as low-pressure systems and/or pipes made of materials that absorb sound (for example, concrete pipes). Also, leak noise correlators are of limited use in systems with relatively few fittings.

The amount of water lost from the distribution system through leakage is only one component of the system's total water losses. Losses due to illegal connections also occur, and meter malfunctions that produce incorrect readings could give the appearance that higher or lower quantities of water have been used. The total amount of water lost from a distribution system from all sources is often referred to as "unaccounted for water" or UFW. The UFW is the difference between the total amount of water produced and the total amount of water consumed. The amount of unaccounted for water lost by a distribution system is usually determined by conducting a water audit.

A water audit is a thorough examination of the accuracy of water agency records or accounts (volumes of water) and system control equipment. Water managers can use audits to determine their water distribution system efficiency. The overall goal is to identify and verify water and revenue losses in a water system. This allows the water utility to select and implement programs to reduce water and revenue losses. Such examinations must be performed annually to update the results of an earlier audit.

Benefits resulting from a water audit can be significant, including:

1. *Reduced Water Losses*—Conducting a leak detection project will identify and locate system leakage. Upon repair of the leaks, water savings will result. Savings are also realized in reduced power costs to deliver water and reduced chemicals to treat water.

2. *Financial Improvement*—A water audit and leak detection program can increase revenues from customers who have been undercharged, lower costs of wholesale supplies, and reduce treatment and pumping costs.

3. *Increased Knowledge of the Distribution System*—The added familiarity of the distribution system gained during a water audit and leak detection project helps a utility to respond more quickly to such emergencies as main breaks.

4. *More Efficient Use of Existing Supplies*—Reducing water losses will help stretch existing supplies to meet increased needs. This could help defer the construction of new water facilities, such as a new well, reservoir, or treatment plant.

5. *Reduced Property Damage*—Improved maintenance of a water distribution system can reduce the likelihood of property damage and better safeguard public health and safety.

6. *Improved Public Relations*—The public appreciates seeing that its water systems are being maintained. Field teams carrying out water audit and leak detection tasks and doing repair and maintenance work make a favorable impression.

7. *Reduced Legal Liability*—Conducting a water audit and leak detection project provides better information for protection against expensive lawsuits.

Waste control or water audit studies are usually conducted when no specific reason can be found for a significant water loss in the system. Routine comparisons of water production and use should be made to determine the amount of unaccounted for or "lost" water. The amount of unaccounted for water that is acceptable depends largely on the conditions in each system. In some systems there is concern when the loss exceeds 10 percent of the water produced while in other systems there is little concern until 20 percent of the water produced cannot be accounted for. The amount of unaccounted for water is affected by leaks, pressures, efficiency of meter maintenance, and the attention given to leakage reduction and unauthorized uses of water. Leakage has already been discussed. Higher pressures not only result in more leakage, but increase the underregistration of meters. Meters also tend to underregister as they get older and if they are not being properly maintained. Utilities that pay attention to finding and eliminating hidden losses of their supply will naturally have a more efficient and cost-effective operation.

Waste control studies basically involve flow measurements beginning at the source of supply and working out into the system. The system's source and master meters are checked out first. Then separate areas ("districts") are isolated by making appropriate valve manipulations. All the water to the isolated district is made to pass through a single pipe where the flow is measured with a meter. Usually, there is an average of about 18 miles (29 km) of mains per district, but this could vary from 4 to 46 miles (6 to 75 km), depending on the situation. If the flow through the pipe is found to be greater than normal, the isolated district is divided into smaller districts to narrow in on the source of the abnormal use, leaks, or wastage. Measurements of water consumption are made in the late evening hours because they are more likely to indicate leakage, waste, or abnormal use of water without the complications presented by normal daytime use. Those areas where unexplained high

Fig. 6.19   Leak detection instrument

(Permission of Heath Consultants, Inc.)

Fig. 6.20   Leak detection
(Permission of Heath Consultants, Inc.)

consumption rates are found are further investigated in detail by visual and sounding methods. Surface areas can be observed for wet spots or depressions, and valves, hydrants, and services can be sounded for typical audible vibrations produced by water escaping from defects in the underground piping.

The most convenient flow measurement device used in studies of this type is the pitotmeter. This device is a reversible (water velocity) pitot (PEA-toe) tube that can be inserted into a main through a one-inch (25-mm) corporation cock (Figure 6.22). The differential pressure (D) caused by the velocity of

the water flowing past the openings to the tubes is calibrated to the average velocity of the water flowing in the main. Recording devices can be used with it to record continuous flow rates over time periods of 12, 24, or 48 hours. This type of meter has a field accuracy of ± 2 percent and can measure flows over a wide range from a few thousand gallons per day to over 200 MGD (750 ML/day).[3]

6.42   Locating Pipes

Ideally, all pipe in a water system would be in standardized, easy to find locations and maps would be available showing

---

[3] 750 megaliters per day or 750 million liters per day.

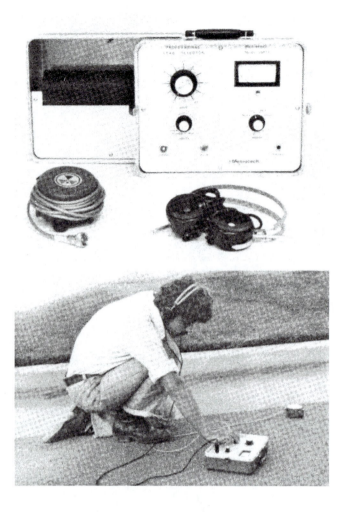

with water flowing in the pipe by using two wire coat hangers. They straighten out the two coat hangers and place a 90-degree bend in each hanger about 6 inches from the end. Holding the 6-inch pieces loosely in each hand and pointing the long pieces in front of their body, they walk toward the suspected location of the buried pipe. When they cross over the pipe, the coat hangers will rotate and align over the buried pipe.

Technology is developing sound-generating devices that could be effective in locating buried nonmetallic pipe. These devices are connected to the pipe, a water meter, a faucet, or a fire hydrant. They use a transmitter to generate a traceable sound that is created by tapping the pipe and a receiver to detect the sound as it moves through the pipe. Thus, the receiver is capable of identifying the location of the buried pipe. This technique may only be effective for about 100 feet because nonmetallic pipe is not a good conductor of sound.

Another approach is the attachment of a type of butterfly valve that is rapidly shut when water is flowing through the pipe. A "water hammer" is generated that moves back and forth down the pipe and can be detected by the receiver. This procedure can detect the water hammer for about 100 feet. A limitation of this procedure is that the water hammer could cause leaks or breaks in the pipe unless properly used by trained persons.

Fig. 6.21   Leak detector
(Permission of Metrotech)

precisely where the installation was made. Unfortunately, this ideal situation rarely exists. Other measures must often be used to locate the pipes while searching for a leak, when a new connection is to be made, or if an excavation must be made in the area to locate or install other nearby facilities. Even when good records are available, an accurate determination of the underground facilities should be made in the field. Numerous devices have been developed to expedite finding buried pipe. One of these devices is shown in Figure 6.23. Electronic pipe finders consist basically of a portable radio-direction-finder receiver. The transmitter induces an electromagnetic field into any buried metallic object within its range. As the receiver is carried across a pipe location, the induced electromagnetic field is detected and produces an audible tone in the earphones used and a deflection on a visual indicating instrument. Both the position and depth of the buried pipe can usually be determined. Another device used is a stainless-steel-tipped shaft which is pushed into the ground to locate the pipe. For future location of nonmetallic pipe, a metallic tracer tape (wire) which is detectable by electronic finders is put on top of the pipe before it is covered.

Locating buried nonmetallic pipes, such as plastic pipes, that do not have a metallic tracer tape (wire) can be very challenging for operators. Some operators can locate buried pipe

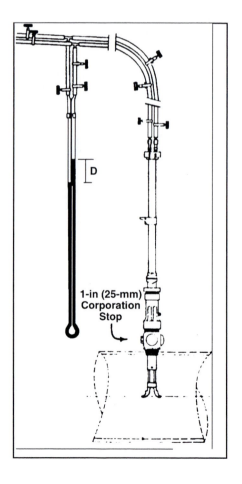

1-in (25-mm) Corporation Stop

Fig. 6.22   Modified pitotmeter
(Reprinted from AWWA *WATER DISTRIBUTION TRAINING COURSE*, by permission. Copyright 1962, the American Water Works Association)

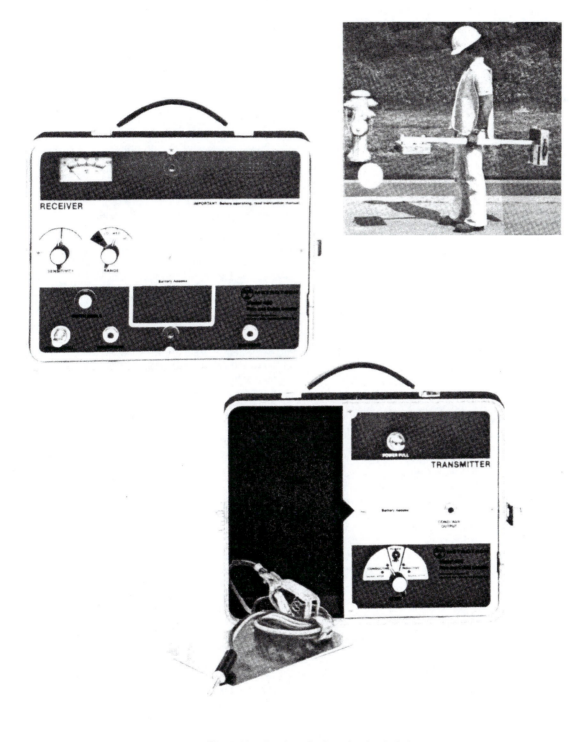

Fig. 6.23   Devices for locating buried pipe

(Permission of Metrotech)

The cost of purchasing a transmitter and receiver may be prohibitive for many water systems. However, a contractor with this equipment may be available to locate the buried nonmetallic pipe. Be sure that the vendor or contractor guarantees the results and performance you desire, in writing, before agreeing to pay for equipment or services. Do not pay unless performance is in agreement with the contract and meets your expectations.

As a last resort for locating buried nonmetallic pipe, cut open the pipe at both known ends. Clean an electrical fish tape with a chlorine-soaked rag. Run the electrical fish tape down the line and trace the fish tape to locate the buried pipe. Another approach could be to insert a "pig" with an electronic transmitter into the line and trace the pig above ground. Remove the pig after the line has been traced.

6.43   Repairing Leaks and Pulled Services

After the leak has been located, route traffic around the work area and take any other necessary safety precautions BEFORE starting excavation. Also try to locate other underground utilities BEFORE starting any excavation. Many phone books list in the "White" pages an "Underground Service Alert" or "One-Call" phone number which should be called BEFORE digging or drilling underground.

A maintenance crew excavates and uncovers the leaky pipe. Sometimes a dewatering pump is also needed to drain the hole before it is possible to work around the pipe. If the main must be isolated before the repairs are made, notify all affected consumers in advance and give them an estimated length of time that the main will be out of service. Leaks at joints or splits or breaks may have to be repaired. Shoring may be required depending on depth of pipe and soil conditions. A good slogan to remember is, "WHEN IN DOUBT, SHORE IT."[4] The simplest repair is accomplished by using repair clamps (Figure 6.24). These devices are short, cylindrical pieces usually made of one piece of pipe or in two halves and bolted together or otherwise fastened around a pipe, covering a break, or making a joint between two pipes. For long splits or other defects, clamps up to 18 inches (450 mm) long with rubber or lead gaskets are available. Repair of cracks and breaks in steel pipe is often done by welding. Joint leaks in caulked bell and spigot joints can be stopped by recaulking, by clamps (Figure 6.24), or the entire joint may be removed and replaced. If the main was taken out of service and drained during the repair job, flush and disinfect the main and test a sample for coliforms before placing the main back in service.

Occasionally a contractor digging another utility trench will hit a service line and pull the corporation cock out of the main line. To repair a break of this type, follow the procedures in this section. Be sure to notify all consumers who will be without water how long they can expect to be without water. Some agencies notify the consumers before any valves are closed to isolate the break while others close the valves first. If extensive damage is occurring (erosion, washouts, and flooding) as a result of the break, close the valves as soon as possible.

6.44   Making Pipe and Service Connections

Every water utility agency should have a policy regarding the installation of services and setting of meters to ensure the consumer of an effective installation and to avoid problems in the future. Perhaps the most satisfactory policy is for the

agency to install all services and meters. If the workload is too great for agency crews, all contractors and plumbers should be notified of required procedures and fittings. Work done in new subdivisions is usually performed by contractors. All installations should be inspected and tested for leaks by the agency BEFORE the installation is covered with backfill.

Connections from existing pipe are often made to a new main or a new service pipe. Making service connections, from a street main to a home, is one of the most frequently performed jobs in a water system. Ideally, when new mains are installed, the connections for the service pipe are made prior to pressurizing the main.

The most common method used in making a connection is "wet tapping" where the connection is made with the main under water pressure. A corporation stop is directly inserted into the main (ductile-iron and PVC thick-wall pipe) using a tapping machine. Although it is called a tapping machine, this device allows three operations to be performed on a main under pressure and should more properly be referred to as a drilling, tapping, and inserting machine.

To insert a tap into a main under pressure, the first step is to excavate down to and around the main. Install shoring if necessary. Clean the main. Install saddle and tapping equipment. Be sure the saddle and equipment are tight.

A combined drill and tap is used to first drill a hole into the pipe (Figure 6.25a). Then, a tap is inserted into the main to thread the hole (Figure 6.25b). Next, still using the tapping machine, the threaded inlet of a corporation stop is threaded into the hole (Figure 6.25c). Wet taps are frequently made with a clamp and corporation stop. Finally, the service line is connected to the corporation stop fitting to be activated when the corporation stop is turned on.

Large service connections are usually made using wet tapping with the water mains under pressure. This is much more convenient for both the water utility and the customer. No customer is out of water, and the job can be done at the convenience of the water utility. Wet tapping also eliminates complaints of dirty water which frequently result when shutting down a section of main. In addition, wet tapping avoids loss of considerable amounts of water.

If you do not have the capabilities for wet tapping, you will have to use a dry tapping machine after closing off the valves and emptying that part of the main that will be tapped. In this operation, attach a service clamp around the main and then thread the corporation stop into it (Figure 6.26).[5] With the corporation stop in an open position, attach the drilling device to the corporation stop's outlet threads and drill a hole or make a shell-cut through the wall of the main. After the main is cleaned, bolt a tapping sleeve to it. A tapping sleeve is a split sleeve or clamp in one-half of which is an opening with a flange or other means of attaching a valve. Figure 6.27 is a picture of one type of tapping sleeve used. Next, attach a tapping valve (a permanent valve installation) to the sleeve outlet (Figure 6.28a). Then attach the drilling machine and adapter to the valve outlet flange (Figure 6.28b). With the tapping valve open, advance the cutter and drill a hole into the pipe; retract the cutter and close the tapping valve (Figure 6.28c). After removing the drilling machine, attach a new lateral to the valve outlet flange and activate it by opening the valve.

---

[4] See Chapter 3, "Distribution System Facilities," Section 3.653, "Excavation and Shoring," in WATER DISTRIBUTION SYSTEM OPERATION AND MAINTENANCE, for details.

[5] Some agencies use this type of equipment for wet tapping.

Pipe clamp for repairing pin holes, cracks, bruises, fractures, holes, and other damage in any type of pipe

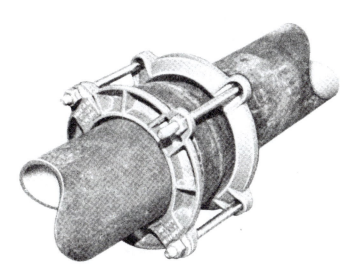

Bell joint clamp for repairing or preventing leaks in cast-iron bell and spigot caulked or rubber ring joints

Fig. 6.24   Leak repair clamps

(Courtesy of Rockwell International Corporation, Municipal & Utility Division)

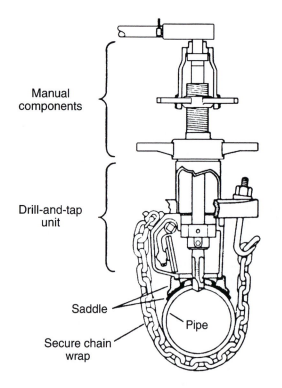

a. With the combined drill-and-tap unit, first drill a hole into the main.

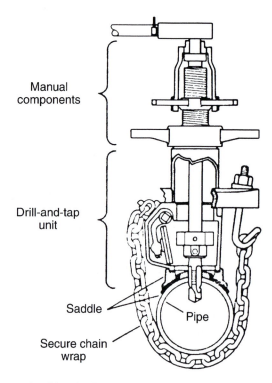

b. After the hole is drilled, insert the tap.

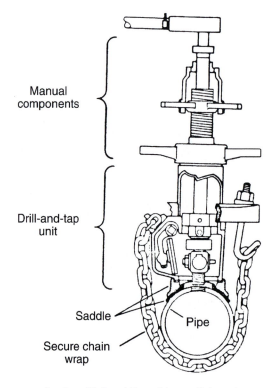

c. Again, with the drill-and-tap unit, insert the threaded inlet of a corporation cock. The service can then be activated.

Fig. 6.25   Wet tapping

(Art reproduced by permission of Mueller Company)

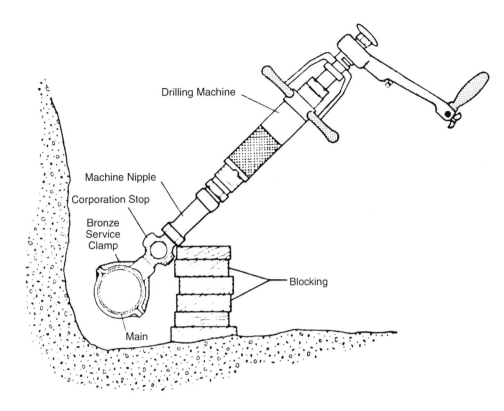

Fig. 6.26   Dry tapping

(Art reproduced by permission of Mueller Company)

Fig. 6.27   Tapping sleeves

(Courtesy of Rockwell International Corporation, Municipal & Utility Division)

a. Clean the main and then bolt the tapping sleeve to it. Attach tapping valve to sleeve outlet.

b. Attach the drilling machine and adapter to valve outlet flange. Position support blocks. Open tapping valve, advance cutter, and drill hole inside of pipe inside the sleeve.

c. Retract cutter and then close tapping valve. Remove drilling machine and attach new line or lateral. Open tapping valve, activating new line.

Fig. 6.28   Drilling machine

(Art reproduced by permission of Mueller Company)

6.5 FIELD DISINFECTION

6.50 Need for Disinfection

Field disinfection of distribution system mains and reservoirs is necessary when they are new, after repairs are made, or whenever there is any possibility of contamination. Under any of these conditions, inadequate disinfection could result in a waterborne-disease outbreak somewhere in the community with your utility agency being legally liable.

6.51 Disinfection of Mains[6]

During the construction of a new water line, or after an extensive repair (involving dewatering), there is a small but real opportunity for contamination of the line, even if special precautions have been taken. Therefore, effective disinfection is necessary before the line is placed into service.

The disinfecting agent most often used is chlorine, which is available in three chemical forms:

1. Liquid chlorine contains 100 percent available chlorine and is packaged in 100-pound, 150-pound, or one-ton (45-, 68-, or 909-kg) steel cylinders. Special equipment and controls, trained operators, and close attention to safety practices are needed when chlorine gas is used.

2. Sodium hypochlorite is a liquid solution. This form of chlorine contains approximately 5 to 15 percent available chlorine and comes in one-quart to five-gallon (1.0- to 20-liter) containers. Precautions must be taken to prevent deterioration of the hypochlorite solution. Store hypochlorite in a cool, dark location and use as soon as possible.

3. Calcium hypochlorite is a dry material containing approximately 65 percent available chlorine; it comes in powder, granular, or tablet form. Calcium hypochlorite is relatively soluble in water and, therefore, adaptable to solution feeding. Storage conditions must be controlled to prevent deterioration or reaction with combustible chemicals or materials.

Disinfection is commonly accomplished using the tablet, continuous feed, or slug methods, depending on the type of chlorine used and specific job conditions.

Tablets are best suited for short sections (a few hundred feet) and small-diameter lines (24 inches (600 mm) or less). Since preliminary flushing cannot be performed, tablets cannot be used unless the main is initially kept clean and dry. As the pipe is laid in the trench, tablets are placed in each pipe section by securely attaching them with an approved adhesive to the top of the pipe. Sufficient tablets are added to provide a dose of 25–50 mg/L chlorine (see Table 6.1). The line is filled slowly (less than one foot (0.3 m) of pipe per second) to prevent the tablets from being flushed away. The chlorinated water is allowed to remain in the line for at least 24 hours. Check the chlorine residual during the test to be sure the residual does not drop below 25 mg/L. Sometimes the tablets will be washed to the far end of the pipe when the pipe is being filled with water. For this reason, samples should be collected from the entire length of pipe and the chlorine residual measured to be sure the chlorine is uniformly distributed throughout the pipe.

In the continuous-feed method, preliminary flushing at not less than 5 ft/sec (1.5 m/sec) is required. A chlorine solution containing not less than 25 mg/L free chlorine is injected into the pipe through a corporation cock or other fitting. The solution is injected as the line is being filled. Table 6.2 gives the amount of chlorine required for each 100 feet (30 m) of pipe of various diameters. At the end of a minimum 24-hour period, properly treated water will have a residual of not less than 10 mg/L free chlorine in all portions of the main.

TABLE 6.1 PIPE DISINFECTION USING TABLETS[a]

Pipe Diameter, in[d]	Number of Five-gram Hypochlorite Tablets Required for a Dose of 25 mg/L[b]				
	Length of Pipe Section, ft[c]				
	13 or less	18	20	30	40
4	1	1	1	1	1
6	1	1	1	2	2
8	1	2	2	3	4
10	2	3	3	4	5
12	3	4	4	6	7
16	4	6	7	10	13

[a] AWWA Standard for Disinfecting Water Mains, ANSI/AWWA C651-92.
[b] Based on 3.25 grams available chlorine per tablet, any portion of tablet required rounded to next higher number.
[c] Multiply feet x 0.3 to obtain meters.
[d] Multiply inches x 2.5 to obtain centimeters.

The slug method is especially advantageous for use with long, large-diameter mains as it reduces the volume of heavily chlorinated water to be flushed to waste and results in significant savings in chlorine costs. Place calcium hypochlorite (granules or tablets) in the main during construction in quantities shown in Table 6.3. This initial chlorine dose will meet the initial chlorine demand. Fill the main completely to remove all air pockets, then flush.

Next, using the continuous-feed method, dose the water to produce and maintain a chlorine concentration of at least 100 mg/L free chlorine. Apply the chlorine continuously for a long enough time period to produce a slug (solid column of water) of highly chlorinated water that will slowly move through the main and expose all interior surfaces of the main to a chlorine

[6] AWWA STANDARD FOR DISINFECTING WATER MAINS, C651-99. Obtain from American Water Works Association (AWWA), Bookstore, 6666 West Quincy Avenue, Denver, CO 80235. Order No. 43651. Price to members, $42.00; nonmembers, $61.00; price includes cost of shipping and handling.

concentration of 100 mg/L as it is being applied and in the main as the slug moves along.

TABLE 6.2 CHLORINE REQUIRED TO PRODUCE 25 mg/L CONCENTRATION IN 100 FEET (30 m) OF PIPE[a]

Pipe Diameter, in [b]	100 Percent Chlorine, lb [c]	1 Percent Chlorine Solution, gal [d]
4	0.013	0.16
6	0.030	0.36
8	0.054	0.65
10	0.085	1.02
12	0.120	1.44
16	0.217	2.60

[a] AWWA Standard for Disinfecting Water Mains, ANSI/AWWA C651-92.
[b] Multiply inches x 2.5 to obtain centimeters.
[c] Multiply pounds x 454 to obtain grams.
[d] Multiply gallons x 3.785 to obtain liters.

TABLE 6.3 PIPE DISINFECTION USING GRANULES[a]

Pipe Diameter, in [c]	Ounces of Calcium Hypochlorite Granules to be Placed at Beginning of Main and at Each 500-ft Interval [b]
	Calcium Hypochlorite Granules, oz [d]
4	0.5
6	1.0
8	2.0
12	4.8
16 and larger	8.0

[a] AWWA Standard for Disinfecting Water Mains, ANSI/AWWA C651-92.
[b] 500 feet is equal to 150 meters.
[c] Multiply inches x 2.5 to obtain centimeters.
[d] Multiply ounces x 28.4 to obtain grams.

If the free chlorine residual in the slug drops below 50 mg/L, stop the flow, add more chlorine to the slug to increase the residual to 100 mg/L and continue. Try to maintain a three-hour contact time as the entire slug moves through the main. When the chlorine slug flows past fittings and valves, operate related valves and hydrants in order to disinfect pipe branches and appurtenances.

After the slug has passed through the main, flush out the chlorinated water until the chlorine concentration in the water leaving the main is no higher than that commonly found in the system. When the disinfection procedures are completed, collect bacteriological samples. Do not put the main into service until the samples are found to be negative for coliform organisms. If positive coliform samples are found, reflush the main and resample. If samples are still positive, the main must be rechlorinated and resampled until satisfactory results are obtained. The 24-hour membrane filter test is commonly used to test for coliform bacteria because test results are available more quickly than with other test methods.

Repair of mains under pressure presents little danger of contamination and disinfection is not required. However, when mains are wholly or partially dewatered, they must be disinfected. In wet excavations, large quantities of hypochlorite are applied to open trench areas to lessen the danger of contamination. The interior of all pipes and fittings used in making the repair must be swabbed or sprayed with a one percent hypochlorite solution before they are installed.

The most practical way of removing contamination introduced during repairs is by thorough flushing. Where it can be done, a section of main, in which the break is located, should be isolated and all service connections shut off. Then the section should be flushed and chlorinated using the slug method as described for new main disinfection except that the dose may be increased to as much as 300 mg/L and the contact time reduced to as little as 15 minutes.

After the chlorination has been completed, flushing is resumed and continued until any discolored water is eliminated and the water is free of noticeable chlorine odor. The main may be returned to service prior to completion of bacteriological testing so that the time customers are out of water will be minimized. Samples should be taken on each side of the main break if the direction of flow in the main was not known at the time of the break. If positive samples are found, daily sampling must be continued until two consecutive samples are negative.

For more details on the disinfection of water mains, see Chapter 6, "Disinfection," in *WATER DISTRIBUTION SYSTEM OPERATION AND MAINTENANCE*.

FORMULAS

To determine the flow in a pipe in gallons per minute, we usually have to calculate the flow in cubic feet per second. The flow in cubic feet per second (CFS) is determined by multiplying the area of the pipe in square feet times the velocity. We have referred to this formula as Q = AV.

$$\text{Area, sq ft} = \frac{(0.785)(\text{Diameter, in})^2}{144 \text{ sq in/sq ft}}$$

We divided by 144 sq in/sq ft to convert the calculated area from square inches to square feet.

Flow, CFS = (Area, sq ft)(Velocity, ft/sec)

or

Flow, GPM = (Flow, cu ft/sec)(7.48 gal/cu ft)(60 sec/min)

EXAMPLE 1

A 6-inch diameter water main is to be flushed at 4 ft/sec before disinfection. What should be the reading on the flowmeter in gallons per minute?

Known	**Unknown**
Diameter, in = 6 in	Flow, GPM
Velocity, ft/sec = 4 ft/sec	

1. Calculate the flow in cubic feet per second.

Flow, CFS = (Area, sq ft)(Velocity, ft/sec)

$$= \frac{(0.785)(6 \text{ in})^2(4 \text{ ft/sec})}{144 \text{ sq in/sq ft}}$$

= 0.785 cu ft/sec

2. Convert flow in cubic feet per second to GPM.

Flow, GPM = (Flow, cu ft/sec)(7.48 gal/cu ft)(60 sec/min)

= (0.785 cu ft/sec)(7.48 gal/cu ft)(60 sec/min)

= 352 gal/min

6.6 PIPE FLUSHING

Flushing is done to clean out distribution pipelines by removing any impurities or sediment that may be present in the pipe. Routine flushing of dead-end lines is often necessary to avoid taste and odor complaints. Many operators use flushing as a short-term solution to distribution system problems. Flushing is commonly practiced after receiving water quality complaints (red water, sand and grit, tastes and odors, cloudy (air) water, and something swimming), when the water in the system appears to have become contaminated, and to clean newly installed or repaired mains prior to disinfection.

Flushing may remove deposits, encrustations, sediments, and other materials. Deposits that have settled out and accumulated in pipelines may result in taste, odor, and turbidity problems. Encrustations may restrict the water flow. Sand, rust, and biological materials cause quality problems and are not uncommon in pipelines. The needed frequency of routine flushing can usually be determined by customer complaints and the types of material found during the flushing procedure. Flushing should not be considered the only solution to distribution system water quality problems. The water utility should always try to prevent water quality degradation through proper design, operation, and treatment.

Water mains should be flushed before consumers start complaining about poor water quality. Flushing should be conducted during periods of low water demand (spring or fall) when the weather is suitable. Prior planning and good communications will allow the flushing crew to conduct the flushing operation quickly and without confusion. Flushing crews consist of two operators. The following procedures are recommended for flushing operations.

1. Preplan an entire day's flushing using the available distribution system maps. Consider flushing at night between 9:00 PM and 5:00 AM to minimize any inconvenience to customers. Night operations encounter little traffic, but traffic must be made aware of the operation if it will be affected by the flushing. Warning devices include lights, traffic cones, barricades, and flaggers.

2. Determine where sections of mains are to be flushed at one time, the valves to be used, and the order in which the pipelines will be flushed.

3. Start at or near a source of supply and work outward into the distribution system. This is referred to as unidirectional flushing.

4. Ensure that an adequate amount of flushing water is available at sufficiently high pressures. A *MINIMUM* flushing velocity of 2.5 ft/sec (5 ft/sec preferred) (0.75 and 1.50 m/sec) should be used. Do not flush a large main supplied by a single smaller one if a choice is possible.

5. Prior to flushing the mains, notify all customers who will be affected of the dates and times of the flushing through billing, newspapers, and local radio and TV announcements. Explain the intent and objective of the flushing program. Notify individuals who might be on dialysis machines and also hospitals, restaurants, laundromats, and others who might be affected while the mains are being flushed.

6. Isolate the section to be flushed from the rest of the system. Close the valves slowly to prevent water hammer.

7. Open the fire hydrant or blowoff valve slowly.

8. Direct flushing water away from traffic, pedestrians, and private lots (Figure 6.29). Avoid erosion damage to streets, lawns, and yards by the use of tarpaulins and lead-off discharge devices. Try to avoid flooding, which can cause traffic problems.

9. Open hydrant fully for a period long enough (5 to 10 minutes) to stir up the deposits inside the water main. Usually lines are flushed for at least 30 minutes.

10. Ensure that system pressures in nearby areas do not drop below 20 psi (138 kPa or 1.5 kg/sq cm).

11. Record all pertinent data regarding the flushing operation as well as a description of the appearance and odor of the water flushed. Figure 6.30 is a sample flushing log sheet that can also be used for a pipeline cleaning operation.

12. Collect two water samples from each flowing hydrant, one in the beginning (about 2 to 3 minutes after the hydrant was opened) and the second sample when the discolored water turns clear (just before closing the hydrant). These samples allow a check on the water quality for certain basic water quality indicators (iron, chlorine residual, turbidity) and the development of water quality trends for comparison purposes.

13. After the flushing water becomes clear, slowly close the hydrant or blowoff valves.

14. In areas where the water does not become completely clear, the operator should use judgment as to the relative color and turbidity and decide when to shut down. A water sample in a clear glass bottle will allow the operator to visually observe the color from time to time.

15. Mark closed valves on a map when they are closed and erase marks after the valves are reopened. Do this promptly and do not depend on memory.

16. After flushing one section of pipe, move on to the next section to be flushed and repeat the same procedures.

FORMULAS

The formulas needed to calculate a desired flowmeter reading in gallons per minute (GPM) to flush a water main are the same formulas we've used before.

To calculate the cross-sectional area of a pipe when the diameter is given in inches,

$$\text{Area, sq ft} = \frac{(0.785)(\text{Diameter, in})^2}{144 \text{ sq in/sq ft}}$$

To calculate the flow in a pipe in cubic feet per second (CFS), we need to know the area in square feet and the velocity in feet per second. This is the familiar formula, Q = AV.

Flow, CFS = (Area, sq ft)(Velocity, ft/sec)

To convert the flow from cubic feet per second (CFS) to gallons per minute, GPM,

Flow, GPM = (Flow, cu ft/sec)(7.48 gal/cu ft)(60 sec/min)

Direct flushing water away from traffic, pedestrians,
underground utility vaults, and private lots.

Deflection tubes keep water and swabs from going into traffic on a busy street.
Without the chain, vibration will break tube.

Fig. 6.29   Diverting flushing water

Date	Time	Location	Press. Zone	Size of Main		Swabs		P Pitot Press, psi	d Disch. Opening, in	Q Flush. Rate, GPM	V Flush. Velocity, FPS	Time Req'd. to Clear, min.	Flushed Water Description
				D Dia, in	L Length, ft	# of Runs	# per Run						

Q = Flushing rate in GPM

d = Diameter of nozzle or opening in inches

P = Pitot gage pressure at nozzle or opening in psi

$Q = 26.8 \, d^2 \sqrt{P}$

V = Flushing velocity in main in FPS

D = Diameter of main being flushed in inches

$V = \dfrac{0.409 \, Q}{D^2}$

Fig. 6.30 Main flushing and swabbing log

EXAMPLE 2

A 15-inch diameter water main is to be flushed at a velocity of 5 ft/sec. What should be the reading on the flowmeter in gallons per minute?

Known	Unknown
Diameter, in = 15 in	Flow, GPM
Velocity, ft/sec = 5 ft/sec	

FORMULA (Q = AV)

Flow, CFS = (Area, sq ft)(Velocity, ft/sec)

1. Calculate the cross-sectional area of the pipe in square feet.

$$\text{Area, sq ft} = (0.785)(\text{Diameter, ft})^2$$

$$= \frac{(0.785)(15 \text{ in})^2}{144 \text{ sq in/sq ft}}$$

$$= 1.23 \text{ sq ft}$$

2. Determine the flow in the pipe in cubic feet per second (CFS).

$$\text{Flow, CFS} = (\text{Area, sq ft})(\text{Velocity, ft/sec})$$

$$= (1.23 \text{ sq ft})(5 \text{ ft/sec})$$

$$= 6.15 \text{ CFS}$$

3. Calculate the flowmeter reading in gallons per minute (GPM).

$$\text{Flow, GPM} = (\text{Flow, cu ft/sec})(7.48 \text{ gal/cu ft})(60 \text{ sec/min})$$

$$= (6.15 \text{ cu ft/sec})(7.48 \text{ gal/cu ft})(60 \text{ sec/min})$$

$$= 2,760 \text{ GPM}$$

6.7 CROSS-CONNECTION CONTROL

6.70 Importance of Cross-Connection Control

BACKFLOW[7] of contaminated water through cross connections into community water systems is not just a theoretical problem. Contamination through cross connections has consistently caused more waterborne disease outbreaks in the United States than any other reported factor. Inspections have often disclosed numerous unprotected cross connections between public water systems and other piped systems on consumers' premises which might contain wastewater; stormwater; processed waters (containing a wide variety of chemicals); and untreated supplies from private wells, streams, and ocean waters. Therefore, an effective cross-connection control program is essential.

Backflow results from either *BACK PRESSURE*[8] or *BACK-SIPHONAGE*[9] situations in the distribution system. Back pressure occurs when the user's water supply is at a higher pressure than the public water supply system (Figure 6.31). Typical locations where back pressure problems could develop include services to premises where wastewater or toxic chemicals are handled under pressure or where there are unapproved auxiliary water supplies such as a private well or the use of surface water or seawater for firefighting. Backsiphon-

age is caused by the development of negative or below atmospheric pressures in the water supply piping (Figure 6.32). This condition can occur when there are extremely high water demands (firefighting), water main breaks, or the use of on-line booster pumps.

The best way to prevent backflow is to permanently eliminate the hazard. Back pressure hazards can be eliminated by severing (eliminating) any direct connection at the pump causing the back pressure with the domestic water supply system. Another solution to the problem is to require an air gap separation device (Figure 6.35, page 210) where the water supply service line connects to the private system under pressure from the pump. To eliminate or minimize backsiphonage problems, proper enforcement of plumbing codes and improved water distribution and storage facilities will be helpful. As an additional safety factor for certain selected conditions, a double check valve (Figure 6.36, page 210) may be required at the meter.

6.71 Program Responsibilities

Responsibilities in the implementation of cross-connection control programs are shared by water suppliers, water users (businesses and industries), health agencies, and plumbing officials. The water supplier is responsible for preventing contamination of the public water system by backflow. This responsibility begins at the source, includes the entire distribution system, and ends at the user's connection. To meet this responsibility, the water supplier must issue (promulgate) and enforce needed laws, rules, regulations, and policies. Water service should not be provided to premises where the strong possibility of an unprotected cross connection exists. The essential elements of a water supplier cross-connection control program are discussed in the next section.

The water user is responsible for keeping contaminants out of the potable water system on the user's premises. When backflow prevention devices are required by the health agency or water supplier, the water user must pay for the installation, testing, and maintenance of the approved devices. The user is also responsible for preventing the creation of cross connections through modifications of the plumbing system on the premises. The health agency or water supplier may, when necessary, require a water user to designate a water supervisor or foreman to be responsible for the cross-connection control program within the water user's premises.

---

[7] *Backflow. A reverse flow condition, created by a difference in water pressures, which causes water to flow back into the distribution pipes of a potable water supply from any source or sources other than an intended source. Also see BACKSIPHONAGE.*

[8] *Back Pressure. A pressure that can cause water to backflow into the water supply when a user's water system is at a higher pressure than the public water system.*

[9] *Backsiphonage. A form of backflow caused by a negative or below atmospheric pressure within a water system. Also see BACKFLOW.*

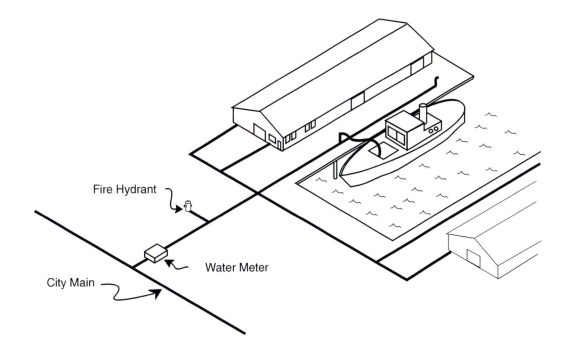

HYDRAULIC GRADIENT

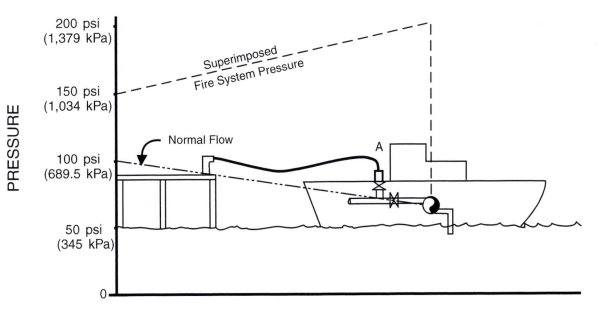

Fig. 6.31   Backflow due to back pressure

(Source: *MANUAL OF CROSS-CONNECTION CONTROL PROCEDURES AND PRACTICES*,
Sanitary Engineering Branch, California Department of Health Services, Berkeley, CA)

DISTRIBUTION SYSTEM

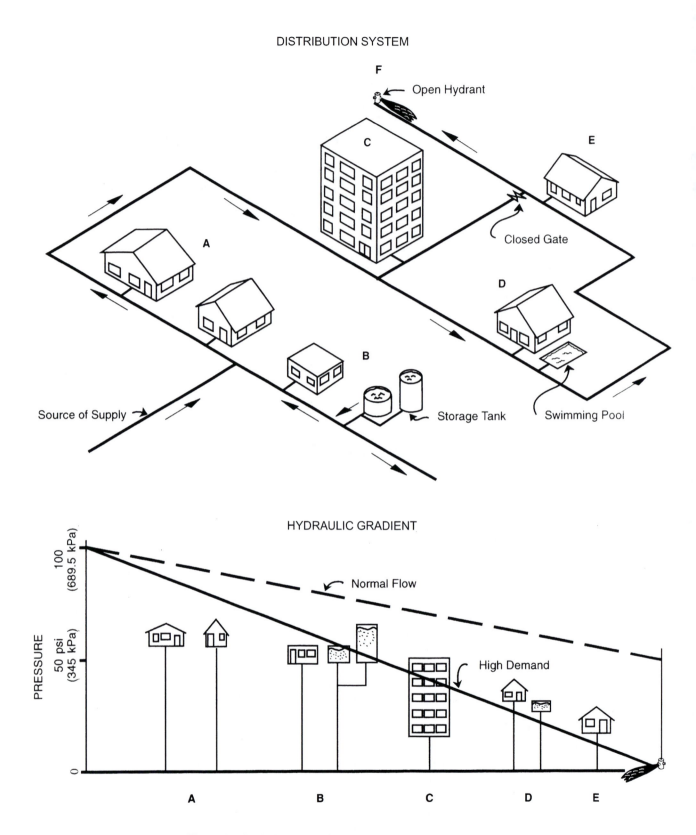

Fig. 6.32   Backsiphonage due to extremely high water demand

(Source: *MANUAL OF CROSS-CONNECTION CONTROL PROCEDURES AND PRACTICES*,
Sanitary Engineering Branch, California Department of Health Services, Berkeley, CA)

The local or state health agency is responsible for issuing and enforcing laws, rules, regulations, and policies needed to control cross connections. Also this agency must have a program that ensures maintenance of an adequate cross-connection control program. The protection of the system on the user's premises is provided where needed by the water utilities.

The plumbing agency (building inspectors) is responsible for the enforcement of building regulations relating to prevention of cross connections on the user's premises.

6.72 Water Supplier Program

The following elements should be included in each water supplier's cross-connection control program:

1. Enactment of an ordinance providing enforcement authority if the supplier is a governmental agency, or enactment of appropriate rules of service if the system is investor-owned.[10]

2. Training of personnel on the causes of and hazards from cross connections and procedures to follow for effective cross-connection control.

3. Listing and inspection or reinspection on a priority basis of all existing facilities where cross connections are of concern. A typical cross-connection survey form is shown in Figure 6.33.

4. Review and screening of all applications for new services or modification of existing services for cross-connection hazards to determine if backflow protection is needed.

5. Obtaining a list of approved backflow prevention devices and a list of certified testers, if available.

6. Acceptable installation of the proper type of device needed for the specific hazard on the premises.

7. Routine testing of installed backflow prevention devices as required by the health agency or the water supplier. Contact the health agency for approved procedures.

8. Maintenance of adequate records for each backflow prevention device installed, including records of inspection and testing. A typical form is shown in Figure 6.34.

9. Notification of each water user when a backflow prevention device has to be tested. This should be done after installation or repair of the device and at least once a year.

10. Maintenance of adequate pressures throughout the distribution system at all times to minimize the hazards from any undetected cross connections that may exist.

All field personnel should be constantly alert for situations where cross connections are likely to exist, whether protection has been installed or not. An example is a contractor using a fire hose from a hydrant to fill a tank truck for dust control or the jetting (for compaction) of pipe trenches. Operators should especially be on the lookout for illegal bypassing of installed backflow prevention devices.

6.73 Types of Backflow Prevention Devices

Different types of backflow prevention devices are available. The particular type of device most suitable for a given situation depends on the degree of health hazard, the probability of backflow occurring, the complexity of the piping on the premises, and the probability of the piping being modified. The higher the assessed risk due to these factors, the more reliable and positive the type of device needed. The types of devices normally approved are listed below according to the degree of assessed risk, with the type of device providing the greatest protection listed first. Only the first three devices are approved for use at service connections.

1. Air gap separation.

2. Reduced-pressure principle (RPP) device.

3. Double check valve.

4. Pressure vacuum breaker (only used for internal protection on the premises).

5. Atmospheric (non-pressure) vacuum breaker.

Figure 6.35 shows a typical air gap separation device and its recommended location. Figure 6.36 shows the installation of a typical double check valve backflow prevention device. These devices are normally installed on the water user's side of the connection to the utility's system and as close to the connection as practical. Figure 6.37 shows a typical installation of pressure vacuum breakers.

Only backflow prevention devices that have passed both laboratory and field evaluations by a recognized testing agency and that have been accepted by the health agency and the water supplier should be used.

For additional information on backflow prevention devices, see Section 3.83, "Backflow Prevention Devices," in *WATER DISTRIBUTION SYSTEM OPERATION AND MAINTENANCE*.

6.74 Devices Required for Various Types of Situations

The state or local health agency should be contacted to determine the actual types of devices acceptable for various situations inside the consumer's premises. However, the types of devices generally acceptable for particular situations can be mentioned.

An air gap or a reduced-pressure principle (RPP) device is normally required at services to wastewater treatment plants, wastewater pumping stations, reclaimed water reuse areas, areas where toxic substances in toxic concentrations are handled under pressure, and premises having an auxiliary water supply that is or may be contaminated. The ultimate degree of protection is also needed in cases where fertilizer, herbicides, or pesticides are injected into a sprinkler system.

A double check valve device should be required when a moderate hazard exists on the premises or where an auxiliary supply exists, but adequate protection on the premises is provided.

Atmospheric and pressure vacuum breakers are usually required for irrigation systems; however, they are not adequate in situations where they may be subject to back pressure. If there is a possibility of back pressure, a reduced-pressure principle device is needed.

---

[10] *A typical ordinance is available in CROSS-CONNECTION CONTROL MANUAL, available from National Technical Information Service (NTIS), 5285 Port Royal Road, Springfield, VA 22161. Order No. PB91-145490. EPA No. 570-9-89-007. Price, $33.50, plus $5.00 shipping and handling per order.*

CROSS-CONNECTION SURVEY FORM

Place:_____   Date:_____

Location:_____   Investigator(s)_____

Building Representative(s) and Title(s):

_____
_____

Water Source(s):_____
_____
_____

Piping System(s):_____
_____
_____

Points of Interconnection:_____
_____
_____
_____
_____

Special Equipment Supplied with Water and Source:

_____
_____
_____

Remarks or Recommendations:_____
_____
_____
_____
_____
_____

NOTE: Attach sketches of cross-connections found where necessary for
       clarity of description. Attach additional sheets for room-by-
       room survey under headings

                                        Description of
       Room Number   Cross-Connection(s)

Fig. 6.33 Typical cross-connection survey form
(From CROSS-CONNECTION CONTROL MANUAL, U.S. Environmental Protection Agency, Water Supply Division)

CODE 03250
15M 7-77 P.O. 30582

MAIL TO: Principal Sanitary Engineer
Department of Water and Power, City of Los Angeles
P.O. Box 111   Room A-18
Los Angeles, California 90051

RETURN NO LATER THAN: _____

MANUFACTURER	MODEL	SIZE	SERIAL NUMBER	SERVICE NUMBER

SERVICE ADDRESS:

LOCATION:

1	2	3	4	5	6	7	8	9	10	11	12	13	14	15	16	17	18	19	20	21	22	23	24	25	26	27	28	29	30	31	32	33	34	35	36	37	38	39	40	41	42	43	44	45	46	47

48	49	50	51	52	53	54	55	56	57	58	59	60	61	62	63	64	65	66	67	68	69	70	71	72	73	74	75	76	77	78	79	80

	CHECK VALVE #1	CHECK VALVE #2	CHECK VALVE #3	DIFFERENTIAL PRESSURE RELIEF VALVE
INITIAL TEST	1. LEAKED* ☐ 2. CLOSED TIGHT ☐	1. LEAKED ☐ 2. CLOSED TIGHT ☐	1. LEAKED ☐ 2. CLOSED TIGHT ☐	OPENED AT _____ LBS. REDUCED PRESSURE. DID NOT OPEN ☐
REPAIRS	CLEANED ☐ REPLACED: DISC ☐ SPRING ☐ GUIDE ☐ PIN RETAINER ☐ HINGE PIN ☐ SEAT ☐ DIAPHRAGM ☐ OTHER, DESCRIBE ☐	CLEANED ☐ REPLACED DISC ☐ SPRING ☐ GUIDE ☐ PIN RETAINER ☐ HINGE PIN ☐ SEAT ☐ DIAPHRAGM ☐ OTHER, DESCRIBE ☐	CLEANED ☐ REPLACED DISC ☐ SPRING ☐ GUIDE ☐ HINGE PIN ☐ SEAT ☐ DIAPHRAGM ☐ OTHER, DESCRIBE ☐	CLEANED ☐ REPLACED: DISC: UPPER ☐ LOWER ☐ SPRING ☐ DIAPHRAGM: LARGE: UPPER ☐ LOWER ☐ SMALL ☐ SEAT: UPPER ☐ LOWER ☐ SPACER: LOWER ☐ OTHER DESCRIBE ☐
FINAL TEST	CLOSED TIGHT ☐	CLOSED TIGHT ☐	CLOSED TIGHT ☐	OPENED AT _____ LBS. REDUCED PRESSURE

The above report is certified to be true.

INITIAL TEST BY _____ CERTIFIED TESTER NO. [| | | |]   DATE | MO. | DAY | YR. |

REPAIRED BY _____ DATE _____

FINAL TEST BY _____ CERTIFIED TESTER NO. [| | | |]   DATE | MO. | DAY | YR. |

Fig. 6.34   Typical backflow prevention device maintenance record form
(Permission of Department of Water and Power, City of Los Angeles)

TANK SHOULD BE OF SUBSTANTIAL CONSTRUCTION AND
OF A KIND AND SIZE TO SUIT CONSUMER'S NEEDS.
TANK MAY BE SITUATED AT GROUND LEVEL (WITH A
PUMP TO PROVIDE ADEQUATE PRESSURE HEAD) OR
BE ELEVATED ABOVE THE GROUND.

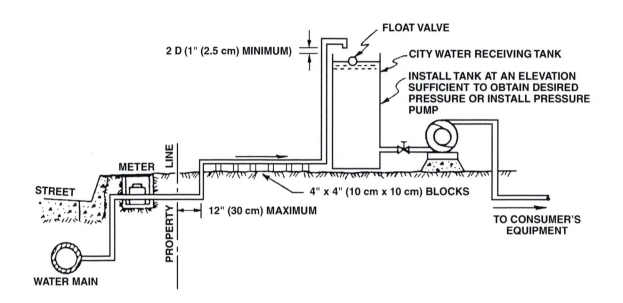

Fig. 6.35   Typical air gap separation

(From *MANUAL OF CROSS-CONNECTION CONTROL PRACTICES AND PROCEDURES*, Sanitary Engineering Branch, California Department of Health Services, Berkeley, CA)

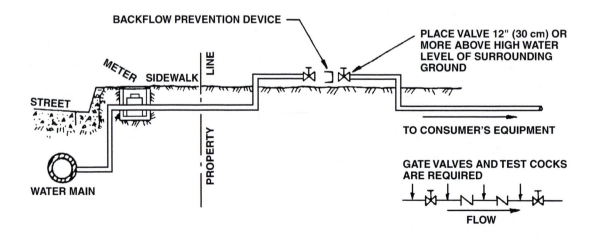

Fig. 6.36   Typical double check valve backflow prevention device

(From *MANUAL OF CROSS-CONNECTION CONTROL PRACTICES AND PROCEDURES*, Sanitary Engineering Branch, California Department of Health Services, Berkeley, CA)

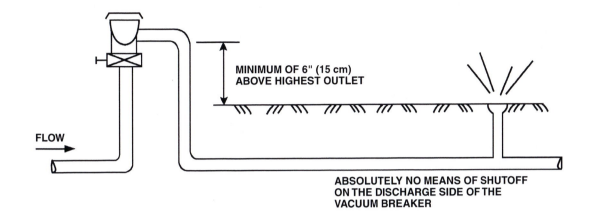

MINIMUM OF 6" (15 cm)
ABOVE HIGHEST OUTLET

FLOW

ABSOLUTELY NO MEANS OF SHUTOFF
ON THE DISCHARGE SIDE OF THE
VACUUM BREAKER

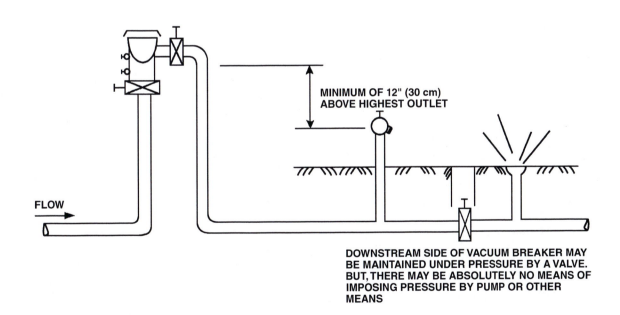

MINIMUM OF 12" (30 cm)
ABOVE HIGHEST OUTLET

FLOW

DOWNSTREAM SIDE OF VACUUM BREAKER MAY
BE MAINTAINED UNDER PRESSURE BY A VALVE.
BUT, THERE MAY BE ABSOLUTELY NO MEANS OF
IMPOSING PRESSURE BY PUMP OR OTHER
MEANS

Fig. 6.37   Typical installations of atmospheric (top) and pressure (bottom) vacuum breakers

(From *MANUAL OF CROSS-CONNECTION CONTROL PRACTICES AND PROCEDURES*, Sanitary Engineering Branch, California Department of Health Services, Berkeley, CA)

6.75   Typical Cross-Connection Hazards

6.750   Importance of Hazard Awareness

Water distribution system operators need to be aware of the types of hazardous chemicals that could enter the water distribution system as well as potential sources of these hazardous chemicals. Operators need to know the types of pollutants or contaminants that are used by consumers that could threaten the public health of consumers if they entered the distribution system. A knowledge of typical industries that have contaminated public water systems through cross connections will help operators protect the quality of the water delivered to consumers through the distribution system.

6.751   Hazardous Chemicals Used by Consumers

Chemicals used by industries may create a hazard to the public when the chemicals are used on site, enter the industry's water distribution system, and then may enter the public water distribution system through a cross connection. This section describes some typical industries and the protection recommended to protect public water distribution systems.

- Agriculture

Agriculture uses many different types of chemicals for different purposes. Toxic chemicals are used by agriculture in fertilizers, herbicides, and pesticides. *Protection recommended:* an air gap separation or a reduced-pressure principle backflow prevention assembly is recommended.

- Cooling Systems (Open or Closed)

Cooling systems, including cooling towers, usually require some treatment of the water for algae, slime, or corrosion control. *Protection recommended:* an air gap separation or a reduced-pressure principle backflow prevention assembly is recommended.

- Dye Plants

Most solutions used in dyeing are highly toxic. The toxicity depends on the chemicals used and their concentrations. *Protection recommended:* an air gap separation or a reduced-pressure principle backflow prevention assembly is recommended.

- Plating Plants

In plating work, materials are first cleaned in acid or caustic solutions at concentrations that are highly toxic. *Protection recommended:* an air gap separation or a reduced-pressure principle backflow prevention assembly is recommended.

- Steam Boiler Plants

Most boiler plants will use some form of boiler feedwater treatment. The chemicals typically used for this purpose include highly toxic compounds. *Protection recommended:* an air gap separation or a reduced-pressure principle backflow prevention assembly is recommended.

6.752   Industries With Cross-Connection Potential

A knowledge of industries that may have cross connections to a public water distribution system will help operators prevent the occurrence of cross connections. The following inspection guidelines list typical hazards and recommend cross-connection protection.

- Auxiliary Water Systems

An auxiliary water system is a water supply or source that is not under the control or the direct supervision of the water purveyor. An approved backflow prevention assembly must be installed at the service connection of the water purveyor to any premises where there is an auxiliary water supply or system, even though there is no connection between the auxiliary water supply and the public potable water system.

Typical auxiliary water systems include water used in industrialized water systems; water in reservoirs or tanks used for firefighting purposes; irrigation reservoirs; swimming pools; fish ponds; mirror pools; memorial and decorative fountains and cascades; cooling towers; and baptismal, quenching, washing, rinsing, and dipping tanks.

Protection recommended: an air gap separation or a reduced-pressure principle backflow prevention assembly is recommended where there is a health hazard. A double check valve assembly should be used where there is only a pollution hazard.

- Beverage Bottling and Breweries

An approved backflow prevention assembly must be installed on the service connection to any premises where a beverage bottling plant is operated or maintained and water is used for industrial purposes.

The hazards typically found in plants of this type include cross connections between the potable water system and steam-connected facilities; washers, cookers, tanks, lines, and flumes; can and bottle washing machines; lines in which caustic, acids, and detergents are used; reservoirs, cooling towers, and circulating systems; steam generating facilities and lines; industrial fluid systems and lines; water-cooled equipment; and firefighting systems, including storage reservoirs.

Protection recommended: an air gap separation or a reduced-pressure principle backflow prevention assembly is recommended where there is a health hazard. A double check valve assembly should be used where there is only a pollution hazard.

- Canneries, Packing Houses, and Reduction Plants

An approved backflow prevention assembly must be installed at the service connection to any premises where vegetable or animal matter is canned, concentrated, or processed.

The hazards typically found in plants of this type include cross connections between the potable water system and steam-connected facilities; washers, cookers, tanks, lines, and flumes; reservoirs, cooling towers, and circulating systems; steam generating facilities and lines; industrial fluid systems and lines; firefighting systems, including storage reservoirs; water-cooled equipment; and tanks, can and bottle washing machines, and lines.

Protection recommended: an air gap separation or reduced-pressure principle backflow prevention assembly is recommended.

- Chemical Plants—Manufacturing, Processing, or Treatment

An approved backflow prevention assembly shall be installed on the service connection to any premises where there is a facility requiring the use of water in the industrial process of manufacturing, storing, compounding, or processing chemicals. This will also include facilities where chemicals are used as additives to the water supply or in processing products. Cross connections may be numerous because of the intricate piping. The severity of these cross connections varies with the toxicity of the chemical used.

The hazards typically found in plants of this type include cross connections between the potable water system and formulating tanks and vats, decanter units, extractor/precipitators, and other processing units; reservoirs, cooling towers, and circulating systems; steam generating facilities and lines; firefighting systems, including storage reservoirs; water-cooled equipment; hydraulically operated equipment; equipment under hydraulic tests; pressure cookers, autoclaves, and retorts; and washers, cookers, tanks, flumes, and other equipment used for storing, washing, cleaning, blanching, cooking, flushing, or for the transmission of food, fertilizers, or wastes.

Protection recommended: an air gap separation or a reduced-pressure principle backflow prevention assembly is recommended where there is a health hazard.

- Dairies and Cold Storage Plants

An approved backflow prevention assembly shall be installed on the service connection to any premises on which a dairy, creamery, ice cream, cold storage, or ice manufacturing plant is operated or maintained, provided such a plant has on the premises an industrial fluid system, wastewater handling facilities, or other similar source of contamination that, if cross connected, would create a hazard to the public system.

The hazards typically found in these types of plants include cross connections between the potable water system and reservoirs, cooling towers, and circulation systems; steam generating facilities and lines; water-cooled equipment and tanks; can and bottle washing machines; and lines in which caustics, acids, detergents, and other compounds are circulated for cleaning, sterilizing, and flushing.

Protection recommended: an air gap separation or a reduced-pressure principle backflow prevention assembly is recommended where there is a health hazard. A double check valve assembly should be used where there is only a pollution hazard.

- Film Laboratories

An approved backflow prevention assembly must be installed on each service connection to any premises where a film laboratory, processing, or manufacturing plant is operated or maintained. This does not include darkroom facilities.

The hazards typically found in a plant of this type include cross connections between the potable water system and tanks, automatic film processing machines, and water-cooled equipment that may be connected to a sewer, such as compressors, heat exchangers, and air conditioning equipment.

Protection recommended: an air gap separation or a reduced-pressure principle backflow prevention assembly is recommended.

- Hospitals, Medical Buildings, Sanitariums, Morgues, Mortuaries, Autopsy Facilities, and Clinics

An approved backflow prevention assembly must be installed on the service connection to any hospital, medical buildings, and clinics. The hazards typically found in this type of facility include cross connections between the potable water system and contaminated or sewer-connected equipment; water-cooled equipment that may be sewer-connected; reservoirs, cooling towers, and circulating systems; and steam generating facilities and lines.

Protection recommended: an air gap separation or a reduced-pressure principle backflow assembly must be installed on the service connection to any hospital, mortuary, morgue, or autopsy facility, or to any multistoried medical building or clinic.

- Laundries and Dye Works (Commercial Laundries)

An approved backflow prevention assembly must be installed on each service connection to any premises where a laundry or dyeing plant is operated or maintained.

The hazards typically found in plants of this type include cross connections between the potable water system and laundry machines having under rim or bottom outlets; dye vats in which toxic chemicals and dyes are used; water storage tanks equipped with pumps and recirculating systems; shrinking, bluing, and dyeing machines with direct connections to circulating systems; retention and mixing tanks; wastewater pumps for priming, cleaning, flushing, or unclogging purposes; water-operated wastewater sump ejectors for operational purposes; sewer lines for the purpose of disposing of filter or softener backwash water from cooling systems; reservoirs, cooling towers, and circulating systems; and steam generating facilities and lines.

Protection recommended: an air gap separation or a reduced-pressure principle backflow prevention assembly is recommended.

- Marine Facilities and Dockside Watering Points

The actual or potential hazard to the utility's water system created by any marine facility or dockside watering point must be individually evaluated. The basic risk to a domestic water system is the possibility that contaminated water can be pumped into the domestic water system by the fire pumps or other pumps aboard a ship. The additional risk of dockside water facilities located on fresh water or diluted salt water is that if backflow occurs, it can be more easily digested because of the lack of salty taste.

Protection recommended: minimum system protection for marine installations may be accomplished in one of the following ways: (1) water connections directly to vessels for any purpose must have a reduced-pressure backflow prevention assembly installed at the pier hydrants; (2) where water is delivered to marine facilities for fire protection only, and no auxiliary water supply is present, all service connections should be protected by a reduced-pressure principle backflow prevention assembly; (3) water delivered to a marine repair facility should have a reduced-pressure principle backflow prevention assembly; (4) water delivered to small boat moorages that maintain hose bibbs on a dock or float should have a reduced-pressure principle backflow prevention assembly installed at the user connection and a hose connection vacuum breaker on all hose bibbs; and (5) water for fire protection aboard ship, connected to dockside fire hydrants, must not be taken aboard from fire hydrants unless the hydrants are on a fire system separated from the domestic system by an approved reduced-pressure principle backflow prevention assembly.

- Metal Manufacturing, Cleaning, Processing, and Fabricating Plants

An approved backflow prevention assembly must be installed on the service connection to any premises where metals are manufactured, cleaned, processed, or fabricated and the process involves used water and/or industrial fluids. This type of facility may be operated or maintained either as a separate function or other facility, such as an aircraft or automotive manufacturing plant.

The hazards typically found in a plant of this type include cross connections between the potable water and reservoirs, cooling towers, and circulating systems; steam generating facilities and lines; plating facilities involving the use of highly toxic chemicals; industrial fluid systems; tanks, vats, or other vessels; water-cooled equipment; tanks, can and bottle washing machines, and lines; hydraulically operated equipment; and equipment under hydraulic tests.

Protection recommended: an air gap separation or a reduced-pressure principle backflow prevention assembly is recommended where there is a health hazard. A double check valve assembly should be used where there is only a pollution hazard.

- Multistoried Buildings

Multistoried buildings may be broadly grouped into the following three categories in terms of their internal potable water systems:

1. Using only the service pressure to distribute the potable water throughout the structure, and with no internal potable water reservoir,

2. Using a booster pump to provide potable water directly to the upper floors, and

3. Using a booster pump to fill a covered roof reservoir from which there is a down-feed system for the upper floors.

Considerable care must be exercised to prevent the use of the suction-side line to these pumps from also being used as the takeoff for domestic, sanitary, laboratory, or industrial uses on the lower floors. Pollutants or contaminants from equipment supplied by takeoffs from the suction-side line may be easily pumped throughout the upper floors. In each of these systems it is probable that there is one or more takeoffs for industrial water within the building. Any loss of distribution main pressure will cause backflow from these buildings' systems unless approved backflow prevention assemblies are properly installed.

Protection recommended: an air gap separation or a reduced-pressure principle backflow prevention assembly where there is a health hazard; a reduced-pressure principle backflow prevention assembly when takeoffs for lower floor sanitary facilities are connected to the suction side of booster pump(s); and a double check valve assembly where there is a non-health hazard. The suction pressure on booster pumps should be limited to prevent drawing water from adjacent unprotected premises.

- Oil and Gas Production, Storage, or Transmission Properties

An approved backflow prevention assembly shall be installed at the service connection to any premises where animal, vegetable, or mineral oils and gases are produced, developed, processed, blended, stored, refined, or transmitted in a pipeline, or where oil or gas tanks are maintained. An approved backflow prevention assembly must be installed at the service connection where an oil well is being drilled, developed, operated, or maintained; or where an oxygen, acetylene, petroleum, or other manufactured gas production or bottling plant is operated or maintained.

The hazards typically found in plants of this type include cross connections between the potable water system and steam boiler lines; mud pumps and mud tanks; oil well casings; dehydration tanks and outlet lines from storage and dehydration tanks; oil and gas tanks; gas and oil lines; reservoirs, cooling towers, and circulating systems; steam generating facilities; industrial fluid systems; firefighting systems, including storage reservoirs; water-cooled equipment; hydraulically operated equipment and equipment under hydraulic tests.

Protection recommended: an air gap separation or a reduced-pressure principle backflow prevention assembly is recommended.

- Paper and Paper Product Plants

An approved backflow prevention assembly must be installed on the service connection to any premises where a paper or paper products plant (wet process) is operated or maintained.

The hazards typically found in a plant of this type include cross connections between the potable water system and pulp, bleaching, dyeing, and processing facilities that may be contaminated with toxic chemicals; reservoirs, cooling towers, and circulating systems; steam generating facilities and lines; industrial fluid systems and lines; water-cooled equipment; and firefighting systems, including storage reservoirs.

Protection recommended: an air gap separation or a reduced-pressure principle backflow prevention assembly is recommended.

- Plants or Facilities Handling Radioactive Material or Substances

An approved backflow prevention assembly must be installed at the service connection to any premises where radioactive materials or substances are processed in a laboratory or plant, or where they may be handled in such a manner as to create a potential hazard to the water system, or where there is a reactor plant.

Protection recommended: an air gap separation or a reduced-pressure principle backflow prevention assembly is recommended.

- Restricted, Classified, or Other Closed Facilities

An approved backflow prevention assembly must be installed on the service connection to any facility that is not readily accessible for inspection by the water purveyor because of military secrecy requirements or other prohibitions or restrictions.

Protection recommended: an air gap separation or a reduced-pressure principle backflow prevention assembly is recommended.

- Solar Domestic Hot Water Systems

An approved backflow prevention assembly must be installed on the service connection to any premises where there is a solar domestic hot water system.

The hazards typically found in a solar domestic system include cross connections between the potable water system and heat exchangers, tanks, and circulating pumps. Contamination can occur when the piping or tank walls of the heat exchanger between the potable hot water and the transfer medium begin to leak.

Protection recommended: the recommended protection depends on whether there is a possible health hazard or a non-health hazard. In either case a reduced-pressure principle backflow prevention assembly will always provide safe protection.

• Water Hauling Equipment

An approved backflow prevention assembly must be installed on any portable spraying or cleaning units that have the capability of connection to any potable water supply that does not contain a built-in approved air gap.

The hazards typically found in water hauling equipment include cross connections between the potable water system and tanks contaminated with toxic chemical compounds used in spraying fertilizers, herbicides, and pesticides; water hauling tanker trucks used in dust control; and other tanks on cleaning equipment.

Protection recommended: an air gap separation or a reduced-pressure principle backflow prevention assembly is recommended.

6.753 Maintenance and Testing Procedures

Backflow prevention programs must require the owners of buildings and facilities with backflow prevention devices to maintain the devices within their buildings and facilities in good working condition. Also, qualified persons must periodically test the backflow preventers for satisfactory performance.

6.754 Acknowledgment

Material in this section was obtained from *RECOMMENDED PRACTICE FOR BACKFLOW PREVENTION AND CROSS-CONNECTION CONTROL* (M14), available from American Water Works Association (AWWA), Bookstore, 6666 West Quincy Avenue, Denver, CO 80235. Order No. 30014. ISBN 1-58321-288-4. Price to members, $69.00; nonmembers, $99.00; price includes cost of shipping and handling.

6.8 RECORDS AND MAPS

6.80 Importance of Records

In too many systems the importance and value of keeping good records are not recognized. Where this occurs, the operators may not know (or be able to find) the construction details of important facilities, where they are located, or what shape they are in. The need for a good record system regardless of the size or complexity of the water system cannot be overemphasized.

Records are needed for many reasons. In general, they promote the efficient operation of the water system. Records can remind the operator when routine operation or maintenance is necessary and help ensure that schedules will be maintained and no needed operation or maintenance will be overlooked or forgotten. Records are the key to an effective maintenance program. They are also needed for those regulatory agencies that require submission of periodic water quality and operational records. Records can be used to determine the financial health of the utility, provide the basic data on the system's property, and prepare monthly and annual reports. Another reason for keeping accurate and complete

records of system operations is the legal liability of the utility. Such records are required as evidence of what actually occurred in the system. Good records can help if the utility is threatened with litigation. Records also assist in answering consumer questions or complaints. Finally, clear, concise records are required to effectively meet future operational needs, that is, for planning purposes.

Records should be tailored to meet the demands of the particular system and only records known to be useful should be kept. Operators should determine what type of information will be of value for their system and then prepare maps, forms, or other types of records on which the needed information can be easily recorded and clearly shown. Records should be prepared as if they will be kept indefinitely. In fact some will be kept for a long time, while other records will not. Records should be put into a filing system that can be easily used and understood by everyone concerned, readily accessible, and protected from damage in a safe environment. The nonpermanent records should be disposed of in accordance with a disposal schedule set up for the different types of records maintained. Good recordkeeping tips can be found throughout these manuals. For additional information on recordkeeping from the viewpoint of the distribution system manager, see Chapter 8, Section 8.12, "Recordkeeping," in *WATER DISTRIBUTION SYSTEM OPERATION AND MAINTENANCE*.

6.81 Maps

Comprehensive maps and sectional plats are used by most utilities. The comprehensive map provides an overall view of the entire distribution system. Important structures are shown, including water intakes, treatment plants, wells, reservoirs, mains, hydrants, and valves. The preferred scale for comprehensive maps is 500 feet per inch (60 m/cm), while the maximum scale recommended is 1,000 feet per inch (120 m/cm). Sectional plats will show various portions of the comprehensive map in much more detail (Figure 6.38). The scale varies from 50 to 200 feet per inch (6 to 24 m per cm). Standard symbols are used to indicate different items on these and other utility maps. Some common symbols are shown in Figure 6.39.

Valve and hydrant maps as shown in Figure 6.40 may cover the same area as up to four sectional maps. They not only show valve and hydrant locations, but provide such information as the direction to open the valve, the number of turns to open, the model type, and the installation date. A valve intersection plat with the valves identified by letters is shown in Figure 6.41.

Other types of maps are also used. Leak survey maps are usually another modification of sectional or valve maps and,

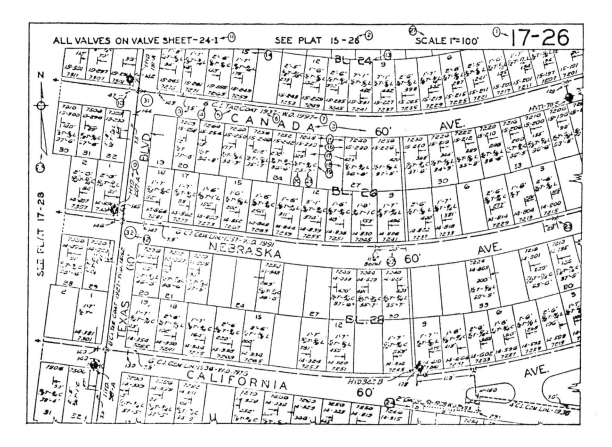

Fig. 6.38   Portion of sectional plat

(Reprinted from WATER DISTRIBUTION TRAINING COURSE, by permission.
Copyright, the American Water Works Association)

where regular leak survey work is conducted, these maps show the valves to be closed and the areas to be isolated. Leak frequency maps show the locations where leaks have been found and pinpoint problem areas. Customer complaints, when indicated on a map, are also very helpful in showing problem areas and the need for follow-up investigations. Locations of leaks and complaints may be marked on wall-mounted maps by pins with colored heads for ease in interpreting location, size, and type of problems.

All maps and drawings should show constructed facilities "as built" (or record drawings). If there was any change whatsoever from the construction plans, the maps and plans used by the utility should show this change. Whenever modifications are made, plans should be changed to show the details of the modification, the date of the modification, and who recorded the modification on the plans. The modified drawings are called "as-builts" or "record drawings."

Plan and profile maps are engineering drawings that show the depth of pipe, pipe location both vertically and horizontally, and the correct distance from a reference starting point. Operators occasionally need to use this type of map. Water gradient contour maps are prepared by taking pressure readings during peak use periods over the system, calculating hydraulic gradients, placing these gradients on the comprehensive map, and drawing in gradient contour lines. They can be used to indicate problem areas with insufficient or excessive pressures.

The geographic information system (GIS) is a computer program that combines mapping with detailed information about the physical structures within geographic areas. To create the database of information, "entities" within a mapped area, such as streets, manholes, line segments, and lift stations, are given "attributes." Attributes are simply the pieces of information about a particular feature or structure that are stored in a database. The attributes can be as basic as an address, manhole number, or line segment length, or they may be as specific as diameter, rim invert, and quadrant (coordinate) location. Attributes of a main line segment might include engineering information, maintenance information, and inspection information. Thus an inventory of entities and their properties is created. The system allows the operator to periodically update the map entities and their corresponding attributes.

The power of a GIS is that information can be retrieved geographically. An operator can choose an area to look at by pointing to a specific place on the map or outlining (windowing) an area of the map. The system will display the requested section on the screen and show the attributes of entities located on the map. A printed copy may also be requested. Figure 6.42 shows a GIS-generated map. This example shows data from an inflow/infiltration analysis, including pipe attributes, hydraulic data, and selected engineering data. The example also shows a map of the system. In most cases computer-based maintenance management system (CMMS) software has the ability to communicate with geographic information

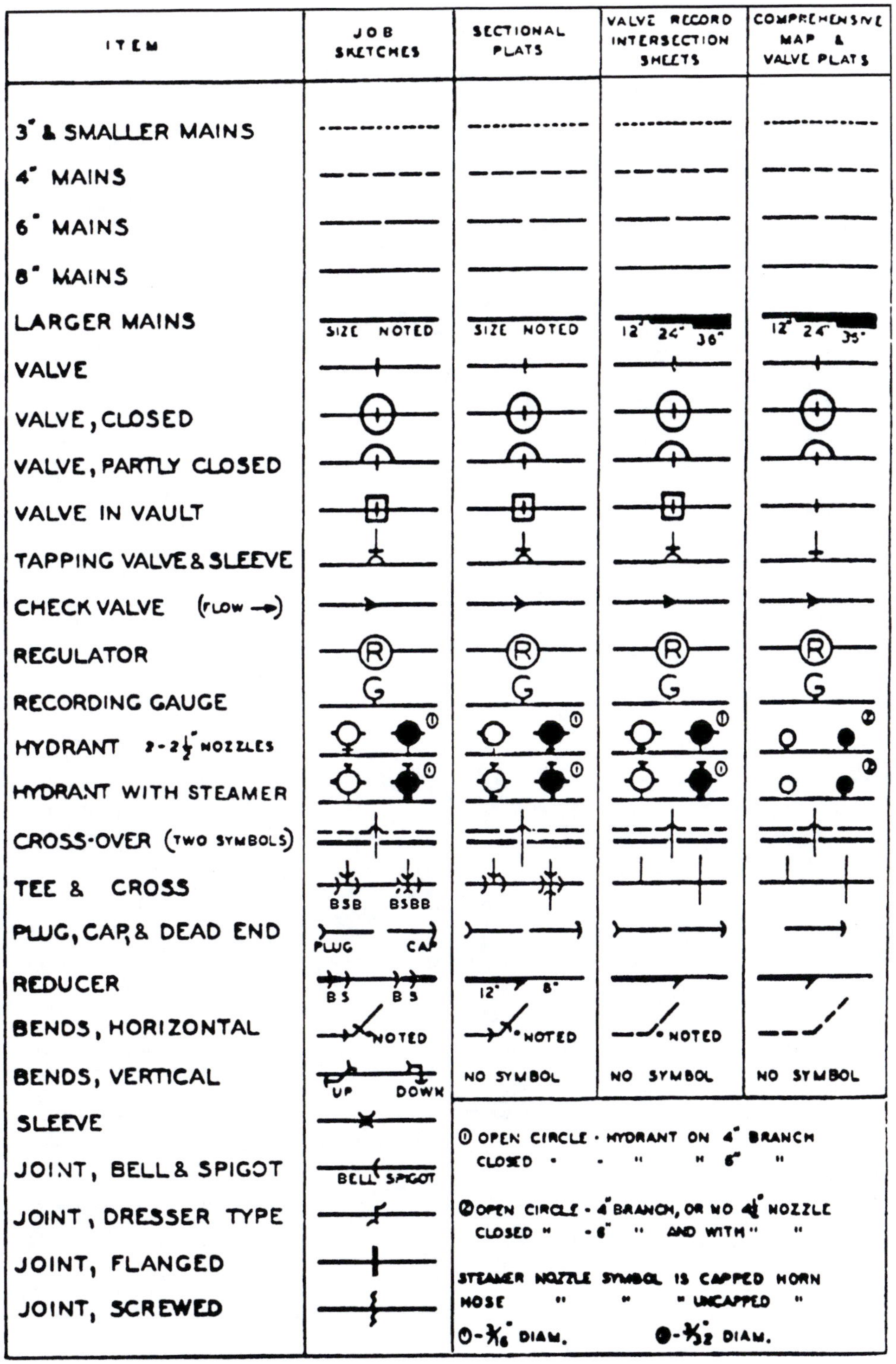

ITEM	JOB SKETCHES	SECTIONAL PLATS	VALVE RECORD INTERSECTION SHEETS	COMPREHENSIVE MAP & VALVE PLATS
3" & SMALLER MAINS				
4" MAINS				
6" MAINS				
8" MAINS				
LARGER MAINS	SIZE NOTED	SIZE NOTED	12" 24" 36"	12" 24" 36"
VALVE				
VALVE, CLOSED				
VALVE, PARTLY CLOSED				
VALVE IN VAULT				
TAPPING VALVE & SLEEVE				
CHECK VALVE (FLOW →)				
REGULATOR				
RECORDING GAUGE				
HYDRANT 2-2½" NOZZLES				
HYDRANT WITH STEAMER				
CROSS-OVER (TWO SYMBOLS)				
TEE & CROSS	BSB BSBB			
PLUG, CAP, & DEAD END	PLUG CAP			
REDUCER	B S B S	12" 8"		
BENDS, HORIZONTAL	NOTED	NOTED	NOTED	
BENDS, VERTICAL	UP DOWN	NO SYMBOL	NO SYMBOL	NO SYMBOL
SLEEVE		① OPEN CIRCLE · HYDRANT ON 4" BRANCH		
		CLOSED · · " " 6" "		
JOINT, BELL & SPIGOT	BELL SPIGOT			
JOINT, DRESSER TYPE		② OPEN CIRCLE · 4" BRANCH, OR NO 4" NOZZLE		
		CLOSED " · 6" " AND WITH " "		
JOINT, FLANGED		STEAMER NOZZLE SYMBOL IS CAPPED HORN		
JOINT, SCREWED		HOSE " " " UNCAPPED "		
		○-⁷⁄₁₆" DIAM. ●-⁷⁄₃₂" DIAM.		

Fig. 6.39   *Common map symbols*

(Reprinted from *WATER DISTRIBUTION OPERATOR TRAINING HANDBOOK*,
by permission. Copyright 1976, the American Water Works Association)

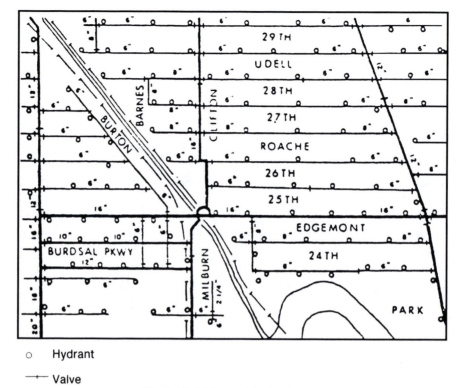

o   Hydrant

———+———   Valve

Fig. 6.40   Valve and hydrant map

(Reprinted from *WATER DISTRIBUTION OPERATOR TRAINING HANDBOOK,*
by permission. Copyright 1976, the American Water Works Association)

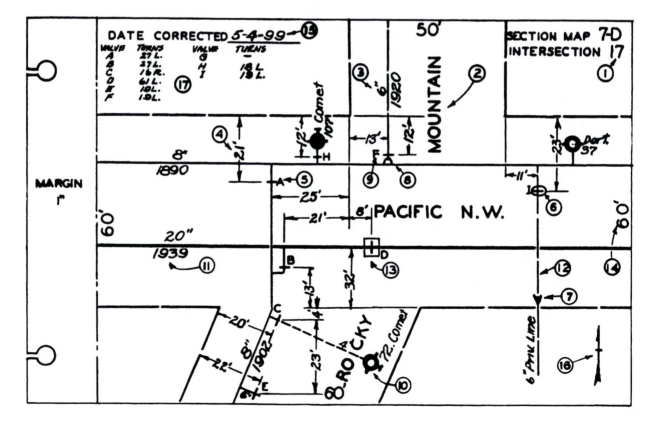

Fig. 6.41   Valve intersection plat

(Reprinted from *WATER DISTRIBUTION TRAINING COURSE,* by permission.
Copyright, the American Water Works Association)

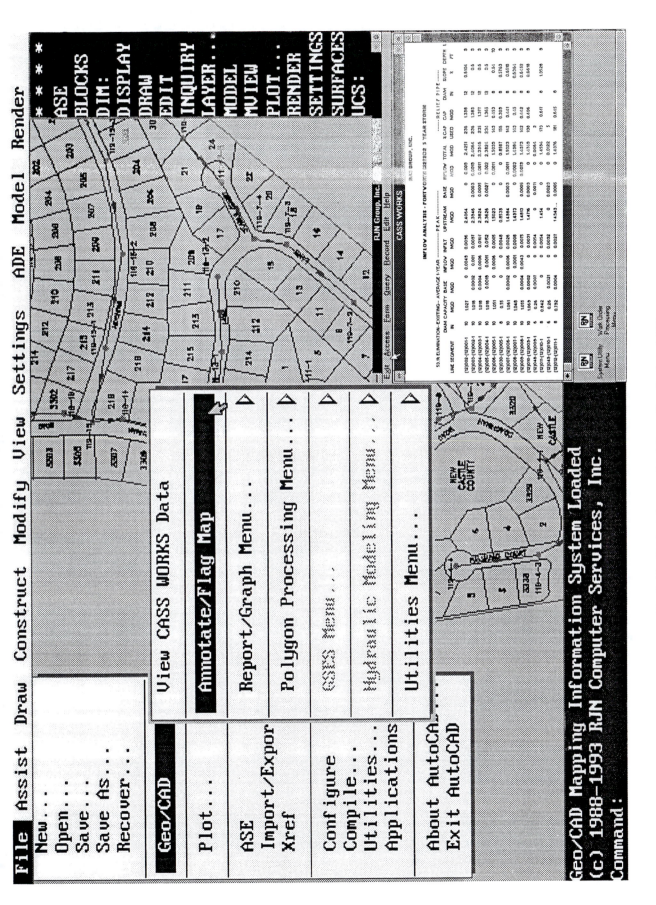

Fig. 6.42   Typical Geographic Information System (GIS) map

systems so that attribute information from the collection system can be copied into the GIS.

A GIS can generate work orders in the form of a map with the work to be performed outlined on the map. This minimizes paper work and gives the work crew precise information about where the work is to be performed. Completion of the work is recorded in the GIS to keep the work history for the area and entity up to date. Reports and other inquiries can be requested as needed, for example, a listing of all line segments in a specific area could be generated for a report.

In many areas GISs are being developed on an area-wide basis with many agencies, utilities, counties, cities, and state agencies participating. Usually a county-wide base map is developed and then all participants provide attributes for their particular systems. For example, information on the sanitary sewer collection system might be one map layer, the second map layer might be the water distribution system, and the third layer might be the electric utility distribution system. In addition to sharing databases with CMMSs, GISs generally now also have the ability to operate smoothly with computer-aided design (CAD) systems.

6.82   Types of Records

Written records should be kept on all facilities in the distribution system. These records should describe the facility, its construction, date installed, repair and maintenance work done, manufacturer, and condition during latest inspection. As new facilities are installed, they should be included in the existing record system. Records should also note those facilities retired from service. Other types of records to be kept include:

1. Results of water quality monitoring,
2. Cross-connection control,
3. Main flushing,
4. Main cleaning,
5. Consumer complaints,
6. Disinfection,
7. Pressure surveys,
8. Leaks,
9. Engineering reports,
10. Any operations done in compliance with the request of the health department, and
11. A daily log kept on any and all unusual events occurring, such as equipment malfunction, unusual weather conditions, and natural or man-made disasters.

Each public water system is required by the Primary Drinking Water Regulations to maintain records of water quality analyses, written reports, variances or exemptions, and actions taken to correct violations of the regulations. The lengths of time these records must be kept are summarized in Table 6.4.

Important distribution system operational records include technical and maintenance information on pumps, meters, valves, and other equipment. Information on design, capacities, and required maintenance should be kept with each major piece of equipment. Each piece of equipment should have its own file containing manufacturer's instructions, repairs made, and the schedule to be followed for routine maintenance. Each valve and hydrant should have a permanent file card such as that shown in Figure 6.43 and an inspection report form such as that shown in Figure 6.44.

TABLE 6.4   MINIMUM TIME PERIODS FOR RETAINING RECORDS

Record	Minimum Years of Retention
Bacteriological analyses	5
Chemical analyses	10
Written reports such as sanitary surveys, engineering reports	10[a]
Variances or exemptions	5[b]
Action taken to correct violation	3[c]

[a] Following completion of surveys and reports.
[b] Following expiration of variance or exemption.
[c] After last action with respect to violation.

Every utility should have a work order system which provides that all additions or changes to, or removal of, any of the system facilities be accomplished using approved work orders. Examples of some work order forms used are shown in Figures 6.45 and 6.46. The work order system should be devised to account properly for all of the physical plant facilities. The work order sketch (Figure 6.46), when completed, is used to revise the distribution maps to record additions, changes, or removals.

6.9   ADDITIONAL READING

To obtain additional information regarding the topics in this chapter, review the appropriate chapters and sections in the following operator training manual:

WATER DISTRIBUTION SYSTEM OPERATION AND MAINTENANCE. Obtain from the Office of Water Programs, California State University, Sacramento, 6000 J Street, Sacramento, CA 95819-6025, phone (916) 278-6142 or visit the website at www.owp.csus.edu. Price, $45.00.

6.10   ACKNOWLEDGMENT

Material contained in this chapter is copyrighted by the California State University, Sacramento Foundation and is reproduced by permission.

Permanent Valve Record

VALVE NUMBER__________ LOCATION__________

MANUFACTURER__________ __________

TYPE__________ VALVE DEPTH__________

SIZE__________ OPENS TO RIGHT OR LEFT__________

DATE INSTALLED__________ TURNS TO OPEN__________

VALVE BOX TYPE__________ NORMAL GATE POSITION__________

DATE OPERATED	COMMENTS

Fig. 6.43 Typical valve record form

(Reprinted from *OPFLOW*, January 1979, by permission. Copyright 1979, the American Water Works Association)

VALVE INSPECTION REPORT

MUNICIPALITY__________ VALVE NO. ______

LOCATION__________

SIZE______ MAKE______ OPER. NUT______

OPENS__________ NO. TURNS______

VALVE IN__________ ROUTE NO.______

CONDITION	INSPECTION DATES					
OPENS						
NO. TURNS						
STEM						
PACKING						
NUT						
BOX or MANHOLE						
VALVE in NOW						
INSPECTED BY						

CONDITION	INSPECTION DATES					
OPENS						
NO TURNS						
STEM						
PACKING						
NUT						
BOX or MANHOLE						
VALVE in NOW						
INSPECTED BY						

CONDITION	INSPECTION DATES					
OPENS						
NO TURNS						
STEM						
PACKING						
NUT						
BOX or MANHOLE						
VALVE in NOW						
INSPECTED BY						

HYDRANT INSPECTION REPORT

MUNICIPALITY__________ HYD. NO.______

LOCATION__________

MAKE__________ SIZE______

$2\frac{1}{2}$" NOZZLES__________ STEAMER NOZZLES______

OPENS______ SIZE MAIN______ SIZE BRANCH______ BRANCH VALVE______

CONDITION	INSPECTION DATES					
PAINT						
CAPS						
CHAINS						
STEM						
PACKING						
DRIP						
TOP NUT						
VALVE						
VALVE SEAT						
CONDITION of WATER						
MINUTES FLUSHED						
STATIC PRESSURE						
RESIDUAL PRESSURE						
FLOW						
INSPECTED BY						

CONDITION	INSPECTION DATES					
PAINT						
CAPS						
CHAINS						
STEM						
PACKING						
DRIP						
TOP NUT						
VALVE						
VALVE SEAT						
CONDITION of WATER						
MINUTES FLUSHED						
STATIC PRESSURE						
RESIDUAL PRESSURE						
FLOW						
INSPECTED BY						

Fig. 6.44 Valve and hydrant inspection report forms

(Reprinted from *WATER DISTRIBUTION TRAINING COURSE*, by permission. Copyright, the American Water Works Association)

INVESTMENT WORK ORDER

FOR PROPERTY ADDITIONS
AND IMPROVEMENTS

Investment Work Order No.   A-80

Charge to Budget (Item C Below) $ 1,652.65

The Metropolitan Water Company
Name of Company

Apply to Budget Item No.   1A-2

Metropolitan City
Location

File No.   -443

DESCRIPTIVE TITLE: Install 400 feet of 6"   pipe on
Main Street south from First Avenue.

PURPOSE: Give complete explanation here, not by letter. Attach extra sheet if necessary. Sketch must accompany changes in distribution system, buildings, pumping equipment and piping. If contribution or refundable deposit toward the cost is to be obtained, state amount thereof, from whom it will be received, and if an agreement is to be entered into submit the signed agreement. If State regulations, franchises, municipal contracts or company rules are involved, state extent.

This installation required to replace a 3/4" galvanized pipe installed in 1926, which has become inadequate due to corrosion and an increased number of customers.

Pressure on Proposed Mains ___60___ psi   Traffic ___light___   Type of Paving ___none___

SUMMARY ESTIMATE OF COST

A. Total estimated cost (per reverse) $ 1,652.65

B. Less: Contributions (non-refundable) $ _____

C. Net direct cost to Company $ 1,652.65

D. Service and meter installations $ _____

E. Total cost $ 1,652.65

If any preliminary investigation costs have been incurred for this project, to what account were they charged?
___None___

Does the proposed work replace any Company owned property? ___Yes___

If yes, what number is assigned to the related Retirement Order? R - 31

In what political subdivision will new property be located? ___Metropolitan City___

RETURN ON INVESTMENT

1. Total Investment cost (Item E) . . . . $ 1,625.65

2. Increase in revenue:

2a. ____ Consumers @ $ ____ . . . $ _____

2b. ____ Consumers @ $ ____ . . . _____

2c. ____ Hydrants @ $ ____ . . . _____

2d. _____ . . . _____

3. Total increase in revenue . . . . . $ _____

4. Decrease in operating expenses . . . . _____

5. Total—Lines 3 and 4 . . . . . _____

6. Increase in expenses:

6a. Operating, maintenance and general taxes, ____% of Line 3 . . . . $ _____

6b. Depreciation ____% of Line 1 . . . _____

7. Total increase in expenses . . . . _____

8. Income before income taxes—Line 5 minus 7 _____

9. Income taxes ____% of Line 8 . . . _____

10. Income available for return—Line 8 minus 9 $ _____

11. Rate of return—Line 10 ÷ Line 1 . . . _____ %

PREPARATION AND APPROVAL

	LOCAL AND DIVISION OFFICES	Date		GENERAL OFFICE	Date
Prepared By:	_____	____		_____	____
Local Manager:	_____	____		_____	____
Budget Approval:	_____	____		_____	____
Division Comptroller:	_____	____		_____	____
Division Manager:	_____	____		_____	____

Fig. 6.45   Typical investment work order form

(Reprinted from *WATER DISTRIBUTION TRAINING COURSE*, by permission.
Copyright, the American Water Works Association)

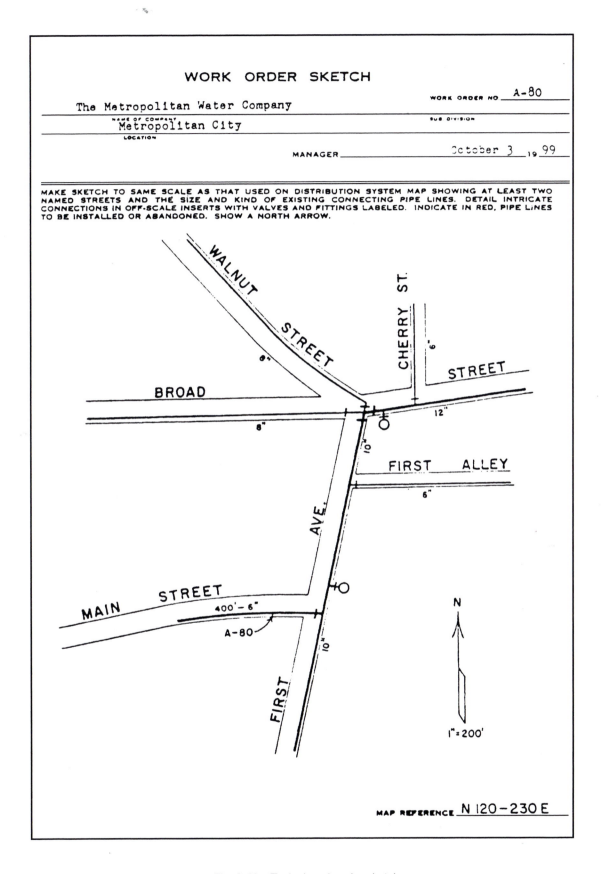

Fig. 6.46   Typical work order sketch

(Reprinted from *WATER DISTRIBUTION TRAINING COURSE*, by permission.
Copyright, the American Water Works Association)

WATER SYSTEMS OPERATION AND MAINTENANCE VIDEO TRAINING SERIES

CHAPTER (VIDEO) 7

APPROACHES TO COMPLIANCE WITH STANDARDS

VIDEO 7 SUMMARY

Video 7, APPROACHES TO COMPLIANCE WITH STANDARDS, provides operators, owners, and decision makers with the knowledge, skills, and abilities they need to keep their water system in compliance with drinking water standards. Information is provided on how to take a systematic approach to identifying and investigating multiple approaches to achieving compliance. Emphasis is placed on evaluating life cycle costs for multiple alternatives to determine the most cost effective selection to achieve and maintain compliance. Procedures are provided for procuring and managing outside expertise to assist with the compliance process.

CONTENTS OF VIDEO 7

APPROACHES TO COMPLIANCE WITH STANDARDS VIDEO

INTRODUCTION

IDENTIFY THE PROBLEM

CONSULT WITH YOUR REGULATOR

EXPLORE APPROACHES

CONSOLIDATION/MERGE SYSTEMS

NEW SOURCE

TREATMENT

    Nitrate (Ion exchange system—leased)

    PCE (Granular activated carbon adsorption system)

TREATMENT CONSIDERATIONS

CONSIDERING ALL ALTERNATIVES

CONTENTS OF CHAPTER 7

**APPROACHES TO COMPLIANCE WITH STANDARDS
LEARNING BOOKLET**

OBJECTIVES

Chapter (Video) 7.   APPROACHES TO COMPLIANCE WITH STANDARDS

Following completion of Video 7 and Chapter 7, you should be able to:

1. Identify areas of non-compliance with drinking water standards,

2. Develop and use a decision tree to solve a problem,

3. Identify resources for assistance in achieving compliance,

4. Identify multiple alternatives for achieving compliance,

5. Evaluate multiple alternatives for achieving compliance,

6. Apply life cycle cost comparisons of alternatives, and

7. Hire and manage a consulting engineer.

LEARNING BOOKLET STUDY MATERIAL

This section of the *LEARNING BOOKLET* contains important information. Read this section after watching the video and before attempting to take the Objective Test for this chapter.

Material covered in this section will help you better understand the material in the video. Also some critical information is easier to present in the *LEARNING BOOKLET*, such as Drinking Water Standards.

Chapter (Video) 7.   APPROACHES TO COMPLIANCE WITH STANDARDS

7.0 INTRODUCTION

Water has many important beneficial uses and each requires a certain specific level of water quality. The major concern of the operators of water treatment plants and water supply systems is to produce and deliver to consumers water that is safe and pleasant to drink. The water should be acceptable to domestic and commercial water users and many industries. Some industries, such as food and drug processors and the electronics industry, require higher quality water. Many industries will locate where the local water supply meets their specific needs while other industries may have their own water treatment facilities to produce water suitable for their needs.

All water treatment plant operators need to be thoroughly familiar with the state and federal laws and standards that apply to domestic water supply systems. These regulations are the goals and guideposts for the water supply industry. Their purpose is to ensure the uniform delivery of safe and aesthetically pleasing drinking water to the public.

Water systems can fall out of compliance with standards due to a change in source water quality or due to a change in the standards. When it becomes known that the water system is, or will be, out of compliance with standards, it is time to act. Decisions must be made about what course of action to take to maintain or to return the system to compliance with standards. It is important to take a measured and organized approach in the decision-making process in order to arrive at the best course of action for the water system. Remember, each water system is unique and each will require a unique solution to the problem of staying in compliance with water quality standards.

7.1 HISTORY OF DRINKING WATER LAWS AND STANDARDS

Up until shortly after 1900, there were no standards for drinking water. The first standards, established in 1914, were designed in large part to control waterborne bacteria and viruses that cause diseases such as cholera, typhoid, and dysentery. These new standards were overwhelmingly successful in curbing the spread of such diseases. However, with time and technology, other types of contaminants, this time chemicals, again stirred public concern. In 1962 the U.S. Public Health Service (the forerunner of the U.S. Environmental Protection Agency) revised the national drinking water standards to include limits on selected organic chemicals.

In 1972, a series of reports detailing organic contamination in the drinking water supplied to the residents of New Orleans from the Mississippi River triggered profound changes in drinking water regulations. A study by the Environmental Defense Fund found that people drinking treated Mississippi River water in New Orleans had a greater chance of developing certain cancers than those in neighboring areas whose drinking water came from groundwater sources. Heightened public awareness and concern regarding cancer became major factors behind the push for legislative action on the issue of drinking water contamination. The finding of suspected carcinogens in drinking water established a widespread sense of urgency that led to the passage and signing into law of the Safe Drinking Water Act in December, 1974.

The Safe Drinking Water Act (SDWA) gave the federal government, through the U.S. Environmental Protection Agency (EPA), the authority to:

- Set national standards regulating the maximum allowable levels of contaminants in drinking water (MCLs);

- Require public water systems to monitor and report the levels of identified contaminants; and

- Establish uniform guidelines specifying the acceptable treatment technologies for removing unsafe levels of pollutants from drinking water.

While the SDWA gave EPA responsibility for promulgating (passing into law) drinking water regulations, it gave state regulatory agencies the opportunity to assume primary responsibility for enforcing those regulations.

Implementation of the SDWA has greatly improved basic drinking water purity across the nation. However, recent EPA surveys of surface water and groundwater indicate the presence of synthetic organic chemicals in 20 percent of the nation's water sources, with a small percentage at levels of concern. In addition, research studies suggest that some naturally occurring contaminants may pose even greater risks to human health than the synthetic contaminants. Further, there is growing concern about microbial and radon contamination.

In the years following passage of the SDWA, Congress felt that EPA was slow to regulate contaminants and states were lax in enforcing the law. Consequently, in 1986 Congress enacted amendments designed to strengthen the 1974 SDWA. These amendments set deadlines for the establishment of maximum contaminant levels, placed greater emphasis on enforcement, authorized penalties for tampering with drinking water supplies, mandated the complete elimination of lead from drinking water, and placed considerable emphasis on the protection of underground drinking water sources.

The 1986 SDWA amendments set up a timetable under which EPA was required to develop primary standards for 83 contaminants. Other major provisions of the 1986 SDWA amendments required EPA to:

1. Define an approved treatment technique for each regulated contaminant,

2. Specify criteria for filtration of surface water supplies,

3. Specify criteria for disinfection of surface and groundwater supplies, and

4. Prohibit the use of lead products in materials used to convey drinking water.

To comply with the provisions of the 1986 SDWA amendments, the EPA, the states, and the water supply industry undertook significant new programs to clean up the country's water supplies.

On August 6, 1996, the President signed new Safe Drinking Water Act (SDWA) amendments into law as Public Law (PL) 104-182. These amendments made sweeping changes to the existing SDWA, created several new programs, and included a total authorization of more than $12 billion in federal funds for various drinking water programs and activities from fiscal year (FY) 1997 through FY 2003.

Topics covered in the 1996 amendments include:

- Comprehensive public health protection through risk-based standard setting
- Reliance on best available science
- Contamination prevention tools and programs
- Consumer awareness and public participation in drinking water issues
- Increased funding to assist with compliance
- Strengthened enforcement authority for EPA
- National minimum operator certification guidelines for states
- Mandatory capacity development programs (managerial, technical, financial) for all water systems including small systems
- Groundwater protection programs and groundwater disinfection
- Authorization for research in selected areas:
  - Arsenic health impacts
  - Disinfectants and disinfection byproducts
  - Estrogenic substances screening
  - Monitoring for unregulated contaminants
  - Waterborne disease studies

For additional information and details see "Overview of the Safe Drinking Water Act Amendments of 1996" by Fredrick W. Pontius, *JOURNAL AMERICAN WATER WORKS ASSOCIATION*, October 1996, pages 22-33 and http://www.epa.gov/safewater/consumer/trendrpt.pdf.

On December 16, 1998, two major regulations were signed into law: the Disinfectants/Disinfection By-Products (D/DBP) (see *WATER TREATMENT PLANT OPERATION*, Volume II (2004), Office of Water Programs, California State University Sacramento, Section 22.23 for details), and the Interim Enhanced Surface Water Treatment Rule (IESWTR) (see *WATER TREATMENT PLANT OPERATION*, Volume II (2004), Office of Water Programs, California State University Sacramento, Section 22.2216 for details). The D/DBP Rule was developed to protect the public from harmful concentrations of disinfectants and from trihalomethanes which could form when disinfection by-products combine with organic matter in drinking water. The goal of the IESWTR is to reduce the occurrence of *Cryptosporidium* and other pathogens in drinking water. This rule was developed to ensure that protection against microbial contaminants is not lowered as water systems comply with the D/DBP Rule.

Operators are urged to develop close working relationships with their local regulatory agencies to keep themselves informed of the frequent changes in regulations and requirements. A summary of the National Primary Drinking Water Standards is presented in Table 7.1. The Safe Drinking Water Act poster included with this booklet is an excellent summary of the standards.

7.2   THE DECISION TREE

When a drinking water system is out of compliance with drinking water standards, action must be taken, and decisions must be made. One method for taking an organized approach to decision making is to use a decision tree. The decision tree organizes the decision process into a defined sequence that guides users through consideration of several alternatives. The process helps ensure that users don't become immediately focused on one solution without considering other alternatives, which may turn out to be far more cost effective for the water system. The decision tree we will be using to describe the process is pictured below (Figure 7.1).

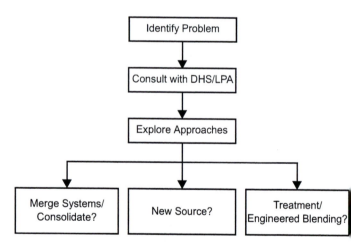

Fig. 7.1   Decision tree

7.3   IDENTIFY THE PROBLEM

Causes of water contamination can be natural or man-made. One example of a natural contaminant of concern is arsenic in groundwater. Arsenic is a naturally-occurring substance in rock and soil layers beneath the surface. If these rock and soil layers are part of an aquifer, the water in contact with the arsenic-containing soils will dissolve some of the arsenic into the water. Wells tapping into the aquifer will produce water containing arsenic. Water with arsenic concentrations above the limit allowable in the standards cannot be used as drinking water without mitigation measures to ensure concentrations of arsenic do not exceed those limits.

TABLE 7.1   NATIONAL PRIMARY DRINKING WATER STANDARDS

Contaminant	MCL	Health Effects
Inorganics		
Antimony	0.006 mg/L	decreases longevity, alters cholesterol and glucose levels
Arsenic	0.05 mg/L 0.01 mg/L (effective January 2006)	skin/nervous system toxicity; possible cancer
Asbestos	7 million fibers/L	possible cancer
Barium	2.0 mg/L	circulatory system effects
Beryllium	0.004 mg/L	bone/lung damage; possible cancer
Bromate	0.010 mg/L	possible cancer
Cadmium	0.005 mg/L	kidney effects
Chlorite	1.0 mg/L	blood; developing nervous system
Chromium	0.1 mg/L	skin sensitization; liver/kidney/circulatory/nervous system disorders and respiratory problems
Copper	1.3 mg/L[a]	nervous system/kidney/gastrointestinal effects; toxicity
Cyanide	0.2 mg/L	spleen/liver/brain effects
Fluoride	4.0 mg/L	brown staining and/or pitting of teeth
Lead	0.015 mg/L[a] (at tap)	interference with red blood cell chemistry; developmental delays in children; blood pressure effects in some adults; toxic to infants and pregnant women
Mercury	0.002 mg/L	kidney disorders
Nitrate (as N) and Nitrite (as N)[b]	10.0 mg/L 1.0 mg/L	Methemoglobinemia ("blue-baby" syndrome)
Selenium	0.05 mg/L	nervous system damage
Thallium	0.002 mg/L	liver/kidney/intestines/brain effects
Organics		
VOLATILE ORGANICS		
Benzene	0.005 mg/L	possible cancer
Carbon tetrachloride	0.005 mg/L	possible cancer
o-Dichlorobenzene	0.6 mg/L	kidney and liver effects; blood cell damage
p-Dichlorobenzene	0.075 mg/L	kidney and liver effects
1,2-Dichloroethane	0.005 mg/L	possible cancer
1,1-Dichloroethylene	0.007 mg/L	kidney and liver damage
cis-1,2-Dichloroethylene	0.07 mg/L	nervous system/liver/circulatory system damage
trans-1,2-Dichloroethylene	0.1 mg/L	nervous system/liver/circulatory system damage
Dichloromethane	0.005 mg/L	possible cancer
1,2-Dichloropropane	0.005 mg/L	possible cancer
Ethylbenzene	0.7 mg/L	kidney/liver/nervous system damage
Monochlorobenzene	0.1 mg/L	kidney/liver/nervous system damage
Styrene	0.1 mg/L	nervous system/liver damage
Tetrachloroethylene	0.005 mg/L	possible cancer
Toluene	1.0 mg/L	nervous system/kidney/liver damage
1,2,4-Trichlorobenzene	0.07 mg/L	adrenal gland and internal organ damage
1,1,1-Trichloroethane	0.2 mg/L	liver/nervous system/circulatory system damage
1,1,2-Trichloroethane	0.005 mg/L	liver/kidney effects
Trichloroethylene (TCE)	0.005 mg/L	possible cancer
Vinyl chloride	0.002 mg/L	possible cancer
Xylenes (total)	10.0 mg/L	liver/kidney/nervous system damage
PESTICIDES AND SYNTHETIC ORGANICS		
Acrylamide	treatment technique	possible cancer; nervous system effects
Alachlor	0.002 mg/L	possible cancer
Atrazine	0.003 mg/L	cardiac/reproductive system damage
Benzo[a]pyrene	0.0002 mg/L	possible cancer
Carbofuran	0.04 mg/L	nervous system/reproductive system damage
Chlordane	0.002 mg/L	possible cancer
Dalapon	0.2 mg/L	kidney/liver damage
Dibromochloropropane (DBCP)	0.0002 mg/L	possible cancer
Di(2-ethylhexyl)adipate	0.4 mg/L	liver/reproductive system effects
Di(2-ethylhexyl)phthalate	0.006 mg/L	possible cancer
Dinoseb	0.007 mg/L	thyroid/reproductive system damage
Diquat	0.02 mg/L	kidney/gastrointestinal damage; cataract risk
Endothall	0.1 mg/L	liver/kidney/gastrointestinal and reproductive system effects
Endrin	0002 mg/L	liver/kidney/heart damage

TABLE 7.1   NATIONAL PRIMARY DRINKING WATER STANDARDS (continued)

Contaminant	MCL	Health Effects
PESTICIDES AND SYNTHETIC ORGANICS (continued)		
Epichlorohydrin	treatment technique	possible cancer
Ethylene dibromide (EDB)	0.00005 mg/L	possible cancer
Glyphosate	0.7 mg/L	liver/kidney damage
Heptachlor	0.0004 mg/L	possible cancer
Heptachlor epoxide	0.0002 mg/L	possible cancer
Hexachlorobenzene	0.001 mg/L	possible cancer
Hexachlorocyclopentadiene	0.05 mg/L	stomach/kidney damage
Lindane	0.0002 mg/L	nervous system/immune system/liver/kidney effects
Methoxychlor	0.04 mg/L	nervous system/reproductive system/kidney/liver effects
Oxamyl (Vydate)	0.2 mg/L	kidney damage
PCBs	0.0005 mg/L	possible cancer
Pentachlorophenol	0.001 mg/L	liver/kidney damage
Picloram	0.5 mg/L	liver/kidney damage
Simazine	0.004 mg/L	possible cancer
Toxaphene	0.003 mg/L	possible cancer
2,4-D	0.07 mg/L	liver/kidney/nervous system damage
2,3,7,8-TCDD (Dioxin)	0.00000003 mg/L	possible cancer
2,4,5-TP (Silvex)	0.05 mg/L	liver/kidney damage
Microbial		
Total Coliform	1 per 100 mL <40 samples/mo — no more than 1 positive >40 samples/mo — no more than 5% positive	indicators of disease-causing organisms
Giardia lamblia	3-log (99.9%) removal[c]	Giardiasis; gastrointestinal effects
Legionella	treatment technique[c]	Legionnaire's Disease; affects respiratory system
Enteric viruses	4-log (99.99%) removal[c]	gastrointestinal and other viral infections
Heterotrophic bacteria	treatment technique[c]	gastrointestinal infections
Physical		
Turbidity[c]	0.5 to 5 NTU	interferes with disinfection
Radionuclides		
Gross alpha particles	15 pCi/L	cancer risk
Gross beta particles[d]	4 mrem/yr	cancer risk
Radium 226 & 228	5 pCi/L	bone cancer
Uranium	30 µg/L	kidney damage; possible cancer
Disinfection By-Products		
TTHMs[e]	0.080 mg/L	cancer risk

[a] Action level for treatment.
[b] Applies to community, nontransient noncommunity, and transient noncommunity water systems.
[c] Applies to systems using surface water or groundwater under the influence of surface water.
[d] Applies to surface water systems serving more than 100,000 persons and any system determined by the state to be vulnerable.
[e] Applies to systems serving more than 10,000 persons and also to all surface water systems that meet the criteria for avoiding filtration.

Nitrate is an example of a contaminant that often results from human activity. One nitrate contamination source, animal stockyards, concentrates large numbers of animals into a relatively small area. Waste from the animals percolates into the ground where soil microbes oxidize ammonia and biological nitrogen contained in the liquid waste to nitrate. Nitrate is highly mobile and will travel with water that percolates through soil layers to aquifers below. The resulting elevated nitrate concentrations can cause water drawn from the aquifer to exceed limits set in drinking water standards.

Over fertilization of agricultural and urban landscaped areas can also cause nitrate contamination of both groundwater and surface water. Soil and aquatic organisms oxidize ammonia-nitrogen contained in fertilizers to nitrate. The highly mobile nitrate is carried by water either percolating down to groundwater or running off to surface water. If these water sources are used for drinking water supplies and the nitrate levels exceed regulatory limits, a non-compliance condition is created.

Chemical spills are another example of human-made causes of non-compliance with drinking water standards. It was common practice in the first half of the 20th century for users to dispose of synthetic organic cleaning solvents by pouring them onto the ground. Many of those solvents percolated down into aquifers, contaminating the groundwater. As the groundwater migrated away from the contamination source area, the solvent contamination was carried along. Wells tapping into the contaminated groundwater produce water containing the contaminant.

7.31   Causes of Non-Compliance With Standards

Non-compliance with drinking water standards can result from changes in the standards or from changing contamination of source water. Recent changes in the standards for arsenic in drinking water are a good example of non-compliance resulting from regulatory changes. The allowable limit for arsenic was reduced from 50 µg/L to 10 µg/L by the U.S. EPA. Water systems that were producing water with arsenic concentrations between 10 µg/L and 50 µg/L were previously in compliance. Although nothing changed in the characteristics of the water the systems were providing, the regulatory change caused the systems to fall out of compliance, and action was required.

Non-compliance can also result from migrating contaminants reaching the source water intake for a water system. In this case, a water system previously in compliance can suddenly fall out of compliance due to a change in source water characteristics. Again, action is required to return the water system to compliance with standards.

7.32   Awareness of Regulatory Changes

If the cause of non-compliance is migrating contamination that reaches a water system's source water, it can sometimes be difficult to foresee the non-compliance. However, in the case of regulatory changes, it is always possible to see potential non-compliance coming. Before regulatory changes are enacted, studies are conducted, proposed regulatory changes are publicized, public comments are requested, and grace periods for compliance are allowed. It is the responsibility of all water system operators and owners to remain aware of potential regulatory changes and to participate in the process. One factor in the decision to implement new regulations is the impact the proposed regulations will have on the regulated community. That information is gathered during the public comment period. If a proposed regulation will have a significant impact on your water system, it is imperative that you communicate that information during the public comment period because it may have an impact on the final regulation.

Notices of proposed regulatory changes are published by the EPA and by state regulatory agencies (in California, Department of Health Services), and are posted on the websites for those agencies. Proposed regulatory changes are also posted on the American Water Works Association (AWWA) website.

7.4   CONSULT WITH DHS/LPA

As soon as you become aware that your water system is out of compliance, or will be out of compliance, it is time to begin the process of bringing the system into compliance with standards. The first step in that process is consulting with your state regulatory agency (in CA, Department of Health Services, DHS) or local primacy agency, LPA. These agencies are wonderful resources to help water systems achieve and maintain compliance with standards. They can provide information, advice, contacts, and even funding to help your water system achieve compliance.

The responsibility of drinking water regulatory agencies is to ensure public health by ensuring safe drinking water supplies. That obviously involves enforcement of water quality regulations. What you may not know, is that it also involves providing assistance, guidance, and sometimes, funding to help water systems achieve and maintain compliance with those regulations.

Because water system regulators are involved with so many different water systems, they have significant experience with methods to achieve compliance. Their mission is to use that experience to assist water suppliers with compliance issues. The guidance they can provide will help water agencies consider all alternatives and select the alternative that affords the greatest potential for success, including maintaining economic viability. By contacting the regulatory agency early in the process, you open lines of communication and obtain access to a valuable resource for information and assistance. The website for the California DHS is http://www.dhs.ca.gov/ps/ddwem/.

7.5   EXPLORE APPROACHES

You are now at the third step in the decision tree process. After identifying the problem and consulting with your regulatory agency, it is time to explore approaches to solving the problem of non-compliance with drinking water standards. It is critically important at this point not to jump to a conclusion about a perceived best solution. By thoroughly investigating several approaches, the likelihood of finding an efficient, cost effective solution is increased significantly.

Water system operators and owners, when faced with a non-compliance issue, often jump to a conclusion of treatment as the solution to the non-compliance. Sometimes, treatment is the best solution. However, often times other alternatives produce much better and much less costly results.

A concept that is critically important when exploring different approaches is that of life cycle cost. Life cycle cost evaluation of an alternative considers not just the capital cost for constructing or purchasing and installing a new system or system component, but also the costs for operation and maintenance, chemicals, energy, waste disposal, and replacement. It is the sum of all of these costs that represents the true cost of an alternative to a water utility. By considering only one component of the life cycle cost, such as the capital cost, a utility runs the risk of locking itself into a decision that can financially compromise or even bankrupt the utility. When evaluating alternatives, the current and future water rates of the consumers must be considered.

The objective of this section is to assist operators and owners to explore all approaches before deciding on one. Some of those approaches will be presented and discussed in the next three sections.

7.51   Consolidate Systems

Many water systems operate within a few miles of an adjacent water system. When a water system is faced with a non-compliance situation, one alternative that should be considered is consolidation with an adjacent system. Consolidation enables the continued use of the water distribution infrastructure of both systems while using the source water from the system that is in compliance with standards.

As with all alternatives considered, the life cycle cost of consolidation must be evaluated to determine the true cost of the alternative. Consolidation might be dismissed out of hand if only the capital cost is considered in the evaluation. The capital cost of constructing an interconnecting pipeline between adjacent systems can be high in comparison to the capital cost for other alternatives such as treatment. However, consolidation can result in significant reductions or elimination of many ongoing costs. For example, once consolidated, the need for duplicate administration and laboratory services is eliminated. By consolidating and avoiding treatment, the chemical, energy, waste disposal, and labor costs associated with treatment facility operation and maintenance are avoided. A comparison of life cycle costs will reveal the current and future true costs of each alternative considered.

7.52 New Source

When a water system is faced with non-compliance, another important alternative to consider is switching to a new water source. The change may involve switching from a groundwater source to a surface water source or vice versa. It may also involve drilling a new well or deepening or re-screening an existing well. As with the system consolidation alternative, the capital cost may appear high. However, by avoiding treatment and its associated perpetual O & M costs, the life cycle cost may be lower for the new source alternative.

It should also be noted here that if non-compliance resulted from contamination reaching the water system source water, consideration should be given to identifying the contamination source to assess the cost of eliminating the contamination source. Some contamination sources involve persistent pollutants that are difficult or impossible to remediate. Others may be local and much more feasible to eliminate such as a small livestock operation adjacent to a well. The bottom line is that by considering all alternatives and determining the life cycle cost for each, the most cost effective alternative can be selected so that water rate increases can be minimized.

7.53 Treatment/Engineered Blending

The last alternative we'll present is treatment. Treatment should always be one of the alternatives considered; however, the treatment alternative should always be considered within the context of a life cycle cost analysis. The treatment alternative always involves O & M additions, which can significantly add to life cycle cost because O & M costs continue for the life of the water system. Some examples of treatment O & M costs are chemical costs, energy, waste disposal, and labor.

Many small systems have basic water supply facilities that require little operator attention. Often, addition of a treatment process requires a significant increase in the amount of operator attention and sometimes in the required grade level of the operator. Labor is usually the greatest cost for a utility and adding a requirement for additional labor, and/or higher certification for an operator can result in significant, ongoing increased expenses for the water system.

Additional ongoing expenses that can occur are chemical purchase costs and costs for disposal of hazardous waste products from the treatment operation. Energy costs to run a treatment system are also incurred. These ongoing expenses are in addition to the initial, or capital, cost for constructing or for purchasing and installing the new treatment system.

The discussion above is not intended to discourage water system operators and owners from considering the treatment alternative. Treatment is sometimes the best, most cost effective alternative. The discussion is intended to encourage deci-

sion makers to consider all alternatives and to consider the true cost, the life cycle cost, of each alternative.

What treatment alternatives are available? There are as many treatment alternatives as there are causes of non-compliance with standards. Often, multiple treatment alternatives are available to treat a particular problem. In some cases, treatment of part of the source water, followed by engineered blending of the treated and untreated water will bring a system into compliance. In other cases, vendors may be available who will lease treatment systems to water agencies and include chemicals and waste disposal with the lease contract. So, how does one sort through the myriad of alternatives?

7.6 HIRING A CONSULTANT

Many water agencies, when faced with a non-compliance issue, will seek outside expertise. The first stop for that expertise should be your state or local primacy regulatory agency. They may have the expertise available to your water agency at no charge.

If, after working with your regulatory agency, you decide that you need to obtain outside expertise, your water agency can consider hiring a consulting engineer. Consulting engineers can provide the expertise required to guide the water agency through the process to achieve compliance with standards. That process includes consideration of all alternatives, not just the treatment alternative.

When selecting a consulting engineer, ask the engineer for references from water utility agencies similar to yours. Contact these water utility agencies and ask the agencies if they were satisfied with the services provided by the engineer. Find out if the consulting fees charged were appropriate and reasonable. Determine if the treatment processes were designed and constructed as proposed and also if they work as expected. Be sure to learn if operation and maintenance costs are at the expected levels. Also find out if a performance bond was provided to ensure expected performance at anticipated costs.

Remember, the consulting engineer is working for your agency. It is your responsibility to define the scope of work for the consulting engineer. Make sure that your engineer understands that your agency wants the engineer's services for investigating all alternatives and you want to compare life cycle costs for each. The consulting engineer can help a water agency investigate and implement the best alternative for your system.

7.7 ACKNOWLEDGMENTS

Material contained in this chapter is copyrighted by the State of California, Department of Health Services. This material may not be reproduced or disseminated without prior written permission from the Department of Health Services.

WATER WORDS

A Summary of the Words Defined

in

WATER SYSTEMS OPERATION AND MAINTENANCE
VIDEO TRAINING SERIES

PROJECT PRONUNCIATION KEY

by Warren L. Prentice

The Project Pronunciation Key is designed to aid you in the pronunciation of new words. While this key is based primarily on familiar sounds, it does not attempt to follow any particular pronunciation guide. This key is designed solely to aid operators in this program.

You may find it helpful to refer to other available sources for pronunciation help. Each current standard dictionary contains a guide to its own pronunciation key. Each key will be different from each other and from this key. Examples of the difference between the key used in this program and the *WEBSTER'S NEW WORLD COLLEGE DICTIONARY*[1] "Key" are shown below.

In using this key, you should accent (say louder) the syllable that appears in capital letters. The following chart is presented to give examples of how to pronounce words using the Project Key.

WORD	SYLLABLE				
	1st	2nd	3rd	4th	5th
acid	AS	id			
coliform	COAL	i	form		
biological	BUY	o	LODGE	ik	cull

The first word, *ACID*, has its first syllable accented. The second word, *COLIFORM*, has its first syllable accented. The third word, *BIOLOGICAL*, has its first and third syllables accented.

We hope you will find the key useful in unlocking the pronunciation of any new word.

Term	Project Key	Webster Key
acid	AS-id	aś id
coliform	COAL-i-form	kō′ lə fôrm
biological	BUY-o-LODGE-ik-cull	bī ə läj′ i kəl

---

[1] *The WEBSTER'S NEW WORLD COLLEGE DICTIONARY, Fourth Edition, 1999, was chosen rather than an unabridged dictionary because of its availability to the operator. Other editions may be slightly different.*

WATER WORDS

>GREATER THAN

DO >5 mg/*L* would be read as DO GREATER THAN 5 mg/*L*.

<LESS THAN

DO <5 mg/*L* would be read as DO LESS THAN 5 mg/*L*.

>GREATER THAN

<LESS THAN

A

ACUTE HEALTH EFFECT

An adverse effect on a human or animal body, with symptoms developing rapidly.

AESTHETIC (es-THET-ick)

Attractive or appealing.

AIR GAP

An open vertical drop, or vertical empty space, that separates a drinking (potable) water supply to be protected from another water system in a water treatment plant or other location. This open gap prevents the contamination of drinking water by backsiphonage or backflow because there is no way raw water or any other water can reach the drinking water supply.

ACUTE HEALTH EFFECT

AESTHETIC

AIR GAP

ALLUVIAL (uh-LOU-vee-ul)

Relating to mud and/or sand deposited by flowing water. Alluvial deposits may occur after a heavy rainstorm.

ALTITUDE VALVE

A valve that automatically shuts off the flow into an elevated tank when the water level in the tank reaches a predetermined level. The valve automatically opens when the pressure in the distribution system drops below the pressure in the tank.

AMPEROMETRIC (am-PURR-o-MET-rick)

A method of measurement that records electric current flowing or generated, rather than recording voltage. Amperometric titration is a means of measuring concentrations of certain substances in water.

ANNULAR (AN-you-ler) SPACE

A ring-shaped space located between two circular objects, such as two pipes.

ALLUVIAL

ALTITUDE VALVE

AMPEROMETRIC

ANNULAR SPACE

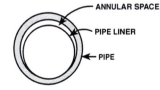

ANODE (an-O-d)

The positive pole or electrode of an electrolytic system, such as a battery. The anode attracts negatively charged particles or ions (anions).

AQUIFER (ACK-wi-fer)

A natural underground layer of porous, water-bearing materials (sand, gravel) usually capable of yielding a large amount or supply of water.

ANODE

AQUIFER

AVAILABLE CHLORINE AVAILABLE CHLORINE

A measure of the amount of chlorine available in chlorinated lime, hypochlorite compounds, and other materials that are used as a source of chlorine when compared with that of elemental (liquid or gaseous) chlorine.

AVERAGE DEMAND AVERAGE DEMAND

The total demand for water during a period of time divided by the number of days in that time period. This is also called the average daily demand.

B

BACK PRESSURE BACK PRESSURE

A pressure that can cause water to backflow into the water supply when a user's water system is at a higher pressure than the public water system.

BACKFLOW BACKFLOW

A reverse flow condition, created by a difference in water pressures, which causes water to flow back into the distribution pipes of a potable water supply from any source or sources other than an intended source. Also see BACKSIPHONAGE.

BACKSIPHONAGE BACKSIPHONAGE

A form of backflow caused by a negative or below atmospheric pressure within a water system. Also see BACKFLOW.

BRAKE HORSEPOWER BRAKE HORSEPOWER

(1)   The horsepower required at the top or end of a pump shaft (input to a pump).

(2)   The energy provided by a motor or other power source.

BREAKPOINT CHLORINATION BREAKPOINT CHLORINATION

Addition of chlorine to water until the chlorine demand has been satisfied. At this point, further additions of chlorine will result in a free chlorine residual that is directly proportional to the amount of chlorine added beyond the breakpoint.

C

CARCINOGEN (CAR-sin-o-JEN) CARCINOGEN

Any substance which tends to produce cancer in an organism.

CATHODE (KA-thow-d) CATHODE

The negative pole or electrode of an electrolytic cell or system. The cathode attracts positively charged particles or ions (cations).

CATHODIC (ca-THOD-ick) PROTECTION CATHODIC PROTECTION

An electrical system for prevention of rust, corrosion, and pitting of metal surfaces which are in contact with water or soil. A low-voltage current is made to flow through a liquid (water) or a soil in contact with the metal in such a manner that the external electromotive force renders the metal structure cathodic. This concentrates corrosion on auxiliary anodic parts which are deliberately allowed to corrode instead of letting the structure corrode.

CENTRIFUGAL (sen-TRIF-uh-gull) PUMP CENTRIFUGAL PUMP

A pump consisting of an impeller fixed on a rotating shaft that is enclosed in a casing, and having an inlet and discharge connection. As the rotating impeller whirls the liquid around, centrifugal force builds up enough pressure to force the water through the discharge outlet.

CIRCLE OF INFLUENCE CIRCLE OF INFLUENCE

The circular outer edge of a depression produced in the water table by the pumping of water from a well. Also see CONE OF INFLUENCE and CONE OF DEPRESSION.

[SEE DRAWING ON PAGE 239]

COLIFORM (COAL-i-form) COLIFORM

A group of bacteria found in the intestines of warm-blooded animals (including humans) and also in plants, soil, air and water. Fecal coliforms are a specific class of bacteria which only inhabit the intestines of warm-blooded animals. The presence of coliform bacteria is an indication that the water is polluted and may contain pathogenic (disease-causing) organisms.

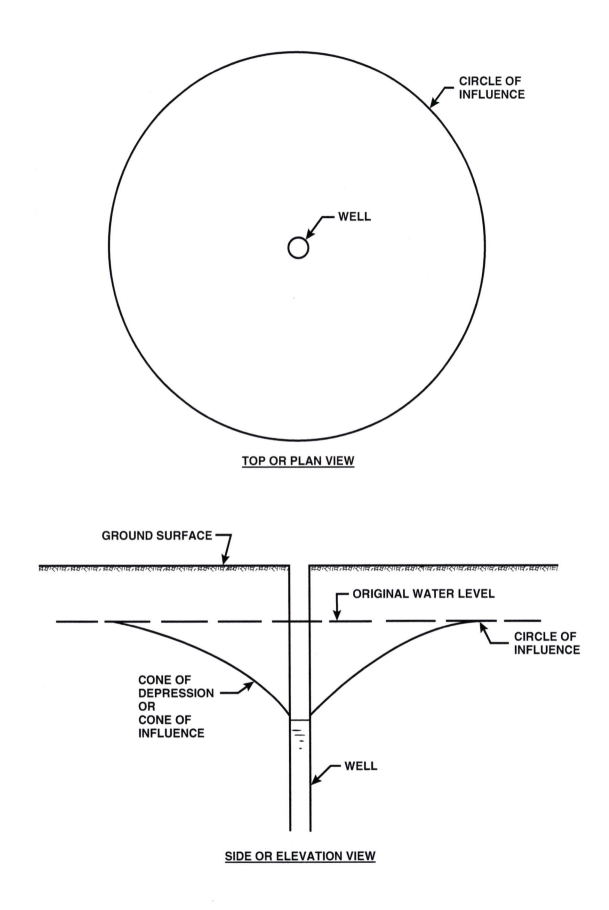

TOP OR PLAN VIEW

SIDE OR ELEVATION VIEW

CIRCLE OF INFLUENCE and CONE OF DEPRESSION/CONE OF INFLUENCE

COMPOSITE (come-PAH-zit) (PROPORTIONAL) SAMPLE
COMPOSITE (PROPORTIONAL) SAMPLE

A composite sample is a collection of individual samples obtained at regular intervals, usually every one or two hours during a 24-hour time span. Each individual sample is combined with the others in proportion to the rate of flow when the sample was collected. The resulting mixture (composite sample) forms a representative sample and is analyzed to determine the average conditions during the sampling period.

CONDUCTIVITY
CONDUCTIVITY

A measure of the ability of a solution (water) to carry an electric current.

CONDUCTOR CASING
CONDUCTOR CASING

The outer casing of a well. The purpose of this casing is to prevent contaminants from surface waters or shallow groundwaters from entering a well.

CONE OF DEPRESSION
CONE OF DEPRESSION

The depression, roughly conical in shape, produced in the water table by the pumping of water from a well. Also called the CONE OF INFLUENCE. Also see CIRCLE OF INFLUENCE.

[SEE DRAWING ON PAGE 239]

CONE OF INFLUENCE
CONE OF INFLUENCE

The depression, roughly conical in shape, produced in the water table by the pumping of water from a well. Also called the CONE OF DEPRESSION. Also see CIRCLE OF INFLUENCE.

[SEE DRAWING ON PAGE 239]

COUPON
COUPON

A steel specimen inserted into water to measure the corrosiveness of water. The rate of corrosion is measured as the loss of weight of the coupon (in milligrams) per surface area (in square decimeters) exposed to the water per day. 10 decimeters = 1 meter = 100 centimeters.

CROSS CONNECTION
CROSS CONNECTION

A connection between a drinking (potable) water system and an unapproved water supply. For example, if you have a pump moving nonpotable water and hook into the drinking water system to supply water for the pump seal, a cross connection or mixing between the two water systems can occur. This mixing may lead to contamination of the drinking water.

D

DPD (pronounce as separate letters)
DPD

A method of measuring the chlorine residual in water. The residual may be determined by either titrating or comparing a developed color with color standards. DPD stands for N,N-diethyl-p-phenylene-diamine.

DRAWDOWN
DRAWDOWN

(1) The drop in the water table or level of water in the ground when water is being pumped from a well.

(2) The amount of water used from a tank or reservoir.

(3) The drop in the water level of a tank or reservoir.

E

EJECTOR
EJECTOR

A device used to disperse a chemical solution into water being treated.

ELECTROMOTIVE FORCE (E.M.F.)
ELECTROMOTIVE FORCE (E.M.F.)

The electrical pressure available to cause a flow of current (amperage) when an electric circuit is closed. Also called VOLTAGE.

EVAPORATION
EVAPORATION

The process by which water or other liquid becomes a gas (water vapor or ammonia vapor).

EVAPOTRANSPIRATION (ee-VAP-o-TRANS-purr-A-shun)   EVAPOTRANSPIRATION

(1) The process by which water vapor passes into the atmosphere from living plants. Also called TRANSPIRATION.

(2) The total water removed from an area by transpiration (plants) and by evaporation from soil, snow, and water surfaces.

F

FLOAT ON SYSTEM   FLOAT ON SYSTEM

A method of operating a water storage facility. Daily flow into the facility is approximately equal to the average daily demand for water. When consumer demands for water are low, the storage facility will be filling. During periods of high demand, the facility will be emptying.

FOOT VALVE   FOOT VALVE

A special type of check valve located at the bottom end of the suction pipe on a pump. This valve opens when the pump operates to allow water to enter the suction pipe but closes when the pump shuts off to prevent water from flowing out of the suction pipe.

FRICTION LOSSES   FRICTION LOSSES

The head, pressure or energy (they are the same) lost by water flowing in a pipe or channel as a result of turbulence caused by the velocity of the flowing water and the roughness of the pipe, channel walls, or restrictions caused by fittings. Water flowing in a pipe loses head, pressure or energy as a result of friction losses. Also see HEAD LOSS.

G

(NO LISTINGS)

H

HEAD LOSS   HEAD LOSS

The head, pressure or energy (they are the same) lost by water flowing in a pipe or channel as a result of turbulence caused by the velocity of the flowing water and the roughness of the pipe, channel walls, or restrictions caused by fittings. Water flowing in a pipe loses head, pressure or energy as a result of friction losses. The head loss through a filter is due to friction losses caused by material building up on the surface or in the top part of a filter. Also see FRICTION LOSSES.

HYDROGEOLOGIST (HI-dro-gee-ALL-uh-gist)   HYDROGEOLOGIST

A person who studies and works with groundwater.

HYDROLOGIC (HI-dro-LOJ-ick) CYCLE   HYDROLOGIC CYCLE

The process of evaporation of water into the air and its return to earth by precipitation (rain or snow). This process also includes transpiration from plants, groundwater movement, and runoff into rivers, streams and the ocean. Also called the WATER CYCLE.

I

INTERSTICE (in-TUR-stuhz)   INTERSTICE

A very small open space in a rock or granular material. Also called a PORE, VOID, or void space. Also see VOID.

ION   ION

An electrically charged atom, radical (such as SO_4^{2-}), or molecule formed by the loss or gain of one or more electrons.

J

(NO LISTINGS)

K

(NO LISTINGS)

L

(NO LISTINGS)

M

MEG   MEG

A procedure used for checking the insulation resistance on motors, feeders, bus bar systems, grounds, and branch circuit wiring. Also see MEGGER.

MEGGER (from megohm)   MEGGER

An instrument used for checking the insulation resistance on motors, feeder, bus bar systems, grounds, and branch circuit wiring. Also see MEG.

MICRON (MY-kron)   MICRON

µm, Micrometer or Micron. A unit of length. One millionth of a meter or one thousandth of a millimeter. One micron equals 0.00004 of an inch.

N

NAMEPLATE   NAMEPLATE

A durable metal plate found on equipment which lists critical operating conditions for the equipment.

O

OVERDRAFT   OVERDRAFT

The pumping of water from a groundwater basin or aquifer in excess of the supply flowing into the basin. This pumping results in a depletion or "mining" of the groundwater in the basin.

OXIDIZING AGENT   OXIDIZING AGENT

Any substance, such as oxygen (O_2) or chlorine (Cl_2), that will readily add (take on) electrons. The opposite is a REDUCING AGENT.

P

PCBs   PCBs

See POLYCHLORINATED BIPHENYLS.

PALATABLE (PAL-uh-tuh-bull)   PALATABLE

Water at a desirable temperature that is free from objectionable tastes, odors, colors, and turbidity. Pleasing to the senses.

PEAK DEMAND   PEAK DEMAND

The maximum momentary load placed on a water treatment plant, pumping station or distribution system. This demand is usually the maximum average load in one hour or less, but may be specified as the instantaneous load or the load during some other short time period.

POLYCHLORINATED BIPHENYLS   POLYCHLORINATED BIPHENYLS

A class of organic compounds that cause adverse health effects in domestic water supplies.

PORE   PORE

A very small open space in a rock or granular material. Also called an INTERSTICE, VOID, or void space. Also see VOID.

POROSITY   POROSITY

(1) A measure of the spaces or voids in a material or aquifer.

(2) The ratio of the volume of spaces in a rock or soil to the total volume. This ratio is usually expressed as a percentage.

$$\text{Porosity, \%} = \frac{(\text{Volume of Spaces})(100\%)}{\text{Total Volume}}$$

POSITIVE BACTERIOLOGICAL SAMPLE   POSITIVE BACTERIOLOGICAL SAMPLE

A water sample in which gas is produced by coliform organisms during incubation in the multiple tube fermentation test. See Chapter 11, Laboratory Procedures, "Coliform Bacteria," in *WATER TREATMENT PLANT OPERATION*, Volume I, for details.

PRIME   PRIME

The action of filling a pump casing with water to remove the air. Most pumps must be primed before start-up or they will not pump any water.

PUMP BOWL   PUMP BOWL

The submerged pumping unit in a well, including the shaft, impellers and housing.

Q

(NO LISTINGS)

R

REDUCING AGENT   REDUCING AGENT

Any substance, such as base metal (iron) or the sulfide ion (S^{2-}), that will readily donate (give up) electrons. The opposite is an OXIDIZING AGENT.

REPRESENTATIVE SAMPLE   REPRESENTATIVE SAMPLE

A sample portion of material or water that is as nearly identical in content and consistency as possible to that in the larger body of material or water being sampled.

RESIDUAL CHLORINE   RESIDUAL CHLORINE

The concentration of chlorine present in water after the chlorine demand has been satisfied. The concentration is expressed in terms of the total chlorine residual, which includes both the free and combined or chemically bound chlorine residuals.

S

SAFE YIELD   SAFE YIELD

The annual quantity of water that can be taken from a source of supply over a period of years without depleting the source permanently (beyond its ability to be replenished naturally in "wet years").

SET POINT   SET POINT

The position at which the control or controller is set. This is the same as the desired value of the process variable. For example, a thermostat is set to maintain a desired temperature.

SPECIFIC GRAVITY   SPECIFIC GRAVITY

(1) Weight of a particle, substance, or chemical solution in relation to the weight of an equal volume of water. Water has a specific gravity of 1.000 at 4°C (39°F). Particulates in raw water may have a specific gravity of 1.005 to 2.5.

(2) Weight of a particular gas in relation to the weight of an equal volume of air at the same temperature and pressure (air has a specific gravity of 1.0). Chlorine has a specific gravity of 2.5 as a gas.

SPECIFIC YIELD SPECIFIC YIELD

The quantity of water that a unit volume of saturated permeable rock or soil will yield when drained by gravity. Specific yield may be expressed as a ratio or as a percentage by volume.

STALE WATER STALE WATER

Water which has not flowed recently and may have picked up tastes and odors from distribution lines or storage facilities.

SUCTION LIFT SUCTION LIFT

The *NEGATIVE* pressure [in feet (meters) of water or inches (centimeters) of mercury vacuum] on the suction side of the pump. The pressure can be measured from the centerline of the pump *DOWN TO* (lift) the elevation of the hydraulic grade line on the suction side of the pump.

T

THM THM

See **TRIHALOMETHANES**.

THERMAL STRATIFICATION (STRAT-uh-fuh-KAY-shun) THERMAL STRATIFICATION

The formation of layers of different temperatures in a lake or reservoir.

TRANSMISSIVITY (TRANS-miss-SIV-it-tee) TRANSMISSIVITY

A measure of the ability to transmit (as in the ability of an aquifer to transmit water).

TRANSPIRATION (TRAN-spur-RAY-shun) TRANSPIRATION

The process by which water vapor is released to the atmosphere by living plants. This process is similar to people sweating. Also see EVAPOTRANSPIRATION.

TRIHALOMETHANES (THMs) (tri-HAL-o-METH-hanes) TRIHALOMETHANES (THMs)

Derivatives of methane, CH_4, in which three halogen atoms (chlorine or bromine) are substituted for three of the hydrogen atoms. Often formed during chlorination by reactions with natural organic materials in the water. The resulting compounds (THMs) are suspected of causing cancer.

TUBERCULATION (too-BURR-cue-LAY-shun) TUBERCULATION

The development or formation of small mounds of corrosion products (rust) on the inside of iron pipe. These mounds (tubercles) increase the roughness of the inside of the pipe thus increasing resistance to water flow (decreases the C Factor).

TURBIDITY UNITS (TU) TURBIDITY UNITS (TU)

Turbidity units are a measure of the cloudiness of water. If measured by a nephelometric (deflected light) instrumental procedure, turbidity units are expressed in nephelometric turbidity units (NTU) or simply TU. Those turbidity units obtained by visual methods are expressed in Jackson Turbidity Units (JTU) which are a measure of the cloudiness of water; they are used to indicate the clarity of water. There is no real connection between NTUs and JTUs. The Jackson turbidimeter is a visual method and the nephelometer is an instrumental method based on deflected light.

U

(NO LISTINGS)

V

VOID VOID

A pore or open space in rock, soil or other granular material, not occupied by solid matter. The pore or open space may be occupied by air, water, or other gaseous or liquid material. Also called an INTERSTICE, PORE, or void space.

VOLTAGE VOLTAGE

The electrical pressure available to cause a flow of current (amperage) when an electric circuit is closed. Also called ELECTROMOTIVE FORCE (E.M.F.).

W

WATER CYCLE   WATER CYCLE

The process of evaporation of water into the air and its return to earth by precipitation (rain or snow). This process also includes transpiration from plants, groundwater movement, and runoff into rivers, streams and the ocean. Also called the HYDROLOGIC CYCLE.

WATER HAMMER   WATER HAMMER

The sound like someone hammering on a pipe that occurs when a valve is opened or closed very rapidly. When a valve position is changed quickly, the water pressure in a pipe will increase and decrease back and forth very quickly. This rise and fall in pressures can cause serious damage to the system.

WATER TABLE   WATER TABLE

The upper surface of the zone of saturation of groundwater in an unconfirmed aquifer.

X

(NO LISTINGS)

Y

YIELD   YIELD

The quantity of water (expressed as a rate of flow—GPM, GPH, GPD, or total quantity per year) that can be collected for a given use from surface or groundwater sources. The yield may vary with the use proposed, with the plan of development, and also with economic considerations. Also see SAFE YIELD.

Z

ZONE OF SATURATION   ZONE OF SATURATION

The soil or rock located below the top of the groundwater table. By definition, the zone of saturation is saturated with water. Also see WATER TABLE.

SUBJECT INDEX

X

(NO LISTINGS)

Y

Z

(NO LISTINGS)